South–South Trade and Finance in the Twenty-First Century

ANTHEM FRONTIERS OF GLOBAL POLITICAL ECONOMY

The Anthem Frontiers of Global Political Economy series seeks to trigger and attract new thinking in global political economy, with particular reference to the prospects of emerging markets and developing countries. Written by renowned scholars from different parts of the world, books in this series provide historical, analytical and empirical perspectives on national economic strategies and processes, the implications of global and regional economic integration, the changing nature of the development project and the diverse global-to-local forces that drive change. Scholars featured in the series extend earlier economic insights to provide fresh interpretations that allow new understandings of contemporary economic processes.

South–South Trade and Finance in the Twenty-First Century

Rise of the South or a Second Great Divergence

Omar S. Dahi and Fırat Demir

A

ANTHEM PRESS

Anthem Press
An imprint of Wimbledon Publishing Company
www.anthempress.com

This edition first published in UK and USA 2019
by ANTHEM PRESS
75–76 Blackfriars Road, London SE1 8HA, UK
or PO Box 9779, London SW19 7ZG, UK
and
244 Madison Ave #116, New York, NY 10016, USA

First published in the UK and USA by Anthem Press 2016

British Library Cataloguing-in-Publication Data
A catalogue record for this book is available from the British Library.

ISBN-13: 978-1-78527-184-7 (Pbk)
ISBN-10: 1-78527-184-9 (Pbk)

This title is also available as an e-book

To my mother

O. D.

To the three joys of life, Dace, Damla and Alnis

F. D.

CONTENTS

FIGURES

TABLES

PREFACE

Tolstoy wrote in *Anna Karenina*: "All happy families are alike; each unhappy family is unhappy in its own way."[1] This is a book about the unhappy families. The countries of the global South, also called developing, un(der)developed, semi-developed, periphery, the Rest, Third World and so forth, are more than ever at the center of attention in the world economy and are shaping the new world order for the twenty-first century. China, India, South Korea and Brazil have become pivotal players in the new era of global production and trade and are increasingly assertive of their newly gained powers in world politics. Other countries of the South seek similar economic gains and more active roles. The rise of the Southern countries has also led to renewed calls for strengthening cooperation among them. In fact South–South cooperation has even become a buzzword to represent anything and everything the North–South economic and political exchanges are (and were) not.

We have written this book to explore both the possibilities and the limits of South–South cooperation in the twenty-first century. In doing so, we have two goals. First, we want to provide an overview of the historical and theoretical context of South–South cooperation. Second, we want to look beyond the "knight in shining armor" versus "dark lord of the east, Sauron" narratives of the rise of the South that we find too often in academic and popular writing. By reexamining the evidence from South–South and South–North economic exchanges, we hope to strip the debate of the excessive pessimism or optimism that biases most analyses of the subject.

Our main premise is that the new multipolarity in the world economy is found within the global South as well as between the North and the South. The rising Southern powerhouses of the world economy, such as BRICS (Brazil, Russia, India, China and South Africa), have had diverse effects on the rest of the developing world, and in this way they appear to replicate the North–South dilemmas and ominous contradictions for the countries we refer to as the Rest of South. Changing the course of this pattern of South–South exchanges requires an honest discussion of the effects of the Emerging South on those countries that continue to struggle for a decent life and, in some cases, simply for survival.

The book emerged from our earlier work on South–South economic exchanges, and in many ways it reflects changes in our analysis of the costs and benefits of South–South economic cooperation. Over the years, our earlier optimistic attitude has given way to a more cautious one. Particularly, the low-growth and low-development trap (in which

---

1. L. Tolstoy, 2014, *Anna Karenina*, Oxford: Oxford University Press (Rosamund Bartlett translation).

most Southern countries became stuck after decades of Washington Consensus experimentation) seems not to be releasing its grip on those countries in the new multipolar world. On the contrary, the rise of a few Emerging South countries appears to have a regressive effect on decades of industrialization efforts by other Southern countries. Changes in trade structures—the skill and technology intensity of products, industrial structure, product and country dispersion, direction and other aspects that form a country's international trade—along with increasing primarization of Southern economies (i.e., an emphasis on exporting raw materials and natural resources rather than manufactured goods) are warning signs for the coming years. Unhappy families indeed.

This book is also influenced by our increasing discontent with the new mainstream development analysis that has emphasized micro-development goals based on representative agents and controlled experiments. The lack of any upward mobility in a majority of Southern countries and the unsustainable nature of most industrialization efforts in leading South countries—concerns ignored or unresolved by much of the mainstream discussion—have helped shape the general framework of this book. However, despite these serious causes for concern, we find reason to hope for a new world economy that is more pluralistic and allows more experimentation in economic policy. Decades of one-size-fits-all orthodoxy are giving way to a more agnostic, less arrogant and more pluralistic economic policy in the South, one that may eventually yield more equitable distribution of the world's wealth while protecting its peoples and resources.

In a nutshell, the book makes the following main points:

1. The nature of South–South cooperation has changed over time and continues to change. It is important to understand how.
2. The treatment of economic theory of South–South cooperation and integration has also changed over time. We describe these changes, along with the similarities and differences between various schools of thought toward South–South economic exchanges, and discuss their implications for the ongoing debate about global economic development.
3. Certain stylized facts and patterns of change in South–South economic exchanges in trade and finance are instructive in analyzing realistically the present state of the economies of countries in the South and those countries' prospects for the future.
4. The widely touted rise of the South is not a homogeneous or linear process, and not all Southern countries have benefited equally from it. The rise of the Emerging South has created both positive and negative prospects for development in the Rest of South.
5. The 55 countries we identify in the Emerging South accounted for 65 percent of the world's population in 2015—4.7 billion people—while 157 mostly smaller and poorer countries in the Rest of South accounted for 1.6 billion people, or 22.6 percent of the world's population. While the economies of the former are growing, many of the latter continue to struggle—even to slide backward. We need to identify the necessary conditions to make South–South exchanges mutually beneficial, allowing for the sharing of knowledge, the upgrading of skills and the enhancement of development in the entire South, not just a part of it.

ACKNOWLEDGMENTS

Many people helped with this book. Anthem Press has been a pleasure to work with and has made the process much easier than it might have been. We thank James Boyce, Mustafa Caglayan, Kevin Gallagher, Ilene Grabel, Jeffrey B. Nugent, Ziya Onis, Arslan Razmi, David Ruccio, Peter Skott, Roberto Veneziani and Mwangi Wa Gĩthĩnji for their feedback on earlier versions of several chapters at different stages of this project. We also thank session participants at the Union for Radical Political Economics/Allied Social Sciences Association (URPE/ASSA) meetings in 2012, 2014 and 2015; the Eastern Economics Association (EEA) meetings in 2012 and 2015; the Analytical Political Economy Workshop at the University of Notre Dame in 2015; and the Southern Economic Association (SEA) meetings in 2012; and thanks to seminar participants at the University of Oklahoma in 2011, Queen's University-Belfast in 2012 and the Central Bank of the Republic of Turkey, Koc University and the University of Massachusetts–Amherst and the World Bank in 2013. We are grateful to two anonymous referees who gave significant feedback on an earlier draft of this book. Several people gave us input on various aspects of the manuscript, including Vivek Bhandari, Bassam Haddad, Salman Hameed, Vijay Prashad, Sayres Rudy, Alejandro Velasco and Lisa Wedeen. We are also greatly thankful to John Stifler for his tireless dedication and excellent help with editing and revisions that made the final product vastly better than it was. We also thank Alexander Gorzewski, Xiaoman Duan, Chenghao Hu, Lord Andzie Quainoo, Wenliang Ren, Souleymane Soumahoro and Ying Zhang for their research assistance. We are also grateful for generous financial support by the South–South Tricontinental Collaborative Programme, International Development Economics Associates (IDEAs), 2013.

We especially need to thank our dissertation chairs, mentors and friends, Amitava K. Dutt and Jaime Ros, for teaching us to think critically about economic issues. They inspired several of our arguments in this book since our graduate school days and always urged us to reject the comfort of dogma for evidence and logic. It was also because of them that we started—for better or worse—coauthoring.

Omar Dahi: I would like to thank the Dean of Faculty Office and School of Critical Social Inquiry at Hampshire College for generous financial support at various stages of writing this book. A fellowship I received from the Whiting Foundation allowed me to conduct research in Buenos Aires, which proved to be very useful for understanding the dynamics of regional integration in the Southern Cone.

I cannot think of a better place to work, teach and conduct research than the School of Critical Social Inquiry at Hampshire College, Amherst, Massachusetts, where my colleagues encourage and inspire me on a daily basis. I have also been fortunate to have incredible students in the South–South Economic Relations course that I offer every spring semester at Hampshire College. Many of their critiques, input, ideas and research have also helped shape my own thinking on South–South relations. Carol Boudreau, Emily Gallivan and Chyrell George: thank you for your help and patience. Over the last decade I have been incredibly lucky to enjoy the friendship and support, personally and intellectually, of Aaron Berman, Vivek Bhandari, Margaret Cerullo, John Drabinski, Eray Duzenli, Viveca Greene, Salman Hameed, Sami Hermez, Yasser Munif, Helena Nassif, Sayres Rudy, Falguni Sheth, Marty and Linda Wolfson, Alejandro Velasco, Jihad Yazigi and Barbara Yngvesson. To Stan Warner and Laurie Nisonoff, I owe a special debt of gratitude for their mentorship and support. I have learned a lot from your kindness and wisdom. Frank Holmquist and Mary Hoyer's boundless generosity and kindness have given me and my family a home away from home. I cannot thank them enough.

I could not have reached this point without the love and encouragement of my parents, Sami and Isaaf, and my brothers, Firas and Ayham. I hope I can return the favor.

Isaf and Ismael taught me once again what unconditional love means. Thank you for bringing such joy into my life every day. Without Cora, I could have not finished graduate school, let alone written a book. You are the love of my life and my best friend. I promise to take a break before my next project.

Firat Demir: I am thankful to my present employer, the Department of Economics at the University of Oklahoma, which provided me with time, resources and generous financial and intellectual support to bring this book to a completion. I am most thankful to my colleagues and undergraduate and graduate students for their inquisitive and right-to-the-point questions, which helped crystallize several of the ideas presented in this book. I owe special thanks to Sohrab Behdad, Gregory Burge, Nilgün Erdem, Suzette Grillot, Alexander Holmes, Gary Hoover, Kwan Kim, Tami Kinsey, Misha Nedeljkovich, Ziya Öniş, Cynthia Rogers, Fikret Şenses, Oktay Türel, Joshua Landis, Samer Shehata and Mitchell Smith for their encouragement and friendship. I also benefited greatly from two sabbatical leave visits to the Faculty of Business and Administrative Sciences at Koc University (Istanbul) and the Department of Economics at the University of Massachusetts–Amherst in spring 2013. Both universities and colleagues in each helped significantly at the earlier stages of this project.

This book was also made possible by a Fulbright scholar grant from the J. William Fulbright Foreign Scholarship Board, which allowed me to spend a very productive year in the Faculty of Economics at the University of Montenegro, where I taught and conducted research during the 2015–16 academic year. I owe special thanks to my colleagues at the University of Montenegro, particularly to Saša Popović, and also to Anica Vujnović and Milena Vučelić at the American Corner in Podgorica, and to Misha Nedeljkovich, Aleksandar Nikolić, Marko Pavlović and Rajko Rakicević, whose friendship, generous help and support made my visit to Montenegro a rewarding and unforgettable experience.

I also want to thank my son, Alnis, and daughter, Damla, for their patience during the writing of this book. Their curious questions and constant interruptions prevented me from becoming a grumpy academic par excellence. My son's goal of writing a book of his own one day also inspired me to write this book. Finally, I would like to thank my wife, Dace, for all her love and support during the whole process of getting ready and then writing this book.

As usual, all remaining errors and omissions are ours.

Chapter One

INTRODUCTION TO
SOUTH–SOUTH RELATIONS

In 2012, a series of posters advertising the London-based HSBC bank caught the eye of international travelers in airports worldwide. Hung on walls alongside moving walkways, the posters featured ironic or humorous photographs, each with a sentence above it starting with the words "In the future." Created by the preeminent international advertising agency J. Walter Thompson and designed to portray HSBC as forward-thinking, the marketing campaign highlighted different ways in which HSBC was at the cutting edge of banking and commerce worldwide.

One poster in particular is relevant to this book. The poster showed a photograph of a gray Chinese terracotta warrior with a steely gaze. Everything about the image was similar to the classic photographs of the terracotta warrior statues except for one detail: instead of boots the warrior wore bright yellow and green flip-flops. Over the photo was the line, "In the future, South–South trade will be norm, not novelty." Additional text elaborated on this line: "Direct trade between fast growing nations is reshaping the world economy. HSBC is one of the leading banks for trade settlement between China and Latin America. There's a new world emerging. Be part of it."[1] The HSBC poster provides an ideal entry point for a critical examination of South–South trade: the ideas conjured by the terracotta warrior photograph and the poster in general are a perfect metaphor for the pervasiveness—and the complexity—of the economic activity that characterizes this whole vast subject.

The virtues of trade between and among countries that belong to what has long been called "the global South" or simply "the South" are now trumpeted not only by giant corporations and major branding agencies but also by public national and international institutions. In 2003, the UN General Assembly decided to observe September 12 every year as the United Nations Day for South–South Cooperation, in recognition of how trade and financial exchanges between two or more countries within the global South is "an important element of international cooperation for development," offering "viable opportunities for developing countries and countries with economies in transition."[2] The assembly chose that particular day in commemoration of the adoption, in Buenos

---

1. http://www.hsbc.com/~/media/HSBC-com/about-hsbc/in-the-future/pdfs/south-south-trade-advert. The authors would like to thank Dana Finkelstein for first bringing this poster to our attention.
2. http://www.un.org/en/events/southcooperationday/

Aires on September 12, 1978, of the Buenos Aires Plan of Action for Promoting and Implementing Technical Cooperation among Developing Countries.

Meanwhile, the World Trade Organization (WTO) dedicated a major section of its 2003 *World Trade Report* to examining the growth of such trade (WTO, 2003). Amplifying the WTO's message, the United Nations Industrial Development Organization (UNIDO) in 2006 published its highly significant study, *Industrial Development, Trade and Poverty Reduction through South–South Cooperation*. Not to be outdone, the World Bank (WB) came up with its *Global Development Horizons 2011* report dedicated to "multipolarity," exploring the effects of the rise of the Emerging South on the rest of the world (World Bank, 2011). Later, it focused its 2015 flagship report for Latin America on the region's performance, with an emphasis on South–South trade, titled *Latin America and the Rising South: Changing World, Changing Priorities* (Torre et al., 2015),[3] and the press briefing for the report called the South "new masters of the global economy."[4] In 2013 the United Nations Development Project (UNDP) named its 2013 Human Development Report *The Rise of the South* (UNDP, 2013), and there is now a separate office for South–South cooperation within the UN itself.

The press was paying attention. The WSJ (Wessel, 2008) hailed the growth of South–South trade as perhaps "the opening of a new epoch of globalization," and *The Economist* Intelligence Unit (2015) dedicated a full issue of its Growth Crossings series, titled *Chain Reactions*, to examining how "trade between emerging markets is reshaping global supply chains." Eventually, the subject of South–South trade and, increasingly, South–South finance reentered mainstream scholarly discussions, doing so after many years in which economics departments in European and North American universities had scorned these subjects as relics of the bygone era of economic nationalism that followed World War II. The number of academic journal articles reflecting this phenomenon has mushroomed, and this proliferation of interest does not even count the (now slightly curbed) general enthusiasm for analyzing the rapidly expanding economies of the BRICS—the popular acronym for Brazil, Russia, India, China and South Africa.

Trade and finance between fast-growing nations are indeed reshaping the world economy—but in what way, and to whose benefit? In the second decade of this millennium, some states are trading profitably and widely while others—typically the least developed—are left out. And so the questions multiply. One obvious and, we think, crucial question is: Can the poorest countries of the global South truly be part of the new emerging world economic order and, if so, how? Less obviously, but with broader implications, do South–South economic exchanges today still hold the promise of an alternative path for development, or has "South–South trade" become just another marketing slogan? Building on a decade and a half of research and publication on South–South economic relations, this book is our attempt to answer these questions. Although by now plenty of studies have examined different aspects of this subject, we are attempting what

---

3. The World Bank also organized a symposium on South–South trade back in 1987, exploring its trade, growth and developmental effects (Havrylyshyn, 1987).

4. http://live.worldbank.org/rise-of-the-south-the-new-masters-of-the-global-economy

we believe is the first study of South–South economic exchanges—both in trade and finance—in a comprehensive framework.

Before describing what this book has to offer, we should ask whether or not this fascination with South–South economic exchanges is really warranted. We believe it is. From the post–World War II decades until the late 1980s, South–South trade represented roughly 5–10 percent of all global trade. However, from 1990 to 2000 this proportion increased from 10 percent to 16 percent. By 2005 it was at 20 percent, and by 2013, 31 percent of all global trade was between or among countries of the South.

Many other statistics illustrate the same economic evolution. Here are a few:

- In 1950, when international trade within the South was in its infancy, exports from the South to the rest of the world already accounted for approximately 30 percent of all world trade, and by 2013 that share had risen to 54 percent.
- Over the same period, the direction of those exports shifted markedly. By 2013, more than 58 percent of all Southern exports were being shipped to other Southern countries.
- The structure of this trade has also changed significantly, as manufactured goods have begun to account for a significant portion of global South exports, both to other countries of the South and to the rest of the world. In 1970, the South accounted for 7 percent of global manufactures exports and only 2 percent of the worldwide export of high-skill and technology-intensive manufactures. In 2012 its share in global manufactures exports surged to 47 percent and, even more importantly, its share in global high-skill manufactures exports climbed to 56 percent. Moreover, by 2012, manufactures accounted for three-quarters of all South–South merchandise exports and more than half of all South manufactures exports to the rest of the world. While the share of high-skill manufactures was a bare 2 percent of South–South exports in 1970, it climbed to 25 percent in 2012.

We see a similar pattern in global financial flows, as banks and industries—with frequent encouragement from their own governments and from those of their intended hosts—have increasingly sought new opportunities in previously neglected places. The share of the South in world foreign direct investment (FDI) inflows, for example, increased from less than 30 percent in 1970 to over 60 percent in 2013. During this period the South has also become a major investor in other countries, increasing its share in global FDI outflows from 0.3 percent in 1970—that is, one-third of 1 percent—to just below 40 percent in 2013, and more than 60 percent of these flows went to other Southern countries. In 2010 Southern countries from Asia accounted for 68 percent of all mergers and acquisitions in Latin America and the Caribbean region—three times their total accumulated acquisitions in this region over the previous two decades. As of 2013, six global South countries were among the top twenty investors in the world, China alone ranking number two in global FDI inflows and number three in outflows.

Another indication of the growing interconnections between different countries is the significant increase in the number of preferential trade agreements (PTAs) and their importance in world trade since the 1990s. From the 1950s through 2014, at least 266

PTAs were reported to the WTO, 88 percent of them signed after 1988. Altogether, by 2014 these agreements accounted for 53 percent of all world trade—and 75 percent of them have been between countries of the South. A parallel development has taken root with investment flows. By 2015, 3,331 bilateral investment treaties (BITs) had been signed and were in force worldwide, 1,292 of them between Southern countries and more than half of those signed after 2000. In these tectonic shifts in global trade and finance we are witnessing a reordering of the global economy as well as of its management, whether it be the management of world finance through the International Monetary Fund (IMF) or development planning through the World Bank or the new BRICS Bank.

Aspects of these changes have been the subject of several valuable books. First are the books examining the rise of BRICS: *BRICS and Development Alternatives* (Cassiolato and Vitorino, 2009), *Building a Future with BRICS* (Kobayashi-Hillary, 2007), *The Rise of the BRICS in Africa* (Carmody, 2013), *BRICS: An Anti-Capitalist Critique* (Bond and Garcia, 2015) and *The BRICS and the Future of Global Order* (Stuenkel, 2015). These books often have a geopolitical bent, and their economic analyses, when present, are of the countries' interactions with one another or with non-BRICS countries. Much of the analysis in these books is useful in understanding how those rising powers are leveraging alliances of all sorts to increase their political and economic clout on a global level. Another category of books homes in on China's economic relations with other countries in the South, such as those many developing countries in Latin America and Africa: *Economic Opportunities and Challenges posed by China for Mexico and Central America* (Peters, 2005), *China and Latin America: Economic Relations in the Twenty-First Century* (Jenkins and Peters, 2009), *New Presence of China in Africa* (Van Dijk, 2010), *The Morality of China in Africa: The Middle Kingdom and the Dark Continent* (Chan, 2013) and *Globalization, Poverty and Inequality: Between a Rock and a Hard Place* (Kaplinsky, 2013). In *The Dragon in the Room: China and the Future of Latin American Industrialization* (2010), Gallagher and Porzecanski's vital examination of China's potentially deindustrializing impact on Latin America underscores some of the arguments we develop in this book. Alice Amsden's body of work in *Rise of the Rest* (2001), *Escape from Empire* (2007) and elsewhere, serves as an important intellectual influence on our study of South–South relations. Finally, numerous books and edited volumes examine either case studies of South–South exchange or regional integration agreements around the globe. These include *Arab Economic Integration* (Galal and Hoekman, 2003), *Trade Policy and Economic Integration in the Middle East and North Africa* (Hakimian and Nugent, 2005), *MERCOSUR: The Common Market of the Southern Cone* (Porrata-Doria, 2005), *The African Union and New Strategies for Development in Africa* (Adejumobi and Olukoshi, 2008), *The Economics of East Asian Integration: A Comprehensive Introduction to Regional Issues* (Fujita et al., 2011), *The Future of South–South Economic Relations* (Najam and Thrasher, 2012), *Regional Economic Integration in West Africa* (Seck, 2013), *Decline of U.S. Hegemony? A Challenge of ALBA and a New Latin American Integration of the Twenty-First Century* (Bagley and Defort, 2015) and *The Politics of Arab Integration* (Luciani and Salame, 2015).

While these scholars' contributions are important valuable to our understanding of various aspects of South–South economic relations, this book undertakes an analysis of the history, theoretical foundations, development trajectories and empirical analysis of

South–South exchanges in trade and finance—all in one comprehensive study. What makes our approach comprehensive is our integration of three elements of analysis that we believe are necessary to fully understand economic phenomena: history (with a focus on power and ideology), theory and empirics. Without a sense of history, an examination of long-term trajectories and how they shaped the current world would not be possible, nor would an appreciation for the rise and fall—and sometimes the recycling—of developmental ideas. A historical perspective also offers us a clearer lens through which to show how power dynamics and shifts in ideology have themselves driven economic outcomes.

Our approach is to examine, from a sympathetic yet critical developmental perspective, the payoff from South–South relations. In doing so, we try to answer the main questions that are crucial to a more complete understanding of South–South exchanges. What have been the areas in which developing countries have forged successful economic partnerships with one another? What are the patterns and characteristics of developing country exports in terms of structure (type of products exported and imported), intensity (amount of trade by volume and dollar value) and direction (to other South or to the North)? Is South–South trade, as many of its advocates claim, relatively concentrated in industrial and more sophisticated products and thus presents higher potential for economic development? Has South–South trade and finance benefited all countries or just a few? What are the possible downsides of South–South trade and finance, and how can developing countries avoid the pitfalls and maximize the benefits?

Advocates of South–South cooperation extol a long list of its benefits: a more level playing field in the global economy and power politics; increased collective bargaining power for countries previously at a considerable disadvantage in almost any trade; enhanced sharing of experience and capabilities in business, technology, communication and other areas; the promotion of national science and technology and of research and development; greater environmental protection; the continued and deepening cultivation of human capital; a greater sense of self-reliance, balanced by cooperation; and more. At the other end of the spectrum there are those who state that some South–South relations are in fact a new form of colonialism, particularly with respect to China's presence in Africa. Many of those discussions are quite polarized, serving primarily as a battleground between diehard supporters of South–South trade and its opponents with partial or incomplete evidence. In this book, we argue the story is more complicated with no knights in shining armor but no evil witches of the East or West, either.

Starting with its past and then examining its present, we show that South–South exchange has tended to be lopsided, dominated by a few countries. Especially since the 1990s, the gaps between developing countries have sometimes become too big to bridge, as some countries have become stuck at—or regressed to—a low level of economic development, with primary commodities and low-skill manufactures dominating their economies, while others have climbed the development ladder. Among the group of countries that we refer to as the Rest of South, for example, 74 percent of their exports in 2012 were of primary commodities—oil, cash crops and so forth—and almost half of these countries depended on one single commodity for more than a third of their export earnings. In contrast, the share of primary goods in total exports of the group we call the Emerging South was less than 20 percent, and while the share of the Rest of South in global technology and skill-intensive exports was only one-third of 1 percent, the Emerging South's share was 55 percent in 2012. In the following pages, we hope to highlight the Rest of South's plight, which usually goes missing during celebrations of the rise of a few.

The definition of what constitutes South versus North is not a settled issue. We have classified countries in three groups: the North (23 countries), the Emerging South (55 countries) and the Rest of South (157 countries).[5] "The North" refers to the industrialized, high-income countries, most but not all of which are in the Northern Hemisphere. "Emerging South" refers to the more advanced and at least partially industrialized countries of the South, most of them from what the World Bank refers to as the middle-income group, and a few from the Newly Industrialized Countries group. The term "developing," in the true sense of the word, refers to these countries. "Rest of South" includes those global South countries not included in the Emerging South category. Most countries of the South (although not most of the population) are in this group. Together, Emerging South and Rest of South make up the global South, a combined total of 6.3 billion people, or 87 percent of the world's population. From here on in this work, we often use the adjective "global" when referring to all countries of Emerging South and Rest of South together. Whenever we use the term "South–South" by itself, we are referring to exchanges within the entire global South (including Emerging South and Rest of South).

In this classification, we have taken into account countries' incomes, production and trade structures, factor endowments and institutional development. For consistency in our analysis, we have kept the group of countries constant and not allowed country switching between groups. Otherwise, we would continuously have to exclude countries that move up the economic ladder, and to do so would introduce a downward selection bias by lowering growth and development rates in the South as a whole. More importantly, moving the new graduates from the global South class would prevent us from understanding how these now-rich countries have become rich. Our rule of thumb in these decisions, therefore, was the timing of a particular country's move up (or down) the development ladder. Argentina, for example, was an upper-income country at the turn of last century, but for most of the twentieth century (and, so far, the twenty-first) it was a low- to middle-income country, and we have therefore classified it as part of the Emerging South rather than as part of the North. On the other hand, South Korea, an upper-income industrialized country, was one of the poorest back in the 1960s, and even as late as the 1990s was still classified by the World Bank as a middle-income country, so it is in the same category as Argentina. Conversely, the North includes Greece, even though on many accounts (including its production and trade structures) that country is more similar to others in the Emerging South. Our main concern in this choice is consistency with other work on the topic. Furthermore, including or excluding a particular country from the North or Emerging South does not change any of our conclusions.

---

5. The full list of countries in each category is included in the Appendix.

There are several limitations to our analysis. Trade analyses in chapters 2–4 include re-exports, a consideration that might be problematic in comparing trade values with value added. Obviously, re-exports as well as intra-firm trade pricing for multinationals create some distortions in data. Besides, exchanges between multinational corporations involving triangular trade and re-exports make up a substantial part of South–South trade. Ignoring these types of exchanges carries the risk of upwardly biasing the real added value of South–South exchanges. More importantly, the analysis in this book does not include an examination of how multinational corporations (MNCs)—whether North- or South-based—are driving or benefitting from these types of exchanges. While we believe such an analysis should be undertaken, particularly in order to get a better picture of this trade's developmental benefits, it is beyond the scope of this book.

We should also note the risk of defining development only with economic wellbeing at the macro level while ignoring gains in other aspects such as gender equality, health, environmental quality and educational outcomes. Likewise, we have omitted a wide variety of exchanges between developing countries, including labor flows, remittances, and other forms of exchange that are crucial to the everyday functioning of economies of all developing countries and to the livelihoods of billions of people. In these respects, this book is very state-centric, focusing on macroeconomic exchanges between countries. Our approach also leaves out the role of South–South social movements (women, labor, environmental and others) in pushing for a more equitable and sustainable world. We have excluded these topics because we had to limit the already-ambitious scope of the book, although we believe this book will be useful to conducting such an analysis, and we intend to shed light on some of those areas in future work.

Finally, we have taken a macro approach in our analysis of the South–South exchanges. This was no coincidence. Unlike adherents to the new micro-based approach in development economics, we follow the older generation of development economists, arguing as did many others before us that the focus away from macro to micro aspects of development hides a thinly disguised ideological bias and allows—indeed, encourages—economists to avoid uncomfortable questions about the reasons for the growing income divergence between the North and the South, or for the increasing deindustrialization (i.e., the declining share of industry output, employment and investment, and the rising share of primary or low-productivity service sectors) of most of the South since the start of the neoliberal project in the early 1980s. According to this new development narrative—fiercely advocated by the international institutions such as the World Bank and various aid agencies—mosquito nets, cash vouchers, lottery schemes and various other micro interventions are the shining path of development through the improvement of human capital, longevity and health, as well as the promotion of individual choices in marriage, pregnancy and family outcomes.

According to these microeconomic analysts, financial incentives can be expected to help individual agents overcome "cultural constraints" such as "fatalism" or "low levels of female bargaining power" in places such as sub-Saharan Africa (Nyqvist et al., 2015). By similar reasoning, they argue that the only barrier to poverty-alleviation is imperfect access to capital markets, since, after all, society is the sum of capitalist entrepreneurs, or representative agents, waiting for some micro credit to pull themselves up by their bootstraps. As the reader will have surmised by now, we disagree with this view. We offer this book as an attempt to bring macroeconomics back to the discussion table, and we hope to convince our readers that economic structures still matter for long-term development and growth.

The book is organized in chapters devoted to the history of global trade and the development of the South, an examination of theoretical frameworks within which to analyze South–South trade and finance, presentation of data on many various aspects of trade and finance both within the South and between the South and the North, and implications for a future in which the right balance between South–South and South–North exchanges will create the greatest economic health for the world.

Chapter 2 explores the political economy of the past, the present and the probable future of South–South relations, providing a historical and institutional context for the broader development debates we discuss in later chapters. Since the mid-1950s, when most developing countries (i.e., the South in general) began to achieve political independence from developed countries (the global North), economists, political leaders and hopeful entrepreneurs of the global South have advocated increasing political and economic integration among these developing countries. Their collective enthusiasm has been based on the belief that such integration is a key to their nations' economic growth, political stability and general well-being and, indeed, a major step toward greater social and economic equality worldwide. The legacy of those attempts not only provides a guide for successes and failures but also helps us understand why the idea of South–South solidarity still holds such prestige in the global South.

Our examination of pertinent economic history begins with the rise and fall of what became known in the 1950s and 1960s as the Third World Movement, a set of institutions, initiatives and proclamations emanating from the South as the world's less developed countries were attempting to come to terms with their own economic underdevelopment as well as with an unequal and dangerously militaristic, confrontational political and global order. We then examine South–South relations in two other realms: lessons learned from the history of regional integration agreements in Latin America, the Middle East and North Africa, sub-Saharan Africa, and East Asia; and the role of South–South blocs in the World Trade Organization (WTO).

The WTO emerged after a pivotal decade, the 1980s, when the debt crisis was followed by a marked shift in bargaining power between the North and the South. Led by the US government, this shift was used as an opportunity to radically transform the agenda, dismantle the state-led development model and redirect economic discourse worldwide towards privatization, deregulation and liberalization in what became known as the Washington Consensus, marching under the banner of TINA ("There Is No Alternative"). As an embodiment of this shift, the WTO nevertheless also provided a space for developing countries to form coalitions to advance their interests. We examine those coalitions and their efficacy in some detail. Then we discuss how countries of the global North have shifted gears and moved outside the WTO to pursue investment treaties, with considerable importance for developing countries. In this final section, the chapter also explores the increasing use of WTO dispute-settlement mechanisms as well as the mechanism for settling investor-state disputes between the North and the South.

In chapter 3 we examine a variety of theoretical frameworks for describing and analyzing South–South vs. South–North trade and finance. Most theories of international and development economics, including both mainstream and non-mainstream approaches, focus on either North–South or North–North interactions while largely neglecting similar interactions between two or more countries of the South. We have mined the vast expanse of economic theory from international economics, development economics and international political economy (IPE), refining from it conceptual frameworks with direct or indirect implications for South–South economic relations. Though the chapter's purpose is theoretical, not empirical, we also provide data to clarify the theoretical discussion and ensure that it is accessible to non-specialists.

Within trade theory, much of the discussion has revolved around the "static" versus the "dynamic" benefits of South–South trade. Modern neoclassical trade theory is based on the Heckscher-Ohlin-Samuelson (HOS) model, which illustrates the gains from trade accruing to countries that specialize according to their comparative advantage at a given time. The HOS and similar approaches are said to be static because they prescribe that countries should specialize eternally in whatever they are better at producing today. Dynamic approaches, on the other hand, study the costs and benefits of repeated exchanges over a long period of time and allow the possibility that a country can change its comparative advantage and move up or down the industrial ladder, depending on the type of policies and exchanges it engages in. We argue that both approaches afford useful insights for understanding South–South trade and finance today.

As a part of dynamic approaches, we also survey structuralist economic models, which have typically indicated that North–South trade may create uneven development, and that South–South trade, capital flows and broader economic integration are, together, a viable alternative. This structuralist view is based on the idea that the closer two countries are in levels of economic development, the more beneficial the economic exchange between them is likely to be. However, it also creates the possibility that certain types of South–South trade may recreate North–South patterns of uneven development. Our theoretical survey also includes Marxian, dependency and world-systems analysis approaches, the last of these being particularly useful as it has created the concept of the "semi-periphery" a category that applies to many of the global South countries with large domestic markets and significant industrial development.

Since one main way that developing countries have advanced trade among themselves on a regional or inter-regional basis has been preferential trading agreements (PTAs), we turn to both economics and IPE approaches to understanding PTAs. By examining issues such as power and policy space, IPE approaches allow us to better understand why South–South PTAs continue to be pursued by countries in the developing world despite the way many such agreements fail to deliver concrete economic benefits. We conclude the chapter by discussing perhaps the least theorized aspect of South–South exchange, that of financial issues, in particular the issue of what impact the level of financial development within the South may have on trade relations.

Chapter 4 provides what we believe is the most thorough empirical comparison available of South–South and South–North economic exchanges, particularly those involving trade. In this chapter we analyze several aspects of South–South trade and finance: (1) the evolution of aggregate South–South trade since 1948; (2) changes in the structure and composition of South–South trade, as observable in five categories, including high-, medium-, and low-technology- and skill-intensive manufactures, resource-intensive manufactures and primary products; (3) the relationship between countries' incomes and their export structures; (4) the connection between export quality and export direction; (5) intra-industry trade, including the direction of this trade, the concentration and dispersion of exports of various products and to various countries; and, finally, (6) changes in South–South finance and the increasing role of the South in global foreign direct investment (FDI) flows. We also provide stylized facts that illuminate discussions in the other chapters of the book.

This fourth chapter reaches several conclusions that we hope will initiate new debates on the future of South–South exchanges. First, we show that there is a great divergence, not just between the North and the South but also between the Emerging South and the Rest of South. In fact, as far as trade structure is concerned, the Emerging South has converged with the North, notably in terms of the variety of both regions' exports and the extent of their influence on global trade. The countries of the Emerging South account for most South–South trade and for most of the world's exports in high-skill manufactured goods. In this respect, as we have already pointed out, the term "South–South" can be misleading, because in 2012 trade within the Emerging South alone accounted for 70 percent of all South–South trade in merchandise goods and 89 percent in manufactured goods. In contrast, the Rest of South is left behind, increasingly forced to remain oriented toward the export of primary goods or, in fact, to return to that orientation, through a transformation called primarization. In 2012, 74 percent of all exports from the Rest of South were of primary commodities. The Emerging South and the Rest of South also stand apart from each other when it comes to their export markets and their product diversification—the Rest of South being confined by a very high concentration in a few areas of production and markets for exports. Another aspect of trade that keeps the Rest of South apart from the Emerging South is its minimal intra-industry trade. Therefore, we argue that while "South–South relations" is still a meaningful term for some exchanges between developing countries, as a concept it is inadequate to capture the great divergence of income levels and economic development between various countries within the South.

In the fourth chapter we also show the importance of trade structure, that is, the type and variety of a country's exports, and we trace how that structure changes over time for Southern countries, both the Rest of South and the Emerging South. We discuss why we should care about trade structure at all, and we highlight the positive correlation between incomes and technology and skill intensity of exports, as well as between technology and skill intensity and export unit prices. We also show that the quality of exported goods is conditional on the incomes of both the exporter and the importer—and not always in a linear, uniform way. We explore increasing regionalism in South–South trade, and we include a discussion of the top export items from the

South and how they change over time. We document how trade barriers remain higher in South–South trade than in any other direction. Last but not least, we explore the changing topography of global finance, with the rise of a few Emerging South countries as major global lenders and investors.

In chapter 5 we synthesize our discussion from the previous chapters to explore what South–South economic exchanges imply for development policy today. We discuss whether the rise of South–South economic integration facilitates or inhibits "new-developmentalist" policy approaches. The starting point for our analysis is to ask two questions. First, what does a non-neoliberal developmental path look like? Second, under what conditions can South–South exchanges become mutually beneficial?

Many scholars have long challenged neoliberal dogmas regarding the role of the state in economic development. Through historical case studies of economic policy among the now industrialized countries as well as the newly industrializing economies, these new developmentalists have demonstrated that industrial policy, with active state intervention in economic development and growth, has been a key factor of these countries' success. In fact, both the first industrialized countries and those that have become industrialized more recently have used the state far more pervasively and systematically in their development than what they advocate for Southern countries today. These interventionist policies have included the state's active participation in human capital formation and infrastructural development as well as protectionist tariff policy and the channeling of domestic credit toward strategic "infant" sectors, technological acquisition, direct measures of support in return for performance requirements, and public-private sector partnerships. The question for the new developmentalists is no longer about the relative importance of the market versus the state but about how states can harness the market for long-term human development and implement effective industrial and agricultural policy.

We examine this new developmentalist literature to determine whether the increase in South–South trade and finance facilitates or inhibits achievement of the desired goals of developmentalist policies in developing countries. On one hand, South–South coalitions within the WTO, South–South PTAs and BITs, and South–South industrial and technology transfers all increase the potential for policy space and effective technological and industrial upgrading. On the other hand, as shown in chapters 2–5, some economies in the South are rising much faster than—and at the expense of—those other Southern countries. Increasingly, a few large Emerging South countries dominate South–South trade and finance, and the rise of these countries is accompanied by the deindustrialization and primarization of large parts of the Rest of South and even many other countries in the Emerging South. This pattern is particularly evident in the case of China's effect on Latin America and Africa. We also note that the rise of the Emerging South has reconfigured economic management within existing multilateral institutions, such as the International Monetary Fund (IMF) and the World Bank, and has also led to the rise of new centers of power such as the BRICS Bank.

The increasing power and influence of the Emerging South has come at the expense, not only of the North, but also of the Rest of the South. We argue that a return to South–South preferential trading agreements that give priority to technology transfer and regional industrialization is the appropriate approach, rather than simply freeing trade for "welfare gains" as the 2013 *Human Development Report* recommends. Chapter 5 ends with a policy framework for South–South relations and the new developmentalism that focuses on eight channels of policy: trade, technology transfer, investment (capital flows), institutional development, trade and investment treaties and policy space, labor rights, environmental rights and global governance. We argue that for South–South economic relations to truly deliver on the promise of a rise that lifts all boats of the global South, it must take into account the impact of relations among these countries through these eight channels.

One further aspect of the HSBC poster is worth mentioning, and is perhaps far more telling than the designers had intended. In the Chinese–Latin American trade relationship implied in the photo, the Chinese have created the mighty warrior and the Latin Americans have made the flip-flops. We hope our analysis contributes to building a world where all the people of the globe have an equal division of labor and distribution of wealth and power, so that they can work in the morning, fish in the afternoon and criticize after dinner, regardless of what they are wearing on their feet.

Chapter Two

SOUTH–SOUTH RELATIONS IN THEIR HISTORICAL CONTEXT

2.1 Introduction

In 1955 heads of state from newly independent Asian and African countries assembled in the city of Bandung, Indonesia, for a six-day summit. It was the first attempt by the global South to form closer alliances and cooperation "on the basis of mutual interest and respect for national sovereignty" (Bandung, 1955). The primary goals of the conference were to condemn colonialism and develop closer Asia–Africa solidarity while criticizing the dangerous nuclear armaments race and militarization of the Cold War struggle between the Soviet Union and the United States. The participants at the Bandung conference bore heavily in mind the devastating legacies of colonialism's economic and social disruption and reorganization, as well as the cultural genocide and marginalization their countries had endured as the result of political and economic imperial practices imposed on them for centuries. The South elites gathered at Bandung had found themselves inheriting largely agricultural societies and a global division of labor with the North whereby they were exporting primary products in exchange for manufactured goods. Buoyed by a rising wave of anti-colonial energies, they were at the same time aware that they were in a dangerous and complex international arena.

The "Final communique of the Asian–African Conference," known more simply as the "Bandung Declaration," heralded the start of a third way, one that followed neither First World nor Second World logic, and later came to be known as the Third World Movement (TWM) (Prashad, 2007). This movement promoted collective self-reliance in the South, including economic cooperation, while formulating sharp critiques of global inequality. Going further, it made bold claims for developing countries as equals in the collective management of the planet. The Bandung Declaration also criticized nuclear escalation and made disarmament an "imperative to save mankind and civilization from the fear and prospect of wholesale destruction" (Bandung, 1955). Thus began the era of modern South–South cooperation.

Five decades later, in 2006, the South American heads of state met in Cochabamba, Bolivia, and there they issued another call for South–South—or more precisely, in this case, Latin American unity. Laying foundations for South American regional integration, the 2006 Cochabamba Declaration resembled the Bandung Declaration in many ways. Both declarations lamented the sharp inequalities between the global North and South; both called for political, economic, and cultural cooperation within the

South; and both spoke of peace and human rights. Yet there were stark differences. In 2006, all the leaders in attendance were democratically elected and oversaw relatively open and free societies, unlike the authoritarian leaders present in Bandung. The Cochabamba Declaration spoke of sustainable development, environmentalism and active and empowered civil society, concepts alien to the assembly in Bandung. In many ways Cochabamba was also far more successful; in the previous 15 years South America's leaders had overseen a period of unprecedented economic and political integration among the countries of the continent in a way that had remained largely an elusive dream in the Third World era. Yet, in many ways Cochabamba was also far less ambitious than Bandung. Calls for unity were limited to one region of the globe, and the group's attempts at integration were more an effort to push back and manage the vagaries of the international economy than anything reflected in the original "spirit of Bandung," in which the South saw itself as a moral force shaping global affairs and making a claim as equals in the global arena. By this time, the term "Third World," once a concise and eloquent way to group many countries that were newly independent and unaligned in the Cold War political landscape, and were un(der)developed, had become obsolete. Even though, from its beginnings, the term Third World was an overgeneralization at best, after the end of the Cold War it went through a metamorphosis and, in modern usage, became synonymous with less-developed countries, a reference to a place rather than a movement with highly ambitious goals of influencing the global political economy.

This chapter provides a historical context for the rest of the book, which focuses on South–South relations in the post–World War II period between the two conferences discussed above. We argue that the current wave of South–South relations, which started in the 1990s, is taking place under conditions that are very different from those of the original Third World Movement. Today, when South–South solidarity is invoked in global fora, it is done with the purpose of appropriating the moral prestige and intellectual appeal that the Third World Movement still holds in the South. Chinese officials, for example, have routinely invoked the legacy of the Movement when starting new ventures in Africa, and the 2000 "Beijing Declaration of the Forum on China–Africa Cooperation" contains several passages that could have been lifted straight out of the Bandung Declaration (Forum on China–Africa Cooperation, 2000). Likewise, in September 2015, Chinese President Xi Jinping, in a roundtable on South–South Cooperation co-hosted by China and the United Nations (UN) at the UN headquarters in New York, stated that "China was a developing nation belonging to the third world." Xi added that South–South cooperation unites "the developing nations together for self-improvement, is featured by equality, mutual trust, mutual benefit, win-win result[s], solidarity and mutual assistance and can help developing nations pave a new path for development and prosperity" (Ministry of Foreign Affairs of China, 2015).

Yet, today's South–South relations are driven by narrower goals, mainly focused on economic interests. We will show how the enormous structural gaps within the South imply that certain types of South–South exchange may be undermining rather than supporting economic development.

Second, we argue that understanding the legacy of South–South relations is important because both mainstream and critical accounts of twentieth-century global capitalist development have largely dwelt on the global North (Harvey, 2005; Panitch and Gindin, 2012). This slanted view misses a fuller picture of the ways the South itself has contributed to shaping the world economy. For example, as discussed in the section below on the Third World Movement, the Group of Seven (G7) was formed in part as a response to the militancy of the Organization of the Petroleum Exporting Countries (OPEC), the Group of 77 (G-77), Non-Aligned Movement (NAM), and the New International Economic Order (NIEO)—all initiatives that emanated from the global South. Even the more recent debates on the reform of the International Monetary Fund (IMF) and the World Bank, and the Western objections to the development of an Asian Monetary Fund (AMF) as a rival to IMF can be seen as a part of this broader picture. More recently, the rise of Investment Treaties such as the Trans Pacific Partnership (TPP) have in part been the result of successful pushback by South–South voting blocs within the World Trade Organization (WTO) against the power of the Quadrilateral Group (Quad): an informal group led by the trade ministers of the United States, European Union, Canada and Japan.

Anyone interested in working toward the goals of more equitable global development should learn from the accomplishments and failures of South–South interactions which today, in a way, function as the Rosetta Stone for our understanding of debates on global economic exchanges. In particular, what we attempt is an approach that measures South–South economic integration against its promise rather than assuming at the outset that it is either beneficial or harmful for the development of any country in the South.

2.2   Postwar Global Landscape

Born out of the Bandung Declaration, the TWM was a series of initiatives by the developing regions with the goal of coming to terms with economic underdevelopment as well as with a highly unequal political and global order shaped by the United States and its allies on the one hand and the Soviet Union and its allies on the other. The desire for collective action was real but should not be viewed as coming at the expense of each state's advancing its own interests—interests that in turn were shaped by these states' various class and social dynamics.

European colonialism had been a brutal experience throughout Asia and Africa at least since the Battle of Ccuta in 1415 when the Portuguese captured their first city in Northern Africa. From that date forward, European colonists would extend their control, in often violent fashion, over much of Africa, Asia and the Americas. Europe then was neither technologically nor industrially superior to all the regions it encountered, but European nations were superior in the one area that was most decisive, military power.[1] According to Maddison's estimates in the year 1500 the "West" (Western

---

1. Findlay (1992), among others, explains the growing North–South income divergence by the comparative advantage of the "West" in the use of violence over the "Rest."

Europe and Western offshoots) had a population of 60 million and a per capita GDP of $753 (in 1990 international dollars), while Asia had a population of 284 million and per capita GDP of $568, a ratio of about 1.3:1. By 1870 the ratio between the West and Asia had increased to 3.7:1, and by 2003, to 5.3:1 (Maddison, 2003). Furthermore, in year 1500, Asia (excluding Japan) accounted for 62.1 percent of world GDP compared to only 17.9 percent for Western Europe. Even as late as 1870 and despite its significantly diminished share, Asia (excluding Japan) still produced 36 percent of world output compared to 33.6 percent for Western Europe and 10.2 percent for Western offshoots (Maddison, 2003).

The history of colonialism is largely a history of violence and pillage. In his classic text *How Europe Underdeveloped Africa*, Guyanese scholar Walter Rodney rejected the "balance sheet" approach to assessing colonialism, which held that while exploitation and oppression characterized European domination of Africa, the colonial governments also did much to benefit and develop that continent: "Colonialism had only one hand—it was a one armed bandit" (Rodney, 1982, p. 205). Contact with Europe resulted in the wiping out of the indigenous population of the Americas, according to some studies up to 95 percent, replacing them with European settlers and slaves shipped from Africa. Meanwhile, in Africa the slave trade and colonial conquest destroyed land, labor and capital, with infamous episodes of ethnic cleansing such as the Belgian conquest of Congo that wiped out around 80 percent of the native population (Maddison, 2003, 2005; Hochschild, 1998). The underdevelopment of the Third World was "made," it was not an original condition (Davis, 2002).

When achieving independence, this legacy of colonialism weighed heavily on the minds of global South elites, as did the fact that they were entering a political and economic arena shaped by the Great Powers. In this arena, four institutions and processes were salient: the Marshall Plan, the Bretton Woods Agreement, the formation of the United Nations and the Cold War.

By the end of World War II the United States had become the world's largest military and economic power, and it took the lead in shaping the world economy—first through the Marshall Plan and, second through the Bretton Woods Agreement. In both cases, US policy was driven by wartime planning to shape the world in a way that reflected US domestic priorities (Panitch and Gindin, 2012).[2]

What this policy meant in practice was that the planners saw a role for the state in the economy that the private sector could not supply, at least in the initial stages of reconstruction or development. As Harry Dexter White argued in some of his plans for the creation of the World Bank, it was "futile" for the private sector at the early stages to supply the necessary capital for reconstruction, given the large investments needed and longer time horizons required for profitability. But the creation of the World Bank was

---

2. Such sentiments were routinely pronounced by US foreign-policy elites, such as diplomat and statesman George Kennan (1948), who wrote: "[W]e have about 50 percent of the world's wealth but only 6.3 percent of its population. [...] Our real task in the coming period is to *devise a pattern of relationships* which will permit us to *maintain this position of disparity* without positive detriment to our national security."

only a temporary solution. Eventually, as White suggested further, "[P]rivate capital will doubtless flow in increasing volume to areas in need of capital" (quoted in Panitch and Gindin, 2012, p. 75).

This emphasis on the eventual role of private capital—protected, to be sure, by government intervention where deemed necessary—would characterize South–North relations for decades following World War II. However, for the United States and other economically powerful actors, the first foreign economic policy priority was to restart economic growth and development in Western Europe since American leaders and their allies saw losing Western European nations to communism as the biggest possible threat to military and economic security. Postwar agreements granted European countries significant independence to shape their own development priorities, but the European Recovery Program, or Marshall Plan, which channeled billions of dollars to Europe (and to Japan), was created with significant US input and distinct geopolitical objectives (Wexler, 1983; Wood, 1986). The United States placed a premium on recovery of European productive capacities, capitalist development to counter the power and relative radicalism of European labor movements, and economic integration within the continent. To this end, the formation of a Western European Union, which encompassed currency and customs union and capital and labor mobility, and which included Britain, was seen as a top priority (Kennan, 1948). In promoting these goals, the Marshall Plan also paved the way for US corporate penetration of Europe and facilitated economic integration between the two.[3]

Another instance of US priorities taking precedence was the Bretton Woods Conference and Agreement of July 1944. This agreement created the World Bank and the IMF, and it gave a dominant position in both organizations to the United States and its European allies. After the International Trading Organization failed to pass as originally envisioned, largely due to objections within the US Congress, the subsequent General Agreement on Trade and Tariffs (renamed the WTO in 1995) became the third pillar of the global economy. The veto power and influence of the United States, as well as the way these three institutions operated, became the basis for key critiques that came from the South and were a major factor in prompting South–South cooperation.[4]

Finally, although its formation was to a large extent driven by the United States, the United Nations would become the major battlefield of international diplomacy for the Third World Movement and the site of some its greatest triumphs. While the UN was (and is) not a fully democratic and independent institution, the South has been attempting to assign it a greater economic and political role, since the UN has been

---

3. See Wexler (1983) and Wood (1986). Many elements of the Plan itself were shaped by internal US corporate interests. For example, Proctor (2012) demonstrates that although cigarettes hardly featured in the requests drawn up by the Europeans, of the $13 billion in total value of goods that the United States shipped to Europe between 1947 to 1951, the value of tobacco was $1billion, and tobacco funding constituted a third of all food-related funding in the Plan (Proctor 2012, pp. 46–48). Also, see Kennan (1948).
4. Even today, with its 16.7 percent voting share, the United States is the only member of IMF with a unilateral veto power. Japan controls the second largest voting share, amounting only to 6.2 percent.

the multinational institution most hospitable to the South's grievances and to the enforcement of international law to which, at least in theory, all states regardless of size and power are bound.

2.3 The Third World Movement

The Third World Movement was complex, often contradictory, and relatively short-lived, announcing itself to the world at Bandung 1955 and effectively ending at the 1982 debt crisis. Calling it a "movement" is somewhat misleading given that it was a state-led project. Its contradictory nature stemmed from the fact that, while attempting collective mobilization for political and economic equality, state elites in the global South were also consolidating power and reflecting what were often narrow class interests. Moreover, the global economy is not simply an open field of opportunities. Just as societies place constraints on individuals, so the world's most powerful players placed constraints on what poor or middle-income large Southern states could do to shape their destinies, even collectively. Those states were attempting to rise in a global economy in which they had little political power and even less economic power, thanks to laws and institutions created by the Northern states. The best way to understand the accomplishments and limitations of the movement is therefore to resist seeing dichotomies of successes and failures, and to avoid viewing the movement as static. Though many of its institutions, particularly the Non-Aligned Movement and G-77 continue to this day, those are mere shells of their former roles, neither having any visible collective impact nor attracting from their member countries any significant investment of political capital.

Nevertheless, in its heyday the Third World Movement was a significant force. The Bandung Declaration of 1955 had signaled the intent of the global South to play a role in global affairs without the presence or tutelage of the colonial powers. The very fact that these countries met was an accomplishment, and two main features of the event are noteworthy. First was the desire of the 29 participant countries to focus on economic development, political sovereignty and peaceful coexistence while establishing a neutral position with regard to Great Power rivalries, even when individual members maintained alliances with one side or the other of the Cold War divide. Second, in contrast, the reaction in the West (and to some extent in the Soviet Union) to the idea of forging alternatives to Western tutelage was at best dismissive and at worst hostile. One *New York Times* reporter gloated about the "rebuffs to the Reds" at the Bandung summit by US allies such as the Philippines, Thailand, Iraq and Iran (*The New York Times*, 1955). Likewise, a *New York Times* editorial chastised the participants for including colonialism and racialism in their list of grievances and expressed the fear that the "whole conference" was turning into a "gigantic anti-colonial football rally." It exhorted the participants to move on:

> Emotionalism over past grievances could easily cloud judgments over *present dangers*. There was—and there still is—the possibility that some of the delegations would be so busy flogging a dead horse that they could not see a live tiger. (*New York Times* editorial, 1955; emphasis added)

One "present danger" was of course, communism, and the live tiger was the Soviet Union. This trend in US and European media of portraying subordination to the United States and other Western powers as natural while regarding any independence attempt as dangerous and naïve, would continue throughout the post–World War II period.[5]

Although Bandung was a historic event for many reasons, undoubtedly the main contribution of the movement to global affairs was its development of the concept of nonalignment. As we argue further below, nonalignment can be described as the ideology of large developing countries on the path to asserting state sovereignty as they navigate the minefield of the global economy and geopolitics. A year after Bandung, this idea of nonalignment was crucially shaped by the 1956 Suez and Hungary crises, at that point constituting the largest postwar confrontation between Third World nationalist leaders and the Great Powers (Willetts, 1978). The aftermath of these crises brought together Tito of Yugoslavia, Nehru of India and Nasser of Egypt, and led to the Belgrade Conference of 1961, where the Non-Aligned Movement would be formally announced to the world.[6]

Containing roughly the same number of participants as Bandung, the Belgrade Conference witnessed a Southern leadership with a more sober and better-defined view of global politics. Their proclamation was derisively referred to as "neutralism" by the US officials at the time. The participants in the movement themselves distinguished between neutrality and nonalignment. Nonalignment was not neutral about all conflicts, just the Cold War. In this way nonalignment was an ideology concerned with the role of states in the international system, and it carried a foreign policy program that

---

5. *The Times* editorial was itself rebuked by a letter from Robert S. Browne, assistant director of the American Committee on Africa, published in *The Times* on April 19, 1955: "The implication of your statement, in context is that, compared to the aggressive ominous threat of communism, the issue of colonialism is both minor and virtually, if not literally, dead. Such a thoughtless statement is typical of the myopic vision which is alienating us ever more from the increasingly important 'uncommitted' bloc of states comprising the major portion of the Bandung Delegates. To expect nations which, just yesterday, were subjected to the humiliating treatment classically rendered to subject colonies to overnight "forgive and forget" is to ignore the realities of human nature. [...] Even more ostrich-like, however, is the implication that "the old type" colonialism is dead, or for that matter, even showing signs of an early expiration. Nothing could be further from the truth, and the nations gathered in Bandung are the first ones to know it. They also are not unaware of the failure of the United States to throw its weight into the destruction of this "old type" colonialism [...] to the more than 125,000,000 Africans who are today denied the right to rule themselves but are instead held in subjection by the leading Powers of the "free world," the characterization of their plight as a "dead horse" can only cause a wince or a sneer. Which of the great Western Powers could come to Bandung with clean hands even now? France? Britain? Belgium, The Netherlands? The United States? Regrettably, not one."
6. Though the concept of nonalignment can be read into earlier documents, including the Bandung Declaration, historian Peter Willets (1978) argues that the Belgrade meeting was the first instance of its announcement as a coherent set of principles, and that nonalignment, as it emanated from Belgrade, was of a more coherent foreign policy of large Southern states, different in nature from earlier declarations.

consisted of peaceful coexistence, equal state relations and cooperation for development and the ending of colonialism (Willets, 1978, p. 29). Ultimately, it emerged from the collision of five forces: the Cold War, interaction between developing countries and the rest of the United Nations, and the issues of disarmament, anti-colonialism and economic development.

The domestic component of nonalignment was developmentalism. In the post–World War II era the development project held the promise that if the South adopted the right policies it might be successful in catching up, or converging, with the North. Keynesian economics reigned supreme and industrialization under the modernization theory was the end goal. Economists of many stripes widely accepted the notion that the private sector or market forces were unable or unwilling to bring about rapid societal transformation. The war mobilization and the success of postwar reconstruction of Western Europe and Japan reinforced confidence in the public sector and planners in their ability to undertake large development projects. Soviet success in transforming an agrarian society into an industrial and technological giant, making it a global power, encouraged other countries of the South to do the same. Raul Prebisch's (and later the Dependency) formulation of the concept of core-periphery and his thesis on declining terms of trade as a result of the colonial pattern of exchanging manufactured goods for primary products formed the intellectual underpinnings of the economic outlook of the Third World Movement.

The countries of the South viewed the Bretton Woods institutions of the World Bank, IMF and the General Agreement on Tariffs and Trade (GATT) as the rich countries' clubs. Since they were just emerging from the colonial era, the African and Asian countries that founded the movement also resented the cultural hegemony and practices of European countries and thought those practices suppressed their own cultural heritage and identity. Examples of their responses include the Negritude movement, the work of poet Aime Cesaire, who rejected French colonial racism and upheld and embraced black identity, and Arab nationalist movements that called for a revival of Arab and Islamic culture.

As noted above, the Third World Movement of the post–World War II period was initiated by heads of state in Egypt (Gamal Abdel Nasser), India (Jawaharlal Nehru), Ghana (Kwame Nkrumah), Indonesia (Sukarno) and Yugoslavia (Josep Tito). Those leaders had been active in, and often at the helm of, various nationalist or socialist anti-imperialist, anti-colonial and pro-independence movements in those countries. Many were staunch critics of European and US hegemony in the global South. Yet, the Third World Movement (and Bandung itself) included pro-Western countries such as the Philippines (under President Carlos Romulo) and Turkey. For several important reasons the Third World Movement brought together a diverse array of countries irrespective of whether their official ideologies were socialist or not, or whether they were allied to either the United States or the Soviet Union.

The first reason was the Third World Movement's focus on "sovereignty," which today is sometimes referred to as "policy space." Whatever their official orientation, the leaders of the global South realized that their countries were weak and underdeveloped. Allying oneself with a big power can buy security and aid, but in too close an alliance one becomes completely beholden to the big power's dictates. All Third Worldist elites were therefore seeking alliances that would prevent them from being too beholden to a single power. Second, even the most authoritarian leaders could not ignore the fact that they must deliver internally on the promise of development and even the most pro-Western of them saw the Bretton Woods institutions and global North policy as completely inadequate in this regard. For example, in a lecture delivered in North Carolina, the pro-US Carlos Romula of the Philippines said that Europe gets a Marshall Plan while Asia gets "chicken feed," and even that little amount is not free:

> What is worse, [aid] comes with the accompaniment of senatorial lectures on how we must be grateful and how imperative it is for us to realize the advantages of the American way of life. And so on. Must Asia and Africa be content with crumbs and must we be told what a great favor is being conferred to us? (quoted in Prashad, 2007, p. 39)

The Third World Movement often combined a radical critique of the world economy with pragmatic reformist demands on multinational institutions, demands that reflected the debate between the more "radical" (or socialist) and "developmentalist" (capitalist) countries and had a significant influence on the twentieth century global landscape. The creation of the United Nations Commission on Trade and Development (UNCTAD), the G-77, the Global System of Trade Preferences (GSTP), a South–South free trade agreement, and the Non-Aligned Movement as well as numerous integration agreements (now known as the "old regionalism") are more well-known examples of South–South cooperation.[7] The G-77 became a major voting bloc in the General Assembly, and countries in the global South took turns supporting each other's causes by voting in unison on resolutions of relevance to each of them. Contrary to assertions that the G-77 was a bloc in name only, studies of voting patterns in the 1970s show that the "defection ratio"—the measure of bloc members voting outside the G-77 consensus as a ratio of total resolutions voted on in any particular session of the General Assembly—was in steady downward decline throughout the 1970s and early 1980s, reaching lows of below 1 percent, and only steadily rising after the debt crisis shattered the Third World Movement in general (Iida, 1988). The G-77 (which at its highest point was actually made up of 128 members) voted on economic as well as political issues, including issues relating to anti-colonial struggles in South Africa and Palestine.

Together the G-77 and other initiatives had a radicalizing influence on the international arena, and particularly in the United Nations to which many of them turned after having been shut out of the Bretton Woods institutions. This influence created a dynamic that is astutely documented by Balakrishnan Rajagopal, who argues that mainstream accounts of the success or failure of organizations such as NAM or institutions such

---

7. There is small strain of literature in the mainstream economics profession that has recently started to explore the importance of power politics in international economic exchanges. Writing in the *American Economic Review*, the highest-ranked journal in economics, Berger et al. (2013), for example, argues that the United States used political influence through CIA interventions during the Cold War to tilt the balance of bilateral trade flows in its favor, even in industries in which it had a comparative disadvantage.

as UNCTAD dwell endlessly on whether or not they achieved their declared goals—and that such accounts thus miss the crucial way in which Southern governments have used these institutions to radicalize the international discourse and make claims and demands against the great powers (Rajagopal, 2003, p. 88).[8]

The zenith of this movement was the unveiling in 1974 of the New International Economic Order (NIEO). The NIEO represented the South's vision of restructuring the global economy in a way that favors the South. The NIEO included institutionalized monitoring of commodity prices at the global level (an attempt to replicate OPEC for other commodities), technology transfer to the developing world, industrialization of the South, democratization of the IMF and the World Bank and restrictions on multinational corporations and foreign direct investment (Cline, 1979). The NIEO represented both developmentalist visions of the developing countries and relative success of South–South cooperation. Even though this new vision of economic development seems radical in retrospect, it was in fact a compromise between the more radical and conservative countries within the G-77.

In many ways the NIEO also represents both the possibilities and limitations of South–South cooperation at that time and the way that the developing countries used international organizations to advance their collective cause. Rajagopal notes that the radicalizing attempts of the Third World movements inside the UN carried within them their own limitations. He observes inherent limitations to the radicalizations of institutions that have their own "internal dynamic for the pace and direction of change in international social life" (Rajagopal, 2003, p. 92). Therefore, Rajagopal reasons, the other side of taking the fight to multinational institutions was the institutionalization of Third Worldist radicalism and solidification of multinational institutions as inherently legitimate terrains of deliberation and policy making.

Among the achievements of the Third World Movement we should also include the inclusion into the GATT of the Generalized System of Preferences (GSP) (1971) and the Enabling Clause (1979). Taken together these clauses further developed the idea of "special and differential treatment," or the notion that developing countries should not be held to the same trade liberalization standards as the rich countries by allowing, among other things, non-reciprocal preferential trade terms to be given by developed to developing countries as well as South–South preferential trade agreements.

Undoubtedly, the Third World Movement embodied many contradictions. As noted before, the movement was led by authoritarian and largely unaccountable elites whose claims for sovereignty were often a response to criticism of their internal suppression of

---

8. Hostile and patronizing attitudes toward organizations such as UNCTAD and economists who work in them can be found also among top mainstream economists. Two quotes from the more liberal segment of the profession might be illustrative of this general attitude. Krugman (1995, p. 514), for example, called "structuralists" as "noneconomists." On the other hand, Easterly called the economic analysis by UNCTAD as "dubious," and "trapped in some kind of intellectual maze" in contrast to the "higher-quality analysis" by the IMF and the World Bank which, according to him, are not subject to the problem of "one nation, one vote" problem. In his book, he further ridicules UNCTAD, claiming that he "may have been the first person to have voluntarily read" some of its works (Easterly, 2006, pp. 202–4).

ethnic minorities and their human rights abuses. As Thandika Mkandawire describes with respect to sub-Saharan Africa, they hung the same banner on their societies' doors: S*ilence, development in progress!* (Mkandawire, 2005). In addition many countries did not practice what they preached in terms of peaceful relations and often found themselves as belligerents against fellow South countries. Internal contradictions within Southern countries reflected different alliances and motivations, parallel to the current divisions among developing countries. Nehru, for example, noted the political intrigues taking place backstage at the Bandung Conference:

> A tightly knit group represented, if I may say so, the United States policy. This consisted chiefly of Turkey, Pakistan, Iraq, Lebanon, the Philippines and Thailand. The last two were at least somewhat moderate in their expression. The other four were quite aggressive and sometimes even offensive. A threat was made out that the Conference would be broken up if their viewpoint was not adopted. [The] object of Pakistan and Turkey especially appeared to be to create as many obstacles as possible. They did not seem to be much interested in agreement or in the success of the Conference. (Nehru, 1955, pp. 50, 62)

Finally, and perhaps most importantly, the gap between promise and achievement remained at its sharpest when it came to economic development and rising living standards.

The eventual demise of the Third World Movement came as a result of a variety of forces. The developed countries, led by the United States, were increasingly exasperated by their own inability to control the UN General Assembly, which the developing countries had democratized. Their exasperation led to the formation of the G7, through which they attempted to provide a forum for economic (and arguably political) deliberation and coordination that was exclusive to the advanced economies and without the meddling of the developing countries (Prashad, 2012). However, the debt crisis of the 1980s and the spread of Washington Consensus market-oriented policies provided fatal blows to the NIEO and the collective bargaining power of developing countries.

The Latin American or Third World debt crisis of 1982 was a massive economic crisis that started when Mexico defaulted on its debt obligations in August of that year. Pretty soon after that, commercial banks ceased lending to the rest of Latin America, leading to the threat of default in several countries in urgent need of refinancing their debts. The crisis was resolved in a way that (a) prevented the US and European commercial banks from sustaining losses by forcing the Latin American countries to nationalize all private debt, and (b) imposing structural adjustment on the Latin American countries through a series of plans referred to as the Baker and then Brady plans, indicating the US secretaries of the Treasury in that time. The plans all involved some sort of debt relief through debt buybacks, debt swaps, low-interest bonds and some debt haircuts (Ocampo, 2013). The economic and social results were severe: regional GDP per capita declined for three years in a row. The poverty rate rose from 40.5 percent to 48.3 percent of the population between 1980 and 1990, real wages declined and income inequality sharpened dramatically. In order to balance their deficits, governments imposed draconian cuts in investment, infrastructure and social spending. As Ocampo shows, the investment rate fell from its peak of 1975–1980 and never recovered, not even today, which at least in that respect is a "lost quarter century" not just a "lost decade," as the crisis is widely referred to (Ocampo, 2013).

The crisis was blamed on Import Substitution Industrialization (ISI) and the inward-oriented policies of those countries. However, as economist Carlos Diaz-Alejandro demonstrated in a cleverly titled famous paper, "I Don't Think We Are in Kansas Anymore," the crisis was largely the fault of external conditions beyond those countries' control. Diaz-Alejandro argued that if one were to examine the financial balance sheets of Argentina, Colombia, Brazil, Chile, Venezuela, and Mexico on the eve of the crisis, none of the countries would indicate as being in serious financial trouble. Moreover, the crisis happened to all six of those countries despite the fact they had very different economic growth performance and trade and financial orientation from relatively open Chile to relatively closed Brazil (Diaz-Alejandro, 1984).[9]

In fact the roots of the debt crisis lie more with changes in the global economy and the three external shocks: the oil-shocks of 1973 (when the price of a barrel of oil rose from $3 to $12) and 1979 (when oil prices rose from $14 to $21 per barrel), the Volcker interest rate shock in late 1979, when the US Federal Reserve raised interest rates, and global rates on borrowing shot to double-digits, and commodity prices declined, which hurt commodity exporting countries' ability to service their debt (copper prices, for example, fell by 50 percent between January 1980 and June 1982). During the 1970s, Latin American debt composition had changed from long-term fixed rates to short-term variable rates as they shifted from borrowing from states and multinational institutions to private commercial banks in the United States and Europe that were flush with oil-exporting country petrodollars and in need of lending targets.[10] (Devlin and French-Davis, 1995; Sachs, 1988). The eventual collapse of oil prices in 1986, as they dropped to $15 from $27 just a year before, turned the situation into a perfect storm by drying up the petrodollars. The situation was made worse for those countries such as Mexico that were dependent on oil exports for a significant part of their foreign exchange earnings (almost half of Mexican exports were from crude oil in 1980).

The spread of Washington Consensus policies through the conditionalities of the IMF, the WB and the WTO as well as massive pressure from the United States (particularly its Treasury department ideologues), led to a wide-spread conversion to the religion of TINA, "there is no alternative," among Third World Intellectuals, economists and policy makers. For example, the push for trade liberalization by these three sisters of Bretton Woods has made it extremely difficult for developing countries to use preferential access to each other's markets, as was the idea of the GSTP. Seeing each other

---

9. This can be contrasted with the situation on the eve of the Great Recession of 2007–08, which contained many red flags that an imminent disaster was highly likely (Roubini and Mihm, 2010).

10. A process known as the "recycling of petrodollars" since the money left those oil-importing countries in the form of higher oil prices, went to the oil-exporting countries which, in turn, due to low absorption rates deposited them in private banks. Finally the "petrodollars" came back to the oil-importing countries in the form of much needed loans so that they could continue with their ambitious development agendas.

as rivals in international trade also did not help. Even today trade barriers between Southern countries are the highest in the world.

Another reason for the end of the Third World Movement was the increasingly accepted view, disseminated by Northern academic and policy circles, that industrial policy is a relic of the ancient past, a view that led to dismantling of decades of work through the state planning organizations and state-owned enterprises (SOEs). The spread of bilateral trade agreements, particularly after the collapse of the Doha round of the WTO, can be seen through the lenses of North–South asymmetry as well. It became obvious to the Northern countries that dealing with one weak Southern state at a time, using myriad incentives and threats such as aid, preferential market access, and so forth, was easier than dealing with them as a whole. The surprisingly small number of WTO cases by the South against the North is an example of this unequal bargaining power that still exists today. Between January 1995 and October 2015, for example, less than 7 percent of trade disputes brought to WTO emanated from low-income countries as opposed to 49 percent from high-income countries. The remaining 45 percent were from middle-income countries. The African members of WTO, on the other hand, do not have even one single dispute filed at the WTO.

By the late 1980s, the Third World Movement was in tatters. When the Non-Aligned Movement met in 1989, they decided to form the G-15, a group of large developing countries that would be strong enough to speak with the G-7 and represent the South's interests at the IMF and the World Bank meetings. The major concern at the meeting was the debt burden of the global South, which was over $1.3 trillion, and the group pledged to find ways to alleviate the debt burden as well as finding financial mechanisms for enhancing trade among the countries of the South themselves. The G-15 was a complete failure however. As Sridharan (1998) argued convincingly, not only did the G-15 not represent the South in any meaningful way, its members showed such little investment in it as a bloc that the group could not even ensure a quorum at several of its summits.

In many ways the twenty-first century again has the potential to become the century of the South. South–South trade and, increasingly, financial flows have reached unprecedented highs and are growing. China, the most notable example of rising Southern power, passed Japan in FDI outflows for the first time in 2010 and has become the second biggest economy in the world, after the United States. South–South economic cooperation is also seeing a resurgence with dozens of new trade and financial agreements and growing bilateral aid flows, both in monetary and in know-how transfers. We will come back to a critical examination of this new resurgence, discussing both its potential and limitations in chapters 3 and 5.

2.4   Regionalism: Old and New

At the same time that developing countries were forming cross-regional alliances in the early post-WWII period, they were also pursuing regional integration that most often took the form of regional preferential trading agreements such as the Latin American Free Trade Area (LAFTA) or Association of Southeast Asian Nations (ASEAN). This integration has had two phases, what is referred to by economists as the "old" and the "new" regionalism. Both kinds of regionalism incorporated assortment of integration agreements. We do not attempt a comprehensive assessment or history of regional integration experiences. Rather we briefly discuss regionalism in Latin America, Middle East North Africa, East and South East Asia, and sub-Saharan Africa with the goal of illustrating a notable feature of South–South regional integration that is illuminated by that region's experience.

2.4.1   Latin America

Several of the earliest examples of regional integration and regional institutions were in the countries of Latin America as far back as the 1820s as a result of those countries' earlier independence and of consequent reciprocal trade ties (Furtado, 1976). Two points stand out from Latin America's integration experience. The first is that the shift between the old and new regionalism not only marked a different kind of preferential trading agreement but broadly signaled the dawn of a new era: the demise of developmentalism and the rise of free trade and capital flows. Second, however, regional integration even under the "new regionalism" still allowed the countries of Latin America maneuvering space to mitigate the worst excesses of globalization.

The Latin American experience with integration in the 1950s and 1960s most concretely exemplifies what is referred to now as the old regionalism because it took place at a time many countries were pursuing import substitution industrialization. The move toward bilateralism and then regionalism first started in Central America after a joint resolution in 1951 at the fourth UN Economic Commission for Latin America and the Caribbean (ECLAC). There, the five Central American governments—El Salvador, Nicaragua, Guatemala, Costa Rica, and Honduras—declared their desire for a Free Trade Area (FTA) that would expand markets and integrate transportation infrastructure. Given the large US influence and the primary product export orientation of the Central American economies, however, meaningful industrial policy coordination remained limited in scope.

The major trade integration agreement from this time period was the Latin American Free Trade Association (LAFTA) signed in February 1960 at the Treaty of Montevideo, which aimed at removing most tariffs in intra-regional trade by 1972. Negotiations had originated with Argentina, Brazil, Chile and Uruguay, and these four were joined by Colombia, Ecuador, Mexico, Peru and Paraguay. By 1968, LAFTA had encompassed all of Latin America. The driving force behind LAFTA's formation was the idea, advanced by Raul Prebisch in ECLAC's 1949 report, that ISI cannot be achieved in just one country, particularly as the Latin American countries were shifting from the "easy" ISI marked by light industry and non-durable consumer goods to the "heavy" phase marked by capital goods and machinery. Many studies commissioned regionally at the time argued that as these countries shifted to the heavy phase, the size of the market became a binding constraint (Furtado, 1976), and so the only way development policies would work was by unifying several countries in the region into a larger market. The pattern of trade structure in Latin America at the time did not leave much room for trade complementarity, and therefore did not support intra-industry trade. For example, it would be absurd to expect major growth in exports to come from Colombia selling coffee to Brazil. Therefore, developing new industries based on the complementarity principle as way of establishing new trade patterns, ones that are more based on manufactures than primary goods, was seen as an imperative.

The problems of integration, however, mirrored those of the Third World Movement. Latin American countries that signed LAFTA, particularly the larger ones, turned out to be more committed to single-country industrialization than regional ISI, and LAFTA's promise for developing new industries on a regional basis never materialized. Cuts on trade barriers were also minimal as, for example, in the first two rounds of negotiations about 7,500 product tariff concessions were negotiated but by the third round the number declined to around 300. Countries had the right to pull out of concessions already negotiated if they so chose, and "national schedules" that listed tariff-reduction obligations by country did not constitute permanent binding obligations. Complementarity agreements designed to allow producers to divide economic activity between countries to maximize market-size benefits were few and were in any case left to the initiative of private producers. As noted even in a secret CIA report, there were also no efforts to develop physical infrastructure to facilitate trade, including new transport routes, or to overcome credit bottlenecks producers face (CIA, 1963). Furtado wrote that "the lengthy and unsuccessful negotiations [...] made it clear that the signatories to the Montevideo Treaty did not really have in mind any drastic changes to their traditional trading patterns" (Furtado, 1976, p. 235).[11] From the viewpoint of trade and regional industrial complementarity LAFTA was thus a failure, as was declared by some of the delegates themselves;[12] however, from the perspective of creating regional institutions and regularizing regional negotiations over joint interest, LAFTA was a success. This point was already raised by the foreign minister of Uruguay, who was quoted saying, "LAFTA was now too important to be left to the economic technicians" (CIA, 1963, p. 6). The United States was also aware that the member countries hoped LAFTA would become "a potentially strong bargainer against the United States, the EEC [European Economic Community], and other continental systems" (CIA, 1963, p. 4). The process of seeking regional solutions to joint problems itself created a path dependency that would have a lasting legacy even under different conditions such as that of the Southern Common Market (MERCOSUR).

The old regionalism era in Latin America, like the Third World Movement, ended with the debt crisis of the 1980s. In its place, a "new regionalism" arose in the 1990s most prominently with the creation of MERCOSUR between Argentina, Brazil, Paraguay and Uruguay.

---

11. Moreover, some countries benefited more than others. The Andean Pact was created through the 1969 Cartagena Agreement by a subset of LAFTA members—Bolivia, Colombia, Ecuador, Peru and Chile (who later withdrew)—who were at lower stages of economic development than LAFTA's largest members—Argentina, Brazil, Mexico—who the signatories believed were disproportionately benefitting from it (Hojman, 1981).
12. Quoted in Bureau of Inter-American Affairs (1974).

Most official histories of MERCOSUR trace its origins back to the 1980s when Argentina and Brazil commenced a process that resulted in the Program for Economic and Political Cooperation (PICE), signed in 1986. However, there are major differences between PICE and MERCOSUR with the latter representing in fact a sharp break from the former (Kaltenthaler and Mora, 2002). PICE had at its core the Capital Goods Protocol, which involved sectoral negotiation such as capital goods, food and nuclear energy. Its spirit and vision were developmentalist and its crafting included input from local researchers, labor and national industries of various sizes. MERCOSUR's core was the Common External Tariff and was free-trade oriented, often referred to as neo-liberal. Its negotiating process was largely secretive and was heavily influenced by big business and multinationals (Gardini, 2006; Botto and Bianculi, 2006).

The 1988 Treaty on Integration, Cooperation and Development formally announced the intention of a Latin America Common Market in ten years. Presidents Carlos Menem of Argentina and Fernando de Mello of Brazil pushed this date forward, and in 1990 they signed the Buenos Aires Act which, moreover, introduced a general approach to integration rather than the original sectoral one. In 1991, Uruguay and Paraguay joined Argentina and Brazil in signing the Treaty of Asuncion. By 1994, the Treaty of Ouro Preto formally ended the transition period, and MERCOSUR fully came into effect. By this time the process of regional integration coincided with a concomitant process of global integration, marked by major steps toward unilateral or across-the-board liberalization in the participating countries.

The Customs Union of MERCOSUR was largely a way to lock in liberalization reforms to be carried out by the Menem administration. Carlos Menem (July 8, 1989–December 10, 1999), a Peronist, came to power on a populist, pro-worker framework as well as a promise to end hyperinflation. Once in power, Menem implemented neo-liberal reforms: privatization of public industries and utilities, liberalization of trade and deregulation of labor and financial markets and, later in 1991 under Domingo Cavallo, the peso was pegged to the dollar. Menem and Brazil's de Mello were ideologically and politically allied to a pro-Western agenda, or at least found in the United States a solution to the crises plaguing their economies. As Bianculi and Botto (2006) note, while the Argentine government was working closely with the IMF, Menem's tariff liberalization went beyond what the IMF recommended. For example, the IMF recommended an average tariff of 25 percent and a maximum tariff of 40 percent while, by mid-1991, average tariff rates had fallen to 12.2 percent. As Menem explicitly stated, MERCOSUR was in a way designed to lock in the liberal reforms: "our commitments to regional integration requires us that we create a macroeconomic and institutional environment that will lead to greater economic efficiency and competitiveness."[13] In the case of MERCOSUR, the most influential private-sector actors were the multinationals and big conglomerates, which "were more involved in the tortuous mechanism of consultation and were also more in favor of integration than small business" (Gardini, 2006, p. 16). The reason is because multinationals saw in regional free trade the capacity for regional export platforms for their already-established subsidiaries. In this way

---

13. Menem (1990), quoted in Kaltenthaler and Mora (2002, p. 121).

regional integration was a means for multinational corporations to reduce costs rather than for national or regional industry to grow.

Nevertheless, the coming to power of left-leaning governments in the early 2000s, primarily in Brazil and Argentina but also elsewhere throughout Latin America, shifted the functions of MERCOSUR towards a relatively developmentalist direction, to the extent allowable under the framework of a Customs Union. As will be discussed in the next chapter, MERCOSUR's existence played a key role in pushing back against the Free Trade Area of the Americas that was being advanced by the Bush II administration. Moreover, Latin America saw the rise of ALBA (Bolivarian Alliance for the Peoples of Our America) and UNASUR (the Union of South American Nations) the former more explicitly developmentalist and reliant on technology transfer and direct aid between Venezuela, Cuba and others, and the latter a political project led by Brazil for a unified stance within the continent (Argentina, Bolivia, Brazil, Chile, Colombia, Ecuador, Guyana, Paraguay, Peru, Suriname and Uruguay, in addition to Venezuela).

Among other issues, this process reveals that regional integration's many steps, the move from free-trade area, to customs union, to common market and so on is not a logical or pre-determined linear path. The move from one to another, what these forms of regional integration are, their function and purpose are constantly being shaped by the interplay of internal and external forces.

2.4.2   Middle East and North Africa

The Middle East and North Africa (MENA) region was historically a thriving center of trade both within and outside the region and enjoyed a comparatively higher standard of living than other regions. It was also as a major hub for trade routes between Europe, East Asia and Southern Africa. Starting in the seventeenth century, however, the region lost its importance for the world economy and experienced a sharp decline in its economic and social development. Its decline in the global economy was accompanied by the rise of Europe, whose industrialization (and accompanying military modernization) instituted a new pattern of trade which, with a few exceptions, remains today. MENA imports manufactures from Europe and exports primary products and raw materials. Over several centuries this process has led to the subsequent decline of the manufactures and crafts production the region had enjoyed, such as textiles in Egypt and Turkey. This decline not only significantly shifted the pattern of production and trade but also disrupted intra-regional trade in agriculture and manufactured goods, which had expanded under the consolidation of the region under Ottoman rule (Owen, 1993). MENA's experience highlights two key aspects of regional integration: first, that regional integration is often either undermined or driven by colonial and postcolonial external intervention, depending on the interests of those powers. Second, that when analyzing regional integration, we should examine factors other than trade and financial flows. In this case, labor flows and remittances were leading factors rather than trade in bringing the countries together. In addition, cultural and ideological commonalities such as a common language or political grievances play a role in binding regions together in ways that pure economic indicators cannot adequately capture (Kadri, 2014).

On the surface, the MENA region is usually considered an anomaly in several respects, including as a holdout against democratization (Diamond, 2010) and also as a region that did not witness regional economic integration in the same way as did Latin America or East Asia. In particular, when evaluating the extent of economic integration in this area of the world, scholars tend to agree that "economic integration has hardly moved beyond the stage of rhetoric" (Aarts 1999, p. 911). However, more than in any other region, integration within the Arab countries of the MENA region has been a highly politicized issue spurred by the rise of Arab nationalist movements. In their various stripes, these movements have implicitly upheld the belief that the countries of MENA, where the Arabic language is spoken, constituted a joint region with common linguistic, cultural and historical traits. Arab nationalism was a matter of political, economic and cultural integration. In this regard, Gamal Abdel Nasser, who was also a prominent leader in the Third World Movement, was a key Arab nationalist. Nasser's popularity skyrocketed in the aftermath of the 1956 Suez conflict with Britain, France and Israel and from then until the 1967 Six-Day War, Nasser and Arab Nationalist sentiments were paramount in the Arab countries.

The entire region's track record is filled with various initiatives, some of them predating all integration agreements in other regions. For example, the League of Arab States formed in 1945 (in large part with the British encouragement), contained a clause for economic cooperation. In 1953, several countries signed the Arab Economic Council, renamed the Arab Economic and Social Council in 1980. While the Arab Economic Council produced the first multilateral agreement on trade liberalization specifically on agriculture and select manufacturing, similar to LAFTA, it included many "escape clauses" and contained no flexible provisions for payment settlement, nor did it interfere with tariffs that individual countries imposed. Integration, in line with the old regionalism in the Arab world, reached its zenith in the late 1950s with the formation of the United Arab Republic (UAR) between Syria and Egypt, a political entity that lasted from 1958 to 1961. Though short-lived and flawed from its inception, the formation of the UAR marked a remarkable achievement in the postcolonial era with the full political union of two formerly independent states.

As in the general evolution of regionalism elsewhere, countries in the MENA region have abandoned the notion of coordinated industrialization and economic development in favor of the simpler idea of liberalization of trade flows (Fawzy, 2003). While outwardly pursuing regional cooperation, most MENA regimes have in fact been interested mostly in political consolidation and state formation. In retrospect, intra-regional trade in MENA has been quite low, averaging 5 percent from 1948–79, 8 percent from 1980–99, and 11 percent from 2000–13 and is the lowest of any region in the world (IMF, Direction of Trade Statistics, 2014). Finally, some scholars have argued that the availability of windfall rents has allowed the regimes of this region to appease domestic constituencies and prevent a formation of coalitions pressuring integration or other deep structural transformations (Carkoglu et al., 1998).[14]

---

14. As Ventura-Dias (1989) shows, Asian countries had high intra-regional trade throughout the colonial period. This allowed "permanent marketing channels to be established" in contrast

However, the focus on trade in goods and services—only one type of economic flow—is a misleading measure of integration; it hides the existence of a regional system that features substantial intra-regional labor, capital and cultural exchange as well as ideological and political contagion effects—something reinforced by the recent wave of Arab uprisings. For example, spillover from intra-regional trade in labor has been a vehicle for transmitting the rents from this trade throughout the region, the rate of that transmission reaching as high as 20 percent of GDP for some countries (e.g., Jordan) and 5–10 percent of GDP for Egypt, Syria, Morocco and Tunisia, and as high as 15–18 percent for Lebanon and the West Bank and Gaza (World Bank WDI, 2015).

Despite the low levels of intra-regional trade in goods and services, the MENA countries were part of a regional system whose economic, political and cultural dimensions provided stability to the governing regimes. Pfeifer (2012) uses the Social Structure of Accumulation (SSA) framework to show how the Arab regimes, both monarchies and republics, initiated public-sector-led development that allowed a conducive framework for capital accumulation.[15] In this view such a framework is supported by three pillars: (a) particular configurations of state–capital and state–labor relations internally that attempted balancing the interests of capital and labor; (b) relations between any regional state and a big power marked by conflict between the conservative and left-wing regimes but also intra-regional transfer of aid and capital flows, mainly from the Gulf, and labor flows from the highly populated republics; (c) regional state-big-power relations that also saw accord and conflict. Pfeifer argues that this regional SSA began to break down in the 1990s and was reconstructed in the 2000s along lines more favorable to Gulf oil capital, which has become dominant at the regional level, spreading its investment capacity throughout the region (Lawson, 2012; Hanieh, 2011, 2013).

2.4.3   East and South Asia

Growth in intra-regional South–South integration was fastest in South and East Asia, propelled by the emergence of newly industrialized and industrializing countries (NICs), including China, Hong-Kong (China), India, Malaysia, Republic of Korea, Singapore, Taiwan and Thailand. Though political and ideological factors played a role—ASEAN was originally formed as a pro-Western block—economic interests, particularly trade in merchandise goods, played the key role in tying the region closer together. The main point illustrated by this region's experience is that absent successful industrial development, regional integration—both as a vehicle for effective economic development as

---

with both MENA and Latin America, where those colonial needs disrupted rather than established intra-regional trade. In empirical trade models known as the "Gravity equation," former colonial linkages always appear as a significant determinant of current bilateral trade flows.

15. The SSA framework was developed by US economists David Gordon, Richard Edwards and Michael Reich (1982) to analyze the development of capitalism in Europe and the United States. Its uniqueness was in analyzing how political, cultural as well as economic institutions create a stable environment for capital accumulation over a certain extended period of time, and analyzes how those institutions fray and new ones form.

well as an alternative to Western economic hegemony—is unlikely to be sustainable within the global South.

In 2013, China alone accounted for 11 percent of world goods trade up from just 2 percent in 1990. Now the biggest trader in the world, it has become a major player in South–South economic exchanges.[16] Additionally, the development experience of NICs, including the earlier-industrialized Japan, have these countries to share know-how and expertise. The countries of the region have experimented with alternative economic policies, often in violation of the traditional Washington Consensus orthodoxy (Amsden, 1989, 2001; Chang, 2002; Rodrik, 1994; Wade, 1990). The diversity of economic policies and the accumulation by these Asian countries of significant experience in industrial policy have also allowed for a new wave of South–South cooperation, not only within the region but also between the countries of this region and the rest of the South.

One clear sign of increasing complementarity in the region is the level of intraregional goods trade, which increased from 31 percent in 1960 to over 57 percent in 2013. While it is lower than the level in Europe and Central Asia, 74 percent, it is nevertheless the second highest level of intra-regional trade in the world, and it accounts for more than 19 percent of all global trade. Furthermore, intra-regional trade accounts for 72 percent of the total trade in South and East Asia, the highest South–South trade of any region in the world, and in 2013 it amounted to 43 percent of the world's total South–South trade.

The efforts for closer economic integration go a long way in Asia. The Asian Development Bank (ADB) was jointly established in 1966 by the United States and Japan to help postwar reconstruction efforts and to finance development projects in the region. It was modeled following the example of the World Bank with the one-dollar, one-vote system, and interestingly its presidents have always been Japanese, similar to the American presidency system in the World Bank.[17] Other noteworthy integration efforts in the region include the formation of the United Nations Economic and Social Commission for Asia and the Pacific (UNESCAP), as well as a number of regional trade and investment agreements signed among the regional countries and aiming at fostering closer integration such as the Bangkok agreement of 1975, as well as the Asian Clearing Union (ACU) in 1974 to facilitate balance-of-payments settlements, currency swaps and central-bank cooperation—also establishing clearing houses to use each other's currencies in current-account transactions.[18] The oldest regional agreement in the region is the Association of Southeast Asian Nations (ASEAN), formed in 1967. Likewise, the

---

16. We discuss the case of China in detail in chapters 4 and 5. The data we refer to henceforth are from the IMF's direction of trade statistics (2014).

17. The United States, Japan and the European Union are the largest shareholders, controlling 15.7 percent, 15.6 percent and 14.4 percent of the capital, and 12.8 percent, 12.8 percent and 15.7 percent of the total vote.

18. The Asian Bond Fund (ABF) is an initiative launched by EMEAP (Executives' Meeting of East Asia–Pacific Central Banks) in 2003. It aims to promote bond market development in the region by diversifying and redirecting the official reserves held by Asian central banks back into the region.

South Asian Association for Regional Cooperation (SAARC) was founded in 1985 by eight countries (Afghanistan, Bangladesh, Bhutan, India, Maldives, Nepal, Pakistan and Sri Lanka).[19]

A turning point in East Asian cooperation came in 1997 with the East Asian crisis, which made the need for regional solutions to regional problems more urgent. The handling of the crisis by the IMF, together with US resistance to any attempts at regional solutions, only sped up these Asian countries' integration efforts and made Asia unique in the global South as the most serious challenge to Western hegemony in international economics. Two such challenges come from the aborted Asian Monetary Fund (AMF) proposal and the Asian Infrastructure and Investment Bank (AIIB).

With an initial budget of $100 billion and ten founding members, the AMF was first proposed by Japan in the aftermath of IMF's mishandling of the Asian financial crisis of 1997. Yet the AMF proposal faced fierce opposition from the IMF and the United States as they argued that such a rival financial institution would cause a rift between Asia and the West and would create moral hazard problem by allowing easier access to its financial resources without undertaking the painful, but allegedly necessary, structural reforms pushed by the IMF through its draconian conditionality requirements. The real motivations are undoubtedly complex but obviously include the desire of the IMF to maintain its monopoly in Asian (and Southern) monetary and economic affairs, and of the United States to protect its hegemony in the region.[20] Establishment of the fund may also offer an alternative to other Southern countries to follow. Interestingly, China and Korea also opposed the AMF proposal, as they feared the motivations of their former colonizer, Japan.[21] In 1997, in the face of the US, IMF and Chinese opposition, Japan dropped the AMF proposal in favor of much smaller initiatives such as the New

---

19. The legacy of the Non-Aligned Movement is visible in many of these regional agreements. Article 1 of SAARC Charter, for example, states that its goals include "promoting peace, stability, amity and progress in the region through strict adherence to the principles of the United Nations Charter and Non-Alignment, particularly respect for the principles of sovereign equality, territorial integrity, national independence, non-use of force and non-interference in the internal affairs of other States and peaceful settlement of all disputes" (SAARC, 2015). Its article 5 states: "Convinced further that economic, social and technical cooperation among the countries of South Asia would contribute significantly to national and collective self-reliance" (SAARC, 2015). For an in-depth discussion of regional cooperation efforts in Asia, see Kumar (2008) and also the Secretary-General of the United Nations address to the 58th session of the General Assembly (2004).

20. US Deputy Secretary of Treasury Lawrence Summers is reported to have called Japanese Vice Minister for International Finance Eisuke Sakakibara and told him, "I thought you were a friend" (quoted in Lipscy, 2003). The main discussion point is argued to be the exclusion of the United States and rivalry with the hegemony of IMF (Lipscy, 2003). Lipscy (2003, p. 95) argues that initially Japan did not inform the United States of its proposal for fears of "stiff resistance." One key sticking point was also on the issue of capital controls, which was opposed vehemently by the United States and IMF. It is interesting that it took a decade for the IMF to allow for this possibility in reports they issued in the aftermath of the Great Recession.

21. For a fuller discussion of the conditions surrounding the AMF proposal, see Bergsten (1998), Hughes (2000), and Hook et al. (2011).

Miyazawa Initiative which offered over $80 billion in total to help countries suffering from the East Asian crisis of 1997.[22]

The most recent challenge to US hegemony in global monetary affairs came from China with the establishment of the Asian Infrastructure and Investment Bank (AIIB), which will be discussed in more detail in chapter 5. The AIIB's successful launch shows, among other things, the diminishing power of the US in Asia and the prospects for deeper regional integration.

2.4.4 Sub-Saharan Africa

The footprints of colonialism are visible throughout the developing world, from the Middle East to Asia and Latin America. However, one could argue that those footprints have been heaviest and most numerous in Africa, where deep inter- and intra-regional divisions were created by the colonial powers as far back as the Berlin Conference of 1884–85, when African nationalities were partitioned by the colonial powers of Europe. The creation of states for the purpose of dividing areas of exploitation and access to resources, has resulted in a bondage relationship between modern African nations and their former colonial masters, who continue to enjoy privileged access to their former colonies and to maintain hegemonic control through economic, political and institutional structures which, in many cases, they molded themselves. To take just one example, the West African and Central African CFA (Financial Community of Africa) francs are currencies created in 1945 by France to be used in its colonies and are still backed by the French treasury today. The CFA franc is used by in 14 countries, 12 of which are former French colonies, as well as a former Portuguese colony (Guinea Bissau) and one former Spanish colony (Equatorial Guinea). As a result, these countries lack independent central banks and any monetary autonomy.

These numerous colonial linkages, together with the lack of a sufficient number of middle-income developing countries, make integration more difficult in this region. As a result, sub-Saharan Africa exports goods to Europe at the highest concentration rate of any region outside Europe itself (34 percent between 1995 and 2009). Its share of exports to Latin America is a bare 4 percent, to MENA 3 percent, and to South Asia 5 percent. It is no surprise that intra-regional trade accounted for only 12.5 percent of its total regional trade during the period 1995–2009. Furthermore, primary products dominate its exports with little value added. Primary products, for example, accounted for 60 percent of total value and 63 percent of the volume of African exports between 1995 and 2009. Resource-intensive-manufactures accounted for 20 percent of the value and 31 percent of the volume of exports. Taken together those figures mean that 80 percent of sub-Saharan African export earnings came from primary products or resource-intensive manufactures, accounting for 94 percent total export volume from the region. In terms of dollar value, less than 2 percent of exports were of high-skill manufactures, the lowest percentage of any region in the world (the data are from chapter 4).

---

22. Japan's own foreign ministry details its contributions toward the Asian crisis, which can be accessed here: http://www.mofa.go.jp/policy/economy/asia/crisis0010.html

Table 2.1 Percentage share of intra-regional South–South PTAs in total PTAs by region

	MENA	South Asia	Sub-Saharan Africa	East Asia & Pacific	Europe & Central Asia	Latin America & Caribbean
1980	7.4	20.8	0.0	37.8	12.9	81.5
1990	14.4	7.0	16.9	25.9	6.0	49.5
2000	46.9	18.9	64.2	28.0	43.5	46.5
2013	40.0	19.0	59.7	32.1	45.0	38.8

Source: WTO (2014) and authors' calculations.
Note: The data refer to the number of PTAs signed between countries.

Nevertheless, sub-Saharan Africa has the highest concentration of intra-regional PTAs among all other developing regions. The share of intra-regional South–South PTAs in total South–South PTAs increased from virtually nothing in 1980 to just below 60 percent in 2013, which is significantly higher than any other region (Table 2.1). The rapid increase in regional trade agreements coupled with the more dynamic growth that the continent has been experiencing in the past decade may be promising for the future of African integration and may contribute to further cooperation in trade, finance and institutional development.

The African Union (AU) was originally established in 2002 as the Organization of African Unity and, with its 52 members, is the most prominent organization in Africa. Among its goals are the creation of a common market, a pan-African parliament, and a court of justice. Another significant initiative first adopted by the Organization of African Unity and launched by the AU in 2002 is the New Partnership for Africa's Development (NEPAD). NEPAD's primary aims include economic and political reform in the region.

African nations have made many recent efforts, some of them successful, to put the region on a more equal footing with other countries in the developing world. The voices extolling Africa's recent growth performance have reached a crescendo (*Economist*, 2011). However, the region's integration with the Rest of South, particularly with China, has ambiguous effects and may jeopardize rather than enhance this continued growth, something we return to in the later chapters.

2.5   WTO and South–South Coalitions

2.5.1   From GATT to WTO

A major challenge for all developing countries was the formation of the World Trade Organization. Paradoxically, the WTO is important because it is perhaps the only remaining organization where South–South coalitions in the mode of the Third World Movement continue, even after they had ceased to be relevant in every other multinational venue. The WTO declares itself mainly a forum for negotiating trade rules but, in fact, it has represented something much more dramatic. In 1944 participants at the

Bretton Woods conference proposed three institutions. Two of these were established—the International Bank for Reconstruction and Development (the World Bank) and the International Monetary Fund—but the third, the International Trade Organization (ITO), was not. The proposed mandate for the ITO extended to employment, economic development, business practices and commodity agreements, and the draft agreement was signed by 53 countries, but it was refused by the most important one, the United States. In 1950 President Truman declared he would not even submit the ITO Charter to Congress for ratification. Given the US importance in the world economy, the ITO never saw the light of day (Matsushita et al., 2003). Instead came the General Agreement on Tariffs and Trade (GATT), which first came into force in January 1948 and was intended to serve as an interim agreement until the ITO was established. The GATT's rules and dispute-settlement mechanism were weak, given its contractual status and lack of legal standing as an international organization (Irwin et al., 2008).

The GATT lasted from 1948 until 1994, when the WTO was launched. The Third World Movement, G-77, NAM and the old regionalism all operated under the GATT. The global South always saw the GATT as a rich man's club and the move to establish UNCTAD and the G-77 was due to the GATT's predominant focus on trade liberalization. In fact, the first four rounds of GATT focused primarily on tariff reductions and it was not until the mid-1960s that anti-dumping and other issues were put on the discussion table.

Nevertheless, the global economy and trade flourished under GATT, with an average annual real growth rate of 5.9 percent from 1948 to 1994, and 5.7 percent from 1995 to 2013 (IMF, 2014).[23] There was no compelling reason solely based on trade for the establishment of the WTO. Rather, the reason was the desire by the so-called Quad (the United States, the European Union, Canada and Japan) to establish global rules on a variety of issues not related to trade. As the leading sectors in the global North shifted away from industrial development the Quad became more interested in providing explicit rules governing services, finance, investment measures and intellectual property rights.

The formation of the WTO was sold to world citizens as a "Grand Bargain" between the global North and South. According to this bargain, the North was getting an expanded mandate that now included investment measures, intellectual property rights and services, and the South was getting access to Northern markets in agricultural and textiles products while also being allowed to continue enjoying special and differential treatment and extended grace periods for implementation of the various WTO accords. In reality, however, the WTO agreement was little more than a unilateral surrender for the South. As mentioned earlier, the organization was established at a time when the bargaining power between the global North and South was at its most lopsided of the postwar period, with the South still reeling from the shock waves of the debt crisis and ensuing structural adjustment programs (SAPs) overseen by the World Bank and IMF. Second, the inclusion of agriculture was, even in principle, an ambiguous victory for the

---

23. The averages are based on total global bilateral exports deflated by (chain-method) US GDP deflator with a base year of 2009.

global South. Some large agricultural exporting countries such as Brazil and Argentina would benefit, but those such as India, more dependent on internal agricultural commerce, would lose. In fact, it turned out to be a total loss for the South as the Blair House Accord of November 1992 between the European Union and the United States shielded the most important subsidies in the global North, including the agricultural protectionism in the European Union under its notorious Common Agricultural Policy (CAP).[24] Perhaps more importantly, the WTO took another leap in the commodification of agriculture, with negative consequences for food sovereignty that had long been a mainstay of global South policy.

Disputes over agriculture would divide the South for some time in the WTO before the nations of the South would unite in agreement over global North subsidies. Another downside of the WTO was its radical reach and dispute-settlement mechanism. The mandate establishing the WTO added the Trade Related Investment Measures (TRIMs), Trade Related Intellectual Property Rights (TRIPs) and the General Agreement on Trade in Services (GATS), in addition to the Agreement on Agriculture. The WTO even included an agreement on public procurement rules which, however, was not part of the Single Undertaking, meaning countries could choose to sign on. In their analysis DiCaprio and Gallagher (2006) have found significant impact from WTO laws and rulings in terms of the shrinking policy space of all countries to conduct industrial policy. Table 2.2 shows the distribution of disputes based on the income levels of complainants and respondents through the Dispute Settlement Mechanism (DSM) of the WTO between 1995 and October 2015. Low-income countries are generally left out of this process given their low trade shares in industrial products, and accounted for only 6.8 percent of all complainants and 6.2 percent of respondents. In contrast 44.6 percent of complainants and 43.8 percent of respondents were lower- and upper-middle-income countries, most of whom are from the Emerging South. Most of the action, however, was between Northern countries (particularly the United States and European Union), accounting for 48.7 percent of complainants and 50 percent of respondents.

The DSM itself was the inverse of that in the GATT. Under GATT all countries, including the respondent country, had to accept the rulings of a dispute-settlement panel for its findings to be implemented. Respondent countries often agreed with rulings

---

24. In the years 2007–13, the European Union spent around 40 percent of its budget on agricultural subsidies. Even during the age of austerity, the share if these subsidies will amount to 38 percent of the EU budget for 2014–20. Adding insult to the injury, here is how the European Commission from their official website responds to the question of whether "the common agriculture policy creates food surpluses and hurts farmers in the world's poorest countries": "Did you know that the average EU farmer receives less than half of what the average US farmer receives in public support? The days of 'wine lakes' and 'butter mountains' are long gone. More than a decade of reforms has made agricultural policy more development-friendly. Today, over 2/3 of its imports of farm products come from developing countries. Bilateral agreements with many countries allow for low tariffs on farm imports, and the 50 poorest countries in the world can export unlimited quantities to the EU duty free. [...] The EU has preferential tariff agreements with many developing countries. [...] Did you know that the EU is not only the biggest donor of development aid in the world but also Africa's largest trade partner?" (European Commission, 2015).

Table 2.2 Percentage distribution of WTO disputes by income, 1995–2015

	Complainants	Respondents
Low Income	6.8	6.2
Lower Middle Income	24.7	24.0
Upper Middle Income	19.9	19.8
High Income	48.7	50.0

Source: ECLAC (2015) based on WTO (2015) data.

because of their desire for reciprocity, but the process left room for countries to object to issues they saw as key for development. In the WTO dispute-settlement mechanism, the reverse is true; the panel's findings must be implemented unless all member countries, including the complainant, vote not to implement its findings. This rule becomes even more important given that almost half (47.5 percent) of all disputes are filed by the trio, United States, European Union and Canada, who are also the main respondents, accounting for 48 percent of the total 495 disputes as of 2015 (WTO, 2015).

Looking at the top ten complainants and respondents, we see a clear picture. The DSM has been dominated by conflict between the Quad and the Emerging South. First, ten countries accounted for 76.6 percent of all disputes filed at WTO, and eight of these ten countries were also at the respondent end (the exceptions were Mexico and Australia). Second, among complainants, six of the top ten countries were from the Emerging South (Brazil, Mexico, India, Argentina, Korea and China), accounting for 25 percent of all disputes filed between 1995–2015 (i.e., 495), and were responsible for 58.5 percent of all filings by the global South. That is, only six Emerging South countries were responsible for more than half of all filings by the South. The Emerging South has also become a major respondent with five of the top ten countries from this group accounting for 21.6 percent of the world total and 51 percent of those from the South.

What is also evident is that the Quad is going after the leading Emerging South countries very aggressively. Furthermore, despite the increasing use of the dispute mechanism by the Emerging South against the Quad, there is still a significant gap between the Emerging South and the North in terms of disputes filed against each other in favor of the latter. Table 2.3 looks at the bilateral distribution of the cases filed by the top North and South countries, which are the United States, European Union and Canada, and Brazil, Mexico and India, respectively. While it is true that the largest number of filings have been between the United States and the European Union against each other, taken together, the total number of cases from the United States and the European Union against the Emerging South have exceeded those against the North. Between 1995 and 2015, the United States filed 59 cases against the global South and 57 against the North. Within the global South, China was the number one target of US complaints (the European Union was number one among the Northern countries). Likewise, the European Union filed 49 cases against the Emerging South and 46 against the North. India was the number one target of the European Union (the United States was number one from the North, and China was number two from the

Table 2.3 Top WTO dispute complainants by respondent pairs, 1995–2015

Northern Complainants			Southern Complainants		
Complainant	Respondent	Disputes	Complainant	Respondent	Disputes
US	North	57	Brazil	North	21
	Emerging South	59		Emerging South	7
	China	16		US	10
EU	North	46	Mexico	North	12
	Emerging South	49		Emerging South	11
	India	10		US	9
Canada	North	26	India	North	16
	Emerging South	8		Emerging South	6
	China	3		US	8

Note: The North refers to Austria, Australia, Belgium, Canada, Denmark, Germany, Finland, France, Greece, Israel, Italy, Japan, Luxembourg, Netherlands, New Zealand, Norway, Portugal, Spain, Sweden, Switzerland, United Kingdom, United States. Emerging South refers to: Algeria, Angola, Argentina, Azerbaijan, Bolivia, Brazil, Bulgaria, Chile, China, Colombia, Costa Rica, Croatia, Cyprus, Czech Republic, Dominican Republic, Ecuador, Egypt, Estonia, Guatemala, Hong Kong, Hungary, India, Indonesia, Ireland, Jordan, Kazakhstan, Korea, Latvia, Lithuania, Mexico, Morocco, Oman, Pakistan, Paraguay, Peru, Poland, Romania, Russia, Singapore, Slovakia, Slovenia, South Africa, Syria, Taiwan, Thailand, Tunisia, Turkey, Ukraine, Uruguay, Venezuela, Vietnam. All other countries are classified as the Rest of South. *Source*: WTO (2015) and authors' calculations.

South). For Canada, 26 cases were against the North, and 8 were against the Emerging South. Interestingly, there were no cases filed against the Rest of South. Looking at the top three Southern countries, we see reciprocity. Brazil filed 21 cases against the North with the United States being top on their list. Other countries in the Emerging South, on the other hand, were targeted with seven complaints. Likewise, Mexico went after the North with 12 cases, nine of which were targeted to the United States. Yet, 11 cases were targeted to the Emerging South. For India the North received 16 cases, with the United States again being top on their list with 8 disputes filed while India went after the Emerging South with 6 disputes filed. As is with the aggregates, none of these countries went after any of the Rest of South countries. What this shows is that the battles over international trade are taking place between the Quad and the Emerging South, with the Rest of South being left out of the battle, not for positive reasons, but for the fact that industrial activity and industrial exports there are minimal.

2.5.2 Rise of South–South Coalitions

Taken together these numerous issues meant that the formation of the WTO signaled a new global reality, one in which the policy options of developing countries declined dramatically. Although the deck was stacked against them in terms of both

Table 2.4 Top 10 WTO dispute complainants and respondents, 1995–2015

Rank	Complainants	Cases	Share	Respondents	Cases	Share
1	USA	107	21.6%	USA	126	25.5%
2	EU	94	19.0%	EU	82	16.6%
3	Canada	34	6.9%	China	31	6.3%
4	Brazil	27	5.5%	India	23	4.6%
5	Mexico	23	4.6%	Argentina	22	4.4%
6	India	21	4.2%	Canada	18	3.6%
7	Japan	20	4.0%	Brazil	16	3.2%
8	Argentina	20	4.0%	Rep. of Korea	15	3.0%
9	Rep. of Korea	17	3.4%	Japan	15	3.0%
10	China	16	3.2%	Australia	15	3.0%
	Total	379	76.6%	Total	363	73.3%

Note: Cases refers to total number of disputes filed by complainants and received by respondents. % Share refers to the percentage share of each country's total cases in total WTO disputes of 495.
Source: WTO (2015).

mandate and negotiation processes developing countries in the WTO enjoyed one major victory. Unlike the World Bank and the IMF, which have disproportional voting power for countries based on the one-dollar, one-vote principle, the WTO is based on the principle of one-country, one-vote. Thus at least in theory, any country can veto a negotiating deal, although in practice few countries, particularly small ones, have had the political or economic muscle to stand against the North. This realization probably is the reason why only 49 of 161 members of the WTO ever filed a dispute and none of them were from Africa. In fact, by 2015, top ten complainants accounted 77 percent of all dispute filings (Table 2.4). The following words from one developing country ambassador are a telling articulation of the limit on an individual country's power:

> The US can block consensus but not [my country]. If you block, the entire weight of the organization comes down on you. The problem is that on other issues I need others to be flexible. If I block on this issue, I am in trouble on the other issue. (Narlikar and Odell, 2003, pp. 3–4)

Nevertheless, the member-driven and more democratic governance structure of the WTO meant that developing countries soon formed effective coalitions. Initially they were driven by necessity: the issues covered in the WTO were so vast and complex that many developing countries were ill-equipped to handle them, and so they turned to other developing countries as a way of sharing technical expertise.

These South–South coalitions date back to the years of the GATT, one example being the Informal Group of Developing Countries (IGDC). Led by Argentina, Brazil, Yugoslavia, Egypt and India the IGDC took the lead in pushing for what eventually became the practice of special and differential treatment for Southern nations, and in coordination with UNCTAD and the G-77, the development of the Enabling Clause (Rolland, 2007).

South–South coalitions became more crucially important, starting when a group of countries known as the G-10 attempted to block the expansion of the WTO mandate to include TRIPs and TRIMs, an unsuccessful endeavor that nevertheless laid the groundwork for future cooperation between developing countries. These coalitions formed at the Singapore Ministerial Meeting of 1996, the Seattle Ministerial of 1999, the Doha Ministerial in 2001 and the Cancun Ministerial in 2003. Three of those four meetings ended with a stalemate or collapse, without a formal agreement, in large part because of South–South alliance success in blocking the Quad from further imposing its agenda. The Doha Ministerial, which gave birth to the now-famous Doha Development Agenda, succeeded in coming to a resolution only as the result of pressure from the United States, which was eager to show some international unity in the aftermath of September 11th. Even then, however, South–South maneuvers played a role in shaping the Development Agenda and almost succeeded in blocking the agreement.

The WTO has been in a stalemate ever since, with the Great Recession of 2007–8 further delaying the prospects of a global breakthrough. The 2005 Ministerial in Hong Kong did result in a joint declaration, but that declaration was limited, calling for the continuation of trade talks. At the 2009 Geneva Ministerial, the WTO preempted the talks by putting out a statement that the "meeting is not intended as a negotiating session[; …] the emphasis will be on transparency and open discussion rather than on small group processes and informal negotiating structures."[25] Developing countries had sufficiently pushed back to grind the WTO to a halt.

Scholars of the WTO have distinguished between two types of coalitions: alliances or coalitions that form around specific issues on the basis of mutual self-interest; and blocs, groups with a shared ideology. Alliances are thought to be more practical, accepting the overall framework and approaching negotiations with the view to seek out points of compromise and mutual benefit; blocs are taken to be reminiscent of the Third Worldist era, more confrontational, and seeking to politicize the debate and make maximalist positions (Draper and Sally, 2005; Narlikar and Odell, 2003; Rolland, 2007).

Initially, during the Uruguay Round negotiations through the first several years of its formation, until the Seattle Ministerial of 1999, all coalitions in the WTO were of the alliance issue-based type, and the lines were not drawn along South–North lines. One of the earliest and most famous was the Cairns Group of Agricultural Exporting Countries, which included Argentina, Australia, Brazil, Canada, Chile, Colombia, Fiji, Hungary, Indonesia, Malaysia, New Zealand, Philippines, Thailand and Uruguay. Formed in 1986 this group focused mainly on addressing subsidies in the United States and the European Union. Cairns was to be one among many. Other coalitions with more colorful names included the Café au Lait, Friends of Services, Friends of the Development Box, Small and Vulnerable Economies Coalition, Friends of Fish, Friends of Geographical Indicators, the Cotton-4 and several more (Hoekman et al., 2002; Rolland, 2007). These coalitions were often formed in response to sensitive issues that arose during the negotiating process, and they often dealt with agricultural matters or with what is referred to as Non-Agricultural Market Access (NAMA), in addition to

25. http://www.wto.org/english/thewto_e/minist_e/min09_e/min09_e.htm

the TRIPs and TRIMS issues mentioned above. The Friends of Fish promoted the end of fishery subsidies; the Friends of Geographical Indicators wanted protection of geographic names to go beyond only wine and spirits; while the Friends of the Development Box advocated maintaining special and differential treatment of agricultural exports from the Least Developed Countries.

Increasingly, however, developing countries grew frustrated, both with the style of negotiations within the WTO, and with the mandate of the WTO itself, which offered little gain in return for the huge concessions these developing countries were expected to offer. Of the groups that started as issue-based but increasingly took on a more militant stance, the best known is the Like Minded Group (LMG). Its initial members– Cuba, Egypt, India, Indonesia, Malaysia, Pakistan, Tanzania and Uganda– formed the LMG to address the "Singapore Issues," an expansion of the WTO coverage advocated by the QUAD in the Singapore 1996 Ministerial. These issues included public procurement, competition policy, trade facilitation and investments. Later the LMG took on the "implementation issues," that is, the extensive financial and technical costs developing countries would have to bear in order to comply with WTO regulations (Eagleton-Pierce, 2012). The "Single Undertaking," a main principle of the WTO, required all domestic laws, customs standards and so on, to be brought into compliance with WTO law, which often reflected the already-existing practices in the global North. Therefore, the adjustment costs would fall predominantly on the global South.

Scholars have had mixed reactions to South–South alliances in the WTO. Some considered issue-specific coalitions a more sensible approach for developing countries and a sign that they had grown up from the obstreperous Third Worldist years. Draper and Sally capture this critical attitude towards old-style negotiating blocs:

> Defensive, one-sided pan-developing country alliances are wrong in principle and unlikely in practice. The G77-type diverse alliances were logical in a world of import substitution policies and the Cold War, but are illogical and archaic in the present setting. Like the UN General Assembly and UNCTAD, they serve little purpose but to highlight Northern iniquities and otherwise indulge in rhetorical flourishes. (Draper and Sally, 2005, p. 30)

Similarly, in their analysis of the collapse at the Doha Ministerial, Narlikar and Odell (2003) blamed the Third Worldist style of negotiations that was advanced by the LMG:

> In raising implementation problems, the LMG went beyond simply opposing. They developed technical expertise and presented detailed proposals on a diverse set of WTO issues including TRIPS, TRIMS, agriculture including the Net Food-Importing Developing Countries, accelerated integration of textiles, customs valuation, and implementation of recommendations of completed reviews and WTO disciplines. All called for concessions by developed countries without offering them any negotiating gain. [...] The LMG did show a willingness to stagger some demands (e.g. its proposals on implementation issues identified some to be addressed before/after Seattle, and others to be addressed in the first year of the negotiations). But otherwise there was little indication of areas in which the LMG was willing to accept less or back down. All the demands seem to have been presented as an all-or-nothing package in which everything was a deal-breaker, rather than a set of prioritized demands on which some negotiation was possible. (Narlikar and Odell, 2003, pp. 9, 13)

The Like Minded Group did indeed fail in the Doha round together with other South–South alliances, as the Quad used a combination of carrots and sticks to divide these coalitions and force through a deal. However, the Cancun Ministerial two years later was a completely different story. In Cancun several coalitions succeeded in maintaining a hard line, increasing rather than decreasing in strength as the meetings went on. One of these was the G-22 (originally so called), a group led by India and Brazil, which formed around agricultural issues specifically (including members from the above-mentioned Cairns Group). At the early stages of the Uruguay Round negotiations, the two countries had been divided in their stance between Brazil's "offensive" position on agricultural liberalization and India's "defensive" posture; however, through successive negotiation rounds and the unfolding of WTO dynamics, both countries were united over the issue of global North subsidies. They agreed that there could be no meaningful discussion over agricultural liberalization so long as the United States and European Union maintained their lavish subsidies and heavily protected their domestic markets. Another prominent group, the African Caribbean Pacific (ACP) is a coalition of middle-to-lower income countries whose origins date back to the 1975 Georgetown Agreement. What essentially binds together these 79 countries (48 from sub-Saharan Africa, 16 from the Caribbean and 15 from the Pacific) is that they had originally signed non-reciprocal trade agreements with the European Union. Due to their low income, they had relied on market access to the European Union that was now under threat in the WTO.

During the 2003 Cancun Ministerial meetings, the G-22, ACP, LMG, and Cotton-4 were joined by other coalitions, including the Africa Group and the Alliance on Strategic Products and Special Safeguard Mechanisms. Together these groups solidified under the formidable G-90. All of these groups had members with diverse and potentially divisive particular interests. The issues they faced were agriculture and a desire to extend Special and Differential Treatment but also, more importantly, the ever-expanding and intrusive WTO mandate. What united them by the end of the Cancun meeting was their shared desire to take a stand against US-EU intransigence.

As mentioned earlier, the Doha Ministerial had resulted in the Doha Development Agenda agreement and a public-relations offensive by the WTO leadership to indicate that there would henceforth be priority during Ministerial summits to both the mandate and process of negotiations in the WTO, particularly on issues of Special and Differential Treatment, examining the roles of debt and of capacity-building for very poor countries. However, the South had accepted a raw deal at Doha. The few gains they extracted were mere promises, while in return the Quad extracted further concessions, particularly a commitment that the Singapore issues would be hammered out in Cancun. They had paid twice in concessions for mere promises (Narlikar, 2003).

In Cancun, in the face of pressure by the Quad, the G-90 stood its ground and the chair of the Ministerial, Foreign Minister Luiz Derbez of Mexico, called the meetings to a close before an agreement was reached. By the end of Cancun, South–South coalitions had moved away from the issue-based alliances that supposedly signified a more mature South and, back to the intransigent Third World bloc-type coalitions. However, this was not a sign that the South was clinging to archaic methods. The developing countries had tried the method of negotiating issue by issue but by now they realized that they were accomplishing little, and what little gains they were achieving they had to pay for with more concessions of their own. In the Hong Kong Ministerial, an even larger block was formed—the G-110, which consolidated all South–South coalitions.

Several processes came together to allow for the disruption at Cancun, and later in Hong Kong, and for the stalemate that has characterized the WTO ever since. First, global South leaders had been jolted into action as the large scope of the WTO's mandate had come to bear on their domestic economies, and on policy space in particular (Gallagher, 2008). Second, in 2001 China entered the WTO and there was some doubt, given China's export orientation, what side of the divide it would join. China has become the third most-accused country in the Dispute Settlement Mechanism, ranking right after the United States and European Union. On the complainants' side, however, it ranks only as number 10 and by and large it has not thrown its weight behind the aggressive postures of the Quad. As shown in Table 2.4, the Quad accounted for 51.5 percent of all disputes filed at WTO between 1995 and 2015. China's ambiguous role, coupled with the rise of larger South economies, particularly India and Brazil, has served to turn the tide of bargaining power further in favor of developing countries.

Ultimately South–South coalitions brought together widely disparate countries of the global South, but it is clear that the leading roles were played by the largest of those emerging countries. As with the Non-Aligned Movement, the display of power was possible due to large South countries carrying the South–South banner, in large part due to their desire to advance their self-interests. This is not an ideal situation for the smaller South countries. The disruptive power gained through South–South coalitions can forestall further concessions, but it cannot reverse the significant loss of economic sovereignty that accompanied the post-debt-crisis era.

In December 2015, Nairobi hosted the 10th WTO Ministerial summit with the hope of overcoming the 14-year impasse on forging a trade deal based on the 2001 Doha Development Agenda. Although the United States and European Union insisted on pushing through issues such as stricter laws on investment (akin to the TPP), the main sticking points remained tied to agriculture, specifically American and European subsidies. A recent study has found that subsidies, including in the 2014 US Farm Bill, will artificially lower global cotton prices by almost 7 percent, costing exporting countries of cotton around the world (most of whom are developing countries) $3.3 billion in losses (Lau et al., 2015). In October 2015 the Cotton-4 countries put forward a proposal for movement on the subsidy issue, but the question is whether they will receive support from other South countries, with Brazil having settled its dispute with the United States in a side deal, indicating the possible fraying of South–South alliances in the WTO (Wise, 2015).

The outcome of the 10th Ministerial, the so-called Nairobi package, was again highly questionable for developing countries and repeated the earlier cycle of compromises by the South in exchange for more promises from the North. This time the much-celebrated breakthrough for developing countries was the pledge by developed countries to eliminate agricultural subsidies, a long-standing demand by many South countries. Special safeguard mechanisms, or tariffs against agricultural import surges to protect domestic farmers, and preferential rules of origin for developing countries to benefit from PTAs were also put on the table, also ostensible gains for the South. On the other hand, the Quad also pushed for discussions on government procurement, investment, e-commerce and so on. In short, the Nairobi Package's benefits are still dubious, but it was not a major gain nor loss for the South. The fact that any joint agreement was reached at all was considered a significant achievement but, given the WTO's track record, it is unclear whether this is a good thing. However, what is clear is that developing countries are feeling the pressure and shadow of bilateral agreements taking place outside the WTO as an incentive (more accurately perhaps a stick rather than a carrot) to remain committed to multilateralism, a topic to which we now turn.

2.6   Bilateral Investment Treaties

In part because of their impatience with multilateralism in the WTO, the United States and several European countries have been turning toward Bilateral Investment Treaties (BITs). Although these treaties have existed throughout the postwar period, they were narrow in scope and usually meant to encourage joint ventures and FDI in targeted sectors. According to Van Harten (2007), starting in the 1990s a new type of investment treaties with far greater reach emerged, signaling a major transformation of international economic law whereby states have given control over core powers to private courts. Many of these treaties concern a wide variety of economic activities across all sectors of domestic economies, and they give private arbitrators the power to award compensation to private businesses for any losses they sustain from routine government regulation. Since the postwar era, developing countries starved for growth and investment were competing with one another for a small slice of the global FDI pie and thus were willing to surrender sovereignty over their economies in an unprecedented fashion. BITs contain seemingly harmless language such as "investors shall at all times be accorded fair and equitable treatment." In practice what this means is to severely restrict government behavior and provide arbitrators great leeway while creating unfair competition against domestic businesses that are not given the same rights. The most notorious example has been the case of CMS Gas Transmission Company versus Argentina. After the devaluation of the peso in the aftermath of Argentina's devastating financial crisis in 2001, CMS sued Argentina under the United States–Argentina Bilateral Investment Treaty. Having pegged its currency to the dollar in a one-to-one basis throughout the 1990s, Argentina was forced to devalue its currency, causing CMS to lose money on its investments.

> Here the tribunal concluded that the standard of fair and equitable treatment, although it was "somewhat vague," required Argentina to maintain a stable legal and business environment in the midst of its financial crisis, and that this was "an objective requirement unrelated to whether [Argentina] has had any deliberate intention or bad faith[…]." On this reading, the tribunal decided that Argentina's devaluation of the peso violated its BIT with the US, requiring payment of a very large award to a US firm that had invested in the privatized gas

Table 2.5 Total number of BITs by country groups, North vs. South, 1959–2015

	Rest of South–North	Rest of South–Rest of South	Emerging South–North	Emerging South–Emerging South	Emerging South–Rest of South	Total
1959–2015	687	278	812	560	803	3,140

Note: The numbers represent the total new BITs signed in each period within country groups and exclude Other Investment Instrument Agreements.
Source: UNCTAD (2015d) International investment agreements database and authors' calculations. http://investmentpolicyhub.unctad.org/IIA Accessed 12/3/2015.

sector, and heightening the prospect of further awards (which have indeed followed) against the country. The *CMS* tribunal, along with other tribunals, rejected Argentina's argument (echoed by other states including the US and Canada) that fair and equitable treatment is merely a component of, and thus limited by, the "minimum standard of treatment" as understood in customary international law. (Khan and Christiansen, 2011 p. 175)

The reach of the treaties is matched by equally large rulings against states, averaging about $98 million, but with a wide range, from $300,000 (Maffezini vs. Spain) to $149 million, in the case of CMS against Argentina, to $1.05 billion in CSOB (a Czech commercial bank) versus the Slovak Republic. On a global scale, Table 2.5 shows the total number of BITs signed by country groups during the period 1959–2015. Consistent with the post-1980s shift in the global economy, BITs spiked during the 1990s and 2000s, reaching 1,542 and 1,049 new agreements, respectively. In contrast, the total number of BITs signed during the previous three decades was only 378 (Table 2.6). In fact, 88 percent of all new BITs signed since 1959 took place after 1990. However, there appears to be a slowdown in the signing of new BITs since 2000. In terms of the distribution of BITs, we see that the largest concentration of BITS are in the Emerging South–North and the Emerging South–Rest of South groups. BITs between the Rest of South and North have also increased substantially since 1990s. The slowest growth has been for the intra-(Rest of) South countries, where the newly signed BITs remained the lowest. North–North BITs, not included in the table, are a minuscule number, totaling four between 1961–83 in large part due to relative harmonization of investment policies between countries of the North.

Data from UNCTAD show that North and Emerging South countries are also using other types of treaties, including PTAs, to introduce laws on investment. This category of treaties is referred to as International Investment Agreements (IIAs), which encompass BITs, but also other types of agreements that include investment clauses. For example, many PTAs now include investment chapters with commitments for nondiscriminatory treatment of foreign investors. UNCTAD has argued that a positive side of recently signed BITs is the inclusion of "public policy interests" aside from investor protection as part of the treaty. This includes issues such as sustainable development, job creation, technology and know-how transfer (UNCTAD, 2015c). Whereas only 11 percent of IIAs between 1962–2011 had such an objective, 67 percent of those signed between 2012–14 included it in the agreement. Likewise, 64 percent of new agreements

Table 2.6 Total number of BITs and ISDS by country groups and decade, South vs. North, 1959–2015

		1959–69	1970–79	1980–89	1990–99	2000–09	2010–15
North–Rest of South							
	BITs	49	30	76	246	252	34
	ISDS	0 (0)	0 (0)	1 (0)	6 (0)	41 (0)	27 (0)
North–Emerging South							
	BITs	19	47	90	487	156	13
	ISDS	0 (0)	0 (0)	0 (0)	26 (1)	212 (3)	120 (6)
Rest of South–Rest of South							
	BITs	2	2	0	75	159	40
	ISDS	0	0	0	1	0	3
Emerging South–Emerging South							
	BITs	0	3	18	363	156	20
	ISDS	0	0	0	3	30	20
Emerging South–Rest of South							
	BITs	1	9	32	371	326	64
	ISDS	0 (0)	0 (0)	0 (0)	0 (0)	12 (4)	22 (15)

Note: Numbers in parentheses for ISDS refer to the number of investor state dispute-settlement cases files in the opposite direction by country pairs. BITs do not include other investment instrument agreements.
Source: UNCTAD (2015c, ch. 5; 2015d, 2015e) and authors' calculations.

include exemptions for public health and environment compared to 8 percent before 2012. Moreover 70 percent of all IIAs after 2011 now allow restrictions on unfettered transfer of funds during serious economic crises, compared to only 9 percent before 2011 (UNCTAD, 2015b). However, on the downside, none of the IIAs signed between 1962 and 2011 have any clarification that the treaty does not "override national development objectives and the State's right to regulate in the public interest (for legitimate policy objectives such as public health, safety, environment, public morals, cultural diversity)" and only 11 percent of those after 2011 have such a clause (UNCTAD, 2015c).

Statistics on Investor–State Dispute Settlements (ISDS), the name for complaints filed under various IIAs, show that between 1998–2014, of 589 disputes that were filed, the South was on the defending end 90 percent of the time. Of 589 total disputes, more than 70 percent were brought by Northern investors against global South countries (with the remainder launched by other countries in the South). While not all outcomes of the ISDS favor investors, the threat of a lawsuit itself is a major deterrent for the South, which dares not employ policies that might be challenged by foreign investors, given the exorbitant amounts of awards involved.[26]

Table 2.6 shows both BITs signed and ISDS by decade. As with the rise of BITs, investor–state disputes increased significantly during the 1990s and particularly during the 2000s, even though the number of new BITs signed in the latter decade was in decline. A striking feature of this period is the increasingly one-sided use of BIT clauses by Northern countries against their Southern partners. For example, during the 2000s

---

26 For a discussion of the key reform areas in current IIA regime, see UNCTAD (2015c, ch. 4).

there were 252 BITs signed between the North and the Rest of South, and 41 cases were brought by Northern investors against the Rest of South governments. Yet there were none brought against the North by the Rest of South during the same period or, indeed, any other period. Likewise, the Northern investors brought 212 charges against Emerging South governments during the 2000s compared to only three charges brought by Emerging South investors against the Northern governments. The figures for 2010–15 period are not any different despite the fact that this is also the period when the Emerging South, as demonstrated in great detail in chapter 4, became a major investor globally.

Interestingly, despite the significant surge in BITs among the global South countries during the 1990s and 2000s, we do not see a similar trend in the use of dispute mechanisms as we do in North–South direction. For example, Emerging South countries signed 363 and 156 BITs with each other during the 1990s and 2000s, and yet filed only 3 and 30 cases against each other during these periods, respectively. The same is true for Emerging South–Rest of South BITs and ISDS. Overall, several trends emerge. First, a majority of BITs are signed between North and South countries. However, the Emerging South and Rest of South countries are also increasingly signing BITs with each other. Second, the North has almost a monopoly in the use of ISDS mechanism with little or no retaliation from all global South investors (whether Emerging South or Rest of South).

Who are these countries? Table 2.7 shows the top ten respondents (i.e., accused) and claimants (accusers) for the total number of cases, just between 1987 and 2014. The United States comes as the world number-one claimant, accounting for more than 20 percent of the cases files. On the other end, Argentina is the top respondent country with 9.2 percent of total cases. The evidence from ISDS cases, which are based on various BITs signed between respondent and claimant states, is not very promising for the Rest of South or the Emerging South. These two groups of countries are the most sued by Northern investors. Almost 9 percent of cases are filed within Emerging South

Table 2.7 Top 10 respondents and claimants in total number of ISDS, 1987–2014

Ranking	Respondents	Freq.	%	Claimants	Freq.	%
1	Argentina	56	9.2	USA	125	20.6
2	Venezuela	37	6.1	Netherlands	54	8.9
3	Czech Republic	29	4.8	UK	42	6.9
4	Egypt	24	4.0	Germany	36	5.9
5	Canada	23	3.8	Canada	33	5.4
6	Ecuador	21	3.5	France	32	5.3
7	Mexico	21	3.5	Spain	27	4.4
8	India	16	2.6	Italy	26	4.3
9	Ukraine	16	2.6	Turkey	18	3.0
10	Poland	15	2.5	Switzerland	15	2.5
	Subtotal	258	42.4	Subtotal	408	67.1
	Total	608	100	Total	608	100

Note: The USA as a respondent shares the same rank (i.e., 10) as Poland does. Freq. refers to frequency.
Source: UNCTAD (2015e).

countries against each other, which is the same percentage as within the North–North group. An additional 5.8 percent is filed against the Rest of South. On the other hand, the Rest of South is responsible for 3.2 percent of total cases filed against the Emerging South. In total, 18.5 percent of total cases are filed by the global South countries against each other, which stands in stark contrast with the number of cases they filed against the North, a bare 1.5 percent of the total.

UNCTAD (2015c, p. 125), has recently emphasized that IIAs are not "harmless political declarations" as they allow Northern investors to "challenge core domestic policy decisions[, …] for instance in the area of environmental, energy and health policies" (UNCTAD, 2015c, p. 125). This is why UNCTAD and other critics of IIAs have been advocating for a new generation of those treaties with clearly defined proposals to make them development-enhancing. Particular issues include governments' "right to regulate" in various aspects of development objectives such as sustainable development, environmental protection, public health or other social objectives. Current IIAs and their dispute settlement mechanisms are also criticized for allowing more rights to foreign investors than to domestic ones, discouraging progressive government regulations, arbitrary and inconsistent settlements and resulting in a lack of transparency (UNCTAD, 2015c). The uneven bargaining power of negotiating partners is also a major stumbling block for a new generation of investment agreements; however, this is an area in which South–South cooperation may make a difference. The new generation of South–South agreements should lead the call for more economic sovereignty and go against the grain rather than swim with the tide of draconian investment treaties. Thrasher and Gallagher (2008) in a comprehensive survey of investment treaties including North–North, North–South (European- and American-based) and South–South agreements do find that indeed the latter provide the most policy space for industrial development.

2.7 Conclusion

In the decade of the 1990s, the "anti-neoliberal globalization" movement brought together social movements from around the world and held the promise of solidarity from below—both South–South and South–North. Those movements that started in Africa, Asia and Latin America as a reaction to social disasters brought by the austerity and free-market policies of the 1980s soon spread to the global North. Bringing together indigenous and landless peasants, unionists, environmental activists and traditional left parties, these movements were also key in helping the developing countries shut down the Seattle Ministerial of 1999. The apex of the anti-globalization movement came in the 2001 Porto Alegre World Social Forum, a mass gathering in the Brazilian city that posed as the alternative to the rich and powerful World Economic Forum. The scale of the gathering led Michael Hardt, one of the more prominent social theorists of that decade, to compare the moment to Bandung:

> Rather than opposing the World Social Forum in Porto Alegre to the World Economic Forum in New York, it is more revealing to imagine it as the distant offspring of the historic

Bandung Conference that took place in Indonesia in 1955. Both were conceived as attempts to counter the dominant world order: colonialism and the oppressive Cold War binary in the case of Bandung, and the rule of capitalist globalization in that of Porto Alegre. [...] Whereas Bandung was conducted by a small group of national political leaders and representatives, Porto Alegre was populated by a swarming multitude and a network of movements. This multitude of protagonists is the great novelty of the World Social Forum, and central to the hope it offers for the future. (Hardt, 2002, p. 112)

However, the September 11, 2001, attacks against the United States and the ensuing global "War on Terror" brought an end to the anti-globalization movement, and the spirit of Bandung along with it. Center-left governments did come to power in Latin America, moving away from the Washington Consensus and leading to initiatives such as those reflected in Cochabamba. Elsewhere, however, elsewhere, free market policies dominated until the Great Recession of 2007–08.

The statistics on disputes within the WTO, as well as those that relate to investment treaties outside it, are revealing of the sharp changes that have occurred in the global economy. This chapter started with the story of two conferences five decades apart: Bandung and Cochabamba. Both contained a spirit of self-reliance, the promise of an alternative development model and solidarity against Northern hegemony—all elements that continue to emerge as drivers of current South–South exchanges. The attempt to forge a more equitable global economy by developing countries through alliances among themselves has undoubtedly shaped economic affairs over the course of the six decades after World War II. However, the optimism of publications such as that of the 2013 *Human Development Report* needs to be tempered with a new reality—that after the great divergence that took place between the North and the South starting in the 1800s (Pritchett, 1997) there is the potential of a new great divergence, this time within the global South itself. What is worse is the possibility that South–South interactions may be factors that propel this new great divergence. We use the words *possibility* and *potential* advisedly. As we demonstrate in the next chapters, there are reasons for both optimism and pessimism, and we stress in chapter 5 the ways in which the benefits of South–South relations can be harnessed and the negative impacts mitigated. However, what is also true is that the 1980s witnessed what seems to be an irreversible fundamental structural transformation in both the world economy as well as within the South itself, particularly a change in the conditions that allowed state-led development and gave rise to the energies that propelled the Third World Movement.

Chapter Three

THEORETICAL FRAMEWORKS
AND EMERGING TRENDS

In the early 1980s Alice Amsden noted that economists' views of South–South trade, when they existed at all, depended largely on their theoretical worldview. She might as well have said *ideological* worldview. She made this observation after the high point of nonalignment and the NIEO had come and gone, and the neoliberal offensive in the aftermath of the debt crisis had begun. In this chapter we explore how different economic theories approach the question of South–South versus North–South economic exchanges and discuss the reasons behind their conflicting conclusions. We will also analyze the impact of short-run versus long-run considerations in shaping how economists approach growth and development in the South. The majority of writings in economics literature is focused on the trade aspect of South–South and South–North economic exchanges, and thus this is what we discuss first in this chapter. In later sections, we will turn to other aspects of South–South exchanges, including finance, which has increasingly become an important aspect of this literature.

The sharpest critics of South–South trade were usually liberal and neoclassical economists who saw South–South integration at the expense of South–North as protectionism and remnants of failed economic models of the central planning era masquerading as economic integration. On the other hand, as shown in the previous chapter, the loudest calls for increased South–South economic exchange emanated from Third Worldist elites, intellectuals, and nationalists as well as left-leaning social movements that saw in South–South exchange both a means of solidarity against Northern hegemony and as an alternative economic model. However, as we argue throughout this book, there are grounds to defend as well as criticize certain types of South–South cooperation on purely developmentalist grounds. On the one hand South–South economic exchanges can be beneficial for Southern development and offer Southern countries a more diverse policy space for experimentation that otherwise would not be possible under the continuation of a Northern-dominated world economy. But, as we discuss later in this chapter, the South–South exchanges share some of the common fault lines that have shaped the South–North exchanges for the last two centuries.

During the heyday of this debate—from the 1950s to the 1970s—most of the discussion was purely theoretical, and any empirical evidence for or against South–South economic exchanges largely remained missing, and for a very simple reason: such exchange was a very small fraction both of South countries' trade and of overall global trade: that is, less than 10 percent (see Figure 4.1 in Chapter 4). This chapter presents some of the theoretical debates within economics, and Chapter 4, using stylized facts, provides a snapshot of the evolution of wider South–South economic exchanges in the post–World War II period. Our goal in this chapter is not to mathematically re-derive or provide a complete anthology of existing economic models developed since 1950s but rather to explain their underlying nature and implications for Southern development. Of course, choosing breadth over depth comes at a cost, which is the loss of nuance within each group of approaches. South–South trade is varied and complex and we shall not try to adjudicate among these theories; rather we present them at face value.

This chapter starts with trade theory itself and the standard "static" Hechkscher-Ohlin-Samuelson (H-O-S) model and then moves to "dynamic" theories of trade and their implications for South–South trade. Trade theory, as we discuss it here, ranges from the standard static H-O-S model to dynamic theories, and each kind of theory has practical implications for South–South trade. In this discussion, moreover, we distinguish between two notions of South–South trade that are often conflated: one is the argument for and against South–South trade; the other, for and against South–South *regionalism*. We take the former to be trade in goods and services between any two developing countries, whether or not they are regional neighbors, while the latter refers to economic exchange specifically under regional trade agreements.

There are two main reasons why this distinction is important. First, as we shall see in later chapters, a large and increasing percentage of South–South trade (and foreign direct investment, FDI) is taking place within and between different regions in the global South. Second, the discussions surrounding South–South regionalism go beyond trade to include a variety of political economic factors relating to bargaining power and policy space for economic development. Given the significant rise of Preferential Trading Agreements (PTAs) since the 1990s, it is also essential to consider the arguments for and against South–South regionalism that go beyond economic theory, namely, arguments from various international political economy approaches.

3.1   Static Neoclassical Trade Model

The modern neoclassical trade theory is based on the so-called Heckscher-Ohlin-Samuelson (HOS) model, which is an extension of David Ricardo's comparative advantage theory from 1817. Ricardo argued that for a *given* level of technology, countries should specialize in producing, and therefore trading, goods with which they have a comparative cost advantage. Like the Ricardian model, the HOS model also illustrates the gains from trade accruing to countries that specialize according to their comparative advantage. However, unlike the Ricardian theory, which explains comparative advantage from cross-country differences in technology, the HOS model explains comparative advantage and the ensuing international trade between two countries as an outcome of their differing relative factor abundance. In countries with a higher abundance of capital relative to labor (i.e., the North) the cost of capital-intensive goods will be lower, while in countries with a higher abundance of labor relative to capital (i.e., the South), the costs will be lower for labor-intensive goods. Through specialization and trade liberalization, the relatively capital-abundant countries (i.e., the North) export more physical capital-intensive products to labor-abundant countries (i.e., the South) and receive more labor-intensive products in return.[1] The same holds true if the factors considered are skilled and unskilled labor: countries with an abundance of skilled labor will export more skill-intensive products and import relatively lower-skill-intensive products from countries with an abundance of that factor of production. In other words, countries should specialize eternally in whatever they are better at producing *today*. In this narrative, based on their initial conditions, either in technology as in the Ricardian model, or in their relative capital and labor supplies, as in the HOS model, international division of labor will put countries into different castes such as potato chip versus computer chip producers.[2] As generations of economics students are taught, this theory is based on pretty strong assumptions that include, *inter alia*, that perfect competition and constant returns to scale prevail in all sectors, that factors of production (land, labor, capital) are fully utilized and that prices are fully flexible. More importantly, however, the Ricardian and its HOS version assume static technology and factor endowments, respectively, without saying anything about how they can be changed in the future.

As countries in the South vary in terms of their levels of development, the HOS model can be extended to explain the trade patterns of the Newly Industrializing Countries (NICs) or the Emerging South, using our parlance, as "middle countries." This approach helps to capture how critics of South–South trade would conceptualize most South–South trade relations. Compared to the model that assumes only two countries with two goods (and two factors of production), the "middle country" formulation, adapted from Deardorff (1987), is a three-country, two-good model in which factor endowments lie on a continuum, with relative labor abundance on one end and relative capital abundance on the other. A "middle" country (i.e., one in the Emerging South) lies some distance from either end of this continuum and tends to import labor-intensive goods from a less-developed Southern country (i.e., Rest of South), capital-intensive goods from a Northern country. This process will be reversed for exports, where the same country will export capital-intensive goods to the low-income Southern country and labor-intensive goods to the Northern country (Krueger, 1977; Baldwin, 1979; Khanna, 1987; Deardorff, 1987). Therefore, a Rest of South (North) country can compete with an Emerging South country in labor-intensive (capital intensive) products but not in capital-intensive (Labor intensive) products (Deardorff 1987).

Tables 3.1 and 3.2 illustrate the type of relationship discussed here. When we look at the top five exports and imports (and their percentage shares in the total) of Brazil, an Emerging South country, to and from Kenya, a Rest of South country, and

---

1. Obviously, with the removal of trade barriers in the South since 1990s the South has become a major importer of agricultural products from the North, which continued to protect its agricultural sectors under heavy protectionism and generous subsidy schemes such as the one under Common Agricultural Policy in European Union. Thus, adding insult to injury, the North emerged as a net exporter of high-skill manufactures as well as agricultural products.
2. Under free trade and even without international factor mobility, the model also predicts factor-price equalization with wages and prices becoming equal between the North and the South.

Table 3.1 Top five exports and imports of Brazil to and from Kenya in 2009

HS 1992	Product description	Value (1,000 USD)	Skill-intensity	Share
Exports				
271000	Oils petroleum, bituminous, distillates, except crude	12,835	Res-Intense-Man	13.0%
870600	Motor vehicle chassis fitted with engine	9,895	Medium-skill	10.0%
870210	Diesel powered buses	9,623	Medium-skill	9.8%
870190	Wheeled tractors nes	6,579	Medium-skill	6.67%
720824	Hot rolled iron or non-alloy steel, coil, width >600mm, t <3mm thick, ne	5,929	Medium-skill	6.0%
Imports				
410519	Sheep or lamb skin leather, tanned or retanned, nes	676	Low-skill	27.7%
210120	Tea and mate extracts, essences and concentrates	533	Res-Intense-Man	21.9%
40210	Milk powder < 1.5% fat	204	Primary	8.4%
410619	Goat or kid skin leather, tanned or retanned, nes	203	Low-skill	8.3%
848140	Valves, safety or relief	168	Medium-skill	6.9%

Note: The product codes are based on HS 1992 classification. High, Medium and low skill refer to high, medium and low capital and skill intensive manufactured goods. Res-Intense-Man denotes to resource intensive manufactured goods. Primary refers to primary goods. The classifications are based on Lall (2000) and are further described in chapter 4. Export values are in current prices.
Source: For Tables 3.1–3.4, BACI and authors' calculations.

the United States, a Northern country, we find some interesting trends. First, in the Brazil–Kenya trading relationship, four of the top five exports of Brazil are medium-level technology and skill-intensive manufactured products, accounting for 32 percent of its exports to Kenya. If we include the top export product (oils, petroleum, etc.) whose share is 13 percent, the total manufactures exports' share becomes 45 percent. Furthermore, the total number of distinct products (at 6-digit HS level) exported are quite limited, totaling 391. In contrast, only one of the top five imported products (valves) is medium-skill and the rest are low-skill and resource-intensive manufactures, or primary goods, together accounting for 73 percent of Brazil's imports from Kenya. Overall the total number of distinct products imported from Kenya is 424.

Table 3.2 replicates Table 3.1 for Brazil and the United States. In contrast to the case with Kenya, Brazil's exports to the United States are dominated by primary goods, which are its top two export items and account for 23 percent of the total. The total share of manufactures exports among top five export items is 9 percent. Yet, Brazil's top imports from the United States are mostly dominated by manufactures, accounting for 13 percent of the total.

Table 3.2 Top five exports and imports of Brazil to and from US in 2009

HS 1992	Product description	Value (1,000 USD)	Skill-intensity	Share
Exports				
270900	Petroleum oils, oils from bituminous minerals, crude	3,086,180	Primary	18.6%
90111	Coffee, not roasted, not decaffeinated	724,209	Primary	4.4%
880240	Fixed wing aircraft, unladen weight > 15,000 kg	527,681	High	3.2%
470329	Chem wood pulp, soda/sulphate, non-conifer, bleached	509,741	Res-Intense-Man	3.07%
720110	Pig iron, non-alloy, <0.5% phosphorus	496,136	Medium	2.99%
Imports				
841191	Parts of turbo-jet or turbo-propeller engines	805,022	Medium	4.0%
270112	Bituminous coal, not agglomerated	770,242	Primary	3.8%
271000	Oils petroleum, bituminous, distillates, except crude	704,140	Res-Intense-Man	3.5%
841112	Turbo-jet engines of a thrust > 25 KN	624,863	Medium	3.1%
300490	Medicaments nes, in dosage	456,238	High	2.3%

Table 3.3 below shows the total trade balance of Brazil with the United States and Kenya based on five product categories classified according to their capital and skill intensities as in Lall (2000). Partly supporting the predictions of the HOS theory, the aggregates suggest that Brazil runs a trade deficit with the United States in high- and medium-skill manufactures while running a surplus in low-skill manufactures and primary goods exports. On the other hand, Brazil enjoys a trade surplus in all groups of products, particularly more so in the medium-skill group, with Kenya.

Table 3.4a below shows the trade balance between and among countries of the Rest of South, Emerging South, and the North directions and its contents resonates with the special case of Brazil shown in Tables 3.1–3.3. First of all, it appears that the Rest of South has a trade surplus only in primary commodities and a deficit in the rest. Second, the Emerging South runs a surplus with the North in all but medium-skill manufactures. We should note, however, that some of these numbers have changed significantly since 1995. Table 3.4b below shows the same trade balance data for

Table 3.3 Trade balance of Brazil with the US and Kenya in 2009 (thousands of USD)

Product groups	Brazil–USA	Brazil–Kenya
High-skill	−2,634,630	3,420
Medium-skill	−6,197,084	58,508
Low-skill	439,187	435
Primary goods	3,703,919	9,385
Res-Intense-Man	1,062,239	24,409

Table 3.4a Trade balance of the Rest of South, Emerging South and the North, 2009 (millions USD)

2009	Rest of South–Emerging South	Rest of South–North	Emerging South–North
High-skill	−16,000	−28,400	85,800
Medium-skill	−117,000	−146,000	−137,000
Low-skill	−81,200	−3,916	304,000
Primary goods	241,000	284,000	202,000
Res-Intense-Man	−39,400	−8,623	5,583

Table 3.4b Trade balance of the Rest of South, Emerging South and the North, 1995 (millions USD)

1995	Rest of South–Emerging South	Rest of South–North	Emerging South–North
High-skill	−5,514	−20,800	−57,800
Low-skill	−19,800	−12,200	64,800
Medium-skill	−24,600	−77,300	−193,000
Primary goods	−9,809	−10,700	−12,400
Res-Intense-Man	−14,600	−17,900	−45,900

1995. Accordingly, while there has been little change for the Rest of South (except in the case of primary goods), there has been a radical change for the countries of the Emerging South. In fact, the Emerging South ran a trade deficit in all but low-skill manufactures back in 1995, which is quite different from the story in 2009. A structural change appears to have occurred in trade and in the competitiveness of the Emerging South countries during this interval, which is discussed further in this and coming chapters.

For many economists the explanation for such a pattern of trade is that, after many years of pursuing Import Substitution Industrialization (ISI) policies, many large developing countries (such as Brazil, Mexico, India) had failed to develop high-quality products that would allow them to compete in Northern markets; and, instead, they sought to unload those products—low quality refrigerators, televisions, tractors, machinery or even cars—on their smaller, less-developed neighbors. Already early on, for example, it was sh own that exports by larger Latin American countries—including Argentina, Brazil, Colombia and Mexico—to other Latin American countries were more "sophis-ticated" with a higher capital and imported component intensity than their exports to the rest of the world. However, it was also argued that much of this intra-regional trade in "sophisticated" exports simply represent an effort to recoup the losses arising from excessive import-substitution of previous years, often at the expense of trade partners (Diaz-Alejandro, 1973, p. 11).

This critique of South–South trade based on the HOS model is therefore also a cri-tique of ISI's impact on the structure of the domestic economy. The standard neoclas-sical critique of ISI is based on static resource misallocation effects (i.e., allocative inefficiency), which emphasized the anti-export, anti-employment and anti-agriculture biases of ISI. The basic idea behind the ISI model is that an undeveloped country can start producing industrial products and substitute them for those that it used to import, allowing it to climb up the industrialization ladder. Thus, by definition, ISI is based on a *dynamic* view of comparative advantage whereby countries can change the bundle of goods that they are good at producing.[3] To achieve this outcome, countries use high tar-iffs and quotas on manufactures imports, along with state subsidies of all sorts to domes-tic producers. The opponents of the ISI model argue that protectionism and subsidies create distortions in the domestic economy, shifting resources towards unprofitable and uncompetitive sectors, while at the same time punishing exporters (particularly those capable of producing labor-intensive products) and current consumers whose welfare is diminished because of the unavailability of higher quality and variety of imported goods. Rather than produce and export cheap textiles and basic manufactures that employed lots of people and enabled them to compete internationally, developing coun-tries tried to produce sophisticated capital-intensive manufactures for the domestic mar-ket (such as consumer durables and machinery) with little hope of competitiveness in the international market. High costs of imported inputs, overvalued exchange rates and financial repression also discouraged exporting activity. Because of the higher cost and lower quality of industrial inputs that had to be procured domestically, protectionism also hurt the agricultural sector.

Viewed from this perspective, South–South trade is not necessarily mutually bene-ficial. For the less-developed Southern country, the net result is not beneficial because that country is receiving low-quality (and overpriced) industrial products instead of high-quality Northern products. And from the perspective of the more developed

---

3. The United States was the first country to actively use ISI as an industrial policy. In fact, Alexander Hamilton himself coined the term "infant industry" in his report on manufactures to the US Congress in 1791. In his report, Hamilton advocated using a combination of protec-tionism for infant industries, imposing an export ban on important raw materials, subsidiz-ing industrial inputs, subsidizing and protecting new inventions, transferring new technology from other countries, providing industrial subsidies, establishing product-quality standards and developing financial and transportation infrastructure.

South, this type of export will not reduce dependency on the North because trading with the South is likely to increase the imbalances in the domestic economy (such as foreign currency bottlenecks, increasing imported input and capital dependence on the North, etc.), whereas trade with the developed countries may serve as a means of exchanging abundant factors for scarce ones. In other words, success in unloading those low quality capital- and import-intensive products provides incentives for their further production, exacerbating the problems their production causes in the first place.

Similar negative opinions of global South–South trade were voiced by other economists who argued that because of the ISI legacy South–South trade was marked by significant price distortions and an inefficient shift to capital-intensive goods. These economists declared that if a Southern country "does a great deal of trade with other developing countries [in capital-intensive products] this is probably a sign that it has distorted domestic prices" (Havrylyshyn and Wolf, 1987). In short, adherents to static theory suggest that any South–South trade in sophisticated goods is costly, unsustainable and is likely to do more harm than good in the long run.

The objections to South–South trade as well as the legacy of ISI have been challenged by economists like Alice Amsden who argue that this approach does not explain intra-industry trade between countries with similar factor-endowments. If a substantial amount of South–South trade is in fact between countries with similar incomes, then another framework is needed to understand its implications. Second, those who explain the South–South trade as a result of NICs trying to recoup their losses from the ISI period (by exporting capital-intensive products to other South countries) argue that this pattern of trade is made possible by preferential treatment of trading partners under various trade agreements and, therefore, causes trade diversion from the North. Otherwise, they argue, these Southern products would not be able to compete with the supposedly higher quality and lower price of Northern alternatives. However, while in the 1970s 50 percent of South–South trade originated in East and South Asia, none of this trade was subject to preferential treatment (Amsden, 1984). As we show later in the chapter, South–South preferential trade as a percentage of total South–South trade, and total South exports remained extremely low until the 1990s (see Figures 3.2 and 3.3). Moreover, even within preferential trading agreements among developing countries, tariff escalation has meant that heavy manufactures and other capital-intensive products were usually the least subject to reduction in tariffs. (As discussed in the next chapter, South–South trade in manufactures suffers from higher trade barriers than trade in any other direction).

3.2   Dynamic Theories of South–South Trade: Neoclassical versus Developmentalist and Structuralist Approaches

The main objection to the static critiques of South–South integration comes from the dynamic theories of South–South trade. The development of new trade theory from within the neoclassical school in the late 1970s and 1980s (e.g., Krugman, 1979) led to a new wave of criticisms of South–South economic and political integration efforts. The mainstream theorists were already aware that most of world trade was between similarly endowed economies, that is, North–North trade rather than North–South trade, and that this pattern contradicted the predictions of the HOS theory. As a result, the earlier assumptions of perfect competition, constant returns to scale, homogeneous products and immobile factors gave way to the assumptions of imperfect competition, including monopoly rights over new technology, increasing returns, differentiated products and mobile capital, with special attention to intra-industry trade, the most dominant form of trade among Northern countries.[4] These theories showed that trade liberalization allows for taking advantage of larger markets abroad, a move that could therefore expand these countries' production and growth. Accordingly, increasing specialization and exploitation of economies of scale, faster adoption of newer and better technologies, managerial practices and operational management, and openness to foreign investment are possible investment- and productivity-enhancing factors, all linked to openness and increased integration with the North that would not be possible under ISI.[5] Viewed from this angle, the South–South exchanges also appeared to be a second-best option to North–South exchanges. However, the growing divergence between the North and the South incomes—see Pritchett (1997) for an earlier discussion on this point—led to a new series of papers that emphasized the importance of initial conditions that can generate differences in incomes and growth rates (Krugman, 1987, 1991a; Lucas, 1988; Becker, 1990; Matsuyama, 1991). These papers stood in stark contrast to the endogenous growth models of around the same period, which argued for a trade-induced conditional convergence in cross-country growth rates (Romer, 1990; Grossman and Helpman, 1991; Taylor 1993). As Feenstra (1996) pointed out, the assumption of perfect international diffusion of knowledge is a necessary condition for the convergence story to materialize. Once we drop that assumption, as in Feenstra (1996), the same models can generate divergence across countries, particularly in the North–South direction (see below), and can help the rise of "convergence clubs."[6]

The North–South interactions are often analyzed through the engine of a global growth metaphor (e.g., Lewis, 1980; Taylor, 1981). According to such analysis, increasing Northern growth moves the terms of trade in favor of the South, leading to faster growth and higher capital accumulation in the South as well. Both the neoclassical camp and those outside it, such as the structuralist tradition, have produced a rich

---

4. We should note that these points, imperfect competition, increasing returns and endogenous technological change (together with surplus labor), were present from the beginning in the classical development theory (see Rosenstein-Rodan, 1943, 1984; Nurkse, 1952, 1953). Yet, the new trade and new growth theory literature completely ignored this literature with no reference cited therein. For a discussion, see, Ros (2000, 2008, 2013 ch. 2).
5. The theoretical and empirical evidence on the dynamic gains critique remains very weak. Despite hundreds of empirical studies on the topic, the link between trade openness or export promotion and productivity growth is sketchy at best (Rodrik and Rodriguez, 1999). Meanwhile, a growing literature shows how the opposite is happening in developing countries, which have started experiencing deindustrialization and losses in productivity (UNCTAD, 2003, 2006; McMillan and Rodrik, 2011; Paz, 2014).
6. Convergence clubs refer to income convergence within certain groups of countries such as the OECD.

variety of these types of North–South trade models. In most of these models, the North–South interaction is destined to be asymmetric and "uneven" because of the structure of trade involved whereby the North produces capital goods while the South produces primary goods (Dutt, 1990; Findlay, 1980, Taylor, 1981).[7] As a result, Southern growth is always dependent on Northern growth and is not self-sustaining. Suppose, for example, that because of technological change the South can produce more, given its capital stock, and therefore can increase its growth, which increases its supply as well as its demand for Northern goods, leading to a fall in terms of trade and a reduction in foreign exchange earnings as well as profits. The growth rate, therefore, slows down. As Dutt (2012) has pointed out, the shock of negative terms of trade occurs for a variety of reasons, including the South's inability to produce capital goods, the price-taker status of Southern producers versus price-maker status of Northern ones, and the presence of surplus labor in the South, which makes real wages inelastic to technological advances (Singer, 1950, Prebisch, 1950, and Lewis, 1969).

In defense of North–South integration, Otsubo (1998) argued that only once countries have liberalized trade with the North and begun producing according to their "real comparative advantage," that is, producing labor-intensive goods, will there be a chance for the expansion of intra-industry trade within the South. In this case South–South trade is the effect and not the cause, and therefore policy makers should not attempt to induce South–South integration. Schiff and Wang (2006) have also suggested that the highest impact on total factor productivity in the South comes from the North *directly* through North–South technology diffusion, and secondarily and to a lesser extent *indirectly* through South–South trade. From this perspective, the potential for technology transfer is actually higher when the technology gap between the trading partners is larger, as in the North–South direction (Findlay, 1978). More recently, and particularly since 2000s, a growing literature has examined the hidden micro dynamics in international trade that lead to heterogeneous outcomes in gains from trade across countries. As discussed in detail in chapter 4, significant evidence shows that export quality is not exogenous to importer characteristics such as income levels or similarity in tastes and preferences. Bastos and Silva (2010) and Manova and Zhang (2012), for example, find that export unit values (a signal for product quality), within the same product category increase with the income levels of importing nations. In fact, Manova and Zhang (2012) show that even the very same firms charge higher prices (i.e., sell higher-quality products) in richer country markets. Therefore, North–South trade may provide additional benefits through productivity and quality improvements for Southern producers.

In addition to trade-induced technology diffusion and productivity spillovers, North–South capital movements, particularly FDI flows, are also a major source of technology transfer, allowing the South to catch up with the North (Lall, 2002). The expected positive spillover effects to the recipient Southern countries include better technology, modern management techniques and managerial skills, more R&D investment, and more experience in the international markets as well as the possibility of learning by watching as in Bhagwati (1994). To a lesser extent, short-term debt and equity flows,

---

7. For an in-depth discussion of this literature, see Ros (2013, ch. 4).

which release foreign exchange bottlenecks, also help the South speed up its industrialization and allow convergence with Northern incomes. These last two points were (and are) among the primary arguments put forward by the IMF advocating capital account liberalization in the South.

Prior to Amsden, economists such as Gunnar Myrdal, Frances Stewart, Arthur Lewis and others advanced a series of arguments in favor of South–South trade based on its dynamic potential. *Dynamic* approaches imply that repeated experience or medium and long-run benefits of trading are more important than one-off gains or losses at a given time, and that therefore the static focus of basic trade theory is inadequate.[8] For these economists, South–South trade and all trade policies in general should be part of a strategic development policy. Specifically, they argue that South–South trade is desirable if it stimulates industrial production and upgrading, technological innovation, backward and forward economic linkages and human capital improvement.

The starting point for most of the advocates of South–South trade is a critique of North–South trade or, more precisely, a critique of the idea that universal trade liberalization creates a positive outcome for all countries. Originally advanced by Raul Prebisch in terms of declining terms of trade, the structuralist critique, for example, pointed to the uneven pattern of trade whereby, to its own detriment, the South (i.e., the periphery) exports primary products and/or simple manufactures in return for advanced industrial products from the North (i.e., the center) and so remains in a constant state of underdevelopment.[9] Accordingly, a rich literature from the structuralist as well as neo-Marxian and Kaleckian traditions shows myriad ways in which North–South interaction creates outcomes more favorable to the North, leaving the South in a subservient and dependent position to the North (Bacha, 1978; Taylor, 1981, 1983; Dutt, 1986, 1987; Findlay, 1980, 1981; Darity, 1982; Kanbur and Vines 1986).

What unifies these approaches is the belief that this exchange has prevented autonomous technological development in the South, which would free it from dependency on Northern technology. Furthermore, according to this argument, the idea of the North as the engine of Southern growth is also destined to fail because of differences in income elasticities of demand, a point first emphasized by the earlier structuralist school tradition of the United Nations Economic Commission for Latin America and Caribbean (ECLAC). Singer (1950, 1959) and Prebisch (1950, 1975), for example, showed that the international division of labor—with the South producing primary goods, or possibly lower-end manufactures (Singer, 1975), and the North producing manufactured goods, or higher-end manufactures—creates uneven development, since income elasticity is high in the North, low in the South.

---

8. For a discussion of the static versus dynamic gains from trade as well as ISI, see Amsden (1989), Chang (2008), Wade (1990). The technology giant Nokia subsidized its electronics business for 17 years before it made a profit. The same is true for the case of Samsung (Chang, 2008).

9. Structuralism in economics emphasizes the interdependence of relations among various economic actors and how institutions and "distributional relationships across its [an economy's] productive sectors and social groups play essential roles in determining its macro behavior" (Taylor, 2004, p. 1). Thus, the structuralists analyze the economy in full as a system rather than taking its micro parts in isolation (Palma, 2008).

Another source of uneven development in the North–South framework is endogenous technological change. In the North, such change can make things even worse through the invention of synthetic substitutes for Southern primary goods (Dutt, 1996). While endogenous growth and increasing returns were at the core of the old development theory, it took a few decades before the neoclassical school woke up to this problem and encapsulated it in the new trade theory. Since then it has become quite mainstream to argue what Myrdal (1956), Kaldor (1967), Amsden (1987), Lall (2001) and Lall et al. (1989) had already argued: not all trade is equal, and what you export matters for long-term development and growth (Antweiler and Trefler, 2002; An and Iyigun, 2004; Hausmann et al., 2007). Particularly, most economists now accept that exports in more technology-intensive industries are likely to generate larger spillovers (such as innovation and physical and human capital accumulation) and linkages for development than lower-technology and labor-intensive exports. An and Iyigun (2004) and Hausmann et al. (2007), for example, find that a higher export concentration in technology and skill-intensive goods generates higher per-capita GDP growth rates. Likewise, Antweiler and Trefler (2002) discuss the importance of scale economies for understanding the factor content of trade resulting from industry-level externalities. Imbs and Wacziarg (2003) also examine the patterns of sectoral concentration within and across countries and find that, up to a threshold level of income, economic development is accompanied by increasing diversification of production rather than specialization, as is incorrectly predicted by the Ricardian and HOS theory. This point about the developmental importance of what you export was also raised by Kaldor (1967) in his three growth laws, which predict a strong positive relationship between the growth of manufacturing output and: (a) the growth of GDP, (b) the growth of labor productivity in manufacturing (i.e. Verdoorn's law), and (c) the growth of productivity in non-manufacturing sectors. Thus, the neoclassical new trade theory has, in some ways, converged to the classical development theory and the structuralist approaches in its acceptance that economic development is a long-run process and dynamic analysis of trade explains the growth and development trajectories of countries better than older static approaches. Even though it may seem obvious to non-economists, it took more than a century for neoclassical economists to accept the fact that, for long-run development, it matters whether a country exports potato chips or computer chips. Even though it is implicit, this acceptance, as is discussed later in this chapter, has significant implications for the modeling of South–South trade if such trade allows technological and skill upgrading, diversification and productivity gains.

Furthermore, according to Vernon's product-cycle theory, innovation and trade in a capitalist system are driven by a series of leading technologically advanced products, which allow a firm to capture monopoly profits for certain periods of time. Eventually the hitherto cutting-edge technology is standardized and replicated by competitors in lower-wage countries, and the production moves to those areas while the technological core moves on to newer, leading-edge products. In this theory, given that it is not a technological innovator, the South is either receiving products after technology has been standardized, in which case profits are lower, or it is investing to replicate Northern technology. The policy implication is that without Southern innovation, the cycle of unequal exchange will continue favoring Northern producers who capture Schumpeterian profits.

This critique of South–North dependency and uneven form of interaction led to a bourgeoning of literature on alternatives including the South–South trade in the early 1980s. In a series of papers, Alice Amsden presented compelling evidence in favor of South–South trade in manufactures (Amsden 1980, 1983, 1984, 1987). Amsden argued that because of both demand and supply conditions, South–South exports in manufactures are relatively skill-intensive and more sophisticated than South–North exports of manufactures, which tended to be more standardized or low-skill. This thesis has consequences for gains from trade: if learning effects, which are the highest among skill-intensive products, are taken to be the major dynamic gains from production and trade, this type of exchange will render the greatest benefits for Southern development.

Amsden's arguments were similar to the "flying geese" approach of Akamatsu (1962) and others who had shown that, in its early post-war industrialization, Japan (and later others such as South Korea) first imported simple Northern consumer goods and then learned to produce them domestically, using a variety of techniques such as reverse engineering.[10] Once it gained the capacity and necessary know-how, Japan exported these products, first to other Southern countries, then into Northern markets. With crucial government support in the build-up of Japan's production capacity, this process continued with gradual progress in the technology and skill intensity of manufactures produced domestically and then exported. Once Japan reached a certain level of maturity in manufactures, increasing labor costs led Japanese firms to move their production overseas in neighboring Asian countries, creating a similar virtuous cycle in those economies as well. Thus the flying geese analogy whereby a leading Southern country opens the way for later comers in development.

As was the case with Japan, so in the South generally, technological activity is such that at certain moments in its growth, a firm turns abroad to foreign sources of technology, and a large part of its activity is dedicated to importing and assimilating those sources, adapting them to suit local conditions. This adaptive engineering gives rise to major productivity gains even if it does not move the firm to the technological frontier. Amsden argues that this was why Southern countries advanced much further in production engineering rather than in systems engineering, that is, in rendering operations more efficient rather than designing new processes (Amsden, 1983). Amsden noted an emerging competitiveness of Southern countries in commodities that are characterized by a high degree of such skill (e.g., ships, precision instruments, machine tools, nonelectrical machinery):

> By comparison with the technology of highly machine-paced and process-centered industries, the skilled trades are smaller in scale and less science-based. Thus, each stage in the manufacturing process is less specialized and more integrated. Capabilities in design engineering and production engineering interact and reinforce each other so that the newly

---

10. For a discussion of how most of today's industrialized countries used similar techniques, see Chang (2008).

industrializing countries are able to move closer to the global technological frontier in such sectors. The abyss between the design of a product and its production is smaller than for other 'sophisticated' manufactures. (Amsden, 1984, p. 125)

Accordingly, Amsden suggested that South–South trade in manufactures allows "learning by exporting" in more sophisticated manufactures in a way that does not take place between South–North trade, given how the vast technological gap in the latter type of exchange prohibits the type of intra-industry trade that would benefit Southern countries. This view challenges the orthodox (neoclassical) view about technology transfer. In neoclassical theory, the greater the gap in technological development between two countries, the greater the possibility for transfer. Amsden is suggesting that the opposite is true: the closer two countries are in technological development, the more likely they are to benefit mutually from trade in manufactures, since the technology is more appropriate for local conditions in each respective country.

In his study of Argentinian and Brazilian exports, Chudnovsky (1983) also noted the divide between those countries' their exports to the South and North into "custom-built" and "series-built" categories. The former are made in small batches with a long production process, high unit values, and strict customer specifications and design requirements. Basic design is usually imported through licensing agreements, but the detailed designs of parts and components are adjusted to local conditions, through a process that requires a "complex fabrication technology" and "a skilled staff to deal with the machining operations and the internal organization of the production process" (p. 225). "Series-built" goods are produced with less regard to such conditions with lower unit value, and customers are more sensitive to their price than they are with custom-built goods.

Stewart (1990) argues that in addition to the disadvantage of being the technological laggard, technological innovation in the North means that the South is dependent on the direction of technological change from the North, which is more capital-intensive and embodies high-income characteristics (p. 81).[11] Stewart suggests that these products are therefore biased against Southern preferences and inappropriate in terms of both techniques of production and product characteristics, each of which the South accepts because it has no alternative. On the other hand, imports from other South countries are more likely to embody "older" technologies more appropriate for South technological development and processes. In many instances these technologies may actually be more beneficial to the host countries than cutting-edge technologies (from the North), which may have been designed for goals that do not match a South country's needs. Likewise, Nelson and Pack (1999) criticize the "accumulation" explanation of

---

11. Following Lancaster's (1971) approach to consumer demand, which posits that consumers desire certain characteristics of goods rather than the goods themselves. Higher-income consumers for example might request a high-definition television versus a standard television for lower-income consumers; thus certain products will have "high" while others will contain "low" income characteristics, in this case, corresponding to preferences in North and South, respectively. See Copeland-Kotwal (1996) and Murphy and Schleifer (1997), for example, on how quality preferences may affect demand for Southern goods.

technological change, as it ignores the "assimilation" aspect, emphasizing the centrality of learning in identifying, adapting and operating imported technologies.

In the opposite camp, the neoclassical approach to technological acquisition, as in the HOS theory, argues that Southern countries have a wide variety of choices in the international technology market and are free to select and incorporate the best technologies with minimal cost or effort. In this narrative, capacity and capability are seen as one and the same thing (Lall, 2000).

The "assimilation" argument of Stewart (1990) and Nelson and Pack (1999) coincides with what Lall refers to as the "capabilities" approach to technological change. Firms in developing countries have imperfect knowledge of technological alternatives, and finding technologies is a difficult and costly process. Once a new technology is imported, its use requires creating new skills and knowledge to master its tacit elements, which vary greatly by the kind of technology in question. Some activities are costlier and more prolonged than others, requiring selective interventions according to type in order to help firms overcome learning costs and coordination problems. Thus, according to this approach, technology adoption depends more on the national ability to master and use technologies than on comparative advantage in factor endowments, as in the HOS theory. From this viewpoint, the greater the gap in tacit technological knowledge required in the production of capital and producer goods, the smaller the possibility for technological acquisition and a deepening of the knowledge base (Lall, 2000, 2001).

Trade between Southern countries is argued to have higher learning effects. In small developing countries, inexperienced workers may prefer goods of "older design, simpler, more rugged, less specialized, and less automated" to those provided by industrial countries (Amsden, 1984). Older vintages or adapted products are similarly uneconomical to produce in the North because equipment suppliers and their subcontractors have "forgotten" the older technologies. So, for much of these Southern producer and capital goods, foreign technology is imported and adapted to local needs and demands: "[D]escaling, converting from mass to batch production, changing from imported to local raw material requirements" (Amsden, 1987, p. 133). Compared to machine-paced and process-centered commodities, these simpler products are more liable to adaptation in design. They are smaller in scale and less science-based, such as precision instruments, machine tools, and so forth. Within and among developing countries, then, capabilities in design engineering and production engineering interact and reinforce each other to produce minor "technological" innovation (Amsden, 1984, 1987; Lall, 2000, 2001; Lall et al., 1989). According to this argument, a South country sees an incentive both to export to another South country and to import from one, given their similarities in technological development. Furthermore, since they are less capital-intensive, older technologies allow Southern countries to use their labor supply more effectively and at lower license costs (Pack and Saggi, 1997).

These arguments are also part of the new structuralist critique of the ISI period in developing countries, which blamed the adoption of inappropriate Northern technologies with different factor endowments (i.e., capital-abundant with high wages) for the rising capital intensity of the technologies employed. In the South, high capital-intensity combined with anti-export bias, in return, led to excess capacity and slow employment creation with low wages in industry. Low industrial labor demand exacerbated underemployment in agriculture and services and kept wage growth low in those sectors as well. As a result, labor transfer from traditional sectors to industry and urban areas remained low and hindered agricultural productivity growth. Mistakes in the choice of protected infant industries also worsened this situation as backward linkages between the hand-picked industries and agriculture were weak, limiting demand growth. The widening gap between the rural and urban areas, along with slow wage growth in industry, worsened the income distribution, shifting the pattern of consumption and production towards consumer goods, which are consumed by only a small segment of the population, that is, the labor aristocracy in urban areas. These mistakes in the choice of infant industries also aggravated the pressures on the balance of payments and foreign exchange bottlenecks as the import intensity increased rather than decreased under ISI. It did so partly because the capital-intensive nature of new industries and the high import-output ratios created a dependent development as the necessary intermediate and final capital goods needed to be imported. Moreover, the newly produced consumer goods were not substitutes for previously imported ones, but were new products, which further increased the import demand.

Another argument in defense of South–South integration came out of Linder's "preference similarity" theory regarding consumer demand structure (Linder, 1967). According to Linder, inventors, innovators and entrepreneurs are stimulated by home demand, and they develop products according to home-market tastes and preferences. Later, they export products to those countries with tastes and preferences similar to those in the domestic market. According to Linder, most global trade is North–North and intra-industry because of the effective demand structure: the incomes, tastes and preferences of developed countries are similar, and therefore they are more likely to buy differentiated but similar products from one another, be it consumer or intermediate goods. High-income Northerners are likely to want to purchase high-end and technologically advanced automobiles, while Southern consumers may have more tolerance for lower-quality automobiles, if they come with a lower price. This difference explains the prevalence in Southern markets of lower-end consumer goods produced by other Southern countries, such as the popularity of Russian, Indian and Iranian cars that are not available in Northern countries. However, since Southern goods face higher trade barriers in other Southern countries, either because of protectionism or colonial-era distortions favoring Northern countries, consumers often buy "inappropriate" Northern goods that do not match their effective demand structure, thereby lowering their own welfare. As Linder writes, the differences between per-capita incomes in the North and the South perpetuates a longstanding imbalance:

[G]oods in demand in advanced countries are atypical for the economic structure of developing countries; their production functions will be disadvantageous in the latter countries. Goods that developing countries are particularly adept at producing are, on the other hand, not demanded in the advanced countries. Owing to lack of foreign demand [by the North], the developing countries therefore cannot export those manufactures they are most efficient at producing. Generally speaking, they are reduced to trying to export manufactures with which they are unfamiliar to markets of which they have no experience. (Linder, 1967, p. 37)

Contrary to what Findlay (1978), Schiff and Wang (2006) and many others have argued, a recent resurgence of empirical and theoretical work has built on and confirmed Linder's theses showing that the levels of institutional and cultural similarity as well as closeness in incomes, endowments, technological and preference structures between countries boost the potential for economic convergence and spillovers through economic exchanges (Bergstrand and Egger, 2013; Dahi and Demir, 2013; Regolo, 2013; Bahar et al., 2014; Cheong et al., 2015; Demir, 2016). Using bilateral trade data, Regolo (2013), for example, finds that endowment similarity between country pairs stimulates greater export diversification. That is South–South as well as North–North bilateral trade appears to enjoy greater export diversification than either achieves in another interregional direction.

Overall, the debates surrounding South–South trade have largely concentrated on the developmental benefits of Southern trade in manufactures.[12] The pros and cons largely depend on a temporal perspective, that is, on whether short-run static costs outweigh long-run dynamic gains. If the process of production and trade in South manufactures (with other South countries) is likely to generate domestic spillovers and to induce positive technological change and upgrading, then such trade is likely to be part of an overall process of industrial development. There is also the question of what countries, if any, will replace the North as the engine of growth for the South. Can China or other South NICs achieve this task? The World Bank and the IMF, particularly after the start of the Great Recession in 2008 seems to think that way, suggesting that decoupling of the South from the Northern business cycles is a positive and desired development that can establish counter-cyclical growth patterns between the two poles of the world economy (World Bank, 2008, IMF, 2011a).

Despite the myriad channels the North–South literature provides through which divergent growth takes place, few prominently feature paths that might lead to outcomes different from the ones described above. Questions such as the conditions and policies under which the Southern countries can avoid the underdevelopment or, at best, the dependency trap, seldom appear. As noted by Darity and Davis (2005, p. 154),

The role of government policy is not at the forefront of most of these papers. If we believe these processes operate and perpetuate international inequality, precisely how do we reverse them? Via industrial policy, South–South trade, South–South finance, autarky? Rarely does the formal literature on North–South trade and growth answer the question of how the world should be changed.

---

12. We should note that the environmental effects of North–South trade did not go missing in this literature. Chichilinisky (1994) and Copeland and Taylor (2005), for example, discuss the environmental degradation effects of this trade on Southern countries, partly due to the natural-resource-based exports of the South.

3.3   Radical Approaches to North–South Interactions

While by no means is it the dominant view, some economic historians and development economists argue that primitive accumulation through slavery and pillage created the initial conditions that allowed the West to rise at the expense of the Rest.
They then explain development of the North–South trade with these initial conditions, which biased bilateral trade relations across countries. As every empirical trade
paper that uses the Gravity model has confirmed, any past colonial relationship is a
significant determinant of current trade patterns between countries.[13] Findlay (1992)
explains income-divergence across countries (particularly between the West and the
Rest) by the comparative advantage of the West in the use of violence over the Rest.
Accordingly, the subjugation of the Americas, Africa and Asia, the creation of monopoly rents allowed by military force, and capital accumulation through slave trade
and new colonial markets were a part of the "intercontinental network of production
and trade that stimulated technical progress and investment in Europe and the New
World" (Findlay, 1992, p. 160).

Findlay (1992) is also quite vocal in criticizing mainstream economists for their dis-
missal of the role played by the use of violence in the rise of the West. Surprisingly, in
the same article he mentions that the slave trade, which allowed the development of
trade and production in Europe, "led to the expansion of predatory coastal states and
the disruption of the hinterland" in Africa.

The neoclassical camp of the debate has also made significant progress admitting
the validity of these critiques, including the path-dependency in development, based
on initial conditions. For example, several well-publicized studies show that colonial
rule and the slave trade have had significantly negative effects on institutional development, democracy, income growth, human capital, trust, income inequality and so forth.
(Acemoglu et al., 2001; Angeles, 2007; Iyer, 2010; Wietzke, 2015). However, acknowl-
edging the significance of the initial conditions and the role of Europeans in creating
and shaping those conditions is the furthest the neoclassicals dare to go.[14] They do not
link in any way the rise of the West with the fall of the Rest, nor do they suggest any
organic connection between the two. The neoclassical narrative usually focuses on the
impact of those initial conditions on subsequent development, and on the lack of it in
the global South. Usually in the neoclassical view, structural change and industrial revolution are exogenous (i.e., Hicks-neutral) and not linked in any way to the use of the
lucrative slave trade for capital accumulation or the exploitation of colonies, either as a
source of primary inputs or as an outlet for the manufactures produced in the center.[15]

---

13. Note that this point was also raised by Myrdal (1956, p. 261), who argued that, because of the
    colonial legacy, "governments and businesses in underdeveloped countries are conditioned
    and trained to negotiate and cooperate with their opposite partners in advanced countries
    but not with the governments and businesses in other underdeveloped countries."
14. For a summary of the colonial roots of underdevelopment, see Bagchi (2008).
15. The only time we see the effect of this not-so-pleasant past on modern trade relations is
    through the colonial past dummies in Gravity regressions, which always appear as statisti-
    cally and economically significant.

In other words, the long-term effects of the slave trade and colonial rule on the South *and* on the North as well as on production and trade structures, are usually ignored if not dismissed altogether by mainstream economists.[16]

Darity (2003) exposes these limitations, arguing that the rise of the West was causally linked with the "lag of the Rest" and that colonial rule together with the slave trade bears responsibility for the growing divergence between the North and the South since then. Also missing in the neoclassical world is the role of power in defining the structure of North–South relations. On the other hand, Marxian and other related radical theories, unlike the neoclassical approach, put the uneven exchange, imperialism and primitive accumulation at the core of their explanation of North–South divergence. It is not our intention here to survey the very large literature on this topic, which has been done comprehensively more than once in the past (see, for example, Brewer, 1990). Instead, we will link these contributions with the discussions above and provide a critical discussion of their implications for the growing gap between the North and the South as well as on the issue of South–South integration.

3.3.1 *Marx and Marxian Theories of North–South Interactions*

The early Marxian theories of North–South interactions, including Marx himself as well as his late disciples such as Rosa Luxemburg, Lenin and Trotsky, focused mostly on advanced capitalist countries and their involvement in feudal and agrarian, unindustrialized countries of the South, including the North's colonies. Since there was no Emerging South or any advanced Southern country or, for that matter, any South country that could challenge the North at the time, the analysis was not extended to South–South interactions. For Marx, the constant urge for capitalist expansion required the North to get in touch with the rest through the development of trade and financial linkages. The rest of the world was a source of raw materials, new sources of labor supply, and also a market for the manufactures produced by the growing excess supply of capital. It probably would be fair to say that, for Marx, North–South interactions, however brutal and oppressing they might be for the Southerners, was a progressive development as these interactions brought in "all, even the most barbarian, nations into civilization" (Marx and Engels, (1848) 1969) and allowed the development of productive forces. Even in his older writings, such as the *Communist Manifesto*, this characterization of North-South relations is very visible when he and Engels argue that "in place of the old local and national seclusion and self-sufficiency, we have intercourse in every direction, universal interdependence of nations" (Marx and Engels, (1848) 1969). It is also possible to distinguish different, and sometimes conflicting, views by Marx on North–South interactions. In the case of British imperialism in India, for example, Marx clearly saw it as a progressive development (more

---

16. Of course, there are exceptions to this rule. For example, Berger et al. (2013) show that the United States used its political influence through CIA interventions in developing countries during the Cold War years to increase its export penetration. Accordingly, this was true even in sectors where the United States had a comparative disadvantage.

on this below). The South, for the most part, was a dark place where tyrants ruled and civilization was not developed. As a result, the arrival of capitalism, even if it was through the British navy, was a positive development allowing the backward Asiatic regions to modernize (including the introduction of private property, which for Marx as for many Eurocentric scholars, was missing in the rest of the world).[17] After all, "the country that is more developed industrially only shows, to the less developed, the image of its own future" (Marx, 1867). On the other hand, especially in his later writings, Marx also discussed the effects of exploitation on the colonies, including uneven trade rules, and adopted a more anti-colonial stance, even while he remained unsure about the effects of "nationalistic and protectionist" development strategies (Sutcliffe, 2008).[18] The effects of monopoly rights enjoyed by the East India Company and its kind, for example, were well discussed. The opening up of the Indian market for cheap British textiles, or the forceful introduction of mono-cropping in Ireland and India as well as the forced one-directional free trade in the colonies, were used to explain the rise of poverty, lack of industrialization and dependent development.

The followers of Marx, including Luxemburg, Lenin and Trotsky, among others, focused on imperialism (i.e., "the highest stage of capitalism," according to Lenin) and argued that the capitalist development in the North (i.e., advanced capitalist nations) required the discovery of new markets outside the capitalist regions, which is followed by their eventual destruction by competition (and with the help of the sword) leading to uneven development (Luxemburg, 1913; Lenin, 1917).[19] The use of monopoly capital (which was seen as inevitable given the increasing concentration of capital) combined with the oppressive colonial rule in the colonies allow the capitalist countries to enrich themselves at the expense of the colonies and, therefore, capitalism in the South was no longer a progressive force. Both Luxemburg and Lenin also discussed the role played by the creditor–debtor relationship between the European countries and their colonies, and how it facilitated the further exploitation of the latter by the former. The rise of finance capital was also central in these theories, allowing the relocation of production overseas to take advantage of proximity to natural resources and cheap labor, which eventually would help develop capitalism in the recipient countries. Similar to Marx, much of the analysis of North–South trade and financial flows is limited with the linking of the South to the world markets through the export of raw materials and provision of cheap labor, and through providing a market for Northern manufactures and surplus capital, both financial and fixed. However, finance capital (i.e., capital

---

17. Marx was not very clear in what he meant by the Asiatic mode of production other than using it as a basket term for all that Europe is not. For a discussion and critique of this view and Eurocentrism in economic analysis, see Frank (1998) and Wallerstein (1997).
18. See, for example, Marx (1853, 1879).
19. See Brewer (1990) for a survey. Also, for both Lenin and Trotsky, uneven development was a natural outcome of the expansion of capitalism to less-developed regions, which would be linked to the world economy based on the conditions written by the center (see, for example, Trotsky's discussion of the "uneven and combined development."

exports) was also seen as a double-edged sword as it drained the resources of debtor countries through profit repatriations and debt service.

3.3.2 Dependency School, World-Systems Analysis and the Semi-Periphery

Dependency theory and World-Systems Analysis (WSA) emerged in the mid- to late twentieth century as critiques of mainstream approaches to international trade as well as of orthodox Marxist concepts of the globalization of capital. Both of them, and WSA in particular, were also challenges to the epistemological approaches of modern European–North American academia, who argue that social reality can only be understood through interdisciplinary approaches. The fundamental aspect of dependency theory is the argument that, when capitalism expanded from Western Europe—through colonialism, unequal trade agreements, and other means—it did not replicate itself and develop in the same way in the other countries as it did in the home countries. Rather, the centers of capitalism in Europe and North America, or the "core" (or metropolis) in dependency terminology, was a location of advanced industrial production marked by profitable monopolistic or oligopolistic production, whereas the colonized countries, the periphery (satellite), became fixed in a position of competitive, unprofitable production and export of raw materials and agricultural goods, leading to the eventual "development of underdevelopment" (Frank, 1966; Furtado, 1964; Baran, 1957; Amin, 1976; Emmanuel, 1972). "Core" and "periphery" therefore referred to production processes that were profitable/monopolistic or unprofitable/competitive. Moreover, economic dependency of the South on the North had social, cultural and political characteristics that were not limited just to the economic sphere (i.e., the production and reproduction of culture and political and legal systems in the image of the North, etc.) (Lall, 1975). Crucially then, exchange between "core" and "periphery" was unequal: the core would gain from free trade and finance more than would the periphery. Over time this led to unequal development, even if both regions experienced increasing growth as a result of international trade. In these aspects, the dependency school shares similarities with the structuralist critique of North–South interactions, particularly regarding the South being an exporter of primary products in return for manufactures from the North, creating a state of perpetual underdevelopment in the South. Overall, according to the dependency school, the use of plunder together with unequal trade and indebtedness were seen as the primary cause of Southern underdevelopment. The dependency school also accepted it as impossible to industrialize and break free from the yoke of Northern dictatorial control over the terms of the exchange between the two regions. This was a breaking point between Marx and the dependency theorists who, unlike Marx, did not see Northern capitalism as ever being a progressive force in the South.[20] The solution

---

20. As noted by Lall (1975) and Sutcliffe (2008), later Marxists such as Lenin and Baran (1957, 1976) considered capitalism as a once-progressive force that ceased to be progressive and, instead, created hurdles inhibiting Southern development and growth.

many suggested was a delinking from the global economy, which would limit the uneven development effects of North–South interactions.[21]

In the second half of the twentieth century it became evident to radical economists in the dependency school tradition that there were countries that had a relatively equal mix of core and peripheral processes of production. These were the large middle-income South countries with substantial resources to carry out large-scale industrialization (loosely what we refer to as Emerging South). So, World-Systems analysts created the category of "semi-periphery" to refer to these countries that were not core—they were not as rich, powerful nor had they the same social indicators as the rich European–North American countries—but they were not periphery, either (Wallerstein, 1976).

For WSA, the semi-peripheral countries were less stable than either the core or the periphery and were potential candidates for social revolution. In the "core" and "periphery" there is an elite cohesion around those production processes that make radical change more difficult. However, in the semi-periphery, the elite are split. At any moment, the core segment of the elite may choose to ally themselves with radical social movements to crush the peripheral elite and take the country on a path towards the core. The semi-periphery has much more chances of becoming the core and that possibility was enticing to elites, intellectuals and other social movements in those countries. At the same time, the peripheral elite was also maneuvering to undermine these movements, as their extractive interests were threatened by nationalization, land reform, price controls, export limitations and so on (Chase-Dunn, 1990).

As a result of these internal collusions, the semi-periphery had to choose their alliances carefully. For World-Systems analysts, the Third World Movement, NAM and other South–South alliances were the foreign policy outcomes of semi-peripheral countries—dominated by an industrializing South core elite—trying to bandwagon against the domination of the global core or global North.

This framework carries ambiguous implications for viewing South–South relations. On the one hand, it provides a "material" basis for South–south solidarity that is more concrete and perhaps sustainable. On the other hand, the basic interest of the semi-peripheral countries is their own rise in the global hierarchy, and the alliances they choose are instrumental and ultimately reflect self-interest. While at one point it may suit them to ally with other South countries, at another point they may abandon that alliance if they have a chance to enter the "rich boys club." The expansion of the G-7 to the G-20 includes India, Brazil, China, Turkey and Argentina, while at the same time those countries still declare South–South solidarity is a clear manifestation of this unstable position. Furthermore, it is not very clear why South–South exchanges would not create the same type of dependency between the core Southern countries and the rest (Radice, 2009; Strange, 2009).

---

21. See, for example, Amin (1990).

3.4   Dynamic Gains from Trade and the Case for South–South PTAs

If South–South trade in manufactures is beneficial from a developmental perspective, then why is there not more of it, and what can be done to promote it? As a solution to the problem outlined in the preceding section, Linder (1967) argued that preferential trade agreements (PTAs) should be established in the South. Linder even went so far as arguing that the effects of South–South regional trading agreements are less ambiguous than those for developed countries, and that trade diversion as a result of South–South integration schemes is beneficial as long as it is trade from the North that is being diverted. We are not quite so positive as Linder about this point, and we shall explore in more detail the merits of the trade diversion/creation argument.

As discussed in section 3.2, Arthur Lewis (1980) argues that Southern growth dependency on Northern growth (which he estimated to be at 0.87 between 1873 and 1973) poses a problem if the income gap between the two groups is to be narrowed. Lewis contends that, as the Northern growth is likely to slow down, it will become more difficult for the South to enter Northern markets, since those markets will likely be more protectionist. Lewis suggested that intra-South trade could serve as a substitute, whether in agriculture or in other capital-intensive products (fertilizers, cement, steel, machinery) through PTA formation.

The benefits of PTAs have, however, been equally contested within economic theory, and arguments for and against PTAs go beyond the purely economic. The General Agreement on Tariffs and Trade (GATT), signed in 1947 and later incorporated into the World Trade Organization in the 1995 Uruguay Round of the GATT, is the governing contract on international trade. According to Article 1 of GATT, each WTO member must grant all members the same advantage, privilege, favor or immunity that it grants to any particular country, a provision known as the most-favored nation (MNF) principle. Although members cannot arbitrarily discriminate in tariff policy, there are three major exceptions to this provision. First, article XXIV of the GATT allows developed countries to be both the granters and recipients of trading preferences so long as the preferences offered are not partial but extend to "substantially all the trade" in products originating in union member countries. In practice, this rule has not been strictly enforced, as in the cases of the North American Free Trade Agreement (NAFTA) and the European Union (EU). The second is one-way trade preferences, the basis of the Generalized System of Preferences (GSP), which developed nations can give developing countries as a means of encouraging the developing countries' exports. The European Economic Community actively engaged in this practice in the 1970s with countries in Africa and Southwest Asia, although these have been systematically phased out in the recent bilateral agreements with the European Union. Finally, the Enabling Clause, added to GATT in 1979 and continued under GATT 1994 within WTO, allows developing countries to exchange preferences amongst themselves.

Much of the theoretical literature on PTAs has been influenced by Jacob Viner's 1950 work, *The Customs Unions Issue*, which presented the analytical concepts of "trade diversion" and "trade creation" and argued that PTAs should be judged according to which effect will outweigh the other. Prior to Viner's writing, economists thought that PTAs facilitated a movement towards universal free trade and thus must be "trade enhancing." Viner disputed this claim. Assuming a vertical demand curve and horizontal supply curves for country A, if prior to the formation of a PTA with another country B, the price-plus-tariff of country C's exports to A is lower than country B's price-plus-tariff, country A will import completely from C, assuming country A's domestic price is higher than both. If a PTA is formed between A and B such that A eliminates B's tariff and keeps C's and the result is that the price of B is lower than price of C plus tariff, all of A's imports are from B. This is trade diversion. On the other hand, if before the PTA is formed, the price of A is lower than the prices of the other countries' goods plus tariff, and if A forms a PTA with B, lowering B's price to below A's, all of A's imports will be from B. This is trade creation. As different commodities have different levels of preexisting tariffs, one cannot tell automatically the net welfare effect; therefore, the trade creation and diversion effects should be weighed.

Trade diversion and creation issues weigh heavily in the debate on South–South PTAs. As discussed earlier in the chapter, neoclassical economists commonly believed that, through South–South PTAs, larger South countries could export low-quality and high-cost manufactures to other South countries in order to offset the losses from failing ISI policies. However, the theoretical and empirical literature on the issue of trade diversion and trade creation is famously ambiguous, as a whole subset of papers shows (Wonnacott and Lutz, 1989; Krugman, 1991b; Frankel et al., 1995; Bhagwati, 1995; Bhagwati and Panagariya, 1996). This ambiguity in the mainstream academic literature prompted the second generation of theoretical treatment of regionalism, pioneered by Bhagwati and considered the dynamic analysis of PTAs. From the perspective of mainstream economic theory, the most desirable outcome for international trade is universal free trade. Therefore, the "dynamic" literature on PTAs in mainstream theory dwells on whether the expanding regionalism is acting as a stumbling block or as a building block for universal free trade (Bhagwati, 1993; Bhagwati and Panagariya, 1996). This strand of analysis typically focuses on how political and economic coalitions may be formed through PTAs that will either block or facilitate further integration (Levy, 1997; Krishna, 1998; Bagwell and Staiger, 1997a, 1997b).

This line of inquiry has merit, particularly when it focuses on market access. In 1996, the European Union began negotiating what it called Association Agreements with every Mediterranean basin country. Since the European Union negotiates as one economic bloc, the agreements are considered bilateral and have created a peculiar system of preferential trading areas whereby a big economic bloc is connected to various countries without those countries being connected to each other. This has been labeled the "hub-and-spokes" system. According to Wonnacott (1996), these emerging schemes pose problems. Compared to a full free-trade agreement, an Association creates more trade barriers, more waste from rent seeking, and excessive transport and content costs. The country that benefits most is the "hub," which has access to all markets, while the "spokes" face competition in each other's markets.

Within the neoclassical trade literature, it is also accepted that PTAs can benefit member states through economies of scale, comparative advantage and increased competition (Schiff, 2003). In this view, however, these positive effects are present only in North–North and South–North PTAs, but not South–South PTAs. Neoclassical theorists argue, first, that similar production and trade structures that are dominated by primary commodities in the South make it more difficult to benefit from economies of scale. Incorrect government interventions during the ISI period in the choice of industries, as well as in their geographical location, is also argued to have made the possibility to enjoy economies of scale a remote possibility (Schiff, 2003). Second, given that the South is further away from the technology frontier and less active in R&D, South–North integration offers a greater diffusion of technology (Schiff and Wang, 2008).[22] Third, South–South integration is likely to create asymmetric benefits favoring more advanced Southern countries and allowing them to export their lower-quality and higher-priced manufactures to other less-developed Southern countries, which instead would be better off entering South–North PTAs. Likewise, these economists also suggest that industries with dynamic development potential are more likely to move to the bigger and richer Southern countries under South–South PTAs, leading to their divergence from the Rest of South (Puga and Venables, 1997; Venables, 2003; Schiff, 2003). North–South PTAs are also argued to facilitate increasing vertical specialization or value-chain fragmentation, what Krugman (1995b) referred to as the slicing up of the value added, thus allowing for faster catching up with the North.[23] Finally, in this view, if larger markets were the key to the kingdom of economies of scale, then universal trade liberalization would allow access to a larger market, the world trade (Schiff, 2003).

Compared to the neoclassical view of South–South PTAs, the classical development theory and, implicitly, the new trade theory, focus more on their long-term developmental benefits through infant industry development, economies of scale and decoupling than on the static welfare gains (from trade creation and diversion), or on the "stumbling block/building block" dichotomy. As long argued in classical development theory and supported by robust empirical work in new trade theory, output expansion in international trade is strongly skill-biased (Antweiler and Trefler, 2002). As a result, increasing market size through South–South PTAs can help the South enjoy scale effects and so increase the skill content of its exports. In addition, the decreasing cost of intermediaries imported from other Southern markets can increase export penetration into Northern markets in industrial goods (Fugazza and Robert-Nicoud, 2006). As advocated by Arthur Lewis (see previous section), increasing South–South trade can also reduce the growth dependence of the South on the North, leading perhaps to decoupling from Northern business cycles. In a surprising twist of events, this once-radical view has become quite mainstream since the Great Recession of 2008 and is now advocated even by the World Bank (World Bank, 2008). Furthermore, as previously discussed, classical development theorists and structuralists see the structure of South–South trade as having dynamic and long-term

---

22. Schiff and Ollareaga (2002) and Schiff and Wang (2008) find that the impact of trade-related technology diffusion on Southern TFP is higher in South–North than South–South trade.
23. Baldwin and Robert-Nicoud (2014) argue that these are perhaps best conceived as trade in *tasks* rather than trade in goods however they appear on official trade statistics as traditional intra-industry trade.

benefits for developing countries on account of its comparatively higher technology and human-capital-intensive factor content (Amsden, 1987; Lall et al., 1989; Demir and Dahi, 2011).

As Linder (1967) initially suggested, similarity in production pattern, resource bases, technological development, consumer preferences and institutions between Southern country pairs should also facilitate more appropriate technology transfer (Amsden, 1980, 1987; UNIDO, 2005; World Bank, 2006; Regolo, 2013; Dahi and Demir, 2013; Bahar et al., 2014; Cheong et al., 2015; Demir, 2016). As discussed in the previous section, this is indeed an active line of research in current empirical studies. Bergstrand and Egger (2013), for example, find that country pairs of similar economic sizes or capital and labor endowments are more likely to engage in bilateral preferential trade and investment agreements. Furthermore, Cheong et al. (2015) show that once such country pairs sign a trade agreement, the gains are significantly larger for partnering countries, particularly for South–South blocs. South–North PTAs may also yield more benefits to Northern countries than to Southern ones because of asymmetries in bargaining power, negotiating capacity and retaliatory capability. Even though these asymmetries are also present between Southern countries, the gap is likely to be smaller. Thrasher and Gallagher (2008), for example, show that South–South PTAs leave greater policy space to "deploy effective policy for long-run diversification and development" than do South–North PTAs.

The effects of PTAs on the structure of trade are of particular importance for long-term growth and development. Development economics and new trade theory provide strong evidence that not all trade is equal and that what you export may matter for long-term economic performance (Kaldor, 1967; An and Iyigun, 2004; Hausmann et al., 2007). Exports in more technology-intensive industries are likely to generate larger spillovers (e.g., innovation and physical and human capital accumulation) and linkages for development than lower-technology and labor-intensive ones (Hausman et al., 2007).[24] Kaldor (1967) has well established the importance of manufactures in his three growth laws, which identify a strong positive relationship between the growth of manufacturing output and the growth of GDP, of labor productivity in manufacturing, and the growth of productivity in nonmanufacturing sectors. Again, the structuralist North–South models have long explored how interactions between countries with asymmetrical economic structures, patterns of specialization and development can lead to uneven development (Findlay, 1980; Darity, 1990; Dutt, 1992).[25]

From a long-term developmentalist perspective, whether or not PTAs are trade-creating or trade-diverting is not a very interesting question, although much of the discussion in trade journals is centered on this issue.[26] To the extent that PTAs

---

24. There are also dissenting voices within the neoclassical school showing that trade-liberalization decisions are endogenous with sectoral productivity levels (Karacaovali, 2011).
25. Also see the survey articles by Findlay (1984), Dutt (1989) and Darity and Davis (2005).
26. For a discussion see Bhagwati et al. (1998) and Panagariya (2000).

enhance the export of manufactures and allow for the upgrading of skill and technological content, we can evaluate the success or failure of PTAs according to their
potential long-term developmental impact. From our perspective the more important
question is whether a PTA allows a Southern country to export more bananas or
manufactured goods. While we do not suggest that these questions are unimportant,
we do see reasons to question the disproportionate attention still given to the classic
Vinerian dichotomy.

First, as Ethier (1998) argued, given that the new regionalism has taken place
under large multilateral liberalization of tariffs, and that marginal PTA liberalization remains rather low, the "Vinerian perspective, though not irrelevant, should be
secondary in theoretical models appropriate to an analysis of the new regionalism"
(Ethier 1998, 1150). Second, since North–North, South–North and North–South
trade barriers for merchandise goods are significantly lower than those in South–
South trade (Kowalski and Shepherd, 2006; also see Kee et al., 2009; Medvedev,
2010), it is unlikely that South–South PTAs are diverting trade from the North, a
possibility that has retrospectively been the main point of contention among trade
theorists on the relative costs and benefits of South–South PTAs.[27] In fact, consistent with Mundell's (1968) assertion that "a member's gain from a free-trade area
will be larger the higher are the initial tariffs of partner countries," the reduction
of South–South trade barriers is found to generate a significant increase in South–
South exports, while no such effect is apparent in the case of North–South, South–
North, or North–North trade (Kowalski and Shepherd, 2006; Dahi and Demir,
2013; Behar and Cirera-i-Criville, 2013). Besides, some empirical evidence shows
that South–South PTAs are no more trade-diverting than other PTAs (Cernat,
2001). Third, since higher transportation costs and former colonial linkages with
Northern countries (always significant in Gravity models of trade), in addition to
higher trade barriers (Kee et al., 2009), continue to limit South–South trade expansion, PTAs may be a way of compensating for such trade barriers that are lower in
South–North, North–South or North–North trade. Last but not least, in the case of
industrial development, what matters are dynamic not static gains. That is if South–
South PTAs are found to enhance industrial development, the long-term gains may
very well outweigh the static short-term losses. For example, South–South PTAs are
shown to have a significantly positive effect on manufactured goods exports of the
South while no such effect is detected in the case of South–North PTAs (Dahi and
Demir, 2013). On the other hand, developing countries that have PTAs with the
North either end up suffering an annual loss or experience no significant change in
volume of their manufactured goods exports.

---

27. Figure 4.29 in chapter 4 shows that even within manufactures, trade barriers are significantly higher in the South–South direction than in South–North and North–North.

3.4.1   Stylized Facts on PTAs

Since the early 1990s, the number of PTAs has increased significantly.[28] As of December 11, 2014, 266 PTAs were reported to WTO, 88 percent of them signed after 1988 and all of them together accounting for 53 percent of world trade (WTO, 2014).[29] The total number of country pairs that have signed PTAs with each other increased from 20 in 1958 to 86 in 1970, to 667 in 1980, to 2,393 in 1990, to 4,039 in 2000 and finally to 7,557 in 2013. While the average annual increase in the number of new PTA pairs was 30 between 1958 and 1988, it was 267 between 1989 and 2013. Furthermore, as Figure 3.1 shows below, an overwhelming majority of these agreements (75 percent) were between Southern countries. The number of South–South PTAs remained zero from 1958 till 1962, when it increased to 12, and that of South–North PTAs was zero all the way till 1971, when it increased to 49. In comparison, in 2013 alone, 222 country pairs signed PTAs with each other: 66 percent of these PTAs between South–South pairs while only 34 percent were South–North.[30] In fact, once we exclude the European Union, which signs PTAs as a collective body, in 2013 the share of North–South PTAs in total PTAs drops to 13 percent while that of South–South increases to 87 percent of all new PTAs.

Figure 3.2 shows the trends in PTA trade since 1958, the earliest year a PTA was reported to the WTO. The straight line, which shows the percentage share of global

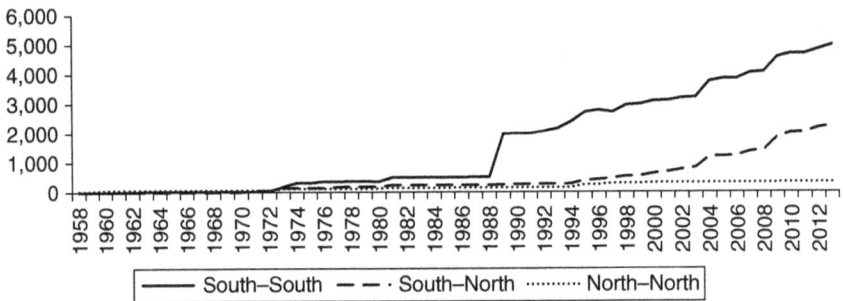

Figure 3.1 Number of preferential trade agreements by country pairs, 1958–2013
Source: WTO (2014).

---

28. Because of incomplete observations on the ratification dates, we used the signing dates as the entry into force for PTA agreements. Similarly, because of lack of data on end-dates once a PTA is signed we assumed it stayed in force in the future. Obviously, these assumptions inevitably create some bias in our figures in this section, such as those for the PTA between Turkey and Syria, which was signed in 2007 but ended in 2011. However, such changes are limited in number.

29. We define PTAs to include bilateral, regional and multilateral trade agreements involving both parties. The list of PTAs reported to the WTO may be incomplete as there is a lag between the signing date and reporting date to the WTO. Also, there are discrepancies among multiple sources of trade agreements such as the University of McGill Trade Agreements Database (http://ptas.mcgill.ca/) and the WTO.

30. Between 1989–2013, 6,293 country pairs signed a new PTA and of this number 67 percent were Southern countries.

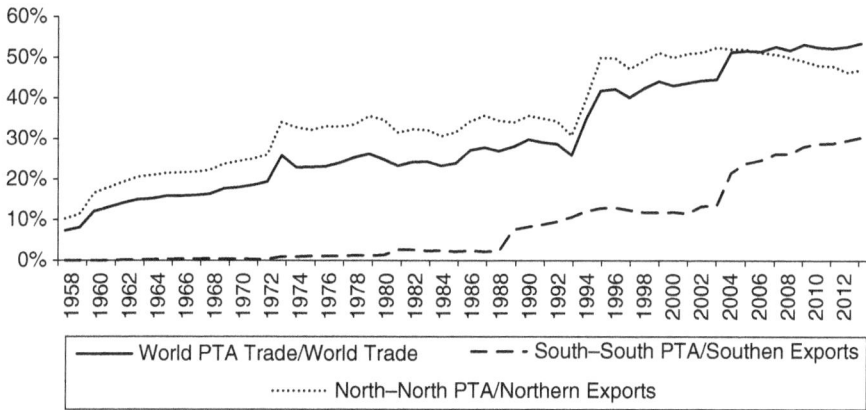

Figure 3.2 The evolution of global preferential goods trade, 1958–2013
Note: "South" refers to the Global South, including the Emerging South. World PTA Trade/World Trade is the share of total PTA trade worldwide as a share of total world trade. South–South PTA/ Southern Exports and North–North PTA/Northern Exports refer to the shares of South–South and North–North PTA exports in total Southern and Northern exports, respectively.
Source: WTO (2014), IMF's Direction of Trade (DOT) statistics, and authors' calculations.

PTA trade between country pairs, suggests that the PTA trade increased from around 7 percent in 1958 to above 53 percent in 2013. While the trend appears clearly upwards, the biggest discrete jump appears between 1993 and 1995, when it increased from 26 percent to 42 percent. We also notice that, while following the world trend very closely, the North–North trade is more PTA-oriented than the world average. As of 2013, 47 percent of all Northern exports were to other Northern countries with which they had an existing PTA relationship. The same figure is much lower for Southern countries, despite a significant increase since 1990. Accordingly, the share of South– South PTA trade was only a small fraction of total Southern exports up until 1988, ranging from 0 percent to 2 percent. Since then, it increased from 8 percent in 1989 to 30 percent in 2013. Historically, therefore, it appears that PTAs have occupied a more central role in Northern exports than for the South.

Figure 3.3 follows up the same data, but this time particularly for Northern and Southern PTA trade as a share of total Southern and Northern PTA exports as well as total South–South and North–North exports. The share of South–South PTA trade in total South–South trade increased significantly from less than 1 percent throughout 1960s and 1970s, to around 6–7 percent during the 80s, to 20 percent in 1989, and to 52 percent in 2013. Overall, 1989 and 2004 appear to be two important dates for the evolution of South–South PTA trade. Looking at the importance of South–South PTAs in total Southern PTA exports, we find different trends for different decades. While up until 1971, the share of South–South PTAs was 100 percent of all Southern PTA trade, the number of South–North PTAs increased significantly. In fact the share of South–South PTAs dropped to 37 percent by 1973 and fluctuated around 40–45 percent for most of 1970s and 1980s. Not until 1989 did South–South PTAs start gaining ground again, reaching as high as 79 percent in 1989 before falling back to 50 percent.

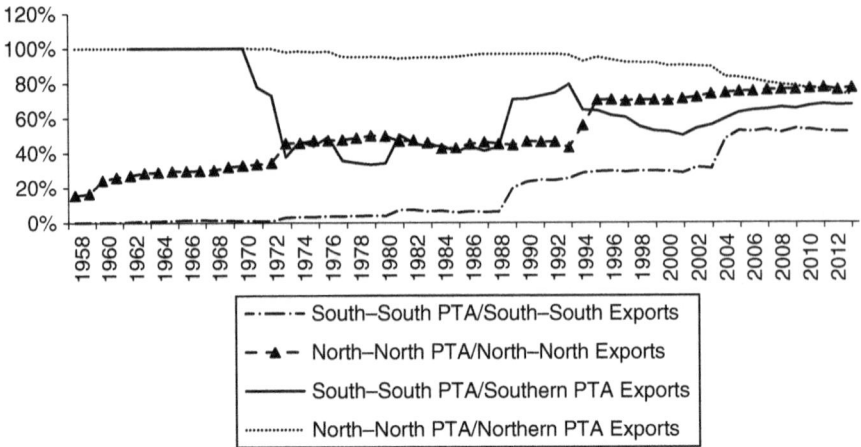

Figure 3.3 The evolution of Southern and Northern preferential goods trade, 1958–2013
Source: WTO (2014), IMF's DOT statistics, and authors' calculations.
Note: "South" refers to the global South, including Emerging South. "South–South PTA/South–South Exports," and "North–North PTA/North–North Exports" refer to the share of South–South and North–North PTA exports in total South–South and North–North exports, respectively. "South–South PTA/Southern PTA Exports" and "North–North PTA/Northern PTA Exports" refer to the shares of South–South and North–North PTA exports in total Southern and Northern PTA exports, respectively.

Since 2001, South–South PTAs have gained momentum again, reaching 68 percent in 2013. While there has been a similar, though steady, decrease in the share of North–North PTA trade (as a share of total Northern PTA exports), dropping to 74 percent by 2013 from 100 percent five decades earlier, it nevertheless still accounts for almost three quarters of Northern PTA exports. We also observe an upward trend in the share of North–North PTA trade in total North–North trade during this period.

Figure 3.4 shows the evolution of bilateral versus multilateral PTAs with a clear upward trend for bilateral agreements in all country groups since the mid-1990s. However, the global South–North PTAs stand in stark contrast to others as almost 100 percent of all PTAs in this group were bilateral in 2013, while only around 45 percent of South–South PTAs were bilateral. These trends partly reflect the new era of North–South PTAs through which developed countries choose to go after individual Southern countries for trade negotiations rather than taking them as a group. As discussed in chapter 2, the asymmetric bargaining power between most Southern countries and the North has been one of the key drivers for increasing Southern coalitions since the Cold War years. As shown in Table 2.3 in chapter 2, the United States, European Union, Canada and Japan, that is, the Quad, was responsible for 51.5 percent of all trade-related disputes filed at WTO between 1995–2015. Therefore, to better understand the motivations of Southern countries entering PTAs with each other we will discuss the political economy of these agreements in the next section.

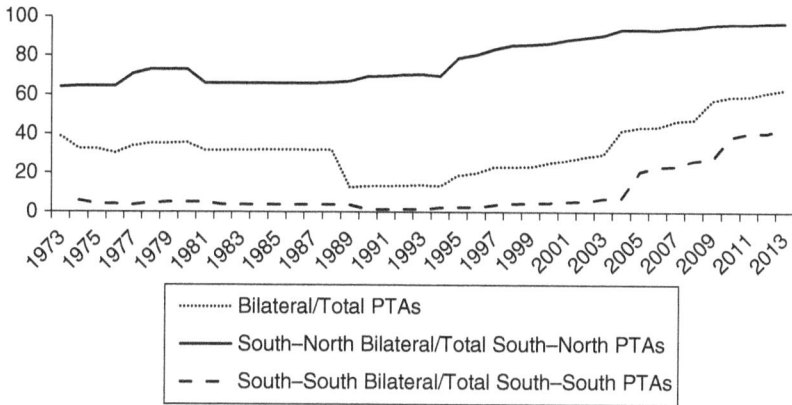

Figure 3.4 Evolution of bilateral versus multilateral trade agreements, 1973–2013
Source: World Trade Organization's RTA database and authors' calculations
Note: Bilateral/Total PTAs refer to the share of bilateral PTAs in total PTAs; South–North bilateral/ Total South–North refers to the share of global South–North bilateral PTAs in total South–North PTAs; and South–South bilateral/Total South–South refers to the share of South–South bilateral PTAs in South–South PTAs. Bilateral PTAs include both PTAs between two countries and PTAs between an existing trade block and an outside country such as the European Union's signing a trade agreement with a country outside the union.

3.4.2 IPE Approaches and South–South PTAs

There are obvious limitations to understanding PTAs through the "stumbling block" or "building block" approach. First, as argued in chapter 2, progress towards universal free trade is not the only or the most appropriate metric for the impact of preferential trading agreements for developing countries. Instead, freer trade should be considered desirable only if it contributes to more specific goals, such as increasing human development, progress towards knowledge-based economies, and industrial development. Second, countries enter into PTAs for complex reasons that include not only economic dimensions such as trade, foreign investment and technology transfer, but also strategic and political goals such as regional hegemony and security. However, an important question raised by the free-trade literature concerns the relationship between "multilateralism" (or "neoliberal globalization," as its critics refer to it) and "regionalism." We explore this relationship in further detail by examining International Political Economy (IPE) approaches. Unlike the literature of mainstream economics approaches, IPE literature has neither the universal free-trade teleology nor the narrow focus on trade and investment volumes but is, rather, interdisciplinary, with insights from comparative politics, international relations, international economics and political economy analysis.

The rapid growth of this literature results from the significant proliferation of PTAs since the 1990s, which led to the term "new regionalism" to distinguish it from the waves of PTAs in the 1960s, during the developmentalist or ISI era. This new wave of regionalism has also led to what many call "spaghetti regionalism" to describe how most countries have become members in multiple PTAs that may in some cases overlap and in other cases be in conflict. The IPE literature on new regionalism is rather large (see Hettne et al., 1999; Shaw and Soderbaum, 2004; Scott 2010); in this section we explore it from the perspective of two questions that we find relevant to the discussion on South–South integration: (a) Should the "new regionalism" be understood as neo-liberalism on a regional scale or, even worse, as an even more extreme form of neoliberalism that is taking place due to the stalling of multilateralism at the WTO? (b) Or, as some literature suggests, is new regionalism shaped by more complex forces and, if so, is there a potential for "new regionalism" to increase policy space for development in the global South?

A good starting place to understand the debates on the "new regionalism" is with Ethier (1998), who argued that in the 1990s PTAs were being signed under new international realities whereby North–North trade in manufactures were dramatically liberalized, developing countries went through substantial liberalization and FDI played a far larger role than before. Ethier noted that most countries that enter into PTAs have already significantly lowered their tariffs, such that the marginal tariff liberalization they may undertake after signing is rather minimal. Nevertheless, the type of integration associated with PTAs is often deeper insofar as it involves policy harmonization and changes to investment policy, particularly relating to investor rights.

This new, deeper regionalism is a natural outcome of trade liberalization: transportation costs have increased relative to total costs of trade, since tariff costs have been reduced. Therefore, rather than ask whether regionalism is a building block or a stumbling block towards multilateralism, Ethier argues that it is multilateralism (in the form of freer trade) that has led to regionalism. Ethier goes on to argue that many countries may enter into PTAs, because the competition for FDI has become fierce. By entering into binding PTAs, developing countries can hope to get a slice of the FDI pie, which they might miss if they remained outside the regional integration circuits proliferating throughout the world.

Though Ethier's analysis lies within the traditional literature on PTAs, it is relevant for the new regionalism debates here, because he concluded that globalization has created the conditions whereby what matters for growth is attracting FDI rather than simply expanding trade, and therefore developing countries starved for growth must keep undertaking market-oriented reforms to "signal" that they are open for business. In a way, this explanation sheds light on why many countries continued with neoliberal reforms even after they have been empirically and intellectually challenged.[31]

According to critics of the new regionalism, the proliferation of PTAs since the 1990s reflects the hegemony of US-pushed neoliberal reforms and the Washington Consensus.

---

31. For example, following the financial liberalization wave, the 1990s witnessed recurring banking and financial crises all over the Southern world. Nevertheless, during 2000–13, an average of 56 countries each year introduced a total of 1,440 regulatory changes in their investment regimes, and 80 percent of them were to promote and facilitate a more favorable environment for foreign investors. The same figure was even higher during the 1990s with 94 percent of a total of 1,035 changes being more favorable to FDI (UNCTAD, 2005b, 2014).

Certainly NAFTA, an early example of the new regionalism, fits this description, and Phillips (2001; 2003ab; 2004) advances this line of argument regarding MERCOSUR which, he argued, functioned as a lubricant for the extension of US hegemony through the Free Trade Area of the Americas (FTAA) agenda. The new regionalism is market-led (based on corporate strategy such as that of automobile companies) not state-led, and threatens to be a mirror image of the process of neoliberalism in the North American hemisphere. And though the new regionalism involves elaborate institutions advocating subregional governance tailored to regional conditions, it is well within the confines of a broadly neoliberal model.

Hettne (2005) disagrees with what he argues are "the simplistic and linear notions of regionalism." He argues that new regionalism is in fact a reaction to and modifier of globalism. Just as neoliberalism may be considered the "second great transformation," the new regionalism can be understood as a sort of double movement, as in Karl Polanyi's Great Transformation. Accordingly, the unfettered expansion of markets under the first phase of globalization is later countered by a more interventionist societal response, that is, regionalization, to limit the impact of dislocations caused by the market penetration into new areas (Hettne, 2005, p. 548).

In this conception, the "new regionalism" is not simply neoliberalism on a small scale but an attempt to come to terms with neoliberalism. As Hveem argues "regionalism would thus be explained not as a result of structural or institutional factors [...] but as an instrument for changing existing international structures and institutions to create new identities, opportunities and alliances" (Hveem, 1999).

Could South–South regionalism then be understood as a "double movement" against globalization and an attempt to bring it under control, or is it simply neoliberalism on a regional scale? Certainly there are many reasons to understand South–South new regionalism as neoliberal. First, South–South new regionalism was directly influenced by the changes in the global economy and by the diminished policy space that emerged after the 1980s debt crisis and subsequent formation of the WTO. If neoliberalism is understood as a process having taken place in a neoliberal era, then most South–South PTAs are certainly aimed in the direction of more liberalization, privatization and deregulation. Within the overall shift of the global spectrum toward markets, however, South–South regionalism seems to have retained more space for developing countries to maneuver than do multilateralism or North–South PTAs.

In a survey comparison of EU and US North–South, South–South and WTO requirements, Thrasher and Gallagher (2008) found that South–South trade agreements are the most likely to secure a large space for industrial and other developmental policy. Another example of the complex impact of South–South PTAs can be found in Doctor's (2007) investigation of the stalled EU–MERCOSUR negotiations to establish an interregional PTA that would have been the largest Free Trade Area in the world. Negotiations between the European Union and MERCOSUR started after the two groups signed the Inter-regional Framework Cooperation Agreement in 1995, and when the European Commission put forward a proposal for a negotiating mandate in 1998. By 2005, after several years of negotiations, the process had reached a dead end and halted, only to be picked up in 2010 and continuing until today.

Doctor argues that, according to standard accounts, the collapse of the negotiations was deemed to be a failure of regionalism and interregionalism. However, that account hid the more complex backstory to the negotiations. At the start of the 2000s, center-left governments had come to power in Latin America and were pushing for a shifting of MERCOSUR towards a more developmental direction. These same governments were also eager to use the institutional weight of MERCOSUR to push for more influence in the region. More crucially, MERCOSUR, led by Brazil, used the EU negotiations as an attempt to counterbalance the then-ongoing negotiations with the United States regarding the FTAA.

The biggest stumbling block in the EU–MERCOSUR negotiations was that MERCOSUR was demanding reforms of the Common Agricultural Policy (CAP) in the European Union, which would have allowed market access for MERCOSUR agricultural goods; and in return the European Union was demanding the dismantling of tariff barriers on industrial products, manufacturing and services. At the same time, the FTAA represented an expansion of NAFTA in a way that heralded wide-ranging market reforms even beyond the EU agreement. Within MERCOSUR, the pushback was led by the services and industrial sectors, particularly those in Brazil which, unlike its counterparts in the other countries, had a history of organized advocacy of their interests. However, the key point is that without the weight of MERCOSUR as a bloc, individual countries in the region, even ones as large as Brazil, might not have been able to push back against both United States and European Union expansion into the region. Using the bloc to balance the United States and European Union ultimately resulted in the "failure" of both FTAA and EU–MERCOSUR, but a failure that in fact preserved policy space and autonomy that might otherwise have been surrendered.

3.5   South–South Finance

The work on South–South economic integration has been disproportionally on the issue of trade; very little is written on the issue of finance—one reason being that the countries of the South did not have much financial integration among themselves. Until the 1990s most Southern countries were in a state of financial autarky with regard to equity flows. Only after the liberalization of capital account of balance of payments and domestic and external financial liberalization did they enter the global financial markets as economic actors. Second, until this time capital flows from Southern countries, both debt and equity, were very limited. Only recently have several major Emerging South countries begun to stand out as major global investors. We will explore the stylized facts on this front in the next chapter; in this section we analyze the theoretical arguments for and against South–South financial integration.

One line of research into recent and new financial elements of economic integration focuses on the role of exchange rate arrangements between developing countries. For example, Eichengreen and Bayoumi (1996), Eichengreen (1998), Mundell (2002) and Bacha (2008) have focused on the optimal currency areas and Southern monetary unions. In an extension of this work, Caglayan et al. (2013) suggest that South–South integration can help developing countries lower their trade exposure to currency fluctuations in key currencies of Northern markets (particularly the US dollar and euro). In the last five years various emerging countries have started negotiations—already finalized in some cases—using national currencies for trade rather than hard Northern currencies, such as the dollar or euro, to escape the negative effects of currency fluctuations. For example, Brazil and Argentina have signed bilateral agreements on using the peso or real in intra-MERCOSUR trade and established futures markets for these local currencies (Phillips, 2009). Similarly, in 2009, Turkey signed a joint agreement with Russia and Iran to use their national currencies for trade instead of the dollar or euro. Likewise, both Turkey and Russia are reportedly preparing to use national currencies in their trade with China as well. They argue that exchange-rate volatility can hamper South–South trade because Southern countries' financial markets are still mostly in an early stage of development while their short-term external liabilities are high. Empirical results using bilateral export data on manufactures from 28 leading emerging markets show that under exchange-rate uncertainty, the direction of trade matters. In most cases they find that exchange rate shocks affect bilateral trade flows only in one direction; that is, either South–South or South–North. Some evidence also suggests that, compared to South–North trade, trade integration between Emerging South economies can further enhance their manufactures export growth (Dahi and Demir, 2013; Caglayan et al., 2013).

Previous research on South–South FDI is also quite limited, despite the fact that, as of 2013, FDI flows to and from developing countries had increased significantly, reaching \$886 billion and \$553 billion, respectively, and corresponding to 61 percent and 39 percent of global inflows and outflows.[32] In fact, in that year, six developing countries were among the top twenty investors in the world (UNCTAD, 2014), and China alone ranked second in global FDI inflows and outflows, right after the United States. Furthermore, within aggregate FDI flows to developing countries, South–South flows increased significantly, reaching around 63–65 percent of all outflows from developing countries in 2010 (UNCTAD, 2011; WB, 2011). In 2013, 53 percent of global merger and acquisition flows came from developing countries, and of this figure, 72 percent went to other developing countries (UNCTAD, 2014: 8). With regard to debt flows, in 2010 China alone loaned to Latin America more than the World Bank (\$14 billion), the IDB (\$12 billion) and the US Export-Import Bank (\$2.2 billion) combined (Gallagher, Irwin and Koleski, 2012). China's lending to Latin America is reported to have picked up speed, \$6 billion in 2008 but then reaching up to \$37 billion in 2010 (Gallagher, Irwin and Koleski, 2012).

While Chinese lending appears to be directed more toward natural resources and infrastructure sectors, and while China tends to impose buy-back conditions, no empirical work has been done on the macro and microeconomic effects of these South–South debt and equity flows (more on this point in chapter 5).[33] Likewise, economists and

---

32. The figures include transition economies. The Southern countries received more than half of world FDI flows during 2012–13.
33. China has also become a major source of development aid, totaling \$14.4 billion between 2010 and 2012 (UNDP, 2015).

political leaders both in the North and the South are paying increased attention to Chinese investments in Africa. According to Strange et al. (2013), China has invested in 1,673 projects in 50 African countries, worth $75 billion in all. However, work on the subject is limited mostly to journalistic accounts of Southern debt and equity flows, and increasingly aid flows, while lacking any empirical or theoretical analysis. One exception is the work of Amighini and Sanfilippo (2014), who test the effect of South–South versus North–South trade and FDI flows on the export structure of African economies at the intensive and extensive margins. They find that South–South FDI flows, unlike North–South flows (where there is no effect), have a positive effect on export upgrading through diversification and quality improvement.

Theoretically speaking, the effects of South–South FDI may differ from those of North–South FDI on host countries' development prospects. In this debate, the neoclassical economists favor North–South FDI over South–South flows, since they assume that Northern firms have better technology, productivity, know-how and managerial skills, better risk-management, and more experience to pass on to host countries. As a result, according to this argument, the potential for knowledge and technology transfer in North–South direction should be higher. In contrast, proponents of South–South financial integration argue that South–South FDI carries a higher potential for technology transfer as the gap between the home and host country technologies is smaller and thus allows for higher absorptive capacity for more appropriate technologies in the host countries. Similarity in tastes and preferences between host and home countries in the South may also allow for easier technology adoption while enabling Southern multinational corporations to address local consumer needs better (UNCTAD, 2011: 42; Amighini and Sanfilippo, 2014).

Differences in sectoral composition of investments are another potential source of heterogeneity in South and North FDI flows. Even though not very explicitly stated, the positive effects of FDI within the neoclassical framework are conditional on several things: (a) the type of FDI (i.e., vertical versus horizontal and greenfield versus merger and acquisitions; (b) the absorptive capacity of host economies; (c) the amount of R&D that is transferred to the host economy; and, perhaps most importantly, (d) the industries into which foreign firms are moving (e.g., services versus manufacturing) (Lall, 2002). Looking at the sectoral distribution of greenfield FDI flows (in dollars) from the rest of the world to the South between 2004 and 2013, we find that most capital flows was to services and primary sectors, 43 percent and 11 percent respectively, while 46 percent was to manufacturing. In terms of total FDI stock in Latin America, for example, in 2012 more than half of FDI was in services, and in the case of South America, once we exclude Brazil, services and primary sectors accounted for more than 85 percent of the total (45 percent services, 40 percent primary sectors), while manufacturing was responsible for only 15 percent of total FDI stock in 2012 (UNCTAD, 2014, p. 63). In the case of Least Developed Countries, 36 percent alone went to primary sectors, mostly in extraction of natural resources (UNCTAD, 2014).

The case with South–South flows, however, appears to be structurally different from those that come from the rest of the world. In the case of Africa, for example, only 3 percent of intra-African greenfield FDI flows between 2009 and 2013 went to primary sectors, compared to 24 percent of flows from the rest of the world to Africa during that time. Likewise, the share of manufacturing flows was 48 percent for intra-regional flows in Africa compared to 32 percent for those from outside the region (UNCTAD, 2014, p. 41). There is also the question of whether there are any differences between Northern and Southern investors' profit repatriation rates and net value added to host economies. Overall, the profitability rate of transnational corporations, the majority of which are from the North, has been much higher than the average GDP growth rate in the North and the South, fluctuating between 5 percent and 8 percent during 2003–13 (UNCTAD, 2014, p. 23). On this account the literature on South–South integration has also focused on the negative role played by Northern multinational corporations (MNCs) that relocate to developing countries and then extract and repatriate profits to the home country without any benefits or value added to the local economy. Accordingly, the MNCs create little or no linkages with the local economy, hire minimal local labor (usually at a low wage) and siphon foreign exchange from the country through profit remittances, royalty payments and increased import demand while facilitating the diffusion of Northern patterns of consumption in developing economies.[34] Nor do MNCs or foreign capital in general significantly transfer technology to the host country, because of their tendency to work in enclaves, their sectoral orientation (i.e., towards services and extractive primary sectors) and also their desire to maintain proprietary ownership of intellectual, technological and material copyrights (Lall, 2002). For example, only a fraction of R&D activities by US majority-owned TNCs are undertaken abroad, just 15.9 percent in 2010. Of this amount, 80 percent was done in Northern countries (NSF, 2014). In fact, total R&D spending of US TNCs in Belgium alone was more than their total spending in Latin America and Africa combined. These observations stand in sharp contrast to the fact that the top two expectations of host countries from MNCs are job creation and transfer of technology (UNCTAD, 2014). This is of course assuming that host countries do not require technology transfer in their agreement with MNCs. Such requirements were a practice advanced by many developing countries, though one that became increasingly difficult under international trade treaties such as the WTO's Trade Related Investment Measures. Thus, it is little surprise that in 2010 only the four countries that resisted the unfettered liberalization—Brazil, China, India and South Korea—received 68 percent of the total R&D done by US multinationals in developing countries (NSF, 2014). Another issue with North–South FDI is that the (imported) capital-intensive nature of foreign firms' investment activities exacerbates balance-of-payments problems and foreign exchange shortages as well as limiting employment growth.

Furthermore, several studies suggest that Southern investors have a comparative advantage in operating in institutionally less-developed and more-risky countries, thanks to their first-hand experience from their home countries (Cuervo-Cazurra and Genc, 2008; Darby et al., 2010; Aleksynska and Havrylchyk, 2013; and Demir and Hu, 2015). This advantage may also help overcome the disadvantaged position of Southern investors in technology, operational and management capabilities, experience (being

---

34. For an earlier view on this, see, for example, Singer (1950).

late comers), internal and external financing sources (including international debt and equity markets), marketing and advertisement, size and colonial linkages (i.e., their lack of it). Last but not least, if entry barriers in the South are lower for other Southern investors, then not only can Southern MNCs enjoy a comparative advantage but also the host countries may be better able to overcome some of the development traps caused by their own comparatively weak institutional development.

Despite such reasons for optimism about these possibilities for South–South finance, ambiguities persist. For example, the increasing South–South financial linkages and the emergence of leading Southern countries as financiers may very well be a double-edged sword if these trends undermine efforts to improve the institutional development of host countries (more on this in chapter 5). In any case, notwithstanding all these theoretical possibilities, empirical evidence to test their validity is lacking. As of now, we simply do not know whether South–South investment flows differ from North–South flows in any significant way with regard to their effects on growth, productivity, employment, value added and export structures.

Perhaps the empirical evidence for any positive effects of FDI remains weak because of the number of "ifs" regarding the conditions under which FDI may improve host economies. Also, as several authors have pointed out, it is quite possible that the self-selection of more productive firms by foreign multinationals may bias empirical results (Aitken and Harrison, 1999; Djankov and Hoekman, 2000; Harris and Robinson, 2002). That is, once we control for the pre-acquisition productivity of domestic firms, the observed positive effect, if any, of FDI may disappear. Aitken and Harrison (1999) find that while FDI is likely to flow into more productive plants in Venezuela, no robust evidence shows any significant productivity improvement in those plants. In fact, the authors report a significantly negative effect from foreign to domestic firms. Harris and Robinson (2002) also find some evidence showing a decline in plant level productivity after the acquisition by foreign firms in the United Kingdom. Even in the case of China which, in 2012 and 2013, was the world's number-two destination in FDI flows, right after the United States, and is the top destination among Southern countries—mainland China accounted for 20 percent of all inflows to the South between 1990 and 2011 (UNCTAD, 2014)—the effects of FDI flows are uncertain. Liu (2008), and Xu, Wan and Sun (2014) find that FDI does not have a significantly positive and unconditional effect on the productivity of Chinese manufacturing firms. Even the former machinery and industry minister of China, He Guangyuan, criticized China's industrial policy of requiring foreign car manufacturers to form local joint ventures:

> It's like opium. Once you've had it you will get addicted forever. [...] From central authorities to local governments, everyone has been trying hard to bring in foreign investment. But so many years have passed and we don't even have a one brand that can be competitive in the auto world. (Reuters, 2012)

Overall, whether South–South FDI flows would be immune from the criticism above is an issue that yet remains to be seen.

3.5.1 South–South Trade and Financial Development

A significant body of research shows that financial development shapes the pattern of specialization in international trade. As discussed earlier, the HOS model predicts the factor endowment to be a determinant of trade patterns. Following that model, Kletzer and Bardhan (1987) argued that credit-market imperfections lead to differential comparative costs even with identical technologies and endowments—a point that has been a central theme in the North–South trade literature.[35] Empirically, a growing number of studies confirm the uneven effect of financial development on industrial and sectoral growth depending on external credit dependence for investment financing. Rajan and Zingales (1998) and Demirguc-Kunt and Maksimovic (1998), for example, show that industries that are more dependent on external finance grow faster in countries with better-developed financial systems. Similarly, Beck (2002, 2003), Svaleryd and Vlachos (2005) and Hur et al. (2006) find that the level of financial development determines the pattern of trade specialization. Accordingly, those countries with lower levels of financial development get a lower share of exports in industries with higher external credit needs. The degree of financial development also determines the credit availability for international trade. As a result, the lack of developed financial systems increases the transaction costs and works as a trade barrier if the trading parties cannot provide trade financing (UNCTAD, 2005a, 2007).

Therefore, the level of financial development is of significant importance for developing countries' exports. However, the research on South–South trade has mostly stayed silent on the trade and finance linkages. To the best of our knowledge only a few papers have explored this line of research. Among these, in Demir and Dahi (2011), we explored the effect of financing constraints on the structure of trade. Based on a two-country/two-sector Ricardian trade model and assuming that primary goods exhibit constant returns to scale while manufacturing goods enjoy increasing returns to scale, we argue that manufacturing sectors suffer more from external credit rationing. That is, even though primary goods producers can continue to operate with an existing technology, the manufacturing sectors need working capital to acquire new technology, the cost of which increases with its quality. Thus, both the HOS model and the Ricardian theory predict that countries with better financial systems have a comparative advantage in industries that depend highly on external finance.

However, in a three-country model, one country in the North and two in the South, the level of financial development may have heterogeneous effects on the pattern and direction of trade. Suppose that country A, in the North, enjoys a perfect capital market, while countries B and C, in the South, have similar yet imperfect capital markets. While country A has a comparative advantage in manufactures exports, particularly those requiring high skill levels, countries B and C specialize in primary goods and low-skill manufactures with less need for external finance. In this setup, even if countries B and C improve their levels of financial development, they are still at a disadvantage as long as those new levels are lower than that of country A. In contrast, when trading with

---

35. See, for example, Krugman (1981) and Dutt (1986).

each other (i.e., in South–South trade) neither B nor C has a comparative advantage in financial development over the other. Besides, any improvement in their financial quality is expected to have a larger marginal effect on their manufacturing industries and their trade shares with each other.

This argument has empirical support. Using bilateral trade data in total and technology-and-skill-intensive manufactured goods for 28 developing countries that account for 82 percent of all developing-country manufactures exports between 1978 and 2005, we find that financial development in the South has an economically and statistically significant positive effect on the share of total and technology-and-skill-intensive manufactures exports in GDP and in total exports in South–South trade. No such significant or robust effect of financial development appears in South–North trade. The positive effect of financial development thus appears asymmetric, favoring South–South trade over South–North. Furthermore, regression analysis suggests that financial development has a significantly stronger positive effect on technology-and-skill-intensive manufactured goods exports than on total manufactures or merchandise goods exports.

3.6 Conclusion

If the purpose of international trade is to enhance domestic efforts at industrial development, then South–South exports in manufactures hold the promise of dynamic gains not available in North–South exports, since gains from North–South exports have tended to be in more standardized products. On the other hand, South–South trade in manufactures risks replicating a pattern of trade that favors the larger Southern country in the same way the traditional North–South trade pattern favors the Northern country. South–South trade then threatens to enable emerging large middle-income Southern countries to capture the lion's share of trade without developmental benefits for lower-income Southern countries. The same critique applies to the future prospects of South–South integration in finance, which is a relatively new comer to South–South literature, for the obvious reason that the development is itself quite new. Particularly, the increasing level as well the increasing share of South–South flows among all global financial flows have led to a new literature on the different developmental effects of these two types of flows. However, the theoretical and empirical research on this topic remains quite thin and leaves much to be explored.

On the neoclassical side, the endogenous growth models of the 1990s, in an attempt to improve the failed static growth models of the earlier period, introduced the idea of human capital, but the ambiguity of the concept meant that these new theories were not much better than the old ones.[36] The new growth models continued to fail in providing an answer to the question of divergence between the North and the South as well as failing to offer any policy solution. The neoclassical new trade theory is much more promising with its acceptance of imperfect competition, increasing returns and technological

---

36. For a review of this type of growth model and their comparison with the classical development theory, see Ros (2013, chaps. 1 and 2).

change as well as in its insistence that the production structure and its scope of economic activities matter for long-term productivity and growth; however, this theory also fails to offer any policy solutions as to how to achieve the virtuous growth path enjoyed by today's industrialized economies. It is equally silent on the heterogeneous effects (if any) of North–South versus South–South interactions.

The radical theories, particularly in the structuralist tradition, or at least in certain branches of it, are a much more vocal defense of South–South exchanges, highlighting their productivity-enhancing aspects. Another active line of research is in the political economy of asymmetries in North–South exchanges and the lack of them in South–South relations, but there are limitations of this research. First, it tends to sideline the asymmetries in production structure, power relations and bargaining powers, as well as the broader divergences among countries in South–South exchanges, if not dismissing those considerations altogether. We return to this point in chapters 4 and 5. Second, for the most part, this literature does not address the general desirability of Northern-style development.

What is distinctive about the renewed attention to South–South exchanges is that, unlike early waves of South–South integration, this subject has been embraced by mainstream multinational institutions. The discussion is not limited just to traditionally development-friendly institutions such as UNCTAD and UNIDO, but extends to such institutions as the WTO, which in 2003 produced a report celebrating the increase in South–South trade and financial flows, even citing favorably Prebisch's hypothesis on declining terms of trade in the context of discussing the importance of manufactures for industrial growth (WTO, 2003). Likewise, the World Bank (2008) pointed out that South–South trade can reduce the South's growth dependence on Northern growth, leading perhaps to the South's decoupling from Northern business cycles. One of the latest celebrations of this phenomenon on a mass scale is the 2013 Human Development Report of the UNDP, titled *The Rise of the South: Human Progress in a Diverse World*, whose authors argue that the rise in South–South linkages indicates a substantial improvement in human development throughout the global South. Interestingly, arguments that were at some point put forward by high development theorists and frowned upon by the mainstream have now been embraced by none other than the same institutions whose mandate is free trade.

Some words of caution are in order here. The heterodox literature usually treats the South as a homogeneous bloc, ignoring the increasing divergence between the Emerging South and the Rest of South. However, to repeat a warning that arises from the discussion of the middle-country framework, unfettered free trade may not be an appropriate way to take advantage of the promise in South–South integration. Also, anyone evaluating the current literature should consider separately the case of countries that export primary goods, particularly fossil fuels.[37] An alternative to unfettered South–South liberalization may be in South–South PTAs, as noted above. As the literature on PTAs is often obsessed with trade volume effects, irrespective of structure, the

---

37. Taylor (1981) develops a good example of a three-country, three-commodity model, including North, South and OPEC.

advantage of South–South PTA is that they may facilitate industrial and technology transfer within the PTA in a way not accomplished by North–South trade; also they may preserve a larger policy space for developing countries to maneuver within the global economy. As the entire global economy has seen a shift towards regional blocs, small developing countries may have little to no option other than attaching themselves to regional hegemons.

Chapter Four

EMPIRICAL ANALYSIS OF THE STRUCTURE OF TRADE AND FINANCE

4.1 Introduction

South–South trade, and increasingly South–South finance, have become major factors in the world economy since the 1990s. In this chapter we undertake a comprehensive empirical analysis of these exchanges both within and between the South and the North. Here, as in the rest of the book, we use the terms South and global South interchangeably to include all Southern countries. Therefore, when we use the term South–South trade we are referring to trade among all countries of the global South. However, we also divide the global South into two subdivisions: Emerging South (55 countries) and the Rest of South (157 countries), and when we refer to trade within those subdivisions, for example Emerging South–Emerging South, we are referring to trade among only those countries. Likewise, South–North exports refer to the exports from the global South to the North whereas North–South exports refers to exports from the North to the global South. The full list of countries is provided in the Appendix. We should point out that even though the Emerging South contains only 55 countries, those countries have a population of 4.69 billion people (or 65 percent of the world population) and two countries, China and India, account for more than half that total, while the Rest of South contains 157 countries and 1.64 billion people (23 percent), and the North contains 23 countries and 930 million (12 percent). The data in this chapter will reveal that the Emerging South has been by far the most dynamic group among the three categories (North, Emerging South, Rest of South), while the Rest of South has been stagnating or in decline. While it is true that the majority of the world's population lives in high-performing South countries (i.e., the Emerging South), which is a positive development, the fact that this improvement may be coming at the expense of other countries in the South is not only alarming, but betrays the promise of South–South trade.

4.2 Evolution of South–South Trade

Previously, for most of the post–World War II period, the share of South–South trade in world trade was marginal, fluctuating around 10 percent, based on the IMF's Direction of Trade Statistics going as far back as 1948, the earliest year for which we have reliable data. As Figure 4.1 indicates, South–South trade in merchandise goods as a share of global trade has increased steadily since the early 1990s, reaching 31 percent of world trade in

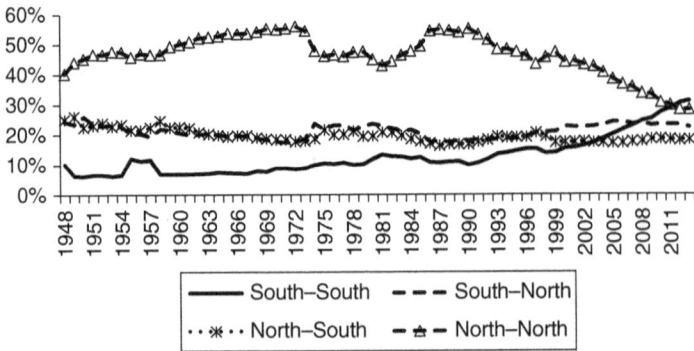

Figure 4.1 The share of South and North in world merchandise goods trade, 1948–2013
Note: South–South, South–North, North–South and North–North refer to the share of each group of exporters in world merchandise exports.
Source: For Figures 4.1–4.3, IMF Direction of Trade Statistics (2014) and authors' calculations.

2013, up from 10 percent in 1990.[1] During this period there has been an accompanying decline in share and dominance of North–North trade in global trade down to 28 percent in 2013 from its peaks of 56 percent in 1972 and 55 percent in 1990. This trend stands in stark contrast with the years from 1948 to 1992 during which time, 23 countries of the North accounted for more than half of world trade, far exceeding the combined exports of 212 South countries. Meanwhile post–World War II trends in North–South and South–North trade stayed quite similar to each other, showing no significant changes from year to year, and moving in a parallel fashion up until the late 1990s (moving around a bandwidth of 20 percent), after which the two diverged with the share of South–North trade exceeding that of North–South by around 4 percentage points.

The increasing shares of South–South and South–North trade hides some significant variations within the South. In particular, the emergence of certain countries, which we refer to as the Emerging South, causes an overestimation of the importance of the South in world trade. Reflecting this distinction, Figure 4.2a separates developing countries into two groups, the Emerging South, comprising 55 countries, and the Rest of South, 157 in all. The line identified as "South–South/global South" indicates what percentage of all exports from the global South is accounted for entirely by exports among countries within the South, as opposed to trade between those countries and countries in the North. As a percentage of global South exports, intra–South–South trade rises steadily, reaching as high as 58 percent in 2013. This trend has been a source of intense debate in economics, and raising the possibility of decoupling, the idea that economic growth in the South is more self-sustaining and no longer dependent on growth in the North. This rise also lends considerable support to the notion that closer integration among developing countries is possible and even inevitable. However, as Figure 4.2a shows, trade among countries of the Emerging South, together with trade between those

---

1. The data for the South include the USSR. However, excluding it from the list of exporting and importing countries makes no difference in terms of qualitative trends discussed, and even the quantitative differences are minimal.

(a)

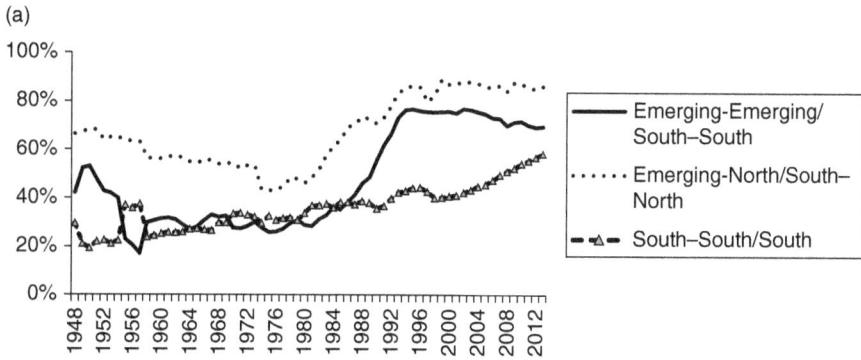

Figure 4.2a Diverging trends within the South: share of Emerging South within South–South and South–North trade, 1948–2013
Note: Emerging-Emerging/South–South refers to Emerging-Emerging country trade in total South–South trade. Emerging-North/South–North refers to the share of Emerging-North trade in total South–North trade. South–South/South refers to the share of South–South trade in total South exports to the rest of the world.

(b)

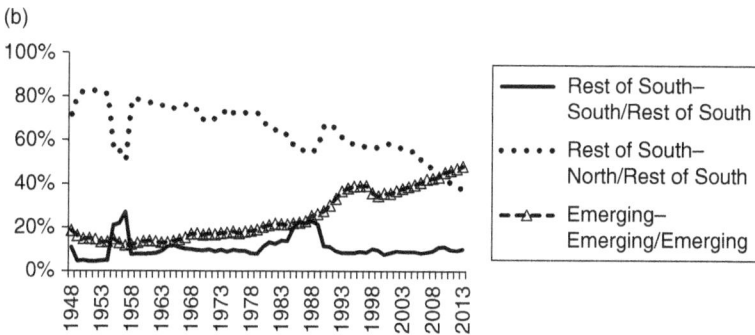

Figure 4.2b Diverging trends within the South: shares of intra-Rest of South and intra-Emerging South exports in Rest of South and Emerging South exports, 1948–2013
Note: Rest of South–South/Rest of South and Rest of South–North/Rest of South refer to the share of the Rest of South–South and Rest of South–North trade in total Rest of South merchandise exports. Emerging-Emerging/Emerging refers to the share of intra-Emerging South trade in total Emerging South merchandise exports.

emerging countries and countries of the North, accounts for most of all trade originating from the South. While the share of intra-Emerging South trade was around 25–30 percent of all South–South trade throughout the 1950s, 1960s and 1970s, in 1981 it began increasing, reaching a high of 77 percent in 1995 and staying around that level for most of the 1990s and 2000s, despite a slight decline after the Great Recession in 2008. Likewise, Emerging South–North trade accounted for an increasing share of all South–North trade, from around 46 percent in 1980 to 86 percent in 2013. In other words, the Emerging South accounts for most of the action in the South since the 1980s.

Figure 4.2b further clarifies the divisions between the Rest of South and the Emerging South. As the emerging countries of the South made greater economic progress, they

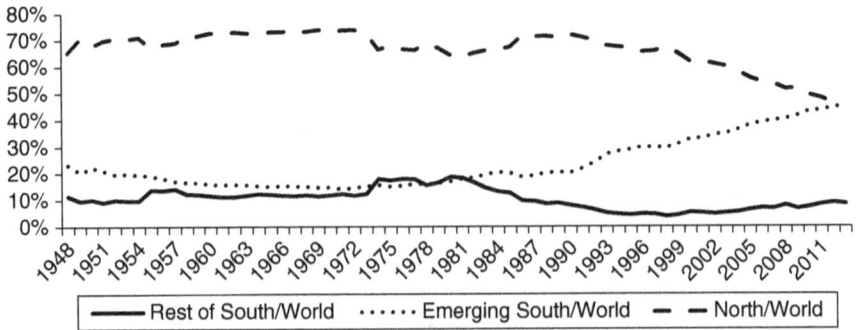

Figure 4.3 Share of the Rest of South, Emerging South and North in world merchandise exports, 1948–2013
Note: Rest of South/World, Emerging/World and North/World refer to the share of the Rest of South, Emerging South and the North in world merchandise trade.

increasingly found markets for their exports in other countries at their own stage of development, not only in the already-developed countries of the North. Thus, the share of intra-Emerging South trade in total Emerging South exports increased steadily, reaching as high as 48 percent in 2013. In contrast, the share of intra-Rest of South trade in total Rest of South exports remained low at around 10 percent, while that of the Rest of South–North trade fell steadily, hitting as low as 37 percent in 2013, accompanied by a steady rise in Rest of South–Emerging South trade, reaching 53 percent. In other words, the Emerging South was making a lot of progress while the Rest of South was stagnating. At the same time, the exports of the Rest of South to the North were being replaced by its exports to the Emerging South.

Figure 4.3 shows the evolution of the shares of these three country groups in world trade since 1948 and confirms the above observation: since 1980 Emerging South country exports have been dynamic, reaching 44 percent of world trade, and almost catching up with the North, whose share fell steadily to 45 percent in 2013. During this period, the share of the Rest of South in world exports declined from its peak of 19 percent in 1980 to a low of 8 percent in 2013. The growth rate of value of trade among countries of the Emerging South has been the highest of all directions of trade, reaching an average of 13 percent (in current dollar prices) between 1980 and 2013 as compared to 6 percent, in both intra-Rest of South and intra-North trade. The next fastest growth was in Emerging South exports to the North, and also to the Rest of South, both averaging 9 percent a year. Rest of South–North exports overall averaged only 3 percent growth a year, while during the same period, North–Rest of South exports averaged 4 percent. Interestingly, both the Rest of South and the North enjoyed their fastest growth in their exports to the Emerging South, both reaching 8 percent a year. Given that the average annual growth rate of world trade between 1980 and 2013 was 6 percent a year (in current prices), these are quite high growth rates for Emerging South exporters and importers.

4.3   Product-Level Analysis of the Structure of South–South Trade

The aggregate trade patterns discussed above may mask structural changes in world trade, especially so for the quality, and technology- and skill-intensity of country exports in the North and the South. As discussed in chapter 3, the structure of trade matters for long-term development and growth, and export-growth per se does not necessarily guarantee export-led growth and industrialization. Therefore, in order to explore the changes in the export structure of the South, we use the CEPII BACI bilateral world trade dataset for the years 1995–2009, the period for which the data are available. The BACI dataset, which is provided by the French research center CEPII, is based on the UN commodity trade statistics database, COMTRADE. While the COMTRADE database has longer data coverage, BACI offers several advantages, including its symmetry (i.e., bilateral flows between exporter country i and importer country j are harmonized), and export unit value information. The dataset provides quantity and price information on bilateral trade flows between 235 exporting and importing countries, at 6-digit 1992 Harmonized System (HS) product classification. For the structure of trade we use Lall's (2000) product group classification, which classifies exports according to their technology and skill intensity into five categories: high-skill- and technology-intensive manufactures (i.e., high-skill), medium-skill- and technology-intensive manufactures (i.e., medium-skill), low-skill- and technology-intensive manufactures (i.e., low-skill), resource-intensive manufactures, and finally primary products.[2] In this structure, turbines, for example, are classified as high-skill while chemicals and clothing are classified as medium- and low-skill, respectively. Likewise, petroleum products are classified as resource-intensive manufactures while crude petroleum is included in primary products. Export structures are path-dependent and slow changing, and yet have significant implications for the future development patterns of Southern countries. High-skill manufactures, such as turbines or aircraft, for example, contain the highest value-added and unit values among all goods, and carry the most potential for industrial development, structural change, and technological upgrading. In contrast, primary goods, such as agricultural produce or crude oil, carry the least potential for industrial upgrading.

The figures below lend support to the idea that a country's successful economic development and long-run growth depends significantly on what it exports. For example, as Figure 4.4a shows, income levels tend to be lower in countries that export mostly primary goods. The figure plots a simple scatter diagram of the relationship between the share of primary products in total merchandise exports and GDP per capita (in constant international dollars) across countries during the period 1995–2009. The diagram suggests a significantly negative correlation between primary goods exporters and their per capita income levels. This is despite the fact that during that period of time there were significant increases in primary goods prices. Figure 4.4b repeats the same exercise for the share of low-skill intensity manufactured goods, and shows a slightly negative relationship.

---

2. The Lall (2000) product classification is based on SITC Revision 2 at three-digit product aggregation. Therefore, we used the HS-1992 concordance table to make the BACI dataset consistent with the SITC Revision 2 at three-digit level in our calculations. The full list of three-digit product classifications is provided in the Appendix.

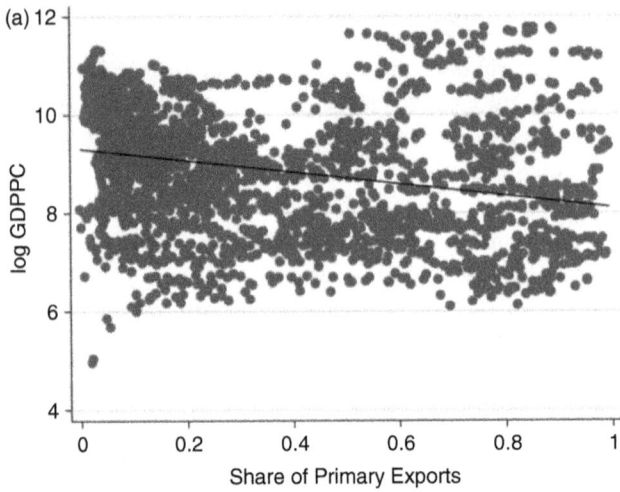

Figure 4.4a The share of primary product exports vs. GDP per capita, 1995–2009[3]
Note: Share of Primary Exports refers to the share of primary products in total merchandise exports of country i at time t. GDPPC is the GDP per capital of country i at time t in constant (2011) international dollars.
Source: For Figures 4.4a–d, BACI, WDI and authors' calculations.

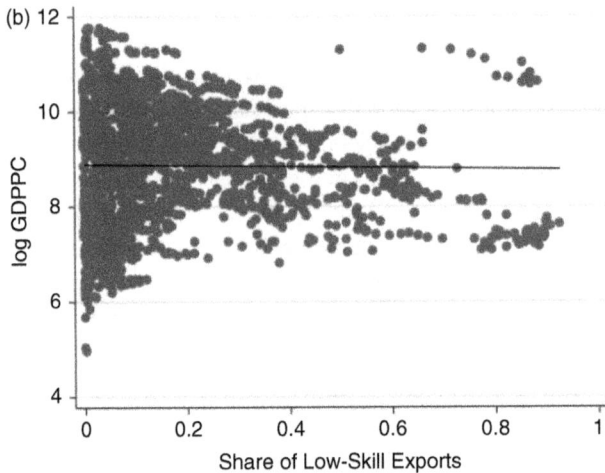

Figure 4.4b The share of low-skill manufactures exports vs. GDP per capita, 1995–2009
Note: Share of Low-Skill Exports refers to the share of low-skill manufactured goods in total merchandise exports of country i at time t.

In contrast, in Figures 4.4c and 4.4d we find a clear, positive relationship between the share of medium- and high-skill-intensity exports and real per capita income levels across countries. This is a well-established finding in other similar works, and it highlights the importance of what kinds of products countries export for their economic development

---

3. The scatter diagrams are based on real PPP dollars. However, using current or constant USD-based GDP per capita series does not change these trends.

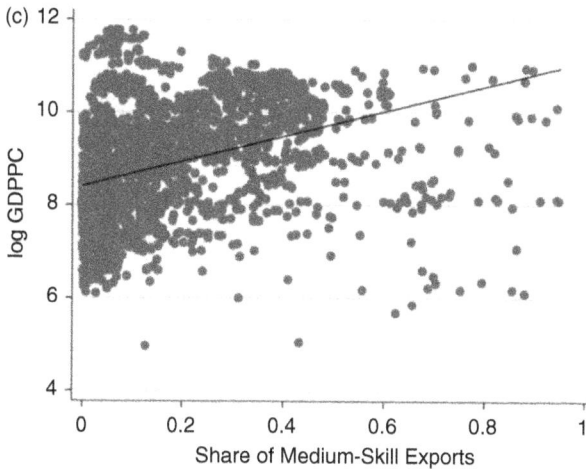

Figure 4.4c The share of medium-skill manufactures exports vs. GDP per capita, 1995–2009
Note: Share of Medium-Skill Exports refers to the share of medium-skill manufactured goods in total merchandise exports of country i at time t.

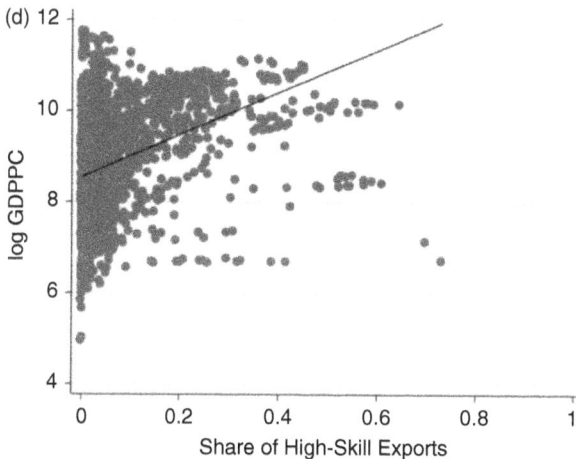

Figure 4.4d The share of high-skill manufactures exports vs. GDP per capita, 1995–2009
Note: Share of High-Skill Exports refers to the share of high-skill manufactured goods in total merchandise exports of country i at time t.

prospects. We use these general trends as the foundation of our more detailed product and region specific analysis below.

4.4 Export Quality and Export Unit Values

The quality and the value-added potential of a country's exports can be captured by the export unit values, which also signal the growth potential of different product groups. For this exercise, we look at the median export unit values (i.e., export value in USD divided

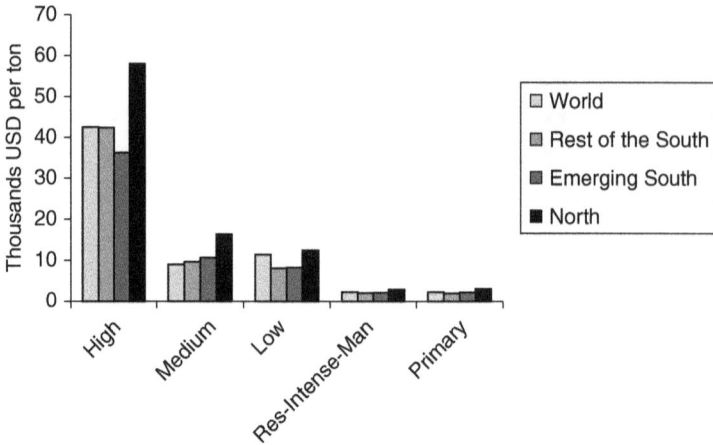

Figure 4.5 Median export unit values across product and country groups, 2009 (current prices)
Note: High, Medium and Low refer to high-, medium- and low-skill intensive manufactured goods. Res-Intense-Man refers to resource intensive manufactures, and Primary refers to primary goods. World refers to the median export unit value for each product group for all countries.
Source: BACI and authors' calculations.

by export volume in thousands per metric ton or equivalent) of each country at the bilateral level with 6-digit HS (1992) product disaggregation. As Figure 4.5 shows, the highest unit value belongs to the high-skill manufactured goods, followed by medium- and low-skill manufactures, at around the same level of unit values. The lowest unit values are in primary and resource-intensive manufactures. We also see that, in each product group, export unit values are highest for those products exported by the North, possibly reflecting superior quality in those products as well as the greater market power of the Northern producers, allowing them to have higher markups in pricing. For high-skill manufactures, for example, the export unit values of Northern exporters are 37 percent and 60 percent higher than the values of Rest of South and Emerging South country exporters.[4]

Table 4.1a shows the median export unit values in 2009 for each exporting country pair, grouped at five levels of skill intensity. We find the following: (a) Export unit values are the highest in high-skill-intensive manufactured goods and the lowest in primary and resource-intensive manufactures product categories for any country pair. (b) For all three exporting country groups—that is, the Rest of South, Emerging South

---

4. Because of the large number of countries with very small export quantities in the Rest of South category, the median export unit values (which is value divided by quantity) appear higher for high-skill goods for the Rest of South than the Emerging South. Once we exclude the lowest 5 percent of exporters in the full dataset based on quantity, which is 0.024 metric ton, the median value for high-, medium- and low-skill manufactures exports from the Rest of South drops to 32, 13, and 8, respectively. In contrast, no significant change happens in the case of Emerging South and North countries.

and North—exports to the North and Emerging South have higher unit values than exports to the Rest of South, regardless of the product group. For example, the median value of the Rest of South high-skill exports to the North is six times the median value of those to the Rest of South. (c) For high-, medium- and low-skill manufactures, the lowest export unit values are found in the Rest of South–Rest of South direction. This particular analysis of export unit values lends support to increasing North–South trade integration on the grounds that such integration is more likely to generate quality- and skills-upgrading for Southern exporters.

A significant price difference for the same product exported by the same country but in different directions suggests heterogeneous product quality. For example, for the Rest of South countries the median value of their high-skill exports to the North is more than six times the value of their exports to each other. We observe the same trend in other product categories except for primary and resource-intensive products, which are by definition more homogeneous. Furthermore, the median value of Rest of South high-skill exports is significantly higher than that of any other product category. Not very surprisingly, there is little price variation in low-value-added product categories such as resource-intensive manufactures and primary products in any of the three country groups in any of the six directions of trade. In contrast, we observe a significant price variation and differentiation among high-, medium- and low-skill manufactures, depending on the direction of trade.

Table 4.1a also shows that the median export unit values of high-skill manufactures are significantly higher for the Rest of South than for the Emerging South exports, or than even the North–North exports when they target Northern markets (see note 4). As discussed later in this chapter, it is also the case that the distribution of manufactures exports of the Rest of South countries is highly skewed, with most exporting very little, and to a limited number of countries. The 50th percentile for the total volume of high-skill manufactures exports was only 371 metric tons for the Rest of South countries in 2009, compared to 105,000 metric tons for the Emerging South. Furthermore, the median Rest of South country exported a positive amount of high-skill manufactures to 58 countries as opposed to 139 for the Emerging South. The situation with medium- and low-skill manufactures is also quite similar. To account for the relatively low levels of exports by the Rest of South, in Table 4.1a we also report in parentheses the median export unit values after dropping the lowest five percentile of exporters based on total export volumes (i.e., 0.024 metric ton). As a result, the export unit values drop for all country groups, but particularly so for the Rest of South, and for the high-skill products. Therefore, the higher export unit values for the high-skill manufactures from the Rest of South appear to result from few countries exporting high value-added manufactures but at lower quantities. This finding also signifies the high level of country heterogeneity within the Rest of South.

To explore changes in a given country's ability to produce more and more valuable exports as time goes by, and as it acquires more technology, experience and trading partners, we compare the percentage changes in median export unit values (in current dollars) in 1995 and 2009 in Table 4.1b and find that during this period the highest increase

Table 4.1a Median export unit values, 2009 (thousand USD per metric ton, current prices)

	High	Medium	Low	Res-Intense-Man	Primary	Total
Rest of South–South	18 (14)	5 (5)	6 (5)	2 (2)	2 (2)	4 (4)
Rest of South–Emerging	57 (34)	10 (9)	17 (15)	2 (11)	2 (2)	8 (7)
Rest of South–North	121 (69)	20 (16)	25 (22)	3 (3)	3 (3)	17 (13)
Emerging–Rest of South	33 (25)	9 (8)	8 (7)	2 (2)	2 (2)	7 (6)
Emerging–Emerging	46 (35)	11 (10)	12 (11)	3 (3)	2 (2)	9 (8)
Emerging–North	66 (49)	14 (13)	19 (17)	3 (3)	3 (3)	13 (12)
North–Rest of South	78 (54)	17 (15)	20 (17)	4 (4)	4 (3)	16 (13)
North–Emerging	84 (66)	18 17)	24 (21)	5 (4)	4 (4)	17 (15)
North–North	85 (72)	18 (17)	25 (23)	4 (4)	4 (4)	16 (15)

Note: High, Medium and Low refer to high-, medium- and low-skill-intensive manufactured goods. Primary refers to primary goods and Res-Intense-Man refers to resource intensive manufactures. Total refers to the median export unit value for all products based on export destination. Values in parenthesis are the median export unit values after dropping the lowest five percentile of exporters based on total export volumes (i.e., 0.024 metric ton).
Source: For Tables 4.1a and 4.1b, BACI and authors' calculations.

Table 4.1b Percentage change in median export unit values (per metric ton), 1995 vs. 2009

Percentage change	High	Medium	Low	Res-Intense-Man	Primary	Total
Rest of South–South	14	21	2	9	26	15
Rest of South–Emerging	73	112	35	40	17	67
Rest of South–North	2	51	6	48	27	36
Emerging–Rest of South	59	26	26	8	16	25
Emerging–Emerging	69	61	32	29	20	46
Emerging–North	43	67	0	27	26	31
North–Rest of South	25	28	3	20	17	17
North–Emerging	25	47	1	24	24	24
North–North	13	44	–21	17	22	12
Average change	36	51	9	25	22	30

Note: The numbers show the percentage changes in export unit values between 2009 and 1995 (based on logarithmic differences). Averages refer to the average change in median values.

was for high- and medium-skill intensive manufactures, while the increase in low-skill, primary or resource-intensive manufactured good prices remained below the average. We also note that, despite the commodity price boom of the 2000s, the export unit prices of primary products increased by only 22 percent (in nominal prices)—that is, by less than half the increase observed for medium-skill export prices. In Table 4.1b we also separate home and host countries and find significant heterogeneity in export value changes across three export destinations. Interestingly, the highest increase in median export values for all three groups (i.e., the Rest of South, Emerging South, and the North) was for exports to the Emerging South countries, at 67 percent, 46 percent, and 24 percent for total exports. The highest increase in the value of these exports is in high- and medium-skill goods categories, reaching 73 percent and 112 percent for Rest of South–Emerging South exports, 69 percent and 61 percent for intra-Emerging South exports, and 25 percent and 47 percent for North-Emerging South exports. Furthermore, for the South, the price (and probably the quality) improvement was the highest for their exports to the Emerging South and the North; the lowest for intra-Rest of South exports. In fact, the Rest of South export unit prices increased a staggering 112 percent for medium-skill manufactures and 73 percent for high-skill manufactures exports to the Emerging South. Emerging South countries, meanwhile, achieved significant quality improvements during this period, particularly with respect to their exports to the Rest of South and to other countries of the Emerging South. Interestingly, export unit values stayed constant for their exports to the North. Northern countries gained the most in the value of medium-skill exports to the Emerging South and to other Northern countries. Overall, it appears that for the Rest of South and the Emerging South countries, Emerging South markets as a destination provided the highest improvement in export unit values and therefore in export quality upgrading.

In a study using data on Chinese manufacturing firms, Manova and Zhang (2014) show that firms differentiate quality of their exports based on the income characteristics of destination countries. That is, they sell higher quality versions of the same product (using higher quality inputs) to rich countries and lower quality to poor countries. Following their work, we explore the effect of exporter and importer country per capita income levels on export unit values at 6-digit disaggregation in 2009. That is, we run the following cross-section OLS regression using log-linearization:

$$ln(\textit{Export Unit Value}_{ijk}) = \alpha + \beta_1 \ln(GDPPC_i) + \beta_2 \ln(GDPPC_j) + V_k + \varepsilon_{ijk} \tag{1}$$

GDPPC refers to the per-capital GDP levels of exporter country i and importer country j, and V refers to product fixed effects. Because the pricing (and quality) decisions of exporters are not exogenous to the choice of destination country, we interpret the results as conditional correlation rather than causality between income levels and export unit values. Our null hypothesis is that increasing income levels of both exporters and importers are correlated with higher quality exports and imports. Table 4.1c below shows the coefficient estimates for β_2 and β_2 from this linear regression, which can be interpreted as elasticities (i.e., the ratio of percentage change in export unit values to percentage change in income per capita). Results in column (1) (Panel A) for the full sample suggest that there is an economically and statistically significant positive correlation between exporter and importer income levels and export unit values, which we interpret as export quality. In terms of the size of the effect, a 10 percent increase in exporter (importer) income increases export unit values by 2 percent (1 percent), which is quite remarkable. However, unlike Manova and Zhang (2014), we do not think that the income effect on quality is linear and homogenous across income groups. In fact, as shown in Hallak (2010), which tests the Linder hypothesis, there are significant differences in importer tastes and preferences across different income levels. We next repeat the same exercise in columns (2) and (3), but this time limiting the sample to the Rest of South–Rest of South, and the Rest of South–Emerging South trade. The results show novel trends that have not been noted in previous studies. We find that export quality is negatively correlated with exporter incomes but positively correlated with importer incomes in Rest of South–Rest of South and Rest of South–Emerging South trade. Accordingly, higher income Rest of South countries export their lower quality products to lower income Southern countries (i.e., the Rest of South and Emerging South). We should note, however, the effect is much smaller for exports destined to Emerging South countries as shown by much smaller coefficient estimates. In contrast, export quality is positively correlated with both exporter and importer incomes in Rest of South–North trade (column 4). In fact, a 10 percent increase in Northern importer income increases export unit price by 3.2 percent. Therefore, there appears to be significant heterogeneity in export quality depending on the direction of trade for the Rest of South.

Turning to Emerging South exports to the Rest of South, we find that a 10 percent increase in exporter (importer) incomes increase export unit prices by 1.8 percent (1 percent) (column 5). We find very similar results in intra-Emerging South trade as well, with almost identical income effects (column 6). The difference between the export quality response of Emerging South countries to the income levels of the Rest of South and the Emerging South appears to be insignificant, with almost identical coefficients. This finding provides support to Linder's hypothesis showing the relationship between similar preference structures and trade between the Rest of South and Emerging South countries. Providing further support to this observation, column (7) shows that a 10 percent increase in Northern importers' incomes increases the Emerging South export quality by 2.7 percent, almost three times the level for the Rest of South importers. That is, Emerging South export quality is much more responsive to income differences in Northern markets than in Southern markets. Last, columns (8–10) present the results for Northern exporters. Northern export quality is much less responsive to the importing Rest of South or Emerging South country incomes, a 0.9 percent or 0.7 percent increase, respectively, in response to a 10 percent increase in incomes. In contrast, in North–North trade the same income effect is found to be 1.7 percent.

The results may also suggest that the Rest of South countries may be better off importing from the Emerging South and the North countries, rather than from each other. The coefficient estimates for importer income effects in Emerging South and North exports to the Rest of South are very close with each other (0.1 and 0.09, respectively) and are significantly lower than the estimate for intra-Rest of South trade (i.e., 0.22), which implies smaller quality differentiation in Emerging South and North exports to the Rest of South at different income levels. This would be especially true for the Rest of South countries at lower levels of income. Besides, higher exporter incomes are correlated with lower product quality in Rest of South–Rest of South and Rest of South–Emerging South trade (columns 2 and 3). Quite the reverse might be true for the Rest of South countries at higher income levels, which might be able to import higher quality products from within the Rest of South. Given that both the Emerging South and the North export their highest quality products to Northern countries, the quality differences might be substantial for the Rest of South importers.

Table 4.1c Export prices across products and importers

	Full	S-S	S-E	S-N	E-S	E-E	E-N	N-S	N-Em	N-N
Panel A	(1)	(2)	(3)	(4)	(5)	(6)	(7)	(8)	(9)	(10)
$\ln Y_i$	0.21***	-0.08***	-0.01***	0.05***	0.18***	0.16***	0.14***	0.32***	0.39***	0.23***0
	(0.00)	(0.00)	(0.00)	(0.00)	(0.00)	(0.00)	(0.00)	(0.01)0	(0.00)	0.0017
$\ln Y_j$	0.10***	0.22***	0.11***	0.33***	0.10***	0.09***	0.27***	0.09***	0.07***	0.17***0
	(0.00)	(0.00)	(0.00)	(0.00)	(0.00)	(0.00)	(0.00)	(0.00)	(0.00)	0.0017
V_k	Yes	Yes	Yes	Yes	Yes	Yes	Yes	Yes	Yes	Yes
Adj R²	0.6117	0.4217	0.6217	0.6317	0.5617	0.6017	0.6517	0.5817	0.6217	0.6917
Pa nell B	(1)	(2)	(3)	(4)	(5)	(6)	(7)	(8)	(9)	(10)
$\ln Y_i$	0.08***	0.13***	0.06***	0.26***	0.09***	0.09***	0.25***	0.09***	0.06***	0.16***0
	(0.00)	(0.00)	(0.00)	(0.02)0	(0.00)	(0.00)	(0.00)	(0.00)	(0.00)	0.0017
V_{ik}	Yes	Yes	Yes	Yes	Yes	Yes	Yes	Yes	Yes	Yes
Adj R²	0.6817	0.610	0.7317	0.7317	0.6617	0.6717	0.7317	0.6317	0.6717	0.7417
Products	4,90417	4,55017	4,62917	4,29517	4,77917	4,88717	4,79617	4,76117	4,87317	4,60917
Obs	6,238,0890	153,00917	149,63017	134,60317	699,5760	1,163,6360	812,0130	772,5730	1,380,39117	972,6580

Note. The dependent variable is (log) export price by country (exporter), destination (importer) and product (HS-6) in $1,000 per metric ton in 2009. Full refers to the full sample, S-S, S-E and S-N refer to Rest of South–South, Emerging South and North trade, and the same rule applies to the rest. Panel A include product fixed effects, and Panel B include exporter-product fixed effects. Exporter GDP per capita drops in Panel B because of collinearity. Y_i and Y_j refer to GDP per capita in exporter country i and importer country j in 2009, and V_k and V_{ik} refer to product and exporter-product fixed effects. *Adj R²* is adjusted R-squared, *Products* is number of different HS-6 product categories, and *Obs* refers to the number of observations. Standard errors are in parenthesis. *** refers to significance at 1 percent level.

Panel B in Table 4.1c repeats the same exercise after replacing product fixed effects, which help control exporter and importer invariant product-specific characteristics, with exporter-product fixed effects, which help control for the effects of exporter specific product characteristics. Exporter-product fixed effects allow us to isolate the effects of importer incomes from the effects of exporter-and-product specific and importer-invariant effects.[5] The results confirm the findings from Panel A, showing that exporters earn more per unit of exports destined to Northern countries.

In Equation 2, we explore the (conditional) correlation between export unit prices and exporter income levels using variation in exporter-product pairs across *destination* countries. That is, we look at the effect of exporter income levels on the average export unit prices of country-product pairs independent of destination countries. To control for exporter-invariant product characteristics, equation 2 also includes product fixed effects. In this equation, β_1 represents variation across exporters within a given product type (HS-6).

$$ln(\text{Export Unit Value}_{ik}) = \alpha + \beta_1\, ln(GDPPC_i) + V_k + \varepsilon_{ik} \qquad (2)$$

In Equation 3, we also explore the variation in export unit prices across different exporter-product pairs. That is: What is the level of variation (measured by standard deviation-sd) in the export unit price of product k by exporter i across different importer country j's? What we are after is to look for any correlation between the identity of the exporter (i.e., the Rest of South, Emerging South and North) and the variation in its prices across different importers. Thus, we test the following regression (3):

$$sd_{ik}\,(ln\ \text{Export Unit Value}_{ijk}) = \alpha + \beta_1\, S_i + V_k + \varepsilon_{ik} \qquad (3)$$

where S_i takes the value of 1 if the exporter is a South country (i.e., the Rest of South and the Emerging South combined). In Table 4.1d we also replace S_i with Emerging South and North to see their effects separately.

The results in column (1) confirm our previous findings that higher income countries charge higher export unit prices, independent of where they export. Columns (2) and (3) suggest that export price dispersion across destinations is lower for the South and the Emerging South exporters, higher for Northern exporters. Depending on destination countries, the product quality may be more variable for Northern exporters than Southern ones. In other words, Northern countries can differentiate product quality and prices better than their Southern rivals, allowing them a considerable leverage in meeting consumer demand. We should note that regressions here include product fixed effects, and that therefore the results are free from any differences across different products.

---

5. Because of collinearity with exporter–product fixed effects, the exporter income variable drops in this set of regressions.

Table 4.1d Average export unit prices across exporters

	Average Export Price	Exporter-product price dispersion	
	(1)	(2)	(3)
ln Y_i	0.10***		
	(0.00)		
Global South$_i$		−0.05***	
		(0.00)	
Emerging$_i$			−0.02***
			(0.00)
North$_i$			0.03***
			(0.00)
Products	4,904	4,866	4,866
Adj R^2	0.65	0.16	0.16
Observations	388,731	313,121	313,121

Note: In column (1) the dependent variable is the average export price of product k for exporter i. For columns (2)–(3), the dependent variable is the standard deviation of export unit price across importers within exporter-product pairs. South, North and Emerging refer to a dummy variable equal to one if country i is in the global South, Emerging South or North. Products refer to the number of distinct products exported.

4.5 Changes in South–South Trade vs. World Trade

In this section, we start analyzing the changes in the structure of world trade, as opposed to changes in aggregate trade. In terms of global export shares, shown below in Figure 4.6, the share of Rest of South in total world manufactures exports stays disappointingly low, with no sign of any change in the trend, an average of 3 percent for the entire period analyzed. In contrast, the share of Emerging South countries has been increasing steadily from 27 percent in 1995 to 43 percent in 2009, with an average of 35 percent for the full period, reflecting the opposite downward trend in Northern manufactures exports.

Total South–South trade has also taken off since the mid-1990s, reaching 26 percent of world trade by 2009, as shown in Figure 4.7. South–South trade in manufactures has also reached 23 percent of world manufactures trade in 2009, almost doubling from its 1995 level of 13 percent. Overall, South–South trade appears likely to continue its upward trend in world trade in the next decades to come, even though it seems to have leveled off after the 2008 Great Recession. The share of South–South manufactures exports in total Southern manufactures exports, on the other hand, reached 52 percent in 2009, displaying a steady increase except for a temporary drop in the late 1990s. Accordingly, as of 2009, more than half (53 percent) of manufactures exports of developing countries were targeted to other developing countries, a percentage that is more than 10 percentage points higher than its 1995 level of 42 percent.

The impressive growth in developing country manufactures exports, particularly those traded within the South, masks the divergence between the Rest of South and

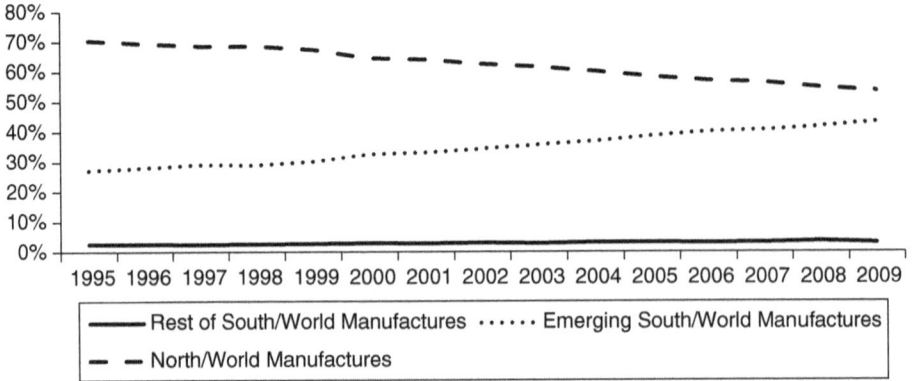

Figure 4.6 The share of the Rest of South, Emerging South and the North in world manufactures exports, 1995–2009
Note: The percentages refer to the share of each group of countries in world manufactures exports.
Source: For Figures 4.6–4.22, BACI and authors' calculations.

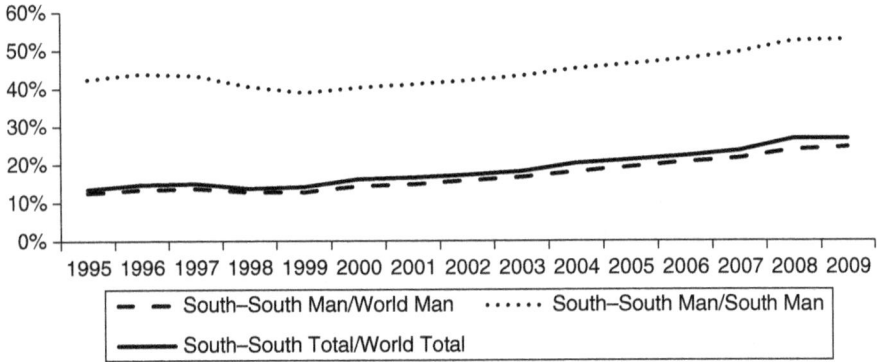

Figure 4.7 The share of the South–South trade in world trade, 1995–2009
Note: South–South/World Man refers to the share of South–South manufactures exports in world manufactures exports. South–South Man/South Man refers to the share of South–South manufactures exports in Southern manufactures exports. South–South Total/World Total refers to the share of total South–South merchandise exports in world merchandise exports.

the Emerging South. In fact, as shown in Figure 4.8, the intra-Emerging South trade accounted for 75–80 percent of all South–South manufactures trade during the period analyzed, with no significant sign of any change in its trend. It appears that, once we drop the 55 Emerging South countries, the remaining 157 Rest of South countries account for at most 27 percent of South–South trade in manufactures in 2009. We find a similar picture if we focus on the total merchandise exports, instead of manufactures exports. However, we also observe a slight decrease in the share of Emerging South in total South–South merchandise goods trade, though this reflects increased primary goods—as opposed to manufactured goods—trade originating from the Rest of South countries.

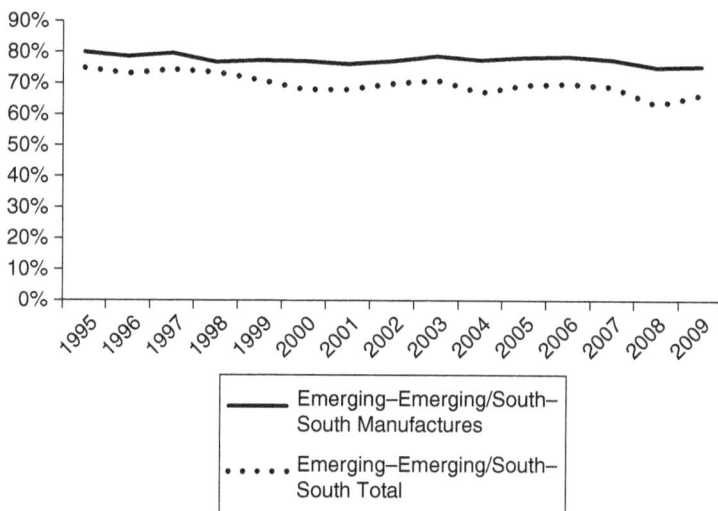

Figure 4.8 Emerging South vs. global South in total and manufactured goods trade, 1995–2009
Note: Emerging-Emerging/South–South Manufactures and Emerging-Emerging/South–South Total refer to the share of intra-Emerging South trade in South–South manufactures and total merchandise exports, respectively.

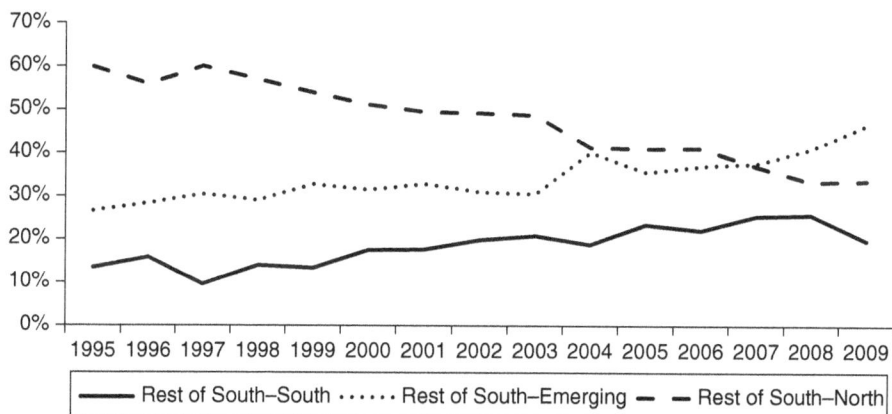

Figure 4.9 Direction of the Rest of South manufactures exports, 1995–2009
Note: Rest of South–South, Rest of South–Emerging, and Rest of South–North refer to the share of Rest of South manufactures exports in each direction. The sums add up to one.

We find a similar gap between the export destinations of the Rest of South countries, showing that intra-Rest of South trade in manufactures is a small fraction of all Rest of South manufactures exports, an average of 18 percent for this period (Figure 4.9). In contrast, manufactures exports from the Rest of South to the Emerging South took off after the late 1990s, reaching 47 percent in 2009 with a period average of 34 percent. In contrast, the share of Rest of South–North exports shows a steady decline from 60 percent in 1995 to 34 percent in 2009 with an average of 47 percent.

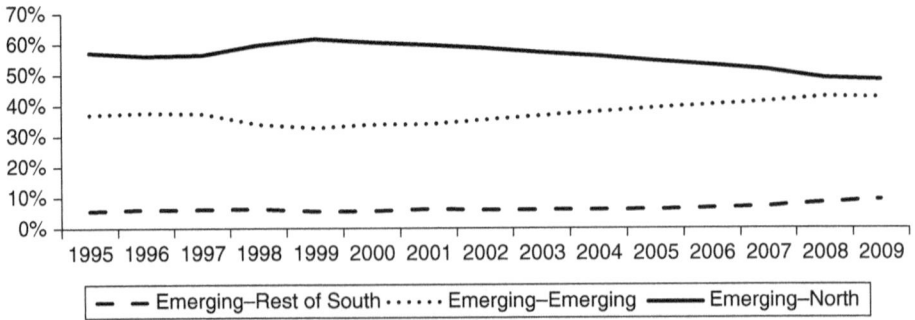

Figure 4.10 Direction of Emerging South manufactures exports, 1995–2009
Note: Emerging–Rest of South, Emerging–Emerging and Emerging–North refer to the share of Emerging South manufactures exports in each direction.

Is the direction of Emerging South exports similar to the direction of Rest of South exports? As discussed in chapters 2 and 3, neoclassical trade theory predicts that trading with Northern frontier countries would generate larger technology and knowledge transfer to the Southern countries, particularly so for the Emerging South countries that have the ability to absorb and adopt superior technology. Structuralist schools, however, suggest otherwise and predict a larger spillover potential between countries with similar endowments, incomes, institutions, and tastes and preferences. According to the trends in Figure 4.10, the Emerging South governments and businesspeople disagree with the neoclassical assessment. Figure 4.10 shows that the share of manufactures trade among countries of the Emerging South increased from 37 percent in 1995 to 43 percent in 2009. At the same time, trade between the Emerging South and the North declined at the same rate, reaching 48 percent in 2009 from a peak of 62 percent in 1999. The share of trade between the Emerging South and the Rest of South, however, seems only marginal averaging 6 percent during the same period.

Next, we start looking into the structure of South–South trade using the product classification of Lall (2000), which groups exports into high-, medium-, and low-skill manufactures, resource-intensive manufactures and primary products. Figure 4.11 shows that the share of Emerging South countries in world high-skill manufactures exports is increasing steadily at a high pace—up from 28 percent in 1995 to 48 percent in 2009—and closing the gap with the North to a bare 3 percentage points. Meanwhile, the North's share of high-skill manufactures exports shows a corresponding steady decline, from 70 percent to 51 percent, particularly after the late 1990s. The high-skill export share of the Rest of South, however, remains disappointingly low, ranging between 1–2 percent since 1995. Overall, the contribution of those 154 developing countries to world high-skill exports remains very limited and stagnant. In 2009 China alone exported almost four times as many high-skill manufactured goods as do those 154 countries combined.

Figure 4.12 shows that the share of high-skill exports in total manufactures exports of the Emerging South has increased steadily since 1995, reaching 26 percent by 2009, 5 percentage points higher than its level in 1995 and 3 percentage points higher than that of Northern countries, as the share of these goods in North's export bundle remained

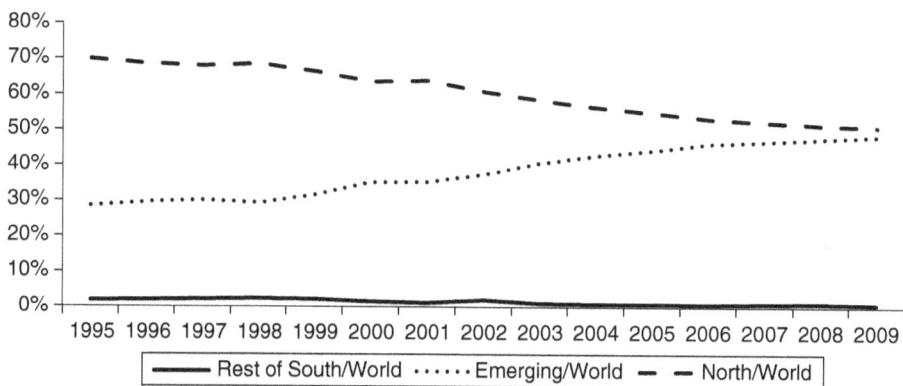

Figure 4.11 Country distribution of global high-skill manufactures exports, 1995–2009
Note: Rest of South/World, Emerging/World and North/World refer to the share of the Rest of South, Emerging South and North in total high-skill manufactures exports in the world.

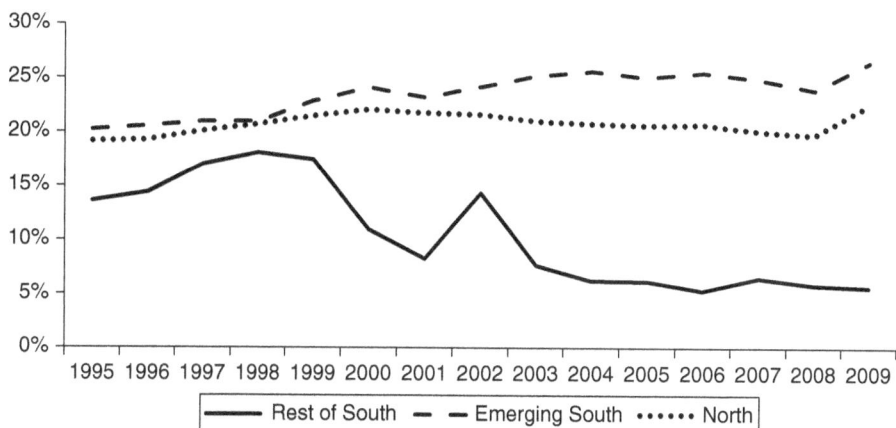

Figure 4.12 Importance of high-skill manufactures in total manufactures exports of country groups, 1995–2009
Note: Rest of South, Emerging South and North refer to the share of high-skill manufactures in total manufactures exports of the Rest of South, Emerging South and the North.

more or less constant during this period, at an average of 21 percent. In contrast, the share of high skill goods in total manufactures exports declined in the Rest of South, from a peak of 18 percent in 1998 to 6 percent in 2009. Figure 4.12 suggests a de-skilling trend in the Rest of South, a point we will discuss further in chapter 5. With only 6 percent of its manufactures exports being classified as high-skill in 2009, the Rest of South appears to have little in common with the Emerging South and promises scant hope for structural change in its export dynamism in the near future. In contrast, the export structures of the Emerging South have practically converged with those of the North.

Where do the global South countries export their high-skill manufactures? Is South–South trade, as suggested by the developmentalist and structuralist scholars, more

(a)

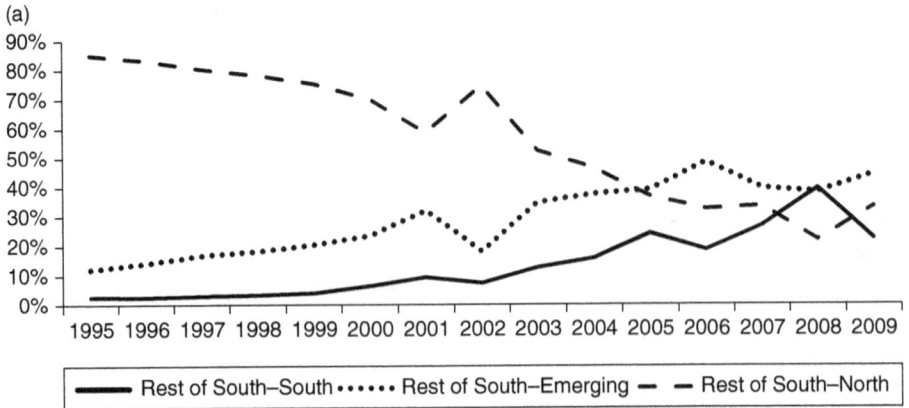

Figure 4.13a Direction of Rest of South high-skill manufactures exports, 1995–2009
Note: Rest of South–South, Rest of South–Emerging, and Rest of South–North refer to the share of the Rest of South, Emerging South and the North in total high-skill manufactures exports of Rest of South countries.

skill-intensive? Even though the Rest of South as a whole exports very little in high-skill goods, perhaps they trade more in such goods with each other, promising skill-upgrading. To answer these questions, we first look at the destination countries for the Rest of South exports in high-skill manufactures. Figure 4.13a shows that, in 1995, 85 percent of high-skill manufactures exports from the Rest of South were shipped to Northern countries. In contrast, in that year, only 3 percent and 12 percent of high-skill goods from the Rest of South were shipped to each other or to the Emerging South, respectively. In other words, there was not much high-skill goods trade between the Rest of South and South countries. Instead, Northern markets were the main outlets for the Rest of South high-skill goods. However, since the mid-1990s, the North gradually lost its importance as a market for the Rest of South high-skill exports, losing its market share from 85 percent in 1995, to 70 percent in 2000, and 33 percent in 2009. The Rest of South, and more importantly, the Emerging South, filled in the space emptied by the North, raising their shares to 23 percent and 44 percent by 2009, respectively. Therefore, the Emerging South countries have become the most important markets for the Rest of South countries, and together with the intra-Rest of South trade, they account for 67 percent of Rest of South exports in high-skill manufactures. This is indeed a significant change and can only be understood in lieu of wider changes in South–South relations during this time. Increasing trade integration through various PTAs and BITs under the flagship of new regionalism has played a role in this change, which provides support to those who favor even closer economic integration among Southern countries. It is also possible that the North has simply stopped importing lower-quality high-skill goods from the Rest of South. As a result, the Rest of South needed to divert this trade to newer markets with closer technological sophistication as well as skill and preference structures to its own. Overall, however, we do not see yet any positive effect on the total volume or share of high-skill manufactures from the Rest of South either in total exports of the Rest of South or in total world trade in such goods. The Rest of South countries as a whole were responsible for less than

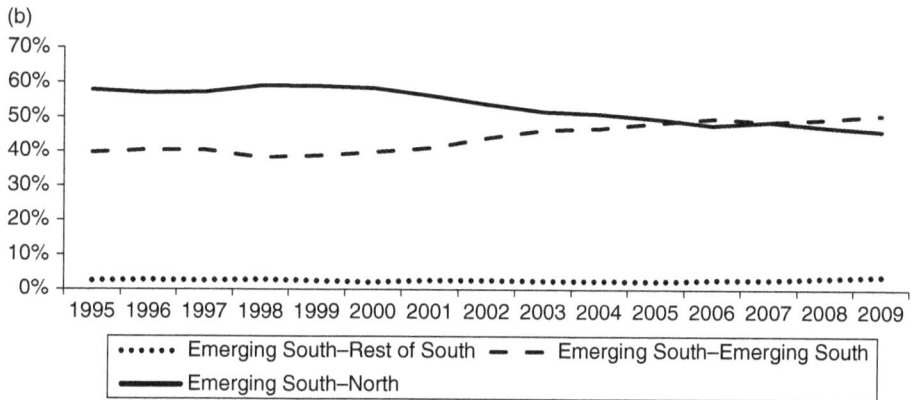

Figure 4.13b Direction of Emerging South high-skill manufactures exports, 1995–2009
Note: Emerging South–Rest of South, Emerging South–Emerging South, and Emerging South–North refer to the share of the Rest of South, Emerging South and the North in total high-skill manufactures exports of Emerging South countries.

1 percent of world exports in high-skill goods in 2009. Furthermore, only 3 percent of the intra-Rest of South trade in 2009 was in high-skill goods, and even a smaller number in Rest of South–Emerging South trade, just 2 percent.

Figure 4.13b shows the same information as in Figure 4.13a but this time for the Emerging South countries. While still absorbing 46 percent of its high-skill exports, the North has become less important of a market for the Emerging South exports. Meanwhile, the intra-Emerging South trade grew steadily, accounting for 51 percent of all high-skill exports of these countries in 2009, thereby surpassing the Emerging South–North trade. The Emerging South, however, exported only a marginal amount of its high-skill exports to the Rest of South, around 2–3 percent of the total, depending on the year. We can expect this trend to continue in the near future with the Emerging South countries becoming even more important for each other as they integrate more.

Looking at the structure of intra-regional trade for these three groups of countries, we find some interesting patterns. Overall, as shown in Figure 4.13c, it appears that the share of high-skill goods among all manufactures exports of the Emerging South to each other is increasing, and that it is around 10 percentage points higher than the level in intra-North trade. In other words, more and more of the trade in manufactured goods between countries of the Emerging South is in high-skill goods, rising to 31 percent of all manufactures in 2009 from 22 percent in 1995. In the Rest of South, we do not see the same pattern. Instead, the share of high-skill goods stayed low, fluctuating between 2 percent and 9 percent, with an average of 5 percent—quite a low number compared to the period averages of 28 percent for the intra-Emerging South and 19 percent for the intra-North trade.

We observe a similar trend in medium-skill manufactured goods. Figure 4.14 shows the Emerging South catching up with the North, whose global trade share in such goods has steadily declined. The Rest of South, however, is stuck at around 1–2 percent of global trade in medium-skill manufactured goods.

(c)

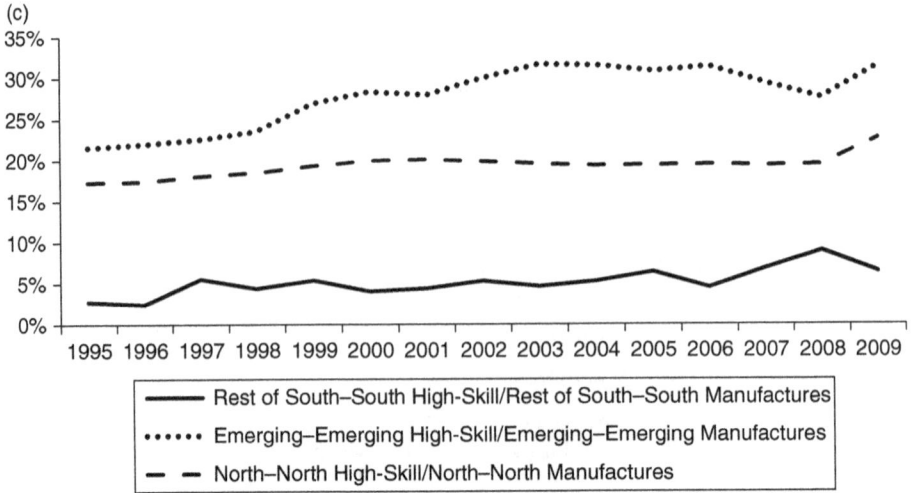

Figure 4.13c Share of intra-group trade in high-skill manufactures exports, 1995–2009
Note: Rest of South–South High-Skill/Rest if South–South Manufactures refers to the share of Rest of South–South high-skill manufactures exports in total intra-Rest of South manufactures trade. Emerging–Emerging High-Skill/Emerging–Emerging Manufactures refers to the share Emerging–Emerging South high-skill manufactures exports in total intra-Emerging South manufactures trade. North–North high-skill/ North–North Manufactures refers to the share intra-North high-skill manufactures exports in total North–North manufactures trade.

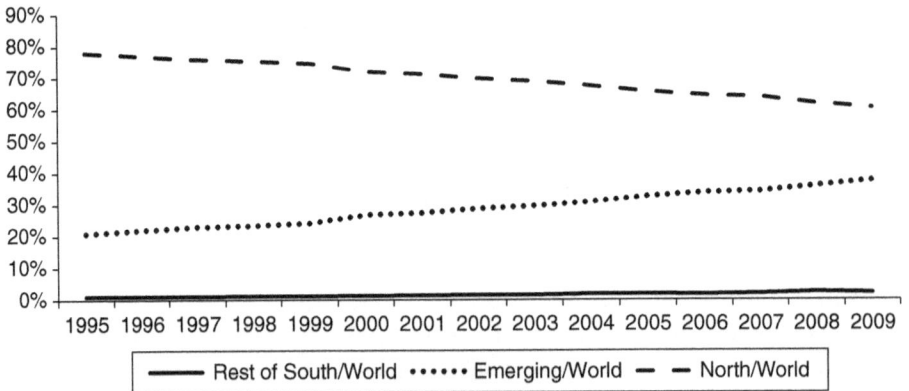

Figure 4.14 Country distribution of global medium-skill manufactures exports, 1995–2009
Note: Rest of South/World, Emerging/World, and North/World refer to the share of the Rest of South, Emerging South, and North in global medium-skill manufactures exports.

The share of medium-skill goods in total manufactured goods exports of the Emerging South and the North has, however, stayed quite stable, averaging 35 percent and 48 percent for those two country groups (Figure 4.15). In contrast, the share of medium-skill goods in the Rest of South manufactures exports increased slightly from 21 percent in 1995 to 26 percent in 2009. We should again note that despite this increase, still the share of the Rest of South in global medium-skill exports has remained low (Figure 4.14).

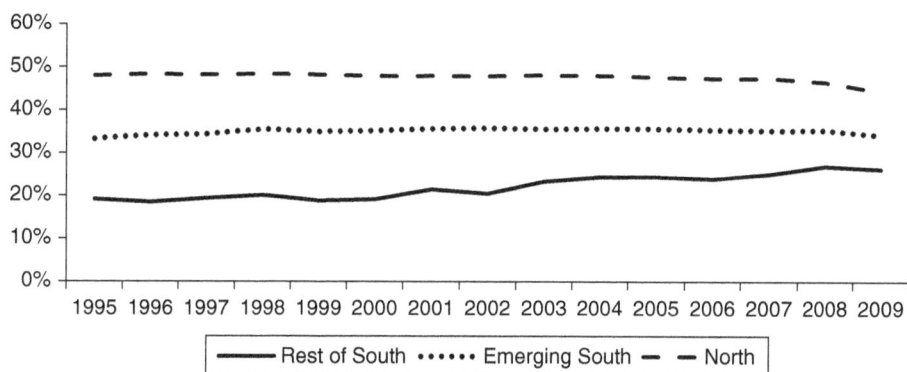

Figure 4.15 Importance of medium-skill manufactures in total manufactures exports of country groups, 1995–2009
Note: Rest of South, Emerging South and North refer to the share of medium-skill manufactures in total manufactures exports of the Rest of South, Emerging South and the North.

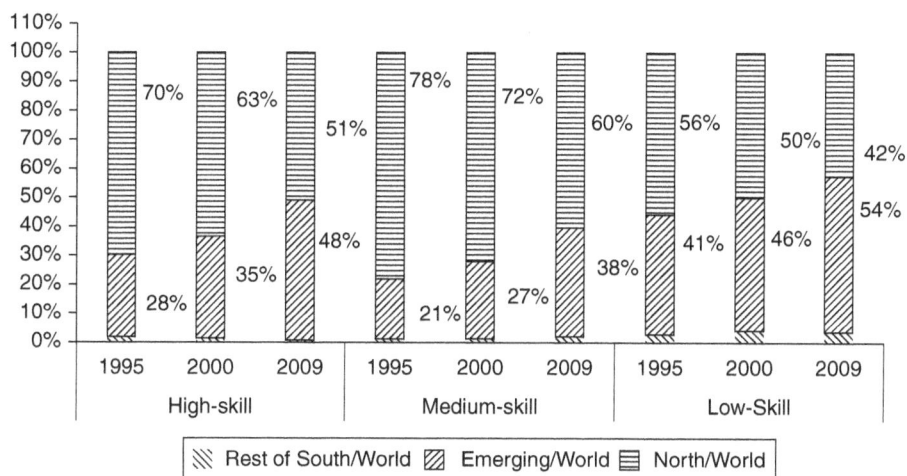

Figure 4.16 The share of the Rest of South, Emerging South and the North in world manufactures exports, 1995, 2000, 2009
Note: Rest of South/World, Emerging/World and North/World refer to the share of the Rest of South, Emerging South and the North in global high-, medium- and low-skill manufactures exports in 1995, 2000 and 2009.

Figure 4.16 presents the general trends in global manufactures export shares of our three country groups based on the skill intensity of products in 1995, 2000 and 2009. In all three product categories, high-, medium- and low-skill, the Rest of South appears to be nonexistent. In contrast, the share of the Emerging South is rising in all three categories while that of the North is falling. In fact, in 2009, 48 percent of high-skill, 38 percent of medium-skill, and 54 percent of low-skill manufactures exports came from the Emerging South countries.

We also see that high- and medium-skill manufactures have increasingly accounted for a larger share of Emerging South exports and converged to the Northern country

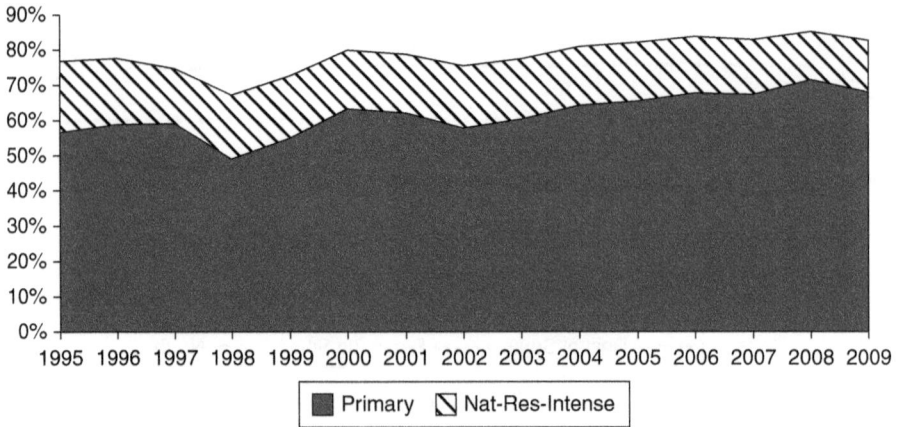

Figure 4.17 Share of natural resource–intensive manufactures and primary goods in Rest of South merchandise exports, 1995–2009

levels. In 2009, 49 percent of Emerging South exports were high- and medium-skill manufactures, while the same number was 43 percent back in 1995. In comparison, 57 percent of Northern exports in 2009 were at the medium- and high-skill level. During this period, the importance of low-skill manufactures in Emerging South exports steadily fell from 22 percent in 1995 to 16 percent in 2009, showing the significant transformation in Emerging South exports, which have increasingly become higher value-added. In contrast, low value-added goods have increasingly dominated the Rest of South exports, a process that goes hand in hand with the deindustrialization and primarization of these economies, and one we discuss further in chapter 5.[6] Figure 4.17 shows that in 2009 primary goods and natural resource–intensive manufactures accounted for 68 percent and 15 percent of total merchandise goods exports from the Rest of South countries. In other words, 83 percent of total exports from the Rest of South were of very low value-added type goods. The export share of these goods remained constant for Emerging South countries, 15–18 percent for primary goods and 14–17 percent for natural resource–intensive manufactures, values that are very close to the Northern country averages.

Comparing the trade structure of Rest of South countries in each direction, as shown in Figure 4.18, reveals some interesting trends. Looking at high-skill goods, we see that 8 percent of Rest of South–North total merchandise exports were in high-skill goods in 1995 as opposed to just 1 percent in 2009. In contrast, their share was 1 percent in Rest of South–South trade in 1995, increasing to 3 percent in 2009. It appears that in the case of Rest of South–North trade, the share of medium- and low-skill goods stayed stable (and low), ranging between 4 percent and 10 percent of their bilateral (group-wise) trade. On the other hand, while exports of medium-skill goods from the Rest of South

---

6. The Emerging South countries are also not a homogenous group and, as we discuss further in chapter 5, several major Emerging South countries are also facing the same problem of deindustrialization.

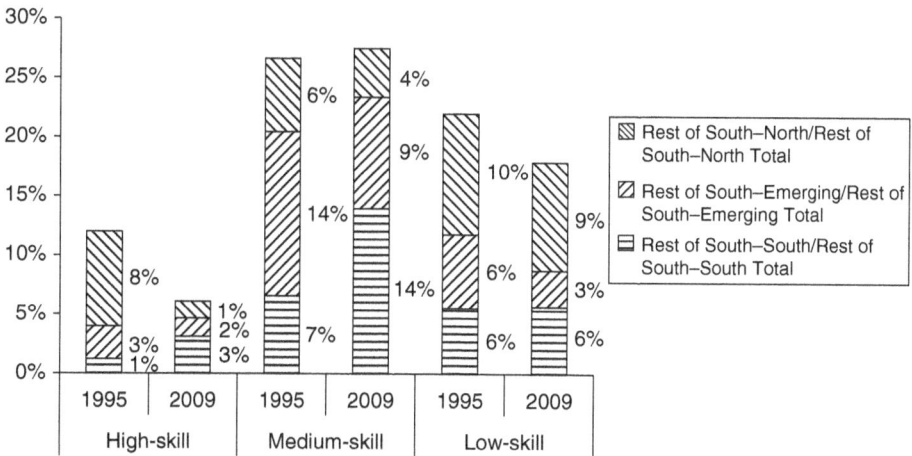

Figure 4.18 Share of high-, medium- and low-skill manufactures in the Rest of South merchandise exports, by export direction, 1995 vs. 2009
Note: Rest of South–Rest of South/Rest of South–South total, Rest of South–Emerging/Rest of South–Emerging total, and Rest of South–North/Rest of South–North total refer to the share of Rest of South high-, medium- and low-skill manufactures exports in its total merchandise exports to each direction.

to the Emerging South fell from 14 percent of its total merchandise trade in 1995 to 9 percent in 2009, their share increased in intra-Rest of South trade, up from 7 percent to 14 percent. However, looking at aggregates we find that the combined share of high-, medium- and low-skill manufactures in total Rest of South exports remained quite low in each direction for Southern exports. In Rest of South–Rest of South, Rest of South–Emerging, and South–North directions, their totals were 23 percent, 14 percent, and 15 percent of their respective merchandise trade in 2009. The rest were in primary and natural resource–intensive manufactured goods.

Unfortunately, mirroring the aggregate trend in Figure 4.17, most of the Rest of South exports in any direction remains in primary goods and resource-intensive manufactures. Figure 4.19 shows that primary and natural resource–intensive goods accounted for 50 percent (56 percent) and 25 percent (31 percent) of total intra-Rest of South exports in 2009 (1995), respectively. Between 1995 and 2009 the share of primary goods in intra-Rest of South exports fell from 56 to 50 percent, while the share of medium-skill goods increased (from 7 to 14 percent). However, this improvement is elusive. During the same period, the share of primary goods in total exports from Rest of South to Emerging South and to the North increased significantly, rising from 54 percent to 69 percent and from 58 percent to 72 percent. In contrast, the export share of every class of manufactured goods in both directions either fell or stayed stagnant. These stylized facts together with those presented earlier suggest a transformation in the economic structures of the South, moving these countries through a (premature) deindustrialization process whereby they become simply primary goods exporters.

The case of the Emerging South and, obviously, of the North is quite different from that of the Rest of South. While primary commodities account for more than half of the

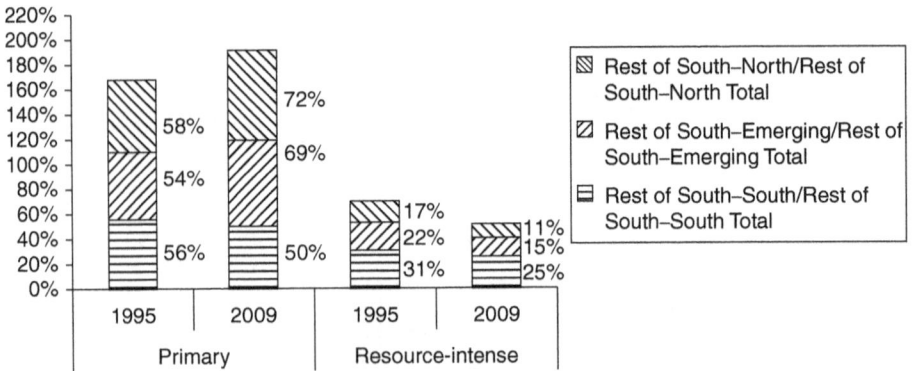

Figure 4.19 Share of natural resource–intensive manufactures and primary goods in Rest of South merchandise exports, by export direction, 1995–2009
Note: Rest of South–South/Rest of South–South total, Rest of South–North/Rest of South–North total, and Rest of South–Emerging/Rest of South–Emerging total refer to the share of primary and resource-intensive manufactures exports in total merchandise exports of the Rest of South to each direction.

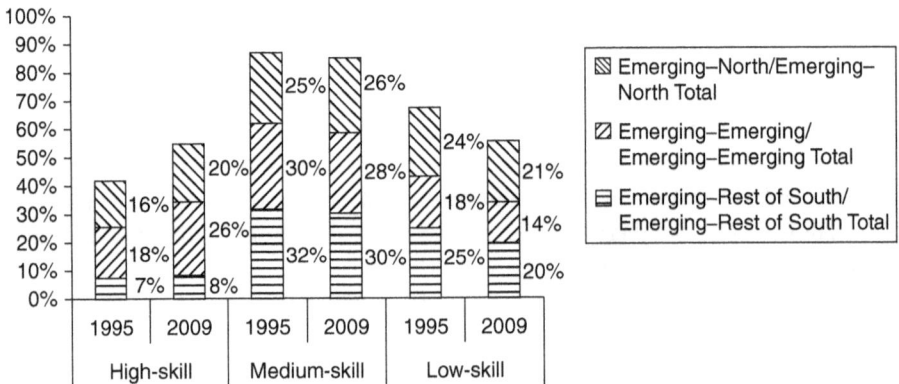

Figure 4.20 Share of high-, medium- and low-skill manufactures in Emerging South merchandise exports, by export direction, 1995 vs. 2009
Note: Emerging-North/Emerging-North total, Emerging–Emerging/Emerging–Emerging total, and Emerging–Rest of South/Emerging–Rest of South total refers to the share of high-, medium- and low-skill manufactures in total exports from Emerging South countries to each direction.

Rest of South exports to other Rest of South, Emerging South or Northern countries, medium- and high-skill manufactures are what Emerging South and Northern countries trade with each other. In intra-Emerging South trade, the share of high-skill goods increased from 18 to 26 percent while the share of low-skill goods decreased from 18 to 14 percent (Figure 4.20). We see the same trend for Emerging South–North trade, where the share of high-skill exports rose to 20 percent from 16 percent while the share of low-skill exports fell from 24 to 21 percent. The share of medium-skill goods stayed stable, accounting for almost one-third of trade volume in all three directions. In Emerging

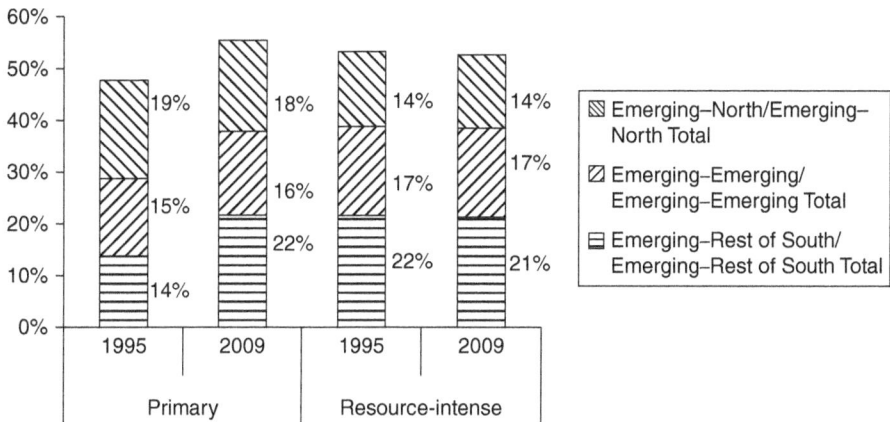

Figure 4.21 Share of natural resource–intensive manufactures and primary goods in Emerging South merchandise exports, by export direction, 1995–2009
Note: Emerging-North/Emerging-North total, Emerging–Emerging/Emerging-Emerging total, and Emerging–Rest of South/Emerging–Rest of South total refers to the share of primary and resource-intensive manufactures exports in total exports from Emerging South countries to each direction.

South exports to the Rest of South, high-skill goods occupied a lower share than in other directions, around 8 percent of their trading volume.

Overall, it appears that Emerging South countries' trade with each other and with the North is more technology- and skill-intensive than that with the Rest of South. In contrast to the higher value-added products, the share of exports of primary goods and resource-intensive manufactures remained more or less constant in Emerging South countries' trade with the North and with each other (Figure 4.21), while increasing in their trade with the Rest of South. Overall, 43 percent of Emerging South exports to the Rest of South in 2009 was either primary or resource-intensive manufactured goods. In contrast, the same share was 33 percent for intra-Emerging South trade, and 32 percent for Emerging South–North trade in 2009.

For a comparison, in Figure 4.22 let us look at the trade structure of Northern countries with each other and with the rest of the world. In 2009, 19 percent and 36 percent of North–North trade was in high-skill and medium-skill goods, as opposed to 3 percent and 14 percent in intra-Rest of South trade, and 26 percent and 28 percent in intra-Emerging South trade. In terms of their export structures, therefore, the Emerging South countries have converged with the Northern countries. Furthermore, the Emerging South has significantly diverged from the Rest of South. When comparing the North and the South, we should remember that the global export share of Emerging South in all three types of manufactures has increased steadily while that of the Rest of South stagnated. Instead of speeding up its industrialization efforts and upgrading the skill and technology intensity of its exports, the Rest of South has fallen into the trap of deindustrialization and has reverted back to a primordial trade pattern, exporting primary goods in exchange for industrial goods. As we discuss in chapter 5 this trend

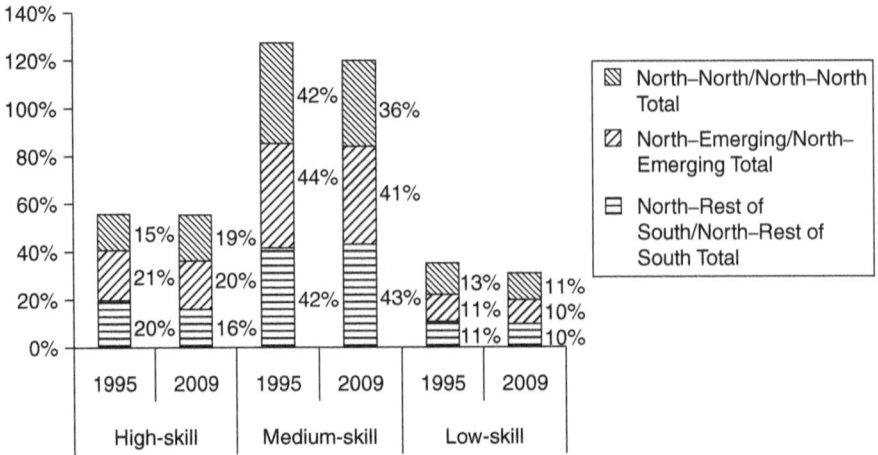

Figure 4.22 Share of high-, medium- and low-skill manufactures in Northern merchandise exports, by export direction, 1995 vs. 2009
Note: North–North/North–North Total, North–Emerging/North–Emerging Total, and North–Rest of South/North–Rest of South Total refers to the share of high-, medium- and low-skill manufactures exports in total exports from the North to each direction.

should be taken into consideration in South–South integration schemes in order to mitigate the imbalances and work on mutually beneficial trade.

4.6   Geographical Structure of South–South Trade

In the previous section, we explored the structure of South–South and South–North trade and demonstrated why using the South as a blanket term when discussing the trade relations Southern countries have with each other and with the North makes little sense given how since the 1990s, the Emerging South has diverged from the Rest of South. However, when it comes to their geographical location, there are significant differences across countries both within the Emerging South as well as the Rest of South, and this is what we will explore in this section. Many of the South–North patterns that have emerged in the previous section are also consistent with the geographical positioning of those countries.

In order to look at regional differences in trade patterns, we classify countries into seven groups based on the World Bank's classification (2014): East Asia and Pacific, Europe and Central Asia, Latin America and the Caribbean (LA), Middle East and North Africa (MENA), North America, South Asia and sub-Saharan Africa. Let us start with the aggregate trade patterns. Table 4.2 below shows the intra- and interregional distribution of total world trade between 1995 and 2009, with boldfaced numbers along the diagonal indicating the percentage share of intra-regional trade in total trade of each region. A couple of observations are in order, which have also been well documented by other studies. First, intra-regional trade is significant, accounting for most

Table 4.2 Geographical distribution of world merchandise exports, 1995–2009

Importing / Exporting region	East Asia & Pacific (%)	Europe & Central Asia (%)	LA (%)	MENA (%)	North America (%)	South Asia (%)	Sub-Saharan Africa (%)
East Asia & Pacific	**49.3**	8.7	10.1	44.0	22.7	23.7	19.5
Europe & Central Asia	19.2	**72.4**	16.4	25.2	20.9	29.1	33.9
LA	4.0	2.4	**18.9**	1.4	16.4	3.0	3.7
MENA	3.3	4.7	2.1	**7.6**	3.3	13.9	3.1
North America	20.6	9.1	50.5	12.9	**34.7**	20.3	22.5
South Asia	2.2	1.1	0.9	6.5	1.0	**5.5**	4.8
Sub-Saharan Africa	1.4	1.5	1.1	2.5	1.0	4.6	**12.5**
Totals	100	100	100	100	100	100	**100**

Note: Columns and rows show exporters and importers, respectively.
Source: For Tables 4.2–4.4, BACI, World Bank (2014), and authors' calculations.

trade in East Asia and the Pacific, Europe and North America. On the other hand, Latin America trades most with North America; South Asia trades most with Europe; sub-Saharan Africa trades most with Europe; and MENA trades most with East Asia and the Pacific. Trade between various countries within Europe is highest of all intra-regional trade worldwide, accounting for almost three-quarters of their total exports.

We find a similar picture when turning to the structure of trade based on its geographical distribution. Table 4.3 below replicates Table 4.2 but this time only for the aggregate sum of medium- and high-skill-intensive manufactured goods. Surprisingly, the distribution of total trade for these goods is almost a one to one, region by region match with the distribution of all trade, except that intraregional trade in MENA and sub-Saharan Africa in these goods is more than twice the share of their aggregate trade—a characteristic that suggests some potential for the expansion of intra-regional trade with positive long term gains. For example, while intra-regional trade account for only 7.6 percent of MENA exports in total merchandise goods, its share is 21.1 percent for exports in high and medium-skill manufactures. The same is true for sub-Saharan Africa.

Regarding the value-added generated by these exports in different product groups, a comparison of export values with export volumes in Table 4.4 may be useful. During the period 1995–2009, in four regions—East Asia, Europe, Latin America and the Caribbean, and North America—high-skill manufactures accounted for 1–5 percent of all export volume but 10–25 percent of all export value. In the case of East Asia, for example, while exports of high-skill goods amounted to 1 percent of all export volume, they took 25 percent of export earnings. In contrast, primary goods were responsible for 40 percent of all export volume but generated only 8 percent of export earnings. This pattern is similar across all regions, and it shows the contrast between primary and resource-intensive manufactures and high- and medium-skill manufactures as comparative sources of exporters' incomes, a point, which we have discussed in sections 4.2 and 4.3. This quite unsurprising pattern also helps explain the growing development and income gap between the Emerging South and the Rest of South. After all, static comparative advantage theory, as argued by David Ricardo, was perhaps not such great advice for developing countries. It appears that whether you export potato chips or computer chips does in fact matter!

Figure 4.23 shows the intra-regional shares of South–South trade (i.e., the Rest of South and Emerging South combined) based on product type and geographical region. With the exceptions of MENA, intra-regional trade in high-, medium- and low-skill manufactures accounted for more than half of all South–South trade for each region in 2009.[7] The regional distribution of South–South trade based on product groups is quite similar to that of total trade distribution. In 2009, for example, 73 percent of all exports of high-skill manufactures from East Asia to the South was intra-regional with an average of 69 percent for all product types. Meanwhile, looking at inter-regional trade, the (unreported) data shows that export destinations are quite mixed. For East Asia the second largest export market is Europe and Central Asia (7.5 percent); for Europe it

---

7. The ratios for the full period of 1995–2009 are very similar.

Table 4.3 Geographical distribution of global medium- and high-skill manufactures exports, 1995–2009

Importing / Exporting region	East Asia & Pacific (%)	Europe & Central Asia (%)	LA (%)	MENA (%)	North America (%)	South Asia (%)	Sub-Saharan Africa (%)
East Asia & Pacific	**46.7**	10.1	5.0	21.5	23.6	21.1	18.3
Europe & Central Asia	19.9	**69.2**	9.3	30.2	23.3	28.3	34.8
LA	4.8	3.0	**19.7**	2.9	16.3	5.3	3.0
MENA	3.3	4.9	1.0	**21.1**	3.5	14.7	3.9
North America	22.3	10.1	63.7	13.4	**31.3**	14.5	11.5
South Asia	1.6	1.0	0.4	5.3	1.0	**7.0**	1.9
Sub-Saharan Africa	1.4	1.7	1.0	5.5	1.1	9.1	**26.7**
Totals	100	100	100	100	100	100	**100**

Table 4.4 Export values vs. export volumes in world trade by geographical location

Skill Intensity / Exporting Regions		East Asia & Pacific (%)	Europe & Central Asia (%)	LA (%)	MENA (%)	North America (%)	South Asia (%)	Sub-Saharan Africa (%)
High	v	25.0	15.8	10.4	3.0	21.5	5.9	1.6
	q	1.0	0.6	1.1	0.1	4.9	0.6	0.0
Medium	v	37.1	38.3	25.1	7.9	38.9	14.5	9.9
	q	11.4	13.9	6.8	5.6	15.1	6.9	3.7
Low	v	17.2	13.5	9.9	4.8	8.6	39.1	4.8
	q	5.0	5.1	2.1	1.0	4.3	7.3	3.0
Primary	v	8.0	12.7	33.0	67.7	13.5	13.0	60.1
	q	40.3	47.2	50.5	73.4	45.8	21.5	62.6
Res-Intense-Man	v	11.7	18.1	20.0	15.9	15.4	26.6	19.8
	q	42.2	33.0	39.5	19.9	29.6	63.7	30.6
Totals	v	100	100	100	100	100	100	100
	q	100	100	100	100	100	100	100

Note. The letters v and q refer to the percentage share of each product group in total value and volume of regional exports between 1995–2009.

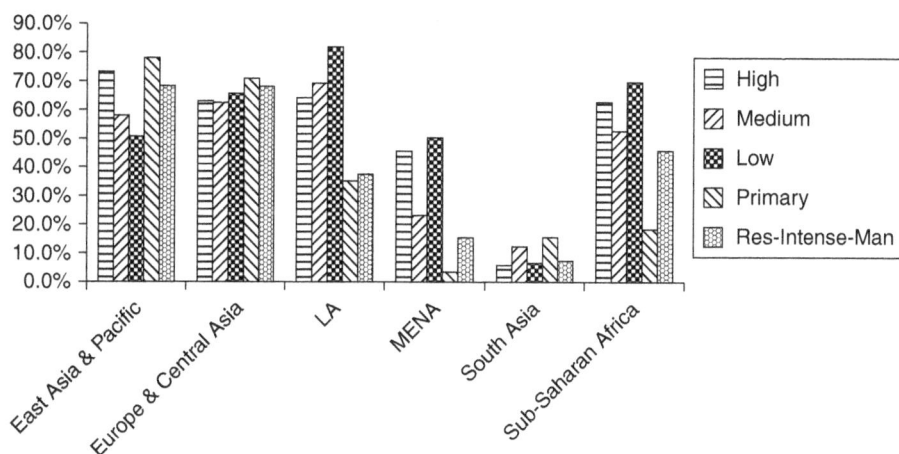

Figure 4.23 Intra-regional South–South trade in 2009
Source: BACI and authors' calculations.

is MENA (12 percent); for Latin America and MENA it is East Asia (20 percent, and 37 percent, respectively). For North America (i.e., Mexico), South Asia and sub-Saharan Africa it is sub-Saharan Africa (22 percent), MENA (32 percent), and East Asia and Pacific (22 percent), respectively. While these trade patterns highlight heterogeneity in trade networks, the high share of intra-regional trade suggests the possibility of further expansion in South–South trade in the coming years.

4.7   Product Structure and Extensive Margins in South–South Trade

In this section we analyze the product structure of South–South trade at the 6-digit HS (1992) classification level. We start with extensive margins, defined as the number of distinct product varieties exported to each destination. Table 4.5 shows that the number of distinct products exported by the Rest of South countries ranges from 20 to 4,203, and those by the Emerging South ranges from 559 to 4,831. The maximum and minimum numbers highlight the country heterogeneity within the global South, which includes countries such as Western Sahara, which exported only 20 different products to the rest of the world in 2009 as well as Serbia, which exported 3,619 different products. The median values show how many distinct products are exported by the median country for each country group, and further underline substantial differences between the Rest of South and Emerging South. The median Rest of South country exported 1,616 distinct products in 2009 while the median Emerging South country exported almost three times more, 4,296 products. As expected, the Emerging South and the North enjoy a higher and quite similar product variety with each other than they do with the Rest of South.

Product variety in intra-group trade in Rest of South–South direction appears to be significantly lower; in fact, the median level of product count in Rest of South–South trade is one fourth of the median for intra-Emerging South and the North-North trade. In 2009, there were 33 Rest of South countries that exported 20 or less products to each

Table 4.5 Extensive margins in world trade in 2005 and 2009: the number of distinct products exported at 6-digit level

	1995			2009		
	Min	Max	Median	Min	Max	Median
Rest of South–World	4	3,619	1,091	20	4,203	1,616
Rest of South–South	1	745	400	1	1,130	461
Rest of South–Emerging	1	1,353	763	9	1,716	965
Rest of South–North	1	1,746	899	1	1,536	820
Emerging–World	146	4,952	4,239	559	4,831	4,296
Emerging–Rest of South	13	1,486	615	35	1,656	699
Emerging–Emerging	33	2,200	1,698	202	2,353	1,883
Emerging–North	99	3,152	2,079	299	2,509	1,637
North–World	1,488	5,015	4,988	1,917	4,839	4,693
North–Rest of South	43	1,233	825	93	1,460	984
North–Emerging	245	2,411	1,965	475	2,538	2,118
North–North	1,200	3,020	2,290	1,138	2,368	1,763

Source: For Tables 4.5–4.15, BACI and authors' calculations.

other. Turkmenistan, for example, exported only 17 different products to the Rest of South while exporting 203 to the Emerging South. We see this trend in the trading relations of Emerging South and Northern countries with the Rest of South as well such that the lowest number of exported product variety occurs in their trade with the Rest of South. For the Rest of South itself, the highest number of product variety (based on medians) is found in their exports to the Emerging South (965) followed by the North (820), while exports to other Rest of South comes last (461). Surprisingly, the pattern is the same both for the Emerging South and the North: the median Emerging South country exports 1,883 distinct products to other Emerging South countries as opposed to 1,637 products to the Northern markets. Likewise, the median Northern country exports 2,118 distinct products to the Emerging South compared to 1,763 to other Northern countries.[8]

Compared to 1995, the extensive margin in Rest of South exports increased in Rest of South–Rest of South and Rest of South–Emerging South directions while it fell in Rest of South–North direction, as shown by their median and maximum levels in Table 4.5. Similarly, the margins for Emerging South countries increased in Emerging–Rest of South and Emerging–Emerging directions while falling in Emerging South–North direction. During this period, the Northern countries also increased their extensive margins in trade with the Rest of South and Emerging South, but experienced a decrease in North–North trade. Between 1995 and 2009, the highest increase in the number of distinct products was for exports to the Emerging South countries from all three directions. For example, while the minimum for extensive margin in intra-Emerging South trade was 33 in 1995, it became 202 in 2009.

---

8. The same patterns exist if one were to use the maximum values rather than medians.

Table 4.6 Top 10 Rest of South exports and their percentage shares in 2009

	Product	Class	Percent
1	Petroleum oils, oils from bituminous minerals, crude	Primary	52.4
2	Oils petroleum, bituminous, distillates, except crude	Res-Intensive Man	8.1
3	Natural gas in gaseous state	Primary	4.2
4	Natural gas, liquefied	Primary	2.9
5	Gold in unwrought forms non-monetary	Unclassified	1.3
6	Propane, liquefied	Primary	1.0
7	Cocoa beans, whole or broken, raw or roasted	Primary	0.7
8	Butanes, liquefied	Primary	0.7
9	Diamonds (jewelry) worked but not mounted or set	Res-Intense-Man	0.5
10	T-shirts, singlets and other vests, of cotton, knit	Low	0.5

Note: Percent shows the percentage share of these products in total export earnings.

However, the extensive margins in the Rest of South trade hide an important detail: the concentration of their export earnings. In 2009, one product type, *petroleum oils*, accounted for a staggering 52.4 percent of all the Rest of South exports, and the top six out of ten exports from the Rest of South were primary goods, accounting for 62 percent of its total exports (Table 4.6). In other words, six primary commodities accounted for more than half of all export earnings of Rest of South countries in 2009. In contrast, the product concentration of Emerging South exports is much lower (Table 4.7). While *petroleum oils* rank as the number one export item of these countries as well, its share in exports is only 6.99 percent and, together with *natural gas*, which ranks number nine, primary goods account for only 8 percent of their total exports earnings. Seven of the top ten exports from the Emerging South are high- and medium-skill intensive manufactures, which account for 11.6 percent of their total exports earnings. These numbers clearly highlight the manufacturing orientation of the Emerging South economies and their high diversification across different product groups. In contrast, the Rest of South exports are highly concentrated in a few primary commodities.

Not only that, but the share of primary goods in the top ten export items of the Rest of South increased from 47 percent in 1995 to 62 percent in 2009. In 1995 *petroleum oils* was also the top export item of the Rest of South countries, accounting for 40 percent of their export earnings, followed by *oils petroleum*, which accounted for 8.8 percent of total exports. The only high-skill export items were *monolithic integrated circuits* and *aircraft parts*, accounting for 2 percent of total exports in 1995. In contrast, in 2009, there were no high-skill exports among the top ten exports of the Rest of South countries. Since 1995, the share of primary goods and resource-intensive manufactures has increased substantially in the Rest of South exports, confirming our earlier observations that these countries are experiencing a deindustrialization. In contrast, the Emerging South displays higher export diversity with a medium and high-skill manufacturing orientation. In 1995, the total share of top-10 export products were 17.7 percent, and five of those being high-skill and three medium-skill,

Table 4.7 Top 10 Emerging South exports and their percentage shares in 2009

	Product	Class	Percent
1	Petroleum oils, oils from bituminous minerals, crude	Primary	6.99
2	Oils petroleum, bituminous, distillates, except crude	Res-Intensive Man	4.23
3	Monolithic integrated circuits, digital	High	2.65
4	Transmit-receive apparatus for radio, TV, etc.	High	1.93
5	Parts and accessories of data processing equipment ne	Medium	1.62
6	Digital computers with cpu and input-output units	High	1.54
7	Color television receivers/monitors/projectors	High	1.46
8	Monolithic integrated circuits, except digital	High	1.43
9	Natural gas in gaseous state	Primary	1.05
10	Optical devices, appliances and instruments, nes	High	0.95

together accounting for 11.2 percent of total exports. In 2009, the share had risen to 11.6 percent.

It is possible that the overall distribution of these product groups differs by direction of exports; therefore, we compare the top ten export products of the Rest of South and the Emerging South in all three export directions. Table 4.8 shows the top ten products in Rest of South–Rest of South and Rest of South–Emerging South trade in 2009. The top two export items, which are primary products and resource intensive-manufactures, accounted for more than half (57 percent) of total intra-Rest of South trade (down from 72.4 percent in 1995). Overall, there appears to be a decline in the share of primary and resource-intensive goods in total intra-Rest of South trade. Still, in 2009 the share of medium-skill manufactures (that was in top ten) was 2.3 percent of total Rest of South exports to each other and 1.5 percent to the Emerging countries, and there were no high-skill exports among the top ten in either of those directions. Likewise, there were no medium or high-skill exports among the top ten export items in Rest of South–North trade. Six of the top ten export items in Rest of South–North trade were primary commodities and resource-intensive manufactures, together accounting for more than 72 percent of their bilateral trade. Primary commodities including *petroleum, natural gas, oils petroleum, cocoa beans* and *propane* accounted for more than 66 percent of total Rest of South–North trade. *Petroleum oils* alone accounted for almost half of Rest of South–North trade in 2009. In Rest of South–Emerging South trade, some interesting trends emerge since 1995. First, the share of primary and resource-intensive manufactures in top ten export items increased, reaching over 72 percent compared in 2009 compared to 57 percent in 1995. The top two export items in 1995 were the same as those in 2009 but accounted for 51 percent of total export value in 1995 as opposed to 66 percent in 2009. We see a similar development in Rest of South–North trade, where the top ten share of primary and resource-intensive manufactures rose to 72 percent in 2009 from 56 percent in 1995 (Table 4.9). While two of the top ten exports in 1995 were

Table 4.8 Top 10 products and percentage shares in Rest of South–South and Rest of South–Emerging South merchandise exports in 2009

	Rest of South–Rest of South			Rest of South–Emerging South		
	Product	Class	Percent	Product	Class	Percent
1	Petroleum oils, oils from bituminous minerals, crude	Primary	40.5	Petroleum oils, oils from bituminous minerals, crude	Primary	58.0
2	Oils petroleum, bituminous, distillates, except crude	Resource Intense Man	16.7	Oils petroleum, bituminous, distillates, except crude	Resource Intense Man	7.6
3	Polyethylene – specific gravity >0	Medium	0.8	Natural gas, liquefied	Primary	1.9
4	Cocoa beans, whole or broken, raw or roasted	Primary	0.8	Gold in unwrought forms non-monetary	Unclassified	1.3
5	Automobiles, spark ignition engine of 1500–3000 cc	Medium	0.7	Propane, liquefied	Primary	1.0
6	Polyethylene – specific gravity <0	Medium	0.7	Butanes, liquefied	Primary	1.0
7	Gold in unwrought forms non-monetary	Unclassified	0.6	Natural gas in gaseous state	Primary	1.0
8	Peat (including peat litter)	Primary	0.5	Diamonds (jewelry) worked but not mounted or set	Resource Intense Man	0.9
9	Gold, semi-manufactured forms, non-monetary	Unclassified	0.5	Ethylene glycol (ethanediol)	Medium	0.9
10	Portland cement, other than white cement	Primary	0.5	Polyethylene – specific gravity >0.94 in primary form	Medium	0.7

Table 4.9 Top 10 products and percentage shares in Rest of South–North merchandise exports in 2009

		Rest of South–North	
	Product	Class	Percent
1	Petroleum oils, oils from bituminous minerals, crude	Primary	49.3
2	Natural gas in gaseous state	Primary	9.6
3	Oils petroleum, bituminous, distillates, except crude	Resource Intense Man	6.0
4	Natural gas, liquefied	Primary	5.0
5	Gold in unwrought forms non-monetary	Unclassified	1.6
6	Cocoa beans, whole or broken, raw or roasted	Primary	1.3
7	T-shirts, singlets and other vests, of cotton, knit	Low	1.1
8	Propane, liquefied	Primary	1.1
9	Pullovers, cardigans etc. of cotton, knit	Low	0.9
10	Men's, boy's trousers & shorts, of cotton, wnot knit	Low	0.8

in the high-skill category, accounting for 3.3 percent of total Rest of South exports to the North, there was none in the top ten list in 2009.

If we exclude *petroleum oils*, *natural gas* and *oils petroleum (hs271000)*, and thereby excluding oil and natural gas rich countries in the Rest of South countries, we find a slightly different picture. Table 4.10 below shows the top ten manufactures exports of the Rest of South in all three directions.[9] A comparison of top ten Rest of South exports of manufactured goods reveals some interesting results. First, there is only one high-skill product on the list in the Rest of South–Rest of South direction, accounting for 1.4 percent of total manufactures exports, and none in Rest of South–Emerging South direction. Likewise, (based on unreported data) in 1995, there was only one high-skill manufactured good in the top ten list, accounting for 1.4 percent of total exports (as in 2009, *medicaments nes, in dosage*). As in 2009, there were no high-skill products in the top ten list in 1995.

In the Rest of South–North direction, while there is only one high-skill product in 2009 with an export share of 1.6 percent (*"medicaments nes, in dosage"*), in 1995 the number two, three, four and seven export items in this direction were high-skill products, accounting for 13.4 percent of total exports (Table 4.11). Overall, in 2009 medium- and high-skill manufactures accounted for 11.4 percent of manufactures exports in the Rest of South–South direction, 17.7 percent in Rest of South–Emerging South, and just 3.2 percent in Rest of South–North directions. In contrast, in 1995 the share of

---

9. To leave out oil-dependent economies, the manufactures exports here exclude "oils petroleum, bituminous, distillates, except crude" (hs 271000), which are classified as resource-intensive manufactures.

Table 4.10 Top 10 products and percentage shares in Rest of South–South and Rest of South–Emerging South manufactures exports in 2009

	Rest of South–Rest of South			Rest of South–Emerging South		
	Product	Class	Percent	Product	Class	Percent
1	Polyethylene – specific gravity >0.94 in primary form	Medium	2.6	Diamonds (jewelry) worked but not mounted or set	Res-Intense-Man	4.2
2	Automobiles, spark ignition engine of 1500–3000 cc	Medium	2.3	Ethylene glycol (ethanediol)	Medium	4.1
3	Polyethylene – specific gravity <0.94 in primary form	Medium	2.3	Polyethylene – specific gravity >0.94 in primary form	Medium	3.1
4	Portland cement, other than white cement	Res-Intense-Man	1.6	Polyethylene – specific gravity <0.94 in primary form	Medium	2.8
5	Medicaments nes, in dosage	High	1.4	Polypropylene in primary forms	Medium	2.3
6	Automobiles, spark ignition engine of >3000 cc	Medium	1.4	Copper ores and concentrates	Res-Intense-Man	2.3
7	Urea, including aqueous solution in packs >10 kg	Medium	1.4	Urea, including aqueous solution in packs >10 kg	Medium	1.8
8	Petroleum bitumen	Res-Intense-Man	1.3	Styrene	Res-Intense-Man	1.8
9	Cigarettes containing tobacco	Res-Intense-Man	1.1	Methyl alcohol	Medium	1.8
10	Bar/rod, iron or non-alloy steel, indented or twisted, nes	Low	1.0	Cargo vessels other than tanker or refrigerated	Medium	1.7

Table 4.11 Top 10 products and percentage shares in Rest of South–North manufactures exports in 2009

	Product	Class	Percent
1	T-shirts, singlets and other vests, of cotton, knit	Low	5.8
2	Pullovers, cardigans etc. of cotton, knit	Low	4.4
3	Men's, boys' trousers & shorts, of cotton, not knit	Low	3.8
4	Women's, girls' trousers & shorts, of cotton, not knit	Low	2.6
5	Pullovers, cardigans etc. of manmade fibers, knit	Low	2.1
6	Diamonds (jewelry) unworked or simply sawn, cleaved	Res-Intense-Man	1.8
7	Methyl alcohol	Medium	1.7
8	Men's, boys' shirts, of cotton, not knit	Low	1.6
9	Medicaments nes, in dosage	High	1.6
10	Jewelry and parts of precious metal except silver	Res-Intense-Man	1.4

medium- and high-skill manufactures in the total top ten Rest of South–Rest of South and Rest of South–Emerging export products were 6 percent and 17 percent but in Rest of South–North trade the share was 13 percent. This change in the shares of Rest of South exports in these three directions suggests a downgrading of South–North export product sophistication and an upgrading in South–South trade. This observation lends support to those arguing that global South–South trade has larger potential for technology transfer and spillovers than South–North trade.

However, as has been suggested throughout this chapter, the Emerging South is fundamentally different from the Rest of South. It also appears that the Rest of South countries trade more technology and skill-intensive products with the Rest of South and the Emerging South than with the North.

Table 4.12 further highlights the differences between the Rest of South and the Emerging South. In 2009 (1995), medium- and high-skill manufactures accounted for four (five), eight (seven) and seven (seven) of top ten products exported in Emerging South–Rest of South, Emerging–Emerging, and Emerging South–North directions. Taken together, these manufactured products accounted for 7.9 percent (9.1 percent) of total Emerging South exports to the Rest of South but 18.4 percent (9.8 percent) in intra-Emerging South trade and 12.5 percent (19.6 percent) in Emerging South–North trade in 2009 (1995) (see Table 4.13). The share of medium- and high-skill manufactures exports in intra-Emerging South exports, eight times their share in intra-Rest of South trade, again shows the significance between these Emerging South countries and the Rest of South.

In 2009, there were five high-skill products among the top ten exports of Emerging South countries to the North, accounting for 11 percent of total exports—up from four high-skill products and 7 percent of all exports in 1995. Similarly, there were six high-skill products among the top ten exports within the Emerging South both in 1995 and in 2009, but their share of total exports increased from 7.4 percent to 15 percent.

Table 4.12 Top 10 products and percentage shares in Emerging South–Rest of South and Emerging South–Emerging South exports in 2009

	Emerging South–Rest of South			Emerging South–Emerging South		
	Product	Class	Percent	Product	Class	Percent
1	Petroleum oils, oils from bituminous minerals, crude	Primary	9.8	Monolithic integrated circuits, digital	High	5.3
2	Oils petroleum, bituminous, distillates, except crude	Resource Intense Man	8.0	Petroleum oils, oils from bituminous minerals, crude	Primary	5.3
3	Natural gas in gaseous state	Primary	3.4	Oils petroleum, bituminous, distillates, except crude	Resource Intense Man	4.9
4	Tankers	Medium	3.0	Monolithic integrated circuits, except digital	High	2.9
5	Cargo vessels other than tanker or refrigerated	Medium	2.5	Parts and accessories of data processing equipment ne	Medium	2.3
6	Jewelry and parts of precious metal except silver	Low	2.1	Optical devices, appliances and instruments, nes	High	2.1
7	Rice, semi-milled or wholly milled	Primary	1.4	Transmit-receive apparatus for radio, TV, etc.	High	1.8
8	Transmit-receive apparatus for radio, TV, etc.	High	1.3	Parts for radio/tv transmit/receive equipment, nes	High	1.5
9	Floating docks, special function vessels nes	Medium	1.1	Parts of line telephone/telegraph equipment, nes	Medium	1.4
10	Diamonds (jewelry) worked but not mounted or set	Res-Intense-Man	1.1	Computer data storage units	High	1.2

Table 4.13 Top 10 products and percentage shares in Emerging South–North exports in 2009

Rank	Product	Class	Percent
1	Petroleum oils, oils from bituminous minerals, crude	Primary	7.9
2	Oils petroleum, bituminous, distillates, except crude	Res-Intense-Man	2.9
3	Color television receivers/monitors/projectors	High	2.4
4	Digital computers with cpu and input-output units	High	2.3
5	Transmit-receive apparatus for radio, TV, etc.	High	2.2
6	Parts and accessories of data processing equipment ne	Medium	1.3
7	Medicaments nes, in dosage	High	2.2
8	Gold in unwrought forms non-monetary	Unclassified	1.2
9	Telephonic or telegraphic switching apparatus	High	1.2
10	Automobiles, spark ignition engine of 1500–3000 cc	Medium	1.0

Meanwhile, there was just one high-skill product among the top ten exports to the Rest of South in 2009—down from two in 1995—accounting for 1.3 percent of total exports (down from 1.9 percent in 1995). Overall, Emerging South countries have increased the skill intensity of the top ten exports with each other and with the North but not with the Rest of South.

In Table 4.14 we look at the top ten manufactures exports of Emerging South countries and find some interesting patterns that raise questions about the future of South–South trade. While there are only two high-skill level products (*transmit-receive apparatus for radio, TV, etc.* and *Medicaments nes, in dosage*) in the top ten manufactures export items of Emerging South countries to the Rest of South in both 1995 and 2009, with only 2.8 percent of total export share in 2009 and 2.3 percent in 1995, the picture is quite different in the other two directions. Namely, in 2009 (1995) seven (eight) of the top ten products in intra-Emerging South trade were high-skill, and they accounted for 20.3 percent (10.7 percent) of these countries' total trade with each other. Likewise, seven (five) of the top ten products in Emerging South–North trade were high-skill, accounting for 14.3 percent (8.7 percent) of their total trade with each other (Table 4.15). Overall, Emerging South countries increased their high-skill exports to other Emerging South and North countries significantly since 1995, while there is no evidence of a similar change in their exports to the Rest of South.

Another way of looking at export diversification is the Herfindahl product concentration index (HCI) that measures trade dispersion across exporters' products. As a country's dependence on a smaller number of products increase, the HCI value will move closer to 1. Similar to the extensive margins analysis, HCI can help evaluate the vulnerability of exporting countries to trade shocks, and also measure changes in their export diversification. The index is measured as the sum of the squares of exported product shares in total exports; that is: $h^i = \sum_{k}^{n} \left(s_k^i \right)^2$ where s_k^j measures the share of product (sector) k in country

Table 4.14 Top 10 products and percentage shares in Emerging South–Rest of South and Emerging South–Emerging South manufactures exports in 2009

	Emerging South–Rest of South			Emerging South–Emerging South		
	Product	Class	II/II	Product	Class	II/II
1	Tankers	Medium	4.31%	Monolithic integrated circuits, digital	High	6.8
2	Cargo vessels other than tanker or refrigerated	Medium	3.60%	Monolithic integrated circuits, except digital	High	3.7%
3	Jewelry and parts of precious metal except silver	Low	3.02%	Optical devices appliances and instruments, nes	High	2.9%
4	Transmit-receive apparatus for radio, TV, etc.	High	1.87%	Parts and accessories of data processing equipment ne	Medium	2.7%
5	Floating docks, special function vessels nes	Medium	1.60%	Transmit-receive apparatus for radio. TV, etc.	High	2.3%
6	Diamonds (Jewelry) worked but not mounted or set	Re- Intense- Man	1.56%	Parts for radio/tv transmit/ receive equipment, nes	High	1.9%
7	Structures and parts of structures, iron or steel, ne	Low	1.15%	Parts of line telephone/telegraph equipment, nes	Medium	1.7%
8	Automobiles, spark ignition engine of 1500–3000 cc	Medium	1.03%	Computer data storage units	High	1.5%
9	Bar/rod, iron or non-alloy steel, indented or twisted, nes	Low	0.98%	Digital computers with cpu and input-output units	High	1.1%
10	Medicaments nes, in dosage	High	0.89%	Iron ore, concentrate, not iron pyrites, unagglorneerate	Re- Intense- Man	1.0%

Table 4.15 Top 10 products and percentage shares in Emerging South–North manufactures exports in 2009

Rank	Product	Class	Percent
1	Color television receivers/monitors/projectors	High	3.1
2	Digital computers with CPU and input-output units	High	3.0
3	Transmit-receive apparatus for radio, TV, etc.	High	2.8
4	Parts and accessories of data processing equipment ne	Medium	1.7
5	Medicaments nes, in dosage	High	1.6
6	Telephonic or telegraphic switching apparatus	High	1.5
7	Automobiles, spark ignition engine of 1500–3000 cc	Medium	1.3
8	Monolithic integrated circuits, digital	High	1.2
9	Computer data storage units	High	1.1
10	Parts of printing machinery and ancillary equipment	Medium	0.9

i's exports.[10] We calculate the HCI at both the 6-digit level and the aggregate product groupings by Lall (2000). The HCI measure for 2009 shows that the highest average concentration, as expected, is among the Rest of South countries, equaling 0.48 as opposed to 0.34 for Emerging South and 0.28 for Northern countries. Furthermore, a quick look at the index in 1995 suggests significant changes in all three country groupings since then. The HCI value was significantly lower in 1995 equaling 0.25, 0.08 and 0.02 for the Rest of South, Emerging South and the North, respectively, which suggest a significant increase in export product concentration during this period.

We can also look at the degree of export dispersion across destination markets to analyze countries' export concentration. For this, we again use the HCI but this time not across products but importers. That is, $h^i = \sum_k^n \left(s_j^i\right)^2$ where s_j^i measures the share of importer j in country i's exports. The HCI value will move close to 1 for those countries whose exports are concentrated in a very few markets, and will move close to 0 for those whose exports are very diversfied across different markets. The index helps signal exporters' dependency on their trading partners, making them more or less vulnerable to demand side shocks from those markets. Looking over time, a fall in this index shows increasing trading partner diversification for exporting countries. The mean value of export market diversification index in 2013 was 0.21 for the Rest of South, 0.12 for the Emerging South, and 0.11 for the North. Consistent with our previous observations before, the Rest of South countries have the highest export market concentration, while the Emerging South and the North have low and similar concentration rates. The variation is also high within the Rest of South, for which the standard deviation of this index was 0.19 while it was 0.10 for both the Emerging South and the North in that year. South Sudan, for example, exported to only three countries in 2013, Australia,

---

10. When HCI is calculated only for "active export lines"—that is, only for positive values of exports—then it captures export concentration at the intensive margin. For more discussion, refer to UNCTAD and WTO, *A Practical Guide to Trade Policy Analysis*.

(a)

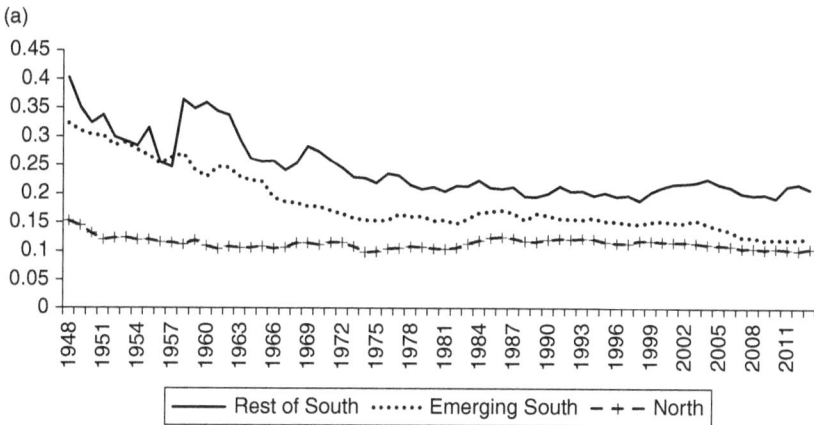

Figure 4.24a Export market diversification by country groups, 1948–2013
Source: For Figures 4.24a and 4.24b, IFS DOT statistics and authors' calculations.

(b)

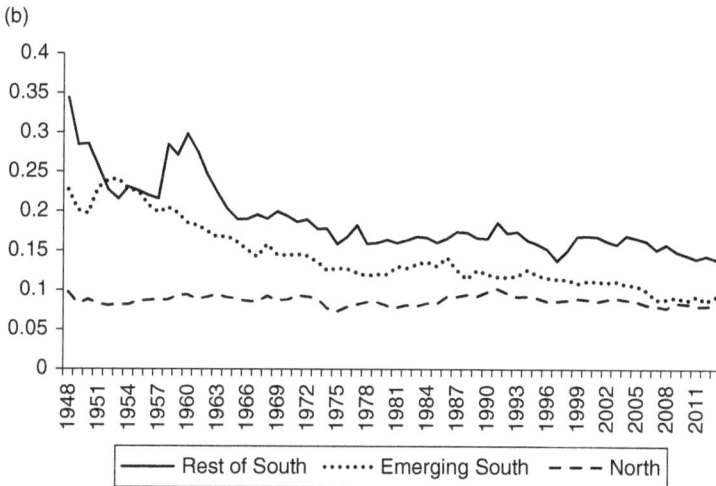

Figure 4.24b Standard deviation of export market diversification within country groups, 1948–2013

China and the United States, with the United States alone accounting for more than 90 percent of its exports. In contrast, Tanzania exported to 138 countries and had an HHI value of 0.08 in that year.

Figure 4.24a shows the average HCI export market concentration index for our three groups of countries between 1948 and 2013. Several observations stand out. First, we see an increasing export market diversification in both the Rest of South and the Emerging South countries. Second, even though the Rest of South had a very similar level of export concentration as the Emerging South did in the late 1940s and early 1950s, the Emerging South diverged from the Rest of South starting in the late 1950s. In fact, the

Rest of South appears to have delinked from many export markets in the late 1950s and early 1960s, leading to a sudden spike in the HCI, perhaps an aftermath shock of the independence movements in most developing countries and the severing of their linkages with their former colonial centers. Third, by 2013, the Emerging South has almost completely converged to the diversification level of the North. The figures using median values, rather than mean values, give almost an identical result. Figure 4.24b shows the standard deviation of the HCI within each country group and highlight both the high level of heterogeneity within the Rest of South and increasing within-group convergence for the Emerging South countries. By 2013, in terms of their export market diversification, the Emerging South countries have become more homogenous and converged to the level of diversity found within the North.

4.8   Intra-industry Trade

For a large number of countries, intra-industry trade is a key driving force for their bilateral trade flows, and it is indeed a prominent feature of trade flows between developed countries. The greater the sophistication of products, the greater the intra-industry trade index. Two countries are likely to import each other's televisions or computers but are unlikely to import each other's crude oil. A widely used method to assess the level of intra-industry trade is the Grubel-Lloyd (GL) index, measured as follows:

$$GL_k^{ij} = 1 - \frac{|X_k^{ij} - IM_k^{ij}|}{X_k^{ij} + IM_k^{ij}}$$

where X_k^{ij} and IM_k^{ij} refer to the exports and imports of i to and from j of product k. The bars in the nominator stand for absolute values.[11] High values of the GL index suggest a high level of intra-industry trade, supporting the monopolistic competition model of Krugman (1979) among others. It is also possible to use this index to capture any convergence/divergence dynamics, as a high value of intra-industry trade between the North and the South suggests convergence in industrial structures. One needs to be careful, however, when interpreting the GL index values, as they tend to increase with the level of aggregation and may, perhaps, reflect the level of vertical trade rather than a convergence of industrial structures. As the South catches up with the North we would also expect the level of horizontal trade to go up reflecting the production of more similar products with the same level of technological and skill sophistication. An increase in intra-industry trade would also suggest possible dynamic gains and technology transfer between trading partners as well as technological upgrading.

---

11. By definition, the GL index takes a value between zero and one. For example, if a country is only an exporter or an importer of a product k, then the second term will equal one, making the index value zero and showing that the level of intra-industry trade is zero. In contrast, if a country exports as much as it imports of product k, then the ratio will equal one, as the second term will equal zero.

Table 4.16a Grubel-Lloyd (GL) index for inter- and intra-regional trade in 2009 at HS 6-digit product level

Exporter/Importer	Rest of South	Emerging South	North
Rest of South	0.024 (0.00)	0.023 (0.00)	0.023 (0.00)
Emerging South	0.023 (0.00)	0.075 (0.00)	0.099 (0.00)
North	0.023 (0.00)	0.099 (0.00)	0.207 (0.025)

Source: For Tables 4.16a–4.18, BACI and authors' calculations. The values in parenthesis refer to median values.

Table 4.16b Grubel-Lloyd (GL) index for inter- and intra-regional trade in 1995 at HS 6-digit product level

Exporter/Importer	Rest of South	Emerging South	North
Rest of South	0.024 (0.000)	0.020 (0.000)	0.016 (0.000)
Emerging South	0.020 (0.000)	0.065 (0.000)	0.076 (0.000)
North	0.016 (0.000)	0.076 (0.000)	0.191 (0.008)

Table 4.17 Average Grubel-Lloyd (GL) index based on skill intensity of exports (at 3-digit level), 1995–2009

Exporter/Importer	Rest of South	Emerging South	North
Rest of South	0.102 (0.00)	0.123 (0.00)	0.165 (0.020)
Emerging South	0.123 (0.00)	0.270 (0.135)	0.389 (0.336)
North	0.165 (0.020)	0.389 (0.336)	0.560 (0.591)

Note: The GL index is calculated based on the five product groups for each country. The group values are based on country averages for each year at HS 3-digit level.

Table 4.16a shows the GL index for 2009 at the 6-digit HS classification level. The values refer to the averages (medians) in each country group. As expected, the highest level of intra-industry trade exists in the North–North direction followed by Emerging South–North and Emerging South–Emerging South directions. The Rest of South trade in all three directions remains quite low. Compared to 1995 (Table 4.16b), there appears to be an increase in intra-industry trade in all three directions but particularly so in Emerging South country trade with the North and with other Emerging South countries.

Table 4.17 measures the average GL index during the period 1995–2009 for product groups at a 3-digit aggregation for five product classifications—high-, medium-, low-skill and resource-intensive manufactures and primary goods—based on the direction of trade. As in Table 4.16a, the highest levels of intra-industry trade are among Northern countries, followed by countries in the Emerging South, and the lowest intra-industry trade is in the Rest of South–Rest of South direction. Emerging South–North intra-industry trade also appears to be higher than within trade among Emerging South

Table 4.18 Average intra-group Grubel-Lloyd (GL) index based on skill intensity (3-digit), 1995–2009

	Rest of South–South	Emerging–Emerging	North–North
High	0.09	0.23	0.56
Medium	0.10	0.28	0.57
Low	0.11	0.29	0.59
Primary	0.10	0.27	0.47
Res-Intense-Man	0.11	0.34	0.63

Source: BACI and authors' calculations at HS 3-digit level.

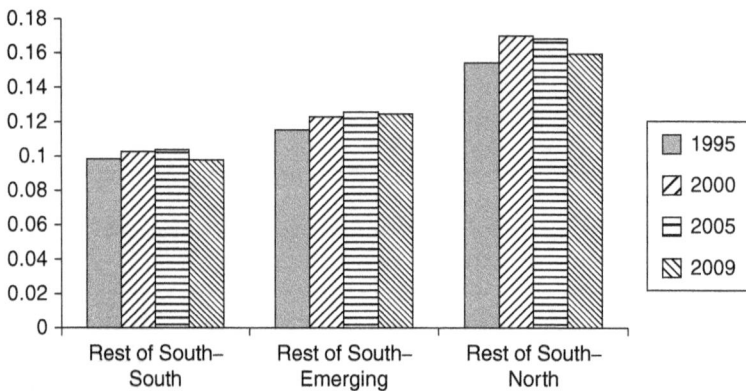

Figure 4.25 Average Grubel-Lloyd (GL) index for the Rest of South based on skill intensity
Source: Figures 4.25–4.27, BACI and authors' calculations at HS 3-digit level.

countries. As in the case of Emerging South countries, the level of Rest of South–North trade is higher than Rest of South trade in other two directions. Overall, the global South trade with the North is more similar than comparable trade within Southern countries, suggesting a higher possibility of knowledge transfers and skill spillovers.

The GL index comparison across product groups yields similar results. In Table 4.18 we present the five product groups based on skill-intensity and their GL index values for intra-regional trade during 1995–2009.

The change in the GL index during the period analyzed is also a major point of interest to understanding structural change in these economies. In the case of the Rest of South trade with others, we observe no significant change in intra-industry trade dynamics in any three country groups (Figure 4.25). Furthermore, we notice that the level of intra-industry trade is higher for Rest of South–Emerging South, and even more so for Rest of South–North directions, than for Rest of South–Rest of South trade.

Overall, the level of Rest of South–South intra-industry trade remains significantly lower than that of intra-group trade among Emerging South as well as Northern countries. The level of Emerging South–North trade in 2009, for example, was more than

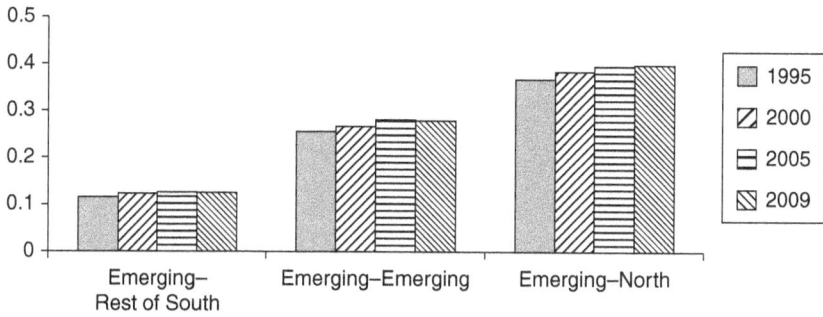

Figure 4.26 Average Grubel-Lloyd (GL) index for the Emerging South based on skill intensity

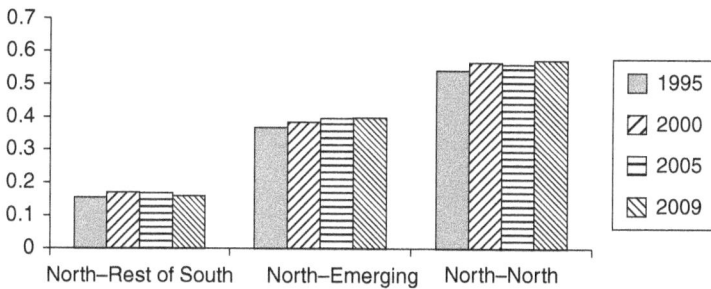

Figure 4.27 Average Grubel-Lloyd (GL) index for the North based on skill intensity

twice as high as Rest of South trade in any direction in 2009 (Figure 4.26). Furthermore, unlike the Rest of South trade, Emerging South intra-industry trade with other Emerging and Northern countries continued its upward trend, approaching the levels of Northern countries (Figure 4.27). Looking at the Rest of South and Emerging South trade with the North, we see that the intra-industry trade is the highest in this direction for these countries. In contrast, the Emerging South–Rest of South trade, as with Rest of South–Rest of South trade is the lowest in any direction. The results also highlight the high level of heterogeneity in developing country exports in terms of destination. While the level of intra-industry trade remains low among developing countries, with no indication of any change in the near future, it is much lower in Rest of South–Rest of South direction than in any other three. In fact, the Rest of South countries enjoy higher intra-industry trade with their Emerging South and North partners than they do with each other.

4.9 The Rise of China vs. the Rest of South

There has been a reshuffling of trade heavyweights since the 1940s, but those at the top still account for much of world trade. Table 4.19 shows the ten biggest exporters in the world in 1950, 1980 and 2013. As of 2013, the top ten countries still accounted for more than half of world trade, and seven of those are Northern countries. The top

Table 4.19 Top 10 exporters of merchandise goods in the world, 1950, 1980 and 2013

	1950	Percent	1980	Percent	2013	Percent
1	US	19.3	US	11.6	China	12.2
2	UK	11.6	Germany	10.1	US	8.7
3	Canada	5.6	Japan	6.7	Germany	7.5
4	France	5.2	UK	5.8	Japan	3.9
5	Germany	3.8	France	5.7	Netherlands	3.6
6	Belgium-Luxembourg	3.2	Saudi Arabia	5.0	Korea	3.1
7	Australia	3.1	Italy	4.0	France	3.1
8	Netherlands	2.6	Netherlands	3.8	Russia	2.9
9	Brazil	2.6	Canada	3.4	Italy	2.8
10	Italy	2.3	Belgium-Luxembourg	3.4	UK	2.7
Total (top 10)		59.4		59.6		50.5
Total (top 20)		75		73.5		70.3

Note: China refers to Mainland in all following discussions. Percentages are calculated using export values in current prices.
Source: For Tables 4.19–4.21, IMF Direction of Trade Statistics and authors' calculations.

20 exporters together accounted for 75 percent of total exports in the world in 1950, 74 percent in 1980, and 70 percent in 2013. Even though the world's current number one exporter, China, is from the global South, accounting for a staggering 12.2 percent of global exports, six of the top ten exporters—the United States, the United Kingdom, France, Germany, the Netherlands and Italy—remained unchanged in the list throughout this period.

In Table 4.20 below we look at the top ten countries in total South–South trade in 1950, 1980 and 2013. As before, we observe a high level of entry and exit behavior in this list. Only one country, (mainland) China, managed to stay in the list for the full period, ranking number one in 2013 and accounting for around 21 percent of total South–South trade. The top ten countries together accounted for 62 percent of total South–South trade. Furthermore, the top 20 Emerging South exporters accounted for 72 percent of total South–South trade in 2013.

The case of South–North trade is similar to that of South–South trade, with a few, mostly Emerging South countries, dominating more than half of the trade in this direction (Table 4.21). In 2013, 60 percent of South–North exports originated from ten countries. The ranking also highlights the changing nature of South–North trade. While, early on, primary commodity exporters such as Saudi Arabia, Libya, Iraq, UAE and Algeria dominated the rankings in 1980, the picture is quite different in 2013. In fact only one country, Saudi Arabia, is a predominantly primary commodity exporter in the top ten list of 2013, and its share fell from 16.6 percent in 1980 to 3.4 percent in 2013. China alone accounted for a quarter of South–North trade in that year.

Table 4.20 Top 10 exporters in South–South trade, 1950, 1980 and 2013

	1950	Percent	1980	Percent	2013	Percent
1	India	12.0	USSR	10.2	China	20.8
2	Hong Kong	10.5	Saudi Arabia	9.5	Korea	7.4
3	China	6.0	Poland	4.5	Hong Kong	6.0
4	Pakistan	6.0	China	4.5	Taiwan	5.2
5	Argentina	5.5	Iraq	4.4	Russia	4.6
6	Iran	5.2	Czechoslovakia	4.1	Singapore	4.2
7	Brazil	4.6	Singapore	4.0	Saudi Arabia	4.0
8	Egypt	4.3	Kuwait	3.6	India	3.6
9	South Africa	4.0	Brazil	3.3	UAE	3.3
10	Yemen, PDR	4.0	Venezuela	3.1	Malaysia	2.9
Total		62.2		51.2		62.1

Table 4.21 Top 10 exporters in South–North Trade, 1950, 1980 and 2013

	1950	Percen	1980	Percent	2013	Percent
1	Brazil	8.9	Saudi Arabia	16.6	China	25.5
2	Argentina	6.7	USSR	5.1	Mexico	8.3
3	India	5.2	Indonesia	4.5	Russia	6.4
4	Cuba	4.8	Libya	4.2	Korea	3.7
5	Venezuela	4.0	Iraq	4.2	Saudi Arabia	3.4
6	South Africa	3.8	UAE	4.1	Poland	3.0
7	Mexico	3.6	Nigeria	3.4	Czech Republic	2.6
8	Indonesia	3.5	Taiwan	3.1	India	2.5
9	Gibraltar	3.0	Mexico	3.0	Ireland	2.4
10	Colombia	2.8	Algeria	2.9	Taiwan	2.3
Total		46.4		51.1		60.1

4.10   Trade Barriers and Tariff Structures

The significant increase in South–South trade has led to renewed discussions on existing trade barriers and how to remove them to expand this trade further, as we discussed in chapter 2. It is often suggested that tariff- and non-tariff-based trade barriers are higher in South–South trade than in any other directions, significantly hampering developing countries' exports to each other. To explore this point further we first use a market access restrictiveness measure developed by Fugazza and Nicita (2011), who estimated the direct market accessibility level for each country as measured by the overall tariff faced by exporters (TTRI, total trade restrictiveness index). The dataset is available from UNCTAD[12] for the period of 2000–09 for 95 countries accounting for 90 percent of

---

12. http://www.unctad.info/upload/TAB/docs/DATA/TTRI_RPM_20002009.zip

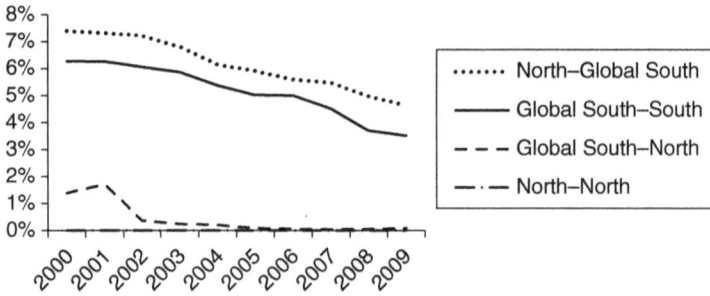

Figure 4.28 Total trade restrictiveness index (TTRI) faced by global South and North exporters, 2000–2009

Note: TTRI is the trade restrictiveness faced by country i in exporting to country j and is calculated as follows: $\dfrac{\sum_{hs} Ex_{ij,hs}\, \varepsilon_{j,hs}\, T_{k,hs}^{j}}{\sum_{hs} Ex_{ij,hs}\, \varepsilon_{j,hs}}$ where Ex are exports, ε is the import demand elasticity, T is the applied tariff rate and hs are HS 6-digit product categories.

Source: Fugazza and Nicita (2011) and authors' calculations

world trade. Figure 4.28 below shows the median TTRI variable for 2000–09 for global South and North countries and confirm the findings of previous research: South–South trade barriers are higher than those in North–North and South–North trade (both of which were near zero in 2009). North–South barriers stand out as the highest among others.

Figure 4.29 below presents the average tariff rates applied to manufactures exports in global South and North trade. In a pattern similar to that of average trade restrictiveness rates for all merchandise goods, as presented in Figure 4.28, South–South manufactures exports face the highest effective tariff rates, followed by North–South exports, while the lowest tariffs for manufactured goods are in North–North, and South–North trade. While the tariff rates fell across the board in all four directions, particularly more so in South–South trade, still South exporters faced the highest trade restriction in their trade with other Southern countries. In fact, the average effective tariff rate in South–South exports was 7.6 percent in 2012, which was respectively 13, 2.9 and 1.2 times higher than the ones present in North–North (0.57 percent), South–North (2.66 percent), and North–global South (6.34 percent) exports.

The fact that South–South tariff barriers remain the highest in all directions may be the reason behind the enthusiasm of both multinational corporations and free trade oriented institutions such as the WTO for increasing South–South trade through trade liberalization. However, as the analysis throughout this chapter indicates, there is good reason to be skeptical about the fact that trade liberalization will deliver the benefits of South–South cooperation. The Rest of South and even many countries in the Emerging South experiencing de-industrialization as a result of free trade should think about agreements that explicitly encourage technology transfer and industrial development rather than those that favor lowering trade barriers and increase investor rights.

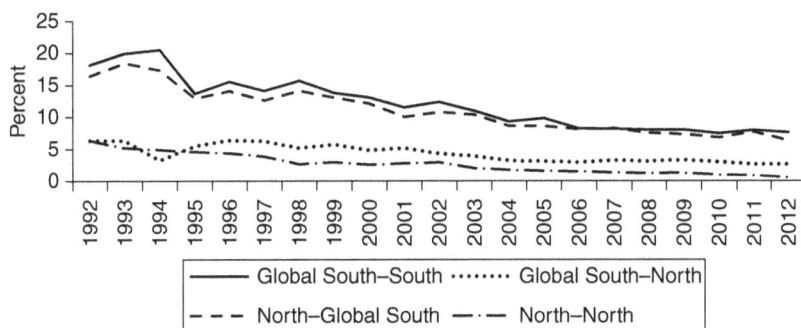

Figure 4.29 Average effectively applied tariff rates faced by total manufactures exports from global South and North, 1992–2013
Note: The y-axis refers to the "effectively applied" average manufactured goods tariff rate faced by export-ers in each direction of exports.[13] The tariff rates for each country in each group are calculated by taking weighted-average tariff rates at HS 6-digit level.
Source: UNCTAD market access statistics available at http://unctadstat.unctad.org/wds/ReportFolders/reportFolders.aspx and authors' calculations

4.11   South–South Finance

In contrast to the case with international trade, the South–South linkages in finance have only been marginally explored in recent literature. The first and probably the most obvi-ous reason is the lack of comprehensive and consistent data on financial flows of various kind between developing countries.[14] While there have been a few attempts to document the magnitude of these flows, we still do not have a very good grasp of bilateral financial flows across countries. Surprisingly, this is a problem found not just in developing coun-tries but across developed countries as well. Furthermore, when the data are available, they usually include significant discrepancies between home and host country statistics, and very rarely are the macro totals equal to the sum of bilateral flows. Nevertheless, it is probable that different types of financial flows have different data-generating properties and some are more difficult to quantify in a consistent manner than others. FDI flows, for example, are arguably measured in a more consistent manner than portfolio flows, espe-cially given the attention they receive in both home and host countries. However, even in the case of FDI flows, the data, to put it mildly, are quite noisy. First, even in the case of Northern countries, there are significant differences in the reported data. For example, let us take a look at the United States and Germany, two of the biggest FDI home and host countries. In 2011, the United States reported $15 billion inflows from Germany, while Germany reported $2.9 billion outflows to the United States. The data for 2008 are

---

13. The global South as the importing region does not include transition economies, which are reported as an aggregate by the UNCTAD. We present the average rates after 1992, as the data prior to 1992 is only available for a limited number of countries.
14. Some recent efforts to overcome this lack of data problem include *AidData*, which tracks Chi-nese development finance to Africa, *LandMatrix*, which reports investment flows to agricultural sector in developing countries, and OECD's resource flows to developing countries statistics.

even stranger with the United States reporting $17 billion inflows from Germany, while Germany reported -$16.8 billion reverse outflows to the United States (i.e., divestment). Surprisingly, the example of the United States and Germany here is not an exception but the rule. Other major country pairs including France or the United Kingdom also yield the same inconsistent results.[15] Thus, even the usual trick of using mirror data or taking the average of inflows and outflows from home and host countries, as is usual in trade flows analysis, is not applicable.

Notwithstanding these difficulties, in this section we attempt to uncover some general trends in global FDI flows, which reached $1.5 trillion in 2013 and averaged as much every year since 2005. FDI flows stand out in economic analysis among other types of financial flows given their expected effects on productivity, employment, fixed capital formation and long-term growth. We explore the case of other types of flows together with FDI flows further in chapter 5. Considering that global FDI flows barely reached $54 billion in 1980 and $208 billion in 1990, these are significant numbers (Figure 4.30). Likewise, FDI flows to and from the global South increased considerably, reaching $934 billion and $599 billion in 2013, corresponding to 64 percent and 43 percent of global inflows and outflows, respectively (Figures 4.30 and 4.31).[16] As of 2013, six developing countries were among the top twenty investors in the world, and China alone ranked number two in global FDI inflows and number three in outflows (Tables 4.22 and 4.24). Furthermore, within aggregate FDI flows to developing countries, South–South flows increased significantly, reaching around 63–65 percent of all outflows from developing countries in 2010 (UNCTAD, 2011; WB, 2011). In 2013, 53 percent of global merger and acquisition flows came from the South, and of this figure 72 percent went to other South countries (UNCTAD, 2014: 8). In the case of Latin America and the Caribbean region, for example, in 2010 South countries from Asia accounted for 68 percent of all mergers and acquisitions (which is three times more than their total accumulated acquisitions in this region over the previous two decades), and intra-regional flows accounted for 17 percent, while Northern countries accounted for only 12 percent of the total (UNCTAD, 2011: 59, 60). Overall, the share of Southern TNCs in this region increased from 8 percent in 2001 to 43 percent in 2010 (UNCTAD, 2011: 60). Likewise, it is reported that in 2013 there were 1,673 investment projects from China worth $75 billion in commitments in 50 African countries (Strange et al., 2013).

In Table 4.22 we provide the list of top ten host countries for FDI flows in the world, in the North and the South in 2000 and 2013. As discussed before, prior to the financial

---

15. Take, for example, the United States and the United Kingdom. In 2010, the United States reported an inflow of $30 billion from the United Kingdom, while the United Kingdom reported -$13.9 billion, which is British divestment from the United States.

16. The figures slightly differ from the aggregate data provided for developing economies in UNCTAD dataset because of differences in the definition of the North. For consistency, we continue to use the same North and South definition throughout the book. The figures and underlying trends, however, are quite similar to those using the South definition from the UNCTAD (including transition economies).

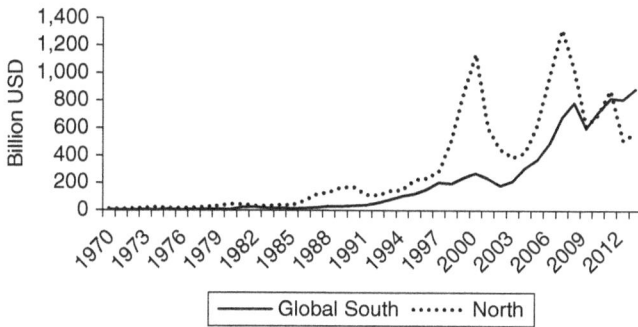

Figure 4.30 Global FDI inflows, 1970–2013
Note: Global FDI inflows (in billions, current dollars) to the North and South where the South includes Transition economies.
Source: For Figures 4.29–4.31, UNCTAD (2015a) and authors' calculations.

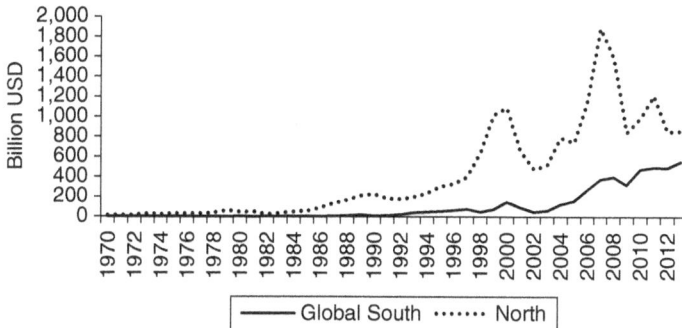

Figure 4.31 Global FDI outflows, 1970–2013
Note: Global FDI outflows (in billions, current dollars) from the North and South where the South includes transition economies.

liberalization wave of the 1990s, global FDI flows were a fraction of what they are today. To give an example, total FDI inflows in 1990 were approximately one-seventh of what they were in 2000. When comparing the year 2000 with 2013, a couple of observations stand out. First, while only two Southern countries were in the world top ten list in 2000, that number increased to six in 2013. We also see a slight change in the composition of the top ten Northern and Southern countries during this period. Six of the top ten North and seven of the top ten South countries remained in the list from 2000. It appears that there is significant path dependency in FDI flows with a few countries remaining as the world's top investment destinations.

Turning to Table 4.23 we find that the distribution of global FDI flows has gone through a major metamorphosis during this period. China, for example, increased its global share of the FDI pie from less than 3 percent in 2000 to 8.5 percent in 2013, although its share within the South remained more or less the same, with a slight increase from 12 percent to 13 percent. The share of the United States, on the other hand, fell

Table 4.22 Top 10 FDI host countries, 2000 vs. 2013 (billions, current USD)

	Top 10 FDI Recipients		Top 10 Northern FDI recipients		Top 10 Global South FDI recipients	
			2013			
1	US	188	US	188	China	124
2	China	124	Canada	62	British Virgin Islands	92
3	British Virgin Islands	92	Australia	50	Russian Federation	79
4	Russian Federation	79	Spain	39	Hong Kong	77
5	Hong Kong	77	U.K.	37	Brazil	64
6	Brazil	64	Luxembourg	30	Singapore	64
7	Singapore	64	Germany	27	Mexico	38
8	Canada	62	Netherlands	24	Ireland	36
9	Australia	50	Italy	17	India	28
10	Spain	39	Israel	12	Chile	20
			2000			
1	US	314	US	314	Hong Kong	71
2	Germany	198	Germany	198	China	41
3	UK	122	UK	122	Brazil	33
4	Belgium	89	Belgium	89	Ireland	26
5	Hong Kong	71	Canada	67	Mexico	18
6	Canada	67	Netherlands	64	Singapore	16
7	Netherlands	64	France	43	Korea, Republic of	12
8	France	43	Spain	40	Argentina	10
9	China	41	Denmark	34	British Virgin Islands	10
10	Spain	40	Sweden	23	Poland	9

Source: For Tables 4.21–4.25, UNCTAD (2015a) FDI database and authors' calculations.

significantly, from a staggering 22 percent in 2000 to less than 13 percent in 2013. The share of top ten Northern host countries also fell from 70 percent to 33 percent during this period, highlighting the structural changes in world economy. As a corollary to the receding share of the North, the top ten South countries increased their share from 17 percent to 43 percent. Globally, the total share of the South in FDI inflows increased to 64 percent. The share of the top ten South countries within the South, however, fell from almost 90 percent to 64 percent in 2013, suggesting a more diverse pool of host countries as FDI destinations. However, the fact that two-thirds of all FDI flows to the South are still clustered in only ten countries shows the uneven nature of development within the South itself.

Next, in Table 4.24 we look at the largest foreign investors in the world in 2010 and 2013. While no South investors made the top ten list in 2000, three Southern countries

Table 4.23 Percentage shares of top FDI host countries in the North and the global South, 2000 vs. 2013

	2000	2013
China/World	2.9	8.5
US/World	22.2	12.9
China/Global South	12.3	13.3
Top 10 North/World	70.2	33.4
Top 10 Global South/World	17.3	42.9
Top 10 South/Global South	89.8	66.6
Global South/World	19.3	64.3
World (billion USD)	1,415	1,452

entered the list in 2013: (mainland) China, Russian Federation, Hong Kong (China, SAR), and the British Virgin Island, given that Hong Kong is a specially administered region of China.[17] In fact, China appeared as the third biggest investor in the world, ranking right after the U.S. and Japan with a total of $101 billion FDI outflows in 2013.[18] The rise of China in global FDI outflows has been remarkable with its share going up from 0.1 percent in 2000 to 7.2 percent in 2013 (Table 4.25). We see a parallel change in its share among Southern investors, reaching almost 17 percent up from 0.6 percent in 2000. The total share of the 10 biggest Southern investors climbed to almost 34 percent in 2013 from less than 12 percent just 13 years ago. The total share of Southern countries in FDI outflows more than tripled since 2000, rising to 42.5 percent in 2013. In terms of the composition of these Southern investors, we again see a high concentration, with the top ten accounting for almost 80 percent of all outward FDI flows from the South. While this concentration has declined since 2000, when it was 92 percent, the data still suggest that an overwhelming majority South–South FDI flows originate from a few Emerging South economies.

4.11 Conclusion

In this chapter we have explored the evolution as well as the structure of South–South trade using aggregate as well as product level data, and a few observations stand out:

---

17. We need to be cautious about the case with Cayman Islands, which is a known tax haven country and therefore FDI inflows and outflows from this location probably reflect flows originating from third countries. Since we do not know the identity of original investors, we still keep it among Southern countries. It is, for example, a common practice for Southern investors to round-trip their own investments (to avoid regulators or taxation) through tax-haven countries, which then enter the balance of payments as capital inflow from abroad (i.e., net borrowing).
18. China and Hong Kong are the biggest investors in each other's economy. We return back to this point in chapter 5.

Table 4.24 Top 10 FDI home countries, 2000 vs. 2013 (billions, current USD)

NI	Top 10 FDI Investors		Top 10 Northern FDI Investors		Top 10 Southern FDI Investors	
			2013			
1	US	338	US	338	China	101
2	Japan	136	Japan	136	Russian Federation	95
3	China	101	Switzerland	60	Hong Kong	92
4	Russian Federation	95	Germany	58	British Virgin Islands	69
5	Hong Kong	92	Canada	43	Korea, Republic of	29
6	British Virgin Islands	69	Netherlands	37	Singapore	27
7	Switzerland	60	Sweden	33	Ireland	23
8	Germany	58	Italy	32	Taiwan	14
9	Canada	43	Spain	26	Malaysia	14
10	Netherlands	37	Luxembourg	22	Mexico	13
			2000			
1	UK	235	UK	235	Hong Kong	70
2	France	177	France	177	British Virgin Islands	34
3	US	143	US	143	Cayman Islands	8
4	Belgium	86	Belgium	86	Taiwan	7
5	Netherlands	76	Netherlands	76	Singapore	7
6	Hong Kong	70	Spain	58	Korea, Republic of	5
7	Spain	58	Germany	57	Ireland	5
8	Germany	57	Canada	45	Chile	4
9	Canada	45	Switzerland	45	Russian Federation	3
10	Switzerland	45	Sweden	41	Brazil	2

Source: UNCTAD (2015a) FDI database and authors' calculations.

1. The biggest jump in in South–South trade took place during the post-1990 period, and this increase was accompanied by a fall in North–North trade, which dominated a majority of world trade till that time.

2. The theoretical evidence predicting developmental dynamic gains from South–South trade is supported by our data, but only partially. These gains are being realized for part of the South that we call Emerging South, and not the Rest of South. The Rest of South is not just growing slowly, it is in fact deindustrializing, partially as a result of the rise of the Emerging South.

3. As point # 2 implies the South is not a homogeneous bloc and there are significant differences between the Emerging South and the Rest of South. The generalizations usually made for the structure of South–South trade may not be applicable across the board for all Southern countries. Indeed, the differences between these two groups of Southern countries are bigger than those between the Emerging South and the North. We expect these differences to grow further in the coming years and to cause the Rest of South to fall further behind Emerging South and the North, as evidenced by the growing gap in the level and sophistication of exports. In terms of

Table 4.25 Percentage shares of top FDI home
countries in the North and the global South

	2000	2013
China/World	0.1	7.2
US/World	11.5	24.0
China/Global South	0.6	16.9
Top 10 North/World	77.5	55.6
Top 10 Global South/World	11.6	33.7
Top 10 South/Global South	92.4	79.4
Global South/World	12.6	42.5
World (billion USD)	1,241	1,411

policy implications, we should start referring to the Emerging South as a separate bloc and stop taking a one-size-fits-all approach to development questions within the South, including those policy prescriptions that advocate a blanket increase in 'South–South economic relations.'

4. The Emerging South contains most of the world's population, about 4.6 billion people (two countries, China and India make up more than half of this number), while the Rest of South contains about 1.6 billion people, with the remainder, about 930 million people, live in the North. The dynamism Emerging South is therefore welcome news from the perspective that it represents a potential that the populations of those countries may benefit from industrial development and technological upgrading. Still, many countries in the Emerging South are at risk of dropping down, joining the Rest of South in their export structure. The Rest of South itself is at risk of becoming a region where serious industrial development is proscribed.

5. Trade within the South now accounts for more than half of all Southern manufactures exports and 58 percent of the total Southern merchandise trade. Yet, the Emerging South is responsible for more than 80 percent of this trade. Moreover, intra-Emerging South trade itself now accounts for 70 percent of total South–South exports, and Emerging South–North trade is almost 90 percent of South–North trade. The share of intra-Rest of South trade itself appears very low in Rest of South merchandise goods exports, remaining at around 10 percent and accompanied by a steady rise in Rest of South–Emerging South trade and a steady decline in Rest of South–North trade. In the case of manufactured goods trade, we find a similar picture, with the share of the Rest of South in world manufactures exports staying steady and low (at around 3 percent) and the share of Emerging South increasing (reaching 43 percent in 2009).

6. We confirm the findings of previous research showing a positive correlation between the structure of a country's exports and its income levels. The higher the percentage share of high- and medium-skill manufactured goods exports in a country's export bundle, the higher is its income. The results from export unit cost analysis confirm these observations. Accordingly, export unit values are found to be the highest for

high-skill manufactured goods across every income group and the lowest for primary and natural resource–intensive manufactures.

7. Export unit values for high-, medium- and low-skill manufactures are the highest for exports directed to the North. It appears that there is significant quality heterogeneity, even within the same product categories, for exports directed to the North, to the Rest of South and to the Emerging South. This product heterogeneity, as reflected by differences in median export values for the same products across different export destinations is the lowest for Northern countries and the highest for Rest of South countries. For example, while the median export unit value for medium-skill manufactures in 2009 is almost the same for North–Rest of South, North–Emerging South, and North–North trade, it is $5, $10, and $20 for Rest of South–South, Rest of South–Emerging South, and Rest of South–North trade. Such differences do not appear significant for the mostly homogenous primary and resource-intensive manufactured goods. Conditional correlation analysis also supports these findings. We show that export quality is negatively correlated with exporter income but positively correlated with importer income in Rest of South–South and Rest of South–Emerging South trade. In contrast, the quality of exports from the Rest of South to the North increases with both exporter's and importer's incomes. Unlike the case with the Rest of South exporters, export quality is positively correlated with both exporters' and importers' incomes when the exporters are from the Emerging South or the North. In other words, more developed Rest of South countries export their lower-quality goods to lower-income Rest of South and, to a lesser extent, Emerging South countries. In contrast, the quality of exports from the Emerging South increases together with the exporting and importing countries' income levels. We also find that the income elasticity of export quality for the Rest of South, the Emerging South and the North is the highest when the importers are Northern countries. In contrast, the elasticities are significantly lower when importers are from the Rest of South or the Emerging South, perhaps providing some support to the Linder hypothesis regarding preference similarities. Northern countries are also found to have a higher product and quality variety than South countries. Overall, our findings also suggest that it is quite difficult for a low-income developing country to produce high-quality exports, and if it does, it is going to be sure to send those goods to high-income Northern countries.

8. Conditional correlation analysis suggests that, controlling for product varieties, export unit prices are positively correlated with the income levels of exporters. Furthermore, once we control for exporter-product pairs within importers, we find that exporter-product price dispersion (measured by the standard deviation of export-unit prices across importers within exporter-product pairs) is higher for Northern countries and lower for the Rest of South and the Emerging South. We also observe significant upgrading in export quality within high- and medium-skill manufactures across countries. The most noticeable change took place in exports to the Emerging South.

9. The structure of trade shows high heterogeneity, although overall reflecting the same general trends discussed above. Particularly, while we observe a significant increase in the skill and technology intensity of Emerging South exports, no such change is visible for the Rest of South. In fact, the average share of high-skill goods in total manufactures exports of the Rest of South fell steadily to around 5 percent in 2009, while going above 20 percent for the Emerging South. Furthermore, the share of high-skill goods in total manufactures exports within Rest of South–Rest of South trade stayed at around 5 percent while that of intra-Emerging South and intra-North trade was above 30 percent and 20 percent in 2009. Nevertheless, within this limited scope, the share of Rest of South–South and Rest of South–Emerging South within Rest of South high-skill manufactures trade increased steadily while that of Rest of South–North decreased, perhaps promising some hope for a future expansion and skills-upgrading. Yet a quick look at the share of primary goods in Rest of South–South trade do not leave much room for optimism, as more than half of Rest of South–South exports in 2009 were in primary and natural resource–intensive manufactures. We see an opposite development with Emerging South countries.

10. A significant portion of international trade remains intra-regional, accounting for 49 percent of East Asia and the Pacific exports, 72 percent of Europe and Central Asia, and 35 percent of North America. The lowest intra-regional trade is found in South Asia (5.5 percent), MENA (7.6 percent) and sub-Saharan Africa (12.5 percent). Furthermore, the intra-regional concentration of trade is even higher in the case of South–South trade, accounting for more than 60 percent of South–South trade in East Asia and the Pacific, Europe and Central Asia and Latin America.

11. High- and medium-skill exports account for a lion's share in export earnings across the world despite their low shares in export volumes. For example, in East Asia and the Pacific, high-skill manufactures are responsible for 25 percent of export revenues yet only 1 percent of export volumes. In contrast, primary goods and resource-intensive manufactures each account for more than 40 percent of this region's export volume but bring in less than 20 percent of its export earnings.

12. Emerging South and North countries export a higher variety of products than the Rest of South. The same trend is found in intra-regional trade as well, with product variety lowest in the Rest of South trade. In fact, in 2009 six primary products accounted for 62 percent of all Rest of South exports with petroleum oils alone responsible for more than half. The Rest of South also has a much higher export market concentration than the Emerging South, making it vulnerable to shocks from their trading partners. The Emerging South has become much more homogenous in terms of its export market dispersion and reached a level that is identical to that of the North in 2013. In 2013, there were 31 (60) Rest of South countries that depended on a single trading partner for more than half (one-third) of their export earnings.

13. We find an increase in intra-industry trade across all country groups though particularly so for the intra-Emerging South and Emerging South–North trade.

14. We observe a significant and dynamic change in the rankings of top South exporters, with the rise of China and South Korea being the most visible. Top ten South countries were responsible for 62 percent of South–South trade in 2013. China alone provided 21 percent of all South–South exports.

15. Despite a significant decrease, trade barriers between the countries of the South remain the highest of any direction.

16. Accompanying the trends in trade, we observe a significant increase in Emerging South's share in global as well as South–South financial flows, both as a host and home country.

Chapter Five

STOPPING A SECOND GREAT DIVERGENCE: A NEW FRAMEWORK FOR SOUTH–SOUTH RELATIONS

5.1 Introduction

The patterns of trade and financial flows that have emerged since the 1990s, as discussed in the earlier chapters of this book, have undoubtedly disrupted the traditional lines of North–North and North–South economic exchanges, which had defined the global economy during the post–World War II period from the 1940s to 1970s. These disruptions are accompanied by a promise of greater economic strength for historically less-developed countries of the South but also have created some undesirable imbalances. The early attempts at South–South integration, under the banner of the Third World and the Non-Aligned Movement, demanded a more equitable world. It now seems quite possible, however, that the current rise in South–South relations through trade, finance and diplomatic and political agreements may reinforce rather than dismantle the traditional global hierarchies. Disparities between the Emerging South and the Rest of South are rapidly replicating the old North–South colonial pattern of trade. These trends, though alarming, are not inevitable or irreversible. In this chapter we present a framework for examining the various transmission channels through which South–South relations operate. Identifying these transmission channels can help us to understand how the positive aspects of South–South economic exchanges can be harnessed and the negative impacts mitigated.

This chapter proceeds as follows. First, we chart the rise of "new-developmentalism" as a progressive response to neoliberal development and argue that, to understand whether South–South relations hold the promise for an alternative model of development, it is worthwhile to explore existing critiques and alternatives. We discuss why the recurring predictions of the end of neoliberalism have repeatedly fallen short and, in any case, what exactly an alternative to neoliberalism may be. We then move to discuss the burgeoning literature on "new-developmentalism," its main tenets and its analysis and critique of neoliberalism. While new-developmentalism provides an accurate critique of the tenets of neoliberal globalization, it fails to take into account the systemic pressures operating in the global economy. In Sections 5.4 and 5.5 we examine South–South Integration and "new-developmentalism and analyze how the rise of China and other Emerging South countries is both hindering effective development in the Rest of South and creating new possibilities for it. Finally, Section 5.6 develops a South–South agenda and policy framework for developing those new possibilities and mitigating the negative factors.

5.2 Twilight of Neoliberalism?

In 1981, the Pakistani writer Eqbal Ahmad wrote a scathing essay on emerging political and economic trends in the global South:

> Closely related to the idea of national security are the ideologically rigged notions of "development" and "modernization." Typically, the neofascist state is deeply committed to economic development; we might even describe this neofascism as "developmental fascism." It views "development" in terms of rates of growth. "Growth" involves the concentration of wealth and power, for both are necessary to the required rate of capital formation. Thus profit = investment = growth = power. The preferred development model favors return to the "free market." But the return is always selective: it does not involve curtailment of monopoly power or of untrammeled investment incentives; it does entail strict controls over wages, labor unions, and prohibition of strikes. A cheap labor force is offered as a primary incentive to capital; the internal market does not expand except for luxury goods. The economy becomes increasingly export-oriented; raw materials, including fancy food products, become the primary export items. Income inequality multiplies. Any resistance to corporate and foreign interests is treated ipso facto as a police problem; anyone questioning this model of development is viewed as a subversive, a terrorist. (Ahmad, 2006, p. 147)

Ahmad's harsh critique was describing the new model of development emerging along-side the gradual dismantling of Import Substitution Industrialization in many places in South Asia, Latin America and the Middle East. While in the case of many countries in the Middle East and the Southern Cone of Latin America this dismantling was being done at the hands of military dictatorships elsewhere it was done through democratic governments, such as in India in the 1990s.[1] His words were prescient, outlining the contours of the era we now refer to as neoliberalism.

Over a decade later, in the introduction to his classic *Embedded Autonomy: States and Industrial Transformation* Peter Evans wrote, "[N]eoliberalism has been refuted, the question is what will replace it." He wrote these words in 1995, just before, or at the beginnings of, the crises in Mexico 1994–95, Turkey 1994, 2001; Argentina 1995, 2001; Russia 1998; South East Asia 1997–98; Brazil 1999; and of course before the Great Recession of 2008 and the European Union debt crisis of 2009. However, neoliberalism appears more resilient than Evans and its other opponents predicted.[2] During the 1990s and 2000s, countries around the world adopted liberalization policies at an increasing

---

1. In many countries the structural shift from the ISI regime to the neoliberal model took place under military rule. It is quite paradoxical that although the new liberal economic paradigm was, and is, (allegedly) based on the assumption of rationality of people and freedom of choice in the marketplace, the political environment was characterized by an assumption of irrationality or inability of people to determine their own fates under free elections with democratic institutions.

2. For a recent discussion of this point, see Mirowski (2013).

pace to attract foreign capital: Between 2000 and 2013, an average of 56 countries each year introduced a total of 1,440 regulatory changes in their investment regimes, 80 percent of which were to promote and facilitate a more favorable environment for foreign investors. The same figure was even higher during the 1990s, with 94 percent of a total of 1,035 changes being more favorable to FDI (UNCTAD, 2005b, 2014).

In the words of scholar Paul Amar, "[T]he end of neoliberalism has been declared again and again over the course of a generation" (Amar, 2013). For example, in a widely disseminated document, "Economic Growth in the 1990s: Learning from a Decade of Reform," the World Bank (2005) humbly admitted that the obsession with privatization, deregulation and liberalization had yielded mixed results and that heterodox economic policies including industrial policy were having positive impacts in many countries. Economist Dani Rodrik summarized the flavor of the report accurately:

> In fact, it is a rather extraordinary document insofar as it shows how far we have come from the original Washington Consensus. There are no confident assertions here of what works and what doesn't—and no blueprints for policy makers to adopt. The emphasis is on the need for humility, for policy diversity, for selective and modest reforms, and for experimentation. "The central message of this volume," Gobind Nankani, the World Bank vice-president who oversaw the effort, writes in the preface of the book, "is that there is no unique universal set of rules. [...] [W]e need to get away from formulae and the search for elusive "best practices" [...]." Occasionally, the reader has to remind himself that the book he is holding in his hands is not some radical manifesto, but a report prepared by the seat of orthodoxy in the universe of development policy. (Rodrik, 2006, p. 974)

The final straw for neoliberalism was supposed to be the Great Recession. In 2008 and later, various scholars and critics from within the left and the mainstream took turns declaring the end of neoliberalism. Even the International Monetary Fund, long considered the biggest culprit among international institutions in advocating austerity policies, recently issued a critical reappraisal of neoliberalism (IMF, 2016). Yet, according to Philip Mirowski, not only did neoliberalism not suffer a mortal blow after the Great Recession, it emerged triumphant (Mirowski, 2013).

Understanding an alternative to neoliberalism requires defining exactly what we mean by the term. It has come to be widely used and overused and has become a key analytical category for anthropologists, development economists, sociologists, political scientists and others. Given this widespread use, it has come to mean many things, and by now there are many surveys of the academic literature regarding neoliberalism.[3] A relatively recent article in a cultural studies journal argues that neoliberalism is "discursive formation, a governmental program, an ideology, a hegemonic project, a technical assemblage, and an abstract machine" (Gilbert, 2013). As is obvious from Gilbert's definition, the term neoliberalism has become a generic term covering everything and at the same time nothing, devoid of substance. Such broad definitions of neoliberalism

---

3. Harvey (2005), Saad-Filho and Johnston (2005), Dumenil and Levy (2004, 2011), Campbell and Pederson (2011), Mirowski and Plehwe (2009).

risk diluting its meaning and give undue support to those deny its existence as a coherent doctrine and political project, as also very convincingly argued by Mirowski (2013).

For our purposes we have found the distinctions offered by Dumenil and Levy useful:

1. In a narrow sense, the term *neoliberalism* can be used to designate a course of events, a set of policies in the broad sense of the term that occurred during the 1980s and 1990s with possible transitional features. It can be interpreted *as an attempt, in the 1980s, by a class of capitalist owners, to restore, in alliance with top management, its power and income after a setback of several decades.* Some of the features recalled above are analogous of 19th century capitalism, but it goes without saying that the notion of restoration does not imply that the new course of capitalism should be identical to any events experienced in the past.

2. In a broader sense, the term neoliberalism can be used to designate a new capitalism, with certain characteristics of sustainability: *the outcome of the restoration of the power and income of a class of capitalist owners in the context of advanced managerial capitalism.* (Dumenil and Levy, 2004, p. 11)

There is of course an ideological component to the discussion of neoliberalism, which seeks to justify neoliberalism and "naturalize" it, as David Harvey and others have observed.[4] The distinction between narrow and broad definitions here demonstrates that the term "neoliberalism" can be used to designate specific sets of policies or to designate an era in which a new form of capitalism emerged to lay down the rules for the global economy. In the narrow sense of policy prescriptions neoliberalism has been summarized in the infamous "Washington Consensus" ten commandments, a term coined by John Williamson in 1989.[5]

Any current understanding of how "neoliberal" the development of new economies is in the twenty-first century is complicated by the experiences of many emerging countries of the South—China, in particular. China has witnessed tremendous economic growth and human development by pursuing policies that do not fit squarely as neoliberal. On one hand, it has adopted development policies that run counter to most of Williamson's ten commandments given its heavy state intervention in industry and controls on capital and financial flows and markets. By the narrow definition, then, China's rise was not neoliberal because it was not due to neoliberal policies. On the other hand, China's rise and continued growth happened in a neoliberal *era* and were made possible by neoliberal reforms in other countries, including substantial trade liberalization, which facilitated the export-led growth model of China and its becoming a hub for FDI to and from other countries. In that broader sense then, China is as neoliberal as any other state because it is operating in a global era in which a particular form

---

4. There is no consensus on the exact definition of neoliberalism. For a comparison see, for example, David Harvey and Philip Mirowski's views on this topic and the longer genealogy of the neoliberal project dating back to the Mt. Pelerin thought collective.

5. For Williamson's own history of the term, see Williamson (2004): The ten points are (1) fiscal discipline, (2) a reordering of public expenditures, (3) tax reform, (4) liberalized interest rates, (5) a competitive exchange rate, (6) trade liberalization, (7) liberalization of FDI flows, (8) privatization, (9) deregulation, (10) property rights.

of economic system reigns supreme. Indeed, as we have shown earlier, the phenomenon of new regionalism itself coincided with the full wave of trade liberalization, privatization and deregulation that started in the 1980s and continued full steam throughout the 1990s. As a part of the new regionalism debate, the rise of China can also be seen through the prism of double-movement analogy, as discussed in the previous chapter. While the neoliberal ladder enabled countries like China to climb fast in the global economic and political order, by doing so, it has also allowed the rise of a more multipolar world, opening more policy space for the Rest of South.

This distinction between different ways of understanding neoliberalism is useful because it allows us to think what an "alternative to neoliberalism" implies. The issue is two questions conflated into one. The first is: What economic and social policies can governments in the South pursue to craft an alternative path of development in place of neoliberalism? This is the question generally answered in the new-developmentalist literature that we discuss below. However, in our view, the answers given by this literature are inadequate, which brings us to the second question that is much more implicit and is too often missed. That is: What are the systematic pressures on South countries that result from operating in a neoliberal global system? The discussions around the first question tend to ignore or minimize the importance of these systematic pressures. In other words, new-developmentalism tends to follow the narrow definition of neoliberalism, treating it as a set of policies that South countries follow by choice, by misguided ideology, or perhaps by elite capture (i.e., domestic elites' and vested interests' shaping of globalization process), while largely ignoring the systematic pressures on individual countries for greater openness in order to attract trade and foreign direct investment.

5.3   What Is New-Developmentalism?

From the 1970s through the 1990s, mainstream development economics shifted its attention from large-scale and transformative macro questions to micro questions with a focus on poverty alleviation, basic needs and good governance. Under the new-developmentalist economics, poverty alleviation in particular, along with other concerns regarding health and education became almost synonymous with development.[6] More recently, pioneered by centers such as the MIT Poverty Action Lab, randomized experiments have become a dominant method to find cures for various ills of un(der) development. These research initiatives, which explicitly posit themselves in counter-distinction to failed large-scale projects, attempt to pinpoint specific, small-scale, narrowly defined interventions, limited in scope, that "work" in a development context (Rodrik, 2008a; Deaton, 2009). Such interventions can range from the impact of timely vaccinations to the introduction of cell phone use, to providing mosquito nets for human capital development, to giving direct cash to school children to postpone marriage and pregnancy or to studying the effect of fertilizer subsidies on fertilizer use.[7] Not only do

6. For a discussion see Rodrik (2008a).
7. Chattopadhyay and Duflo (2004), Banerjee et al. (2007); Duflo et al. (2009), Baird et al. (2010), Nyqvist et al. (2015).

these studies narrow the analytical focus of development economics, moving away from studies of large structures, institutions and social forces but also they are built on a view of development quite commensurate with neoclassical economic theory.[8] In this view, society is made up of entrepreneurial individuals whose good judgment needs to be assisted and harmful type interventions by government need to be replaced with beneficial ones.[9] The focus away from macro to micro aspects of development also allows economists to avoid uncomfortable questions about such things as the reasons behind the growing income divergence between the North and the South and the increasing deindustrialization faced by most of the South since the start of the neoliberal project in the early 1980s.

---

8. Independent of how convincing and robust (i.e., replicable) their results (which often is not the case: see, for example, Deaton, 2009 for a discussion), the micro-based studies of development, including the so-called randomized experiments, are byproducts of the obsession of neoclassical economics with micro foundations. In this setting, a society is nothing but the sum of rational and self-interest maximizing rational individual agents who are endowed with perfect (and in some cases imperfect) information and perfect foresight. Everything is then boiled down to either individual choice or external shocks that yield a certain outcome for each agent. The micro-development school, therefore, "portrays the dynamics of development/ underdevelopment primarily as outcomes of individual decisions, behaviors and interactions. Underdevelopment and poverty are seen as ultimately caused by government failures arising from rent-seeking behavior or market failures arising from opportunism that exploits information asymmetries, or a combination of the two, that call for corrective interventions at the individual level. As such, the field of development and underdevelopment (that is poverty) is divorced from the more structural dynamics and processes that shape, constrain or overpower individual behavior" (Akbulut et al., 2015, p. 750). The micro-credit bonanza, for example, now replaces more fundamental and structural causes of poverty and inequality, or causes of asymmetry in credit market access, or the fact that domestic and international capital market access is highly segmented and is biased towards the North and a few privileged Southern elites and multinationals. All they need, after all, is—no not love—but a bit of micro-credit or external push in millennium villages.

9. See, for example, the debate around the Millennium Development Villages (MDVs) project of Earth Institute at Columbia University and the UNDP, pioneered by Jeffry Sachs. The project claims to aim "the root causes of extreme poverty" and end "poverty trap" using 14 sites in Africa as guinea pigs. Its critics claim that the research design did not include a control group initially, which had to be implanted three years after the project started. More importantly, there is substantial doubt as to whether or not MDVs worked at all and how much of it is applicable to other parts of the world. In a well-publicized study Wanjala and Muradian (2013) analyzed the in MDV in Sauri, Kenya and found that "reducing reliance on agriculture [...] provide[s] a pathway out of poverty." According to their results, "specialization in agriculture as the main source of income negatively affects total cash income" and that the effect of the interventions on household income, saving or investment was insignificant and had little effect on the wider macro-economy (pp. 157–58). Masset and Barnett (2015) also found no difference in poverty rates or changes in per capita incomes between MDV and control villages in Northern Ghana. There was also no significant change in migration dynamics to the MDV, showing that they did not become a center for attraction for other villages.

One reliable indicator of the state of development economics is the development of the Millennium Development Goals (MDGs).[10] This ostensibly well-intentioned, even visionary, set of principles shows how far we have in fact come to downgrade our expectations of what is possible. In this regard, much has changed, and perhaps not for the better, since the Bandung Conference, when development was thought of as a vehicle to transport the South to the living standards of the North, and the Afro-Asian countries were not basket cases asking for a pittance, but growing nations asking for a say in running global affairs and making demands on the Big Powers for disarmament and technology transfer.

Critiques emerging from postmodern schools of thought that have their roots in French philosophy and cultural studies, strongly influenced by the works of Michel Foucault and Edward Said, have also targeted developmentalism. From the postcolonial subaltern studies school to the post-development-critique literature of Arturo Escobar[11] and others, these bodies of work have criticized all previous existing development models as inherently serving a destructive and hegemonic colonizing project by the Northern and Southern elites against the peasantry, working classes and marginalized groups in the South. According to Escobar:

> Development has to be seen as an invention and strategy produced by the "First World" about the "underdevelopment" of the "Third World," and not only as an instrument of economic control over the physical and social reality of much of Asia, Africa and Latin America. Development has been the primary mechanism through which these parts of the world have been produced and have produced themselves, thus marginalizing or precluding other ways of seeing and doing. To think about "alternatives to development" thus requires a theoretico-practical transformation of the notions of development, modernity and the economy. (Escobar, 1992, p. 22)

Therefore, although post-development critique, as in Escobar (1992, 1995), is sympathetic to developmentalist critiques of neoliberalism, it implicates both schools of thought in this technical-political project to reorder society. In addition to Escobar's work, that of James Scott has argued that the combination of modernist ideology and authoritarian governance has led to large-scale disasters that inflict violence on complex economic, social and political ecosystems (Scott, 2000).

The only mainstream development research agenda that retains a macro-level approach is the New Institutionalism school, which includes Dani Rodrik, Daron Acemoglu and James Robinson.[12] A major element of the literature produced by this school of thought is the discussion about how to link institutional formations to

---

10. The MDGs were announced in 2000 at the Millennium Summit of the UN and include eight goals: (1) eradicate extreme hunger and poverty; (2) achieve universal primary education; (3) promote gender equality and empower women; (4) reduce child mortality; (5) improve maternal health; (6) combat HIV/AIDS, malaria and other diseases; (7) ensure environmental sustainability; (8) develop a global partnership for development.
11. See, for example, Escobar (1995, 2000).
12. Dani Rodrik can also be considered in the camp of new-developmentalists.

long-term economic growth and to associate development and underdevelopment with a society's ability to create inclusive versus exclusive institutions. Still, Rodrik, at various forums, has stated that there is no one-size-fits-all kind of institution when it comes to economic development in a particular country or region much of the debate, and most of the actual development activity in the world is still informed by a sense that the ideal institutions for the purpose are in the advanced capitalist West. In other words, development, whether economic, social or political, is measured by "the distance travelled towards an idealized capitalist economy with secure property rights, legal regulations and well-functioning markets" (Akbulut et al., 2015, p. 23).

New-developmentalism shares some of the features of the new institutionalism but has its intellectual roots in the classical or high-development theory of Rodenstein-Rodan, Nurkse, Lewis and Hirschmann. Like early-development thinking, new-developmentalism views "poverty as a symptom and the real issue as the ability to generate high-quality jobs in increasing returns industrial activities" (Khan, 2011 p. 258). The most fundamental agreement between new institutionalism and new-developmentalism, therefore, is the belief that large-scale transformations to radically improve human development in the South are both desirable and possible. In that sense, new-developmentalism is clearly distinct from both the mainstream poverty-alleviation approach and the radical post-development approach. Moreover, it also agrees with high-development theory that the private sector alone in the South is unwilling or unable to bring about equitable and effective human development, and that state intervention is therefore required, not just to provide infrastructure and good governance, as in the liberal neoclassical paradigm, but to implement active industrial policy. State and markets are seen not as rivals but partners with a high level of potential complementarity.

However, most new-developmentalists would find the textbook definition of industrial policy, defined as "imposing tariffs, subsidies, and tax breaks that imply distortions beyond the ones associated with optimal taxes or revenue constraints," too limited (Harrison and Rodriguez-Clare, 2010, p. 4041). For new-developmentalists these policies only begin to scratch the surface of the state–private sector collaboration that took place in Japan and the Asian Tigers—collaboration that ran the gamut of picking and heavily investing in national industries, funneling massive credit, severely constraining the role of multinationals, actively acquiring technology through reverse engineering and other policies.

Khan (2011) argues that new-developmentalism departs from classical development theory in recognizing how heavy-handed state intervention and politicized ISI can degenerate into crony capitalism and underperforming noncompetitive industries, points also raised by the structuralist school. New-developmentalism also incorporates a critique of the idea that growth is synonymous with development, and in that respect it welcomes the ecological and environmental sustainability movements' contributions, a perspective that was lacking in early development theory. Comparative appraisal of Latin America's, the Middle East's and East Asia's experiences with state intervention—the former two being failure stories and the latter a success story—offers useful lessons in assessing what kind of interventions work.

Partly because of the neoliberal assault in the 1980s and partly because of their own failures (see chapter 2), the dismantling of the older-school Keynesian-cum-nationalistic protectionist models gave way to a more nuanced industrial-policy school, one in which the importance of experimentation, knowledge spillovers, human capital and suitability has moved to the central stage. Through historical case studies of economic policy among the older industrialized countries as well as in the newly industrializing economies, these new- developmentalists have demonstrated that industrial policy, with active state intervention in economic development and growth, has been a key factor of these countries' success.[13] The late developers, which include the so-called Asian Tigers, have used the state pervasively and systematically in their development, just as most of today's industrialized countries used it when they were developing (Amsden, 1989; Wade, 1990; Chang, 2002, 2008).[14] The question is no longer about the market versus the state but about how states can harness the market for long-term human development and, and in order to do so, can implement effective industrial and agricultural policy.

The late developers, including Taiwan and South Korea, have attracted significant attention in the new-developmentalist writings. This literature convincingly shows that these late developers were able to create control mechanisms whereby the state technocracy would provide subsidies in return for "monitorable performance standards that were redistributive in nature and results-oriented" (Amsden, 2001, p. 8).[15] These states could avoid the politicization of the economic bureaucracy for short-term gains— something that had happened in many failed ISI countries—since they interfered only minimally with short- and long-term planning aspects, including employment, as well as management of industrial factories. At the same time, the states carried through on their threat to withdraw subsidies and allow businesses to fail if they did not meet output and export expectations.

A prime example of these policies is the case of South Korea, where investors and owners were allowed to fail while the plant and physical infrastructure and labor expertise were moved to new domestic ownerships so as to avoid squandering accumulated inputs and fixed costs (Chang, 2006). Large conglomerates benefited from national development banks that funneled subsidized credit in their direction, and they acquired foreign exchange through large labor-intensive exports. At the same time, the role of FDI, just as in China today, was carefully managed and limited to strategic sectors and the state greatly encouraged technology transfer through reverse engineering and other methods.

---

13. According to Khan (2011) the call for a "new-developmentalism" first originated from Alice Amsden during the February 2000 UNCTAD "High Level Round Table on Trade and Development" Conference in Bangkok.

14. As Chang (2002, 2008) shows, most of Northern countries, including the United Kingdom and the United States, had activist governments that used industrial policy to industrialize. Alexander Hamilton, after all, coined the term "infant industry" in his report on manufactures to the US Congress in 1791.

15. This notion is similar to Peter Evans's concept of the "embedded autonomy" of the private industrial sector (Evans, 1995).

The new-developmentalist policy advice includes the use of trade barriers—tariffs, quotas, subsidies and so forth—to protect domestic, infant firms as a part of an industrial policy toolset, just as Alexander Hamilton advocated in 1791. Accordingly, new-developmentalists see industrial development and promotion of advanced industries with high value added as the way to increase productivity and, eventually, living standards in developing countries in the long run. The success of such investment activities, however, depends on whether or not domestic firms can be induced to achieve high and sustained productivity growth and governments can deliver complementary support mechanisms through better education and infrastructure development (Grabel and Chang, 2004, pp. 66–70). Choosing the "right" industries based on a dynamic comparative advantage for long-run productivity growth and social welfare requires a selective industrial policy and the use of temporary protectionism, which were lacking in the initial ISI experiences in most Southern countries. Another necessary component of a holistic approach to industrial policy is a well-functioning financial system with long-term credit availability and low asset market volatility. Financial regulation and controls on short-term capital flows would also help achieve stabilizing the financial system.

Picking the right industries and sectors, however, is challenging, and requires experimentation (Mukand and Rodrik, 2005; Rodrik, 2008a). The new- developmentalist as well as structuralist critiques of the old ISI era also suggest that the earlier emphasis on capital-intensive heavy industry impeded industrial employment growth and consequently wage growth, given that available technologies were imported from Northern countries with different factor endowments (i.e., they were capital-biased). Slow employment creation in industrial sectors meant that the transfer of labor from agriculture was also slow, thereby exacerbating the population pressure on land and retarding agricultural productivity growth by delaying modernization and the adoption of capital-intensive production methods. The demise of ISI only made things worse by directing the labor surplus—created by the collapse of domestic industries and elimination of agricultural subsidies—to low-productivity service industries in urban areas, in turn leading to premature deindustrialization and dooming productivity growth (UNCTAD, 2003, 2006; McMillan and Rodrik, 2011). Another result of this deindustrialization process is the undeniable large divergence dynamic across countries. Rodrik (2013) provides evidence showing that, while labor productivity converges within manufacturing industries across countries, what is lacking in some of the neediest of these countries is industrialization, itself, the result being productivity- (and consequently income-) divergence between the North and the South. Moreover, the diffusion of Northern consumption patterns has caused domestic producers in the South to move into consumer goods that were not previously imported and had very high imported input content. The high import dependency ratios (i.e., imported input per unit of output) of these new consumer goods meant a worsening of the balance of payments problems in these economies.

Admittedly, both the development and the eventual monitoring of performance targets imposed on public and private firms require a competent public bureaucracy,

Table 5.1 Necessary conditions of new-developmentalism

Development-minded political leadership and economics bureaucracy not blinded by neoliberal ideology and are free from rent-seeking coalitions
Active industrial policy
Bureaucracy capable of overcoming coordination failures and able to provide right incentives
Embedded central bank; active exchange-rate management and avoiding overvaluations; capital controls and prudential financial regulation
Tariff protection, subsidies and directed credit for infant industries
No constraining trade or investment treaties
Emphasis on high value added exports and limits on balance of payments disequilibrium
Favorable investment climate: Macroeconomic equilibrium; low debt service and indebtedness; low macroeconomic volatility and uncertainty; complementary public investments for crowding-in
Institutional experimentation
Social policies for poverty and inequality reduction
Human capital build-up with labor acquiring skills necessary for infant industries

Source: Adapted from Grabel and Chang (2004), Rodrik (1994, 2001, 2004), Wade (1999), Chang (2008), UNCTAD (2003, 2006).

which is obviously lacking in most developing countries (Grabel and Chang, 2004, pp. 79–80). Though all now-rich countries suffered from corruption and cronyism, in many countries today a politicized economic bureaucracy makes the development and implementation of an active industrial policy more difficult, if not impossible. The question of how to enhance the quality of civil service or how to create an administrative bureaucracy, not subject to lobbying or cronyism, is not easy to answer, nor is the broader question of how to achieve institutional reform.[16] Even though the experiences of a number of countries (mostly in East Asia) suggest that such pressures and barriers can be overcome, the replicability of their experiences is questionable at best. While the older structuralist school argued for a virtuous cycle of economic growth and institutional reform, each reinforcing the other and both initiated by an external investment push orchestrated by the state planners through industrial policy, the experience of Southern countries during and after ISI raises serious doubts on this vision.

Table 5.1 summarizes the necessary but not sufficient conditions for a successful industrial policy in the South based on a survey of a wide variety of new developmentalist academic and policy literature. The new-developmentalist checklist in this table represents the antithesis of the Washington Consensus. In brief, it argues for the state as a leader and markets as a means for achieving effective development.

The markets as a means rather than as master is a principal theme in new-developmentalist theories, characteristics they share with the old Keynesian dictum

---

16. We can of course refer to the augmented Washington Consensus debate with a new 10 sets of commandments mostly targeting institutional reform and social safety nets, but we doubt this approach would work any better than the initial Washington Consensus. For a discussion, see Rodrik (2006).

that markets make good servants but bad masters. However, in order to master markets, states must have policy space or room to maneuver, to develop local industries. As discussed in chapter 2, one key reason why neoliberalism continues is that the rise of the WTO and subsequent trade and investment treaties have placed constraints on states' ability to implement such a meaningful industrial policy. The hope, therefore, is that by readjusting global governance, opening new channels for trade and finance and facilitating knowledge and capabilities sharing, the rise of South–South relations can both open up policy space and facilitate industrial policy.

5.4 South–South Integration and New-Developmentalism

What role might the growing integration of countries of the South play in the twenty-first century development landscape? How does the reality of South–South relations measure up against the hopes expressed in previous chapters? Lately, silent undercurrents in economics have moved the dominant views on South–South economic integration towards a reformulation that is more sympathetic to heresy in economic policy. The change did not happen overnight but has been in the making at least since early 2000s as the leading Emerging South countries such as Korea and China have become more vocal in their objections to the dogmatic policy prescriptions of the Washington Consensus and its flag bearers. A growing scholarship by dissenting economists has also made it clear that the rules of the game in economic exchanges between the North and the South are rigged, and the North, instead of helping the South, is indeed "kicking away the ladder." In this transformation, the World Bank and IMF, the two flag bearers of the economics orthodoxy, also played a role. The World Bank, for example, changed its perspective on South–South trade by suggesting that perhaps the old structuralist "non-economists" might have known a thing or two regarding knowledge and technology spillovers potential in South–South trade. In their flagship reports the World Bank suggested that increasing South–South integration may facilitate the delinking of the South from Northern business cycles, allowing for more stability in world trade and growth during downturns in the North, a point already argued by Lewis (1980).[17] The rise of China and other leading emerging economies including Brazil, Turkey, India and the newly industrialized South Korea has contributed to this tectonic shift as their weight in global trade and finance has become too great to ignore.

On the other hand, particularly after the dynamic economic growth of China, advocates of South–South integration have also revised their positions, taking a more critical

---

17. World Bank (2011, p. 47), for example, argued that "a more diffuse distribution of growth poles will mean a world that better weathers shocks and is more resilient to crises." For a discussion of other positive effects South–South interactions, including the more greenfield-oriented nature of FDI flows in between as opposed to acquisition-oriented North–South flows, rising multi-polarity, wider availability of key currencies, trade credit, international aid and so forth, see, for example, World Bank (2011), Akin and Kose (2011) and IMF (2011).

attitude toward South–South economic exchanges. The rise of China, along with that of the Emerging South in general, has created a sharp split within the South. With respect to trade and financial flows it no longer makes sense to speak of a South, nor of "South–South" as a whole. As studies have shown, the rise of China has had a multitude of effects on the Rest of South. Kaplinsky (2008) develops a framework for analyzing China's impact on developing countries through analysis of trade, investment, aid, global governance, environment and migrants with either complementary or competitive channels that operate directly or indirectly. For example, if China's growing exports of textiles to the United States undercuts South African exports to the United States, the result is a competitive trade channel that indirectly affects South Africa. The crowding out of Southern exporters, increasing price competition while decreasing manufacturing terms of trade in Southern exports, increasing the level and volatility of commodity prices fueled by the growing input demand in China, the sale of national firms to Chinese investors, increasing "land-grabbing" in Africa and Latin America and undercutting of environmental and labor standards as well as civil rights and democratization have all been cited as key concerns, both for political leaders and economists in the affected countries and for the would-be architects of a more equitable global agora.

The answer we propose to the question at the beginning of this section is that the rise of South–South relations is both a hindrance and a facilitator in promoting a new-developmentalism and that, far from being a silver bullet for the ills of the developing and underdeveloped South, it may result in significant setbacks. In this section we discuss both these aspects of South–South relations, and we conclude by identifying the conditions under which we think the former can be minimized and the latter maximized.

5.5   The Rise of China and the South: Nemesis or Savior

The main problem with the rise of the South in world economy is that it is dominated by a few countries. As Figure 4.11 in chapter 4, shows, for example, the Rest of South countries account for less than 1 percent of world exports in high-skill manufactures as opposed to 48 percent by Emerging South in 2009. The case with medium- and low-skill manufactures is also very similar. Likewise, according to Tables 4.20 and 4.21, 10 countries accounted for 62 percent of total (global) South–South trade in 2013 and China alone was responsible for 21 percent of this total. Moreover, these 10 countries were responsible for 60 percent of total South–North trade in 2013, with China accounting for more than 25 percent of the total. The case of global financial flows is also very similar to those in trade, with the Rest of South being hardly noticeable. In this section, therefore, we begin with China, the most dominant of all Southern countries, and we pay particular attention to the effects of increasing trade and financial linkages between China and the North, and between China and the South.

5.5.1   *Crowding in or out of Southern Industrialization*

The effects of the rise of China as a manufacturing powerhouse on other Emerging South countries are for the most part worrisome. The empirical evidence so far suggests the following:

- The "Rise of the South" is in fact a bifurcation of the South into two distinct groups, the "Emerging South" and the "Rest of South."
- The rise of China is leading to the primarization of goods exports in many developing countries, including many emerging powers in the South.
- The reconfiguration of South–South trade relations has exacerbated the division of labor within the South.
- Global power dynamics, including representation in multilateral institutions and the use of international trade and investment agreements for dispute resolution, have changed significantly.

Matching its two-digit growth rates since the 2000s, China (including Hong Kong) increased its demand for primary products and is now the world's leading consumer of a multitude of minerals and agricultural goods, accounting for more than a third of world consumption of all metals, 50 percent of global coal consumption, 12 percent of global oil demand, 62 percent of global soy beans demand and 25 percent of world demand in natural rubber (MIT Media lab, 2015; UN COMTRADE, 2014; BP, 2015). The effects of this growing Chinese consumption have been twofold: On the one hand it has led to a primarization of Southern exports, particularly in those countries with a previous history of industrialization, such as Chile. Increasing demand for primary products and favorable terms of trade encourage Southern countries to specialize in primary goods and to move away from industrialization efforts.

On the other hand, for those countries that lacked primary goods, particularly commodities, the increasing cost of production has created a shock to their industrialization efforts. Besides, increasing export competition from China also has crowded out other Southern manufactures exporters. These effects have further aggravated the destructive impacts of widely implemented orthodox economic policies under privatization, deregulation and liberalization on Southern countries' industrialization efforts. The result is a structural transformation in most Southern economies so that, unlike the Northern countries, most Southern countries have now started experiencing a transition from manufacturing and industrial production back to primary sectors and, in some, to services. This is the process that is generally referred to as the deindustrialization and primarization of Southern economies.

Thus, deindustrialization refers to the declining share of industry employment, output and investment and a downgrading to less technology-and-skill-intensive, low-productivity activities, mostly in primary or service sectors. The increasing share of the primary sector, in turn, is called the primarization of economic activities. The earlier wave of this downward trend in Southern industrialization efforts, a result of orthodox economic policies of the 1980s and 1990s, is dubbed "premature deindustrialization (UNCTAD, 2003, 2006;

McMillan and Rodrik, 2011). What we observe since the 2000s appears to be a continuation of this trend but this time fueled by the China's vast growth.

The fact that 74 percent of the Rest of South's exports were in primary commodities in 2012, compared to 64 percent in 1970 (and 76 percent in 1980) suggest the return of the traditional center–periphery relationship that has engulfed the South since the rise of the North (see Prebisch, 1950).[18] In fact, the top export item for the Rest of South, petroleum oils,[19] accounted for 57.5 percent of all their exports in 2012 (MIT Media Lab, 2015). The increasing competition and the crowding out of Southern manufactures exports, combined with unfavorable terms of trade for manufactures and favorable terms for primary goods, speed up the deindustrialization process in many Emerging South countries and make it more difficult for them to climb up the value chain in industrial outputs. The increasing reliance on primary goods exports also makes Southern countries vulnerable to price swings and resulting pro-cyclical boom–bust cycles in goods and asset markets. As noted by Ros (2013), with the rise of China and changing terms of trade in favor of primary goods during the 2000s, we observe the opposite of the Prebisch-Singer hypothesis, as the Southern exporters of primary goods are outperforming those of manufactures exporters. However, this is a cursed growth. While it occurs in a considerable spurt, it also leads to deindustrialization. During times of downturn or slow-down in the global economy, as has occurred since the Great Recession of 2008, the prices of commodity products plunge and, with less industry to fall back on, those countries hitherto reliant on Chinese markets for exports are hit hard.[20] In 2013, 24 countries relied on China for more than a quarter of their total exports, including countries such as Iran (34 percent), Mongolia (91 percent), South Africa (38 percent) and Turkmenistan (69 percent) (IMF, Direction of Trade Statistics, 2014).

In 2012, the share of Chinese exports in world trade increased to over 15 percent, while in 1990 it had been only 4.2 percent. Likewise, during the same period China's share of imports rose to 12.3 percent from below 4 percent (Table 5.2). Furthermore, in terms of their composition, we see a radical change in the structure of these exports. While, in 1990, China exported only 3 percent of the world's high-skill goods, this number increased to just below 29 percent in 2012. We see a similar increase in both low- and medium-skill manufactured goods as well as natural resource–intensive manufactures. The share of primary goods in Chinese exports stayed relatively constant, and low. In its import shares, however, China now accounts for 10.6 percent of world demand for primary goods and 14.6 percent of natural resource–intensive manufactures, up from 2.4 percent and 3.1 percent in 1990. The increase in China's high-skill manufactures imports stayed lower than its exports of such goods, which increased more than ninefold compared to five for the imports.

Table 5.3 shows that, in 2012, primary goods accounted for less than 3 percent of China's total exports, a significant decrease from 10.8 percent in 1990. In contrast, they accounted for almost 14 percent of its import demand, compared to 10 percent in 1990.

---

18. Also, see Ros (2013).
19. SITC codes: 3330, 3340, 3341, 3342, 3343, 3350, 3354.
20. Interestingly, these warnings are also raised by IMF (2012a, 2013a).

Table 5.2 Percentage share of Chinese exports and imports in world trade, 1990, 2003 and 2012

	Exports			Imports		
	1990	2003	2012	1990	2003	2012
Total	4.2%	9.4%	15.1%	3.9%	8.0%	12.3%
Primary	2.7%	2.6%	2.2%	2.4%	5.5%	10.6%
Nat-Resource Intensive	1.8%	4.0%	7.5%	3.1%	6.4%	14.6%
Low-Skill	13.3%	24.2%	32.4%	6.4%	8.5%	7.3%
Medium-Skill	2.6%	5.8%	11.3%	4.1%	7.1%	9.3%
High-Skill	3.0%	13.4%	28.8%	4.1%	12.9%	20.1%

Note: Based on Lall (2000), *Total, Primary*, and *Nat-Resource Intensive* refer to the export (import) shares of total merchandise goods, primary commodities and natural resource–intensive manufactured goods in world trade of these goods. *Low-skill, Medium-skill* and *High-skill* refer to low-, medium- and high-skill manufactured goods. In the trade tables from now on China includes Hong Kong. Exports and imports are valued fob and cif, respectively. For the definition of sub-categories of skill intensity levels, refer to chapter 4. The trade data are based on SITC Rev. 2.
Source: For Tables 5.2–5.8, MIT Media lab (2015) based on Feenstra et al. (2005), UN COMTRADE, and authors' calculations.[21]

There is no doubt, however, that the biggest transformation has taken place with regard to the structure of China's manufactured goods exports, wherein the share of medium- and (particularly) high-skill exports increased while that of low-skill goods decreased significantly. We see the same process for its imported manufactured goods.

To observe the effect of China on South, let us take a closer look at its relationship with Latin America, beginning with an example with one country and one commodity, China's trade in copper with Chile. Table 5.4 shows that, in 2012, China accounted for 28.4 percent of copper,[22] 25.8 percent of nickel,[23] 62.5 percent of iron[24] and 15.4 percent of zinc[25] imports in the world. The growing hunger of China for these commodities seems to be insatiable indeed. In 1990, China demanded only 2.8 percent and 3.8 percent of world imports in copper and iron, but by 2012 those numbers had grown tenfold and sixteen-fold, respectively. The growth in other commodities in Table 5.5 is no less impressive. Likewise, in the case of Chile, as shown in Table 5.5, one single commodity, copper was responsible for 55 percent of its total export earnings in 2012 and 37 percent of that copper went to one single country, China. In fact, copper accounted for 78 percent of all Chilean exports to China in 2012 compared to 21.2 percent in 1990. Given

Table 5.3 Product composition of Chinese exports and imports, 1990, 2003 and 2012

	Exports			Imports		
	1990	2003	2012	1990	2003	2012
Primary	10.8%	4.0%	2.8%	10.3%	10.0%	13.9%
Nat-Resource Intensive	7.2%	6.3%	6.8%	13.4%	11.8%	16.5%
Low-Skill	50.2%	39.0%	29.0%	25.8%	16.1%	8.2%
Medium-Skill	19.5%	19.0%	22.5%	33.1%	27.4%	23.5%
High-Skill	10.5%	29.7%	37.0%	15.2%	33.7%	31.8%

Note: The percentage totals do not add up to 100% due to the excluded category of "other goods."

Table 5.4 Share of Chinese imports in total world trade of selected commodities: copper, nickel, aluminum, iron and zinc, 1990 vs. 2012

	1990	2012
Copper	2.8%	28.4%
Nickel	0.8%	25.8%
Aluminum	2.1%	6.3%
Iron	3.8%	62.5%
Zinc	1.8%	15.4%

Note: The SITC codes are as follows: copper (2871, 6820, 6821, 6822), nickel (2872, 6830, 6831, 6832), aluminum (2873, 6840, 6841, 6842), iron (SITC 2810, 2815, 2816) and zinc (2875, 6860, 6861, 6863).

the growing hunger of China for primary goods, the highest price increase took place in those commodities for which China's consumption increased the most, including minerals, ores and metals (particularly iron ore, copper and zinc) and oil (Figures 5.1 and 5.2, Jenkins, 2009, p. 54; IMF, 2013).

The changes in global copper demand, and the consequent rise in its price, have significant implications for those countries that are heavily dependent on exporting it. Particularly, as even the IMF (2012a) admitted, countries such as Chile lack any counterweight mechanism to shelter them from the storm during downswings in commodity prices. In one year, for example, from January to December 2008, copper prices fell from above $7,000 per ton to $3,100. Despite this serious problem for the exporting (and, indeed, importing) countries, very little is done at the global level to reduce the vulnerability among commodity exporting countries. Instead, during the upturn we observe a very pro-cyclical monetary and fiscal policy that further escalates distortions in domestic asset markets.

We see similar patterns in the region as a whole. Latin America and the Caribbean accounted for 1.6 percent of Chinese exports and 1.8 percent imports in 1990. By 2012, its share in Chinese trade had increased steadily to 5.8 percent for exports and

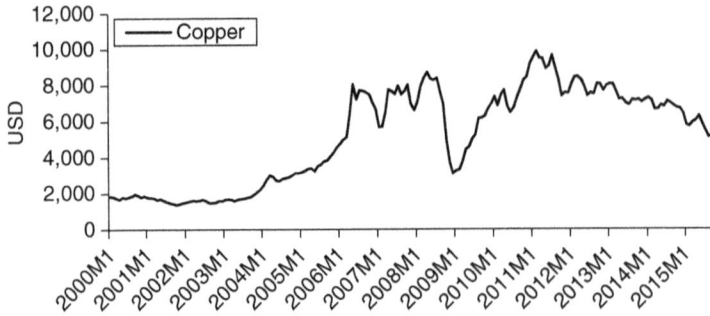

Figure 5.1 Copper prices, USD, 2000:1–2015:9
Note: Copper is grade A cathode, LME spot price, CIF European ports, USD per metric ton.
Source: IMF (2015). http://www.imf.org/external/np/res/commod/External_Data.xls. Downloaded on 10/15/2015.

Table 5.5 Importance of copper for Chilean exports, 1990 vs. 2012

	1990	2012
Share of copper in total Chilean exports	41.7%	55.2%
Share of copper exports in total Chilean exports to China	21.2%	77.9%
Share of China in Chilean copper exports	0.4%	37.3%

Note: Total includes "other" goods.

5.7 percent for imports. However, as shown in Table 5.6 below, it is in the structure of this trade that we see the most dynamic change. While primary goods imports accounted for 13.9 percent of China's total imports from the rest of the world in 2012, they accounted for 45.5 percent of its imports from Latin America. We see the same trend in natural resource–intensive manufactures: of total Chinese imports, natural resource–intensive manufactures accounted for 13.4 percent in 1990 and 16.5 percent in 2012, but the shares of these goods in Chinese imports from Latin America increased from 31.4 percent in 1990 to 41.6 percent in 2012. As a result, primary goods and natural resource–intensive manufactures accounted for a staggering 87 percent of Chinese imports from the region. In contrast, high- and medium-skill manufactured goods were responsible for only 11.7 percent of Chinese imports from Latin America in 2012, displaying a declining trend particularly after the accession of China to the WTO in 2002. Turning to Chinese exports to Latin America, we see that high- and medium-skill manufactures accounted for over 63 percent of these exports, while the share of low-skill manufactures and primary goods declined steadily. This is exactly what many economists, particularly those on the structuralist side, were afraid of: a vicious cycle of increasing deindustrialization and primarization process in the South.

Table 5.7 below shows the same figures as Table 5.6 for selected Emerging South countries, including Argentina, Brazil, Chile, Mexico, South Korea and Turkey. The

Table 5.6 Structure of China–Latin America trade, 1990, 2003 and 2012

	Exports to Latin America			Imports from Latin America		
	1990	2003	2012	1990	2003	2012
Primary	10.4%	1.9%	2.3%	31.8%	36.9%	45.5%
Nat-Resource Intensive	7.2%	8.5%	7.9%	31.4%	31.7%	41.6%
Low-Skill	46.2%	29.8%	25.4%	19.0%	8.5%	1.6%
Medium-Skill	28.0%	21.9%	28.4%	16.1%	11.2%	4.2%
High-Skill	7.6%	37.0%	35.0%	1.4%	11.6%	6.5%

Note: Latin America includes the Caribbean.

transformation in each of these major emerging South economies is radical, to put it mildly. Except for the case of South Korea, these countries have shared a common transformation in their trade structures vis-à-vis China, though a transformation much worse for some than others. The experiences of five of these six countries also suggest that *export growth* does not necessarily mean *export-led growth*. As many others have pointed out, the export-led growth model, at least as it was implemented in most developing countries, did not lead to a virtuous growth path; exports grew, but not in a growth-stimulating way. What we see in primary goods-exporting Latin American countries such as Argentina and Chile is an increasing concentration of those exports, in 2012 accounting for 73.5 percent of Argentine and 60.8 percent of Chilean exports to China. Together with natural resource–intensive manufactures, primary goods accounted for 92.6 percent of Argentine and 99.5 percent of Chilean exports to China in 2012. In 1990 the sum of these two groups was 83.2 percent for Argentina and 82.9 percent for Chile. In contrast, high skill manufactures accounted for a bare 0.5 percent of Argentina and 0.1 percent of Chilean exports to China in 2012.

Even in the case of more successful industrializing countries such as Brazil and Mexico the numbers are worrisome. In 2012, 44.3 percent and 47.8 percent of Brazilian exports to China were of primary goods and natural resource–intensive manufactures, for a total of 92.1 percent, a significant jump from 50.6 percent back in 1990. In the case of Mexico, in 2012 primary goods were responsible for 13.4 percent and natural resource–intensive manufactures for 37.8 percent of its exports to China, for a total of 51.2 percent, compared to just 14.3 percent in 1990. In contrast, the share of low- and medium-skill manufactures dropped, from 20.3 percent and 55.3 percent of Mexican exports to China in 1990 to 2.2 percent and 23.8 percent in 2012. The share of high-skill manufactures exports to China doubled from 9.9 percent in 1990 to 20 percent in 2002, but this improvement probably was a result of the global production chain management that placed China and Mexico in the same ladder. We should note that during the same period Mexican imports of high-skill manufactures, as a share of its total imports from China, increased from 10.6 percent to 51.4 percent.

For each country in question, we see a similar trend, with the share of high-skill manufactures imports from China increasing and that of primary goods and

Table 5.7 Composition of exports and imports of China to and from six Emerging South countries, 1990, 2003 and 2012

	Chinese Exports			Chinese Imports		
	1990	2003	2012	1990	2003	2012
Argentina						
Primary	2.0%	0.9%	1.1%	68.4%	56.5%	73.5%
Nat-Resource Intensive	24.6%	21.6%	9.9%	14.8%	28.0%	19.1%
Low-Skill	37.4%	20.1%	19.7%	8.9%	11.2%	5.2%
Medium-Skill	21.5%	25.0%	34.0%	7.1%	4.0%	1.6%
High-Skill	14.4%	32.2%	35.1%	0.8%	0.5%	0.5%
Brazil						
Primary	39.5%	5.0%	2.2%	17.6%	35.0%	44.3%
Nat-Resource Intensive	10.3%	20.7%	9.8%	33.0%	35.9%	47.8%
Low-Skill	13.3%	13.2%	24.0%	26.6%	11.7%	1.8%
Medium-Skill	26.0%	19.5%	31.8%	22.0%	15.4%	3.1%
High-Skill	10.9%	41.2%	31.8%	0.8%	1.7%	2.4%
Chile						
Primary	2.4%	1.0%	1.1%	42.8%	63.5%	60.8%
Nat-Resource Intensive	8.5%	5.3%	6.7%	40.1%	34.8%	38.7%
Low-Skill	48.6%	57.5%	46.8%	7.5%	0.4%	0.2%
Medium-Skill	25.9%	19.7%	25.2%	2.2%	1.4%	0.2%
High-Skill	14.2%	16.0%	20.2%	0.5%	0.0%	0.1%
Mexico						
Primary	15.1%	1.2%	3.5%	5.2%	1.5%	13.4%
Nat-Resource Intensive	4.2%	4.3%	5.2%	9.1%	11.4%	37.8%
Low-Skill	45.5%	19.5%	16.0%	20.3%	8.4%	2.2%
Medium-Skill	23.7%	18.7%	21.5%	55.3%	29.6%	23.8%
High-Skill	10.6%	54.7%	51.4%	9.9%	49.3%	20.0%
Korea						
Primary	13.1%	18.0%	6.6%	5.9%	2.5%	2.8%
Nat-Resource Intensive	10.8%	11.1%	10.4%	9.9%	10.9%	9.6%
Low-Skill	22.4%	21.4%	22.4%	27.5%	14.5%	6.3%
Medium-Skill	20.7%	14.0%	23.9%	38.2%	27.2%	28.7%
High-Skill	32.2%	29.5%	36.0%	17.5%	42.9%	50.6%
Turkey						
Primary	46.2%	5.2%	1.4%	10.5%	20.8%	31.8%
Nat-Resource Intensive	5.7%	8.0%	6.3%	28.4%	7.1%	37.5%
Low-Skill	19.0%	28.7%	27.7%	22.7%	21.9%	15.6%
Medium-Skill	14.3%	27.8%	34.3%	37.9%	40.9%	7.6%
High-Skill	14.4%	29.9%	29.9%	0.3%	1.2%	2.5%

natural resource–intensive manufactures decreasing significantly. That is, as China climbed up the industrialization ladder, it has moved away from exporting primary goods to importing them and, in return, exporting higher-skill manufactures. Take Turkey, for example, where primary goods accounted for 46 percent of its imports from China in 1990. In 2012, this number was a bare 1.4 percent. In contrast, the share of high-skill manufactures in its total imports from China increased from 14 percent in 1990 to just below 30 percent in 2012. In 2012, high- and medium-skill manufactures together accounted for over 64 percent of Turkish imports from China. Likewise, in Brazil primary goods were responsible for 39.5 percent of its import bill from China in 1990 but just 2 percent in 2012. Meanwhile, the share of high-skill manufactures in its imports from China increased from 10.9 percent in 1990 to 31.8 percent in 2012 and together with medium-skill goods, accounted for over 63 percent of its imports from China in 2012. As noted by many others, the only country in this group that managed to escape the primarization curse is South Korea. Chinese imports from Korea are skill-intensive with high- and medium-skill categories accounting for 79 percent of its total import bill. Its exports are also mainly high-skill, with primary and natural resource–intensive categories accounting for only 17 percent of its exports. In contrast to the Latin American case, exports from South Korea to China have increasingly become of a high-skill nature, going up from 17.5 percent of total Korean exports in 1990 to 50.6 percent in 2012 while the share of low-skill manufactures exports fell from 27.5 percent to 6.3 percent.

Table 5.8 shows the growing importance of trade with China for the Rest of South and the Emerging South trade. Among the Rest of South countries, China accounted for 12 percent of their exports and 17.6 percent of their total imports in 2012. In 1990 the same figures were only 2.1 percent for exports and 4.8 percent for imports. In other words, by 2012 almost a fifth of all Rest of South imports were from one country, China, while for exports we observe an increased concentration on China across all commodity groups, including an increase of twenty-eight-fold in the case of primary goods exported to China from the Rest of South. In 2012, almost a fifth of the total exports from the Rest of South in high-skill (18.6 percent) and natural resource–intensive manufactures (17.5 percent) went to China. Except for low-skill manufactured goods, the importance of China for the Rest of South increased significantly, accounting for 12.3 percent of primary goods and 14.3 percent of medium-skill manufactures exports. However, aside from these exports, the significance of China increased the most for the Rest of South imports. In 2012, the Rest of South countries imported more than a fifth of their high-skill manufactures from China alone. The figure for low-skill manufactures was even higher, reaching more than a third of all their imports.

The figures for the countries of the Emerging South are similar with the importance of China for their primary goods and natural resource–intensive manufactures increasing significantly and the same upward trend in exports for high-skill manufactured goods. Overall, the changes are bigger for imports than exports. China increased its market share in the Emerging South more than the Emerging South countries raised their share in China. Regarding low-skill manufactures, for both the Rest of South and Emerging South, the importance of China as an export market diminished while as a

Table 5.8 Importance of China in Rest of South and Emerging South trade by product groups, 1990 vs. 2012

Share of China in Rest of South:

	Exports		Imports	
	1990	2012	1990	2012
Total	2.1%	12.0%	4.8%	17.6%
Primary	0.4%	12.3%	4.8%	4.1%
Nat-Resource Intensive	2.0%	17.5%	2.8%	11.8%
Low-Skill	4.1%	3.2%	14.2%	37.4%
Medium-Skill	11.1%	14.3%	2.8%	16.0%
High-Skill	5.9%	18.6%	2.2%	21.9%

Share of China in Emerging South:

	Exports		Imports	
	1990	2012	1990	2012
Total	10.3%	17.3%	10.3%	18.3%
Primary	3.5%	14.6%	5.5%	4.0%
Nat-Resource Intensive	7.1%	17.5%	4.7%	8.5%
Low-Skill	15.2%	9.0%	31.3%	34.8%
Medium-Skill	16.9%	11.2%	8.2%	14.1%
High-Skill	9.9%	30.3%	7.4%	32.3%

Note: The percentage values refer to the export and import share of China in total exports and imports of Rest of South and Emerging South countries. The total trade includes the product category of "other goods."

source of their imports increased. For the Emerging South, the same downward trend is visible for medium-skill manufactures exports.

The changes discussed above support arguments both for and against the growing importance of China for the South trade. Southern countries increasingly depend on China as a market for their exports, and this dependence makes them subject to the same criticisms as were raised by the North–South models, including a concern about these countries' increasing growth dependence on China, also about the terms of trade effects on primary goods versus high-skill manufactures. Likewise, China has greatly increased its export penetration into Southern countries, creating significant trade imbalances for the South.

It is also possible that the growing export penetration of Southern countries into the second-largest (and soon to be the largest) market in the world may have positive effects on their export structures and skills upgrading, but so far the evidence is not encouraging. Table 5.9 shows the structure of South–China trade in 1990 compared to 2012. Supporting the general findings in chapter 4 and those above, we see an increased primarization of exports from the Rest of South to China. In fact, 75 percent of these countries' exports to China were of primary goods in 2012, compared to only

Table 5.9 Structure of global South–China trade, 1990 vs. 2012

Rest of South

	Exports		Imports	
	1990	2012	1990	2012
Primary	13.0%	75.2%	14.1%	3.0%
Nat-Resource Intensive	18.4%	11.2%	9.1%	9.8%
Low-Skill	16.3%	1.7%	48.2%	37.8%
Medium-Skill	46.6%	8.7%	22.6%	34.1%
High-Skill	5.4%	2.0%	5.5%	14.3%

Emerging South

	Exports		Imports	
	1990	2012	1990	2012
Primary	8.5%	15.6%	8.1%	3.3%
Nat-Resource Intensive	12.2%	12.9%	7.7%	6.7%
Low-Skill	39.4%	9.0%	43.4%	21.8%
Medium-Skill	27.5%	15.8%	27.1%	24.2%
High-Skill	11.4%	42.8%	12.2%	40.4%

Note: Exports and imports are the percentage shares of each product group in total Southern exports and imports to and from China. Here and elsewhere the percentage totals do not add up to 100 percent because of the excluded category of "other" goods.

13 percent in 1990. The manufactures exports from the Rest of South fell radically across all skill levels, while the share of primary goods skyrocketed. For example, the share of medium-skill manufactures in exports from the Rest of South to China fell from 46.6 percent to 8.7 percent during this period. Likewise, the share of high-skill manufactures fell from 5.4 percent to 2 percent. Meanwhile, imports from China to the Rest of South also went through a structural change, with the share of primary goods, and low-skill manufactures falling and that of medium- and high-skill manufactures rising. These changes also reflect the structural transformation in the Chinese economy, as the country moved away from primary goods and resource-intensive and low -skill manufactures.

The second part of Table 5.9 shows the case of Emerging South economies, which went through a similar transformation in their economic structures to that of China. Therefore, it is no surprise that we see a similar upward trend in their exports of high-skill manufactures and a steep decline in low-skill manufactures. These changes are mirrored on the imports side, the share of high-skill manufactures increasing (as a reflection of increasing Chinese export sophistication) and medium- and low-skill goods decreasing. The trends reflected in this table confirm the findings in chapter 4, suggesting that the future for the Rest of South looks grim and that, when discussing South–South relations, we should be careful to separate this group of countries from

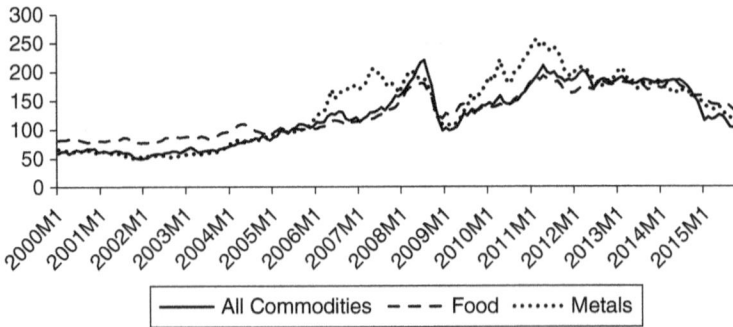

Figure 5.2 All commodities, food and metal commodity price index (2005=100), monthly, 2000:1–2015:9

Note: All commodities refer to all commodity price index, 2005 = 100, includes both fuel and non-fuel price indices. Food refers to food price index, 2005 = 100, includes cereal, vegetable oils, meat, seafood, sugar, bananas and oranges price indices. Metals refer to metals price index, 2005 = 100, includes copper, aluminum, iron ore, tin, nickel, zinc, lead and uranium price indices.
Source: IMF (2015). http://www.imf.org/external/np/res/commod/External_Data.xls Downloaded on 10/15/2015.

the Emerging South. These two groups of countries have radically different economic structures and are very likely to continue to diverge very much in the North–South pattern. Naturally, therefore, the impact of China should also be expected to differ between these two groups of countries.

As discussed above for the case of Chile and Latin America, the growing Chinese import demand for commodities led to significant price volatility. As shown in Figure 5.2 below, the average price index for all commodities increased by more than 250 percent between January 2000 and July 2008 (from an index value of 62 to 220), then fell to less than half of its value in March 2009 with an index value of 98. It then reached a peak of 210 in April 2011 before falling to 103 in September 2015. Likewise, the average price index for all metals increased by more than 200 percent from 66 to 201 between January 2000 and March 2008, then fell by almost half to 106 in March 2009, then again more than doubled to 256 in February 2011 before collapsing by half to 121 in September 2015. Average food prices show a similar trend.

Figure 5.3 shows the same trends as in Figures 5.1 and 5.2 but this time for four commodities of significance for many Southern countries. Cocoa prices, for example, increased from $918 per ton in 2000 to over $3,200 in 2015. Likewise, soybean prices increased from $118 in January 2000 to over $620 in August 2012 before falling to $324 in September 2012. Such sharp price swings, obviously, have a very strong destabilizing effect on the macro and microeconomic fundamentals in these countries, including monetary aggregates, fiscal policy and asset prices. The sudden fluctuations in oil and coffee prices are very similar.

Figure 5.4 shows the evolution of three metal prices in international markets since 2000, and here we encounter the same picture. Like other key commodity prices,

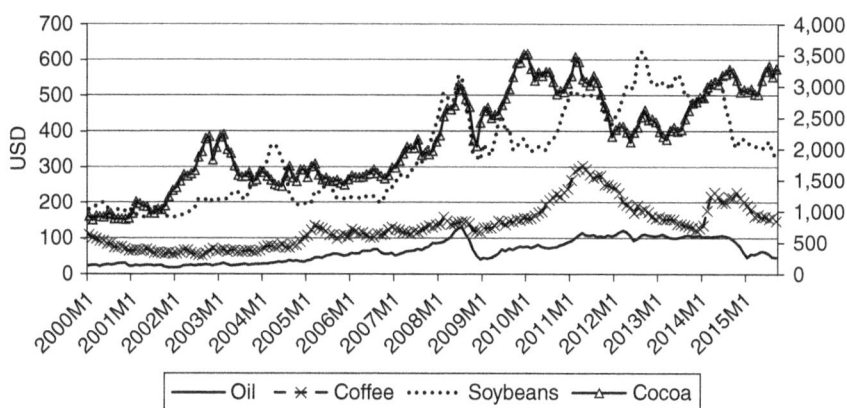

Figure 5.3 Oil, coffee, soybeans and cocoa prices, USD, monthly, 2000:1–2015:9
Note: Oil, coffee and soybeans are on the left axis, cocoa on the right axis. Oil refers USD per barrel, coffee refers US cents per pound, soybeans refers to USD per metric ton, cocoa refers to USD per metric ton.[26]
Source: IMF (2015). http://www.imf.org/external/np/res/commod/External_Data.xls Downloaded on 10/15/2015.

metal prices endured significant upward pressure in the 2000s, until a sudden crash after the 2008 Great Recession, recovering but then collapsing again after 2014. Iron ore prices, for example, increased from $12 per metric ton in January 2000 to a peak of $187 in February 2011 before falling to $52 in September 2015. What is so obvious in these three figures is that during this period international commodity prices display very erratic behavior, with high volatility being the norm rather than the exception.[27]

The reconfiguration of South–South trade relations has also made the division of labor within the South more pronounced. Many East Asian countries have become increasingly integrated with China in terms of their interdependence in trade, leading to the development of a triangular production network and significant intra-regional trade and investment flows. As the aggregate data above suggest, there is substantial division of labor in several industries between China and leading Southern countries such as Brazil. Countries in the Rest of South have become suppliers of primary commodities, agricultural, metal ores and oil, to China, intensifying their deindustrialization and

---

26. Oil refers to Dubai, medium, Fateh 32 API, fob Dubai crude oil (petroleum), Dubai Fateh Fateh 32 API, USD per barrel. Coffee refers to other mild Arabicas, International Coffee Organization New York cash price, ex-dock New York, US cents per pound. Soybeans refers to Soybeans, U.S. soybeans, Chicago Soybean futures contract (first contract forward) No. 2 yellow and par, USD per metric ton. Cocoa, right axis, refers to Cocoa beans, International Cocoa Organization cash price, CIF US and European ports, USD per metric ton.
27. As has become obvious to many, a significant part of these movements is caused by pure speculation conditional on expectations about the growth of the world economy and emerging markets, particularly that of China.

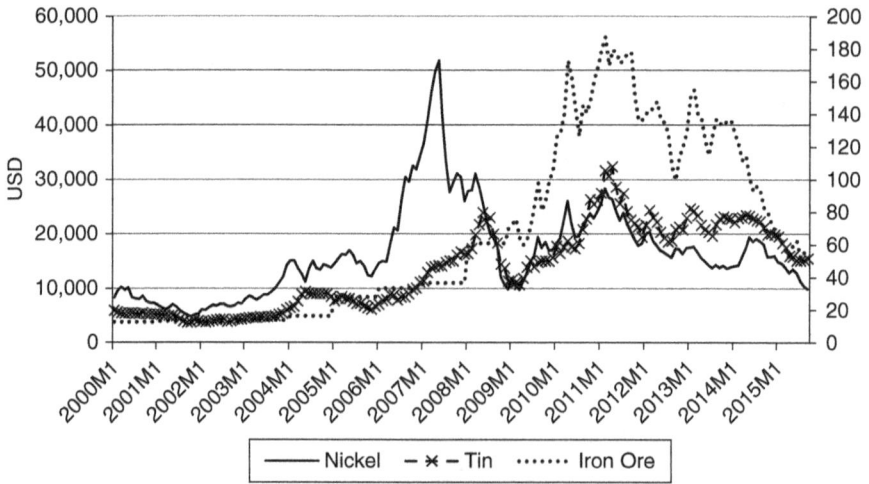

Figure 5.4 Nickel, tin and iron ore prices, USD, monthly, 2000:1–2015:9
Note: Nickel and tin are on the left axis, iron ore is on the right axis; all are USD per metric ton.[28]
Source: IMF (2015). http://www.imf.org/external/np/res/commod/External_Data.xls Downloaded on 10/15/2015.

triggering a primarization in their economies. The growing dependence of the South on the Chinese market also exposes these countries to fluctuations in the terms of trade when the Chinese economy goes through ups and downs, as has been the case since the 2008 global financial crisis.

5.6   Investment Flows and Financial Market Access

China emerged several years ago as a major investor in Southern countries, providing debt and equity flows as well as humanitarian and development aid. In 2010, for example, bilateral lending to Latin America from China reached $37 billion, surpassing that of the World Bank, the Inter-American Development Bank and the US Export-Import Bank combined (Gallagher et al., 2012). In addition, China's two major development banks, the China Development Bank and China Export-Import Bank, have become major sources of funding for infrastructure projects to secure oil and gas deliveries to China and for opening credit lines to foreign energy companies in exchange for long-term energy contracts (Manochehr and James, 2013). On the aid front, China has emerged as a key player since the mid-1990s, providing a total of $14.4 billion between 2010 and 2012 alone, of which 52 percent went to least developed countries of the South (State Council, 2014). While this is a smaller amount than provided by Northern donors such as the United States with $91.6 billion and the United Kingdom with $41 billion during the same period, it marks a significant change in China's approach to development

---

28. Tin is standard grade, LME spot price, USD per metric ton. Nickel is melting grade, LME spot price, CIF European ports, USD per metric ton. Iron ore, right axis, refers to China import Iron Ore Fines 62 percent FE spot (CFR Tianjin port), USD per metric ton.

in the South (OECD, 2015). Furthermore, the sectoral distribution of Chinese aid flows are substantially different than that of Northern donors. Reflecting China's own development experience, Chinese aid flows prioritize economic infrastructure and industry as necessary preconditions for economic development (Warmerdam, 2015). By the end of 2009, 61 percent of concessional loans from China to the South targeted economic infrastructure projects, particularly those in transport, power supply and broadcasting and telecommunications, and 16 percent targeted industry. In contrast, traditional DAC lenders target more social and administrative infrastructure, which received 42 percent of their total commitments while industry received only 1 percent (Warmerdam, 2015, p. 111).

China has also made a major push to increase intra-regional integration within Asia through developing infrastructure and expanding existing trade and finance linkages (Asian Development Bank and Asian Development Bank Institute, 2009).[29] Particularly significant developments that are spearheaded by China are the Asian Infrastructure Investment Bank (AIIB), established in 2015 by 57 countries to help finance infrastructure development in Asia with an authorized capital of $100 billion and headquartered in Beijing, and the New Development Bank BRICS (NDB BRICS), established by Brazil, Russia, India, China and South Africa in 2014 and headquartered in Shanghai with an authorized capital of $100 billion. The AIIB's purposes in Article 1 of its agreement are listed as to "(i) foster sustainable economic development, create wealth and improve infrastructure connectivity in Asia by investing in infrastructure and other productive sectors; and (ii) promote regional cooperation and partnership in addressing development challenges by working in close collaboration with other multilateral and bilateral development institutions." While 22 Asian countries established the AIIB, it now has 57 members, including both developed and developing countries.

Since its inception, Northern policy makers and economists saw the AIIB as a rival institution to the monopoly of the World Bank. For example, Japan opted out of its membership, either under US pressure or because of its suspicions about China's expanding role in the region, or both (*Economist*, 2015). Joseph Stiglitz has suggested that, in order to defend its global hegemony, the United States pressured other countries to stay away from the AIIB (Stiglitz, 2015). Even the former chief economist of the International Monetary Fund, Kenneth Rogoff, openly mocked the US criticisms of the AIIB and the leading role China played (Rogoff, 2015).[30] It is also possible to interpret the Northern

---

29. There are other efforts by China to develop its collaboration with Southern countries. For example, Saudi Arabia and China collaborated to build King Abdullah University of Science and Technology in Saudi Arabia, opened in 2009 with Chinese students making up the largest part of the student body, followed by Indian students.

30. The United States defends its opposition to AIIC on governance and transparency grounds, and fearing that China may use the bank to extend its economic and political muscle. As Rogoff (2015) rightly pointed out, it is difficult to preach good governance when the president of the World Bank is arbitrarily handpicked by the United States, and that of the IMF by the European Union.

objections to China's growing role in international finance as the usual resistance of a cartel to the rise of new world hegemon.

The BRICS bank claims to offer "an alternative to the existing US-dominated World Bank and International Monetary Fund," as stated by its president, K. V. Kamath. Unlike the one-dollar-one-vote management system of the World Bank and the IMF, the BRICS bank has adopted a one-country-one-vote system, allowing its members, particularly smaller Southern ones, equal voice in its management. Furthermore, unlike the IMF and the World Bank, which grant the United States a unilateral veto power, the BRICS allocates no veto power to any of its members.

The BRICS bank has put the South–South cooperation as the foremost of its goals, and in Article 1 of its agreement stated its primary purpose as "mobilizing resources for infrastructure and sustainable development projects in BRICS and other emerging economies and developing countries." We find it promising that the BRICS bank has emphasized the common development goals of the Emerging South and the Rest of South, without lumping them in one group. On the other hand, despite the expressed claim of its president, members of the BRICS Bank are not equal. According to its articles of agreement, the bank's president will be "elected from one of the founding members on a rotational basis" and the membership of the bank is conditional on an affirmative vote of four its five founding members together with an affirmative vote of two-thirds of the members. Furthermore, it is not clear whether the bank is actually based on a one-country, one-vote system. While it is true that each of the founding members has equal capital shares, and therefore equal votes, since "[T]he voting power of each member shall be equal to the number of its subscribed shares in the capital stock of the Bank," in actuality it is not much different from the operations of the IMF or the World Bank. In fact, Article 8 of the agreement clearly states that the capital share (i.e., the voting power) of new members will be decided by the founding members. The same article also states that the founding members will retain a control of 55 percent of the votes no matter how many new members are admitted. In the case of the Asian Infrastructure Investment Bank, we find a similar story, with China controlling just below 30 percent of total shares. We should also note that the mercantilist trade policies of the last 30 years have significantly contributed to this new interest on the part of China in Africa and elsewhere. China's heavy reliance on the US dollar for its international trade and its unprecedented accumulation of dollar reserves—more than a third of all global reserves as of 2014—have compelled China to diversify away from the dollar by investing in other countries' assets.

As discussed in chapter 4, six developing countries were among the top twenty foreign investors in the world in 2013, with China number two in global FDI inflows and number three in outflows. In fact, once we include Hong Kong, which was number four in inflows and number six in outflows, China becomes number two in both inflows and outflows.[31] Furthermore, South–South FDI flows accounted for 63–65 percent of all outflows from developing countries in 2010 (UNCTAD, 2011; WB, 2011). We also see an increased

---

31. When this book was in press, China and Hong Kong surpassed the United States and became number one and number two in FDI inflows in 2014 (UNCTAD, 2015a). Likewise, Hong Kong became number two in FDI outflows and China number three.

speed of merger and acquisitions (M&A) among Southern countries. In 2013, for example, 53 percent of global M&A flows came from developing countries, and of that number 72 percent went to other developing countries (UNCTAD, 2014: 8). In the case of Latin America and the Caribbean region, for example, in 2010 developing countries from Asia accounted for 68 percent of all M&A (more than three times their total accumulated investments in this region over the previous two decades), and intra-regional flows accounted for 17 percent, while developed countries accounted for only 12 percent of the total (UNCTAD, 2011: 59, 60). Overall, the share of developing country TNCs in this region increased from 8 percent in 2001 to 43 percent in 2010 (UNCTAD, 2011: 60). Likewise, it is reported that there were 1,673 investment projects from China in 50 African countries worth $75 billion in commitments (Strange et al., 2013).

In the case of FDI inflows, (mainland) China has increased its global share significantly, from less than 3 percent in 2000 to 8.5 percent in 2013. What is surprising, however, is that this increase came at the expense, not of the Rest of South, but of the North. In fact, the share of FDI inflows to China in global flows to the South remained almost flat with a slight increase from 12 percent to 13 percent between 1990 and 2013. In contrast, we see a further diversification of flows to the Southern countries with the share of top ten destination countries in global flows to the South falling from 90 percent to 67 percent. With regard to outflows, however, we continue to see a high concentration, with 10 Southern countries accounting for 80 percent of all outflows. China alone accounted for 17 percent of all Southern outflows in 2013, reaching $101 billion, third largest in the world.

The rise of China as a major investor in Southern economies has unlocked more possibilities for development planning and experimentation in the South. It has also increased competition and opened new credit channels in global financial markets, reducing the monopoly positions of Northern financial institutions (particularly the IMF and the World Bank) and private banks. Some evidence also suggests that Chinese lending comes with lower conditions (more on this later), and with lower borrowing costs (Gallagher et al., 2012).

However, the growing influence of China in FDI flows should not be exaggerated either. At the end of 2013, the total stock of Chinese foreign investments was $660 billion (in current prices) with over 87 percent of those investments being in South countries, a point emphasized in the press (Table 5.10). Yet, over 57 percent of its total FDI stock was in one country, Hong Kong, which is a specially administered region (SAR) of China. Once we exclude Hong Kong and Macau, another SAR, the share of the South drops to 28 percent. Overall, 68 percent of the total outward stock of FDI from China was in Asia (including Hong Kong) and 13.3 percent was in Latin America. Yet, even in the case of Latin America, two countries, the British Virgin Islands and the Cayman Islands—well-known tax-havens—were responsible for almost 90 percent of these Chinese overseas investments in that region. Despite the heavy coverage in the media, the share of Africa in total Chinese FDI stock was only 4 percent at the end of 2013 (China Statistical Yearbook, 2014).[32]

---

32. Of the remaining FDI stock, 8 percent was in Europe and 4 percent was in North America, 3 percent being in the United States alone.

Table 5.10 Outward FDI flows and stocks from China by region and country, percentage shares, 2013

	Flow	Stock
Asia	70.1%	67.70%
Hong Kong (SAR)	58.3%	57.10%
Africa	3.1%	4.0%
Europe	5.5%	8.0%
Latin America	13.3%	13.0%
Cayman Islands	8.6%	6.4%
British Virgin Islands	3.0%	5.1%
North America	4.5%	4.3%
United States	3.6%	3.3%
Oceania	3.4%	2.9%

Source: China Statistical Yearbook (2014).

As Table 5.10 shows, the flow numbers are not any different. Furthermore, in the case of Hong Kong, China appears as its top FDI destination, accounting for 55 percent of its total outward FDI stock (at book value) and 84 percent of its FDI outflows in 2013.[33] The next largest destination country for Hong Kong is the British Virgin Islands, which held 21 percent of its outward FDI stock and 6.4 percent of its outflows in 2013 (External Direct Investment Statistics of Hong Kong, 2014). It is highly likely that in both China and Hong Kong, the FDI flows to tax havens are a way for domestic firms to bypass financial regulations in China by investing in entities in those countries, which may actually be established by the very same firms.

We should not exaggerate the potential spillover effects from Chinese FDI to host economies, either. As shown in Table 5.11, manufacturing accounts for only a small percentage of Chinese investments abroad, in terms of both flows and stock. A majority of Chinese investments are concentrated in three sectors, leasing and business services, financial intermediation and mining, jointly accounting for 63.4 percent of all FDI stock abroad in 2013. The case of Hong Kong is also quite similar with the "investment and holding, real estate, professional and business services" category accounting for 80 percent of all its FDI outward stock (at book value) in 2013, while the share of manufacturing was less than 3 percent (External Direct Investment Statistics of Hong Kong, 2014).

5.6.1 Land Grabs: Myth or Reality?

FDI in agriculture, in both North–South and South–South directions, has triggered a public debate in recent years, although its share in global FDI flows remains small, (at less

---

33. The numbers exclude outward FDI to non-operating enterprises set up by Hong Kong companies in offshore financial centers. If we include those, then the share of China in Hong Kong's outward FDI stock and flows in 2013 drops to 41 percent and 48 percent while those of British Virgin Islands rise to 39 percent and 35 percent, respectively.

Table 5.11 Outward FDI flows and stocks from China by sector, percentage shares, 2013

% Share in flows		% Share in stocks	
Leasing and Business Services	25.1%	Leasing and Business Services	29.6%
Mining	23.0%	Financial Intermediation	17.7%
Financial Intermediation	14.0%	Mining	16.1%
Wholesale and Retail Trades	13.6%	Wholesale and Retail Trades	13.3%
Manufacturing	6.7%	Manufacturing	6.4%
Rest	17.6%	Rest	16.9%

Source: China Statistical Yearbook (2014).

than 1 percent of total FDI flows between 2003–2013 (World Bank, 2007; UNCTAD, 2015c). Particularly, responding to fast-growing home demand, both for final consumption and as input for biofuels and animal feed, rising import bills and high price volatility and erratic supply conditions, countries of the Emerging South, together with leading Northern countries, have become major investors in the agricultural sector in other Southern countries. China, for example, together with other countries—most notably Brazil but also the United Arab Emirates, Qatar, South Africa and Saudi Arabia—is either directly purchasing or signing long-term leases for significant amounts of land in the Rest of South. While foreign investment in agriculture, just as in other sectors, has the potential to boost productivity, create employment, increase capital formation and modernize agricultural sectors in Southern countries that are in dire need of new investment, serious questions remain as to its net effect on host economies, and many observers refer to such investments as modern-day land grabbing or recolonization (World Bank, 2007; UNCTAD, 2009).

The situation in Africa is particularly complicated by the question of whether China and other countries intend to turn the continent into a food basket and thereby ensure its own food security, as around half of the world's uncultivated arable land remains in Africa. Despite widespread food deprivation across Africa, countries such as Sudan and Mozambique are on the way to become food suppliers to leading Southern countries. For example, the ProSavana project, described by many as the largest land grab in Africa is a Brazil-Japan-Mozambique development project aiming at turning 85 million acres of savannah lands in the Nampula valley of Mozambique into mega soybean farms (Wise, 2014a, 2015). This project was conceived in the expectation of replicating Brazil's success in transforming its own savannah into productive agricultural land, but it also shows the limits of South–South cooperation. Despite the initial majestic claims, the project now appears much smaller, only 700 thousand hectares, and is facing significant obstacles, including local farmers' resistance to land grabbing and the accompanying displacement of inhabitants, as well as the incompatibility of land and the necessary seed and agricultural technology between the Nampula valley and Brazil's Cerrado region. Furthermore, as is the case in Mozambique, having a more democratic government and an activist citizenry may make it more difficult to implement such top-down mega projects in countries (Wise, 2015). Lack of transparency and the top-down nature of such South–South projects limit their applicability in democratic Southern countries.

Data as of October 2015 from the Land Matrix Project (2015), an independent land monitoring initiative, indicate that 1,069 transnational land agreements have been concluded since 2000, covering 96 million acres of land. Of the total number of negotiations, only seven have failed, and another 198 agreements are planned. Table 5.12 shows the top ten investor and host countries in terms of number of land deals that involve the acquisition of land through purchase, lease or concession, and that involve 200 or more hectares (494 acres). It is notable that half of the top ten investors are from the Emerging South (South Africa and the Republic of Korea rank 11th and 12th) and if we merge Hong Kong with mainland China, China appears as world number one with a total of 131 land deals, accounting for 9.4 percent of global total. These ten countries jointly account for 47.3 percent of a total of 1,389 land deals in the world. In terms of the number of deals, Indonesia and Cambodia are the top targets, accounting for over 20 percent of all such deals in the world. We should note that Southeast Asia, East Africa and South America appear to be the top destinations for global investors, with Southeast Asia appearing to be the world's number one, accounting for over 28 percent of global deals, followed by Eastern Africa with over 21 percent and South America with over 15 percent. If we treat Africa as a single unit, it accounts for over 42 percent of all land deals in 2015.

Table 5.13 shows the top ten crops that are involved in these land deals. As many feared would be the case, cash crops dominate the picture with palm oil, corn and rubber the top three, jointly responsible for more than a quarter of global land deals. The excessive dependence on monoculture, the likely contribution of these lands deals to food shortages, and the possibility of environmental devastation are the most publicized effects of this type of agricultural initiatives.

Table 5.14 replicates Table 5.12 but this time by land size rather than by number of land deals. The rankings change quite a bit this time with the United States appearing by far the biggest investor, accounting for 18 percent of all deals, followed by China and Malaysia. Among the top target countries, South Sudan, Papua New Guinea and Indonesia appear as the top three. Unfortunately, and unsurprisingly, quite a few of the target countries are also conflict zones, including South Sudan, DR Congo, Congo, Ukraine and Liberia.

Looking at the United States alone, we find that more than 29 percent of its concluded land deals are in one country, D.R. Congo (Table 5.15). Two countries, both conflict zones, D.R. Congo and South Sudan account for almost half of all US acquisitions (19 million acres in all) of land overseas.

Chinese land deals have quite a different target, mostly in Southeast Asia. The Philippines and Indonesia alone account for 26 percent and 14.5 percent of all Chinese land deals overseas (10 million acres in all), and the top four Asian countries account for more than 61 percent of all Chinese land deals overseas (Table 5.16). Despite all the discussion in the media and the criticism it continues to receive, China, at least on its own as the sole contract owner and not in a joint consortium, is not engaging in much "land

Table 5.12 Land run in the twenty-first century: top ten cross-border land acquisition agreements by investor and target country

	Investor country	Region	Deals (#)	%
1	UK	Northern Europe	110	7.9%
2	China	Eastern Asia	96	6.9%
3	Malaysia	Southeast Asia	96	6.9%
4	USA	North America	91	6.6%
5	India	South Asia	52	3.7%
6	Viet Nam	Southeast Asia	49	3.5%
7	Singapore	Southeast Asia	46	3.3%
8	Canada	North America	43	3.1%
9	France	Western Europe	39	2.8%
10	Hong Kong (China, SAR)	Eastern Asia	35	2.5%
	Total number of deals		1,389	47.3%
	Target country	Region	Deals (#)	%
1	Indonesia	Southeast Asia	118	11.0%
2	Cambodia	Southeast Asia	100	9.4%
3	Mozambique	Eastern Africa	72	6.7%
4	Ethiopia	Eastern Africa	60	5.6%
5	Lao PDR	Southeast Asia	55	5.1%
6	Brazil	South America	48	4.5%
7	Uruguay	South America	39	3.6%
8	Papua New Guinea	Melanesia	38	3.6%
9	Ghana	Western Africa	33	3.1%
10	UR Tanzania	Eastern Africa	31	2.9%
	Total number of deals	Northern Europe	1,069	55.6%

Note: % refers to the percentage share of each country in total land deals in the world. The *Total number of deals* refers to the sum of global land deals and the percentage share of top ten countries in that total.
Source: Land Matrix (2015), downloaded on October 16, 2015, and authors' calculations.

grabbing" in Africa. Furthermore, the share of agriculture in Chinese FDI outflows remain marginal, 1 percent of total FDI stock at the end of 2013.

We also find that almost all but two of 135 Chinese land deals are through leasing or concession while half the time those of the United States are through direct purchase. China also appears to be more likely to form partnerships with target countries while the United States is unilateral in its acquisitions in all cases.

Despite its small share in global investment flows, the modern version of land grabbing in both North–South and South–South directions may create serious problems for host countries. First of all, as Table 5.13 shows, most crops produced in these lands are not for staple food production but are either for biofuel or animal feed, and they are not intended for the domestic consumers, who continue to struggle to meet their daily calorie needs. Therefore, food security remains a serious issue for these home countries. Second, serious doubts remain as to how many linkages—agricultural modernization, technology and know-how transfer, supply-chain management improvement,

Table 5.13 Top ten crops in cross-border land deals

	Crop	Deals (#)	%
1	Oil palm	208	11.1%
2	Corn (Maize)	152	8.1%
3	Rubber	134	7.1%
4	Soya Beans	109	5.8%
5	Jatropha	91	4.9%
6	Wheat	91	4.9%
7	Sugar Cane	87	4.6%
8	Rice	77	4.1%
9	Trees	68	3.6%
10	Eucalyptus	62	3.3%
Total			57.5%

Source: Land Matrix (2015) and authors' calculations.

Table 5.14 Top ten investor and target countries in cross-border land deals, by million acres

	Targets	Land size (million acres)	%	Investors	Land size (million acres)	%
1	South Sudan	10.1	9.7%	USA	19.0	18.2%
2	Papua New Guinea	9.3	8.9%	China	10.0	9.6%
3	Indonesia	8.5	8.1%	Malaysia	7.5	7.2%
4	DR Congo	6.8	6.5%	Singapore	6.8	6.5%
5	Congo	5.3	5.1%	UAE	6.1	5.9%
6	Mozambique	5.3	5.0%	India	5.7	5.5%
7	Russia	4.4	4.2%	UK	5.1	4.9%
8	Ukraine	4.2	4.1%	Canada	4.5	4.3%
9	Brazil	3.9	3.8%	Saudi Arabia	3.8	3.6%
10	Liberia	3.7	3.5%	Rep. Korea	3.4	3.2%

Note: We use only concluded cross-border land deals and only those for which the investor's nationality is known. We also exclude those cases where more than one investor country, other than target country, is involved. Land size refers to million acres. % refers to the percentage share of referring country in world total. China includes Hong Kong.
Source: Land Matrix (2015) and authors' calculations.

introduction of new and diversified commercial crops, developing marketing and distribution channels, market access, job creation, shifting from subsistence to commercial farming and so forth—these foreign investments have with the local economies. Empirical evidence is simply lacking on any of these fronts (World Bank, 2007, 2010; UNCTAD, 2009; Deininger and Byerleee, 2011.). Third, in the absence of democratic governance or transparency in and between target and investor countries, these projects are likely to displace small farmers and local communities. The host-country institutional environment, therefore, is a significant determinant of the distribution of

Table 5.15 Top five US cross-border land deals by target country

	Target country	Land size	%
1	D.R. Congo	5.6	29.3%
2	Papua New Guinea	5.0	26.6%
3	South Sudan	3.5	18.2%
4	Ukraine	1.1	6.0%
5	Argentina	0.6	3.2%

Note: Land size is in millions of acres. % refers to the percentage share of referring country in total US land deals where the United States is the sole contract owner.

Table 5.16 Top five Chinese cross-border land deals by target country

	Target country	Land size	%
1	Philippines	2.6	26.1%
2	Indonesia	1.4	14.5%
3	Papua New Guinea	1.2	12.3%
4	Viet Nam	0.9	8.7%
5	Argentina	0.8	8.3%

Note: China includes Hong Kong. % refers to the percentage share of referring country in total Chinese land deals where China is the sole contract owner.

economic benefits. Last but not least, the fast and furious nature of these foreign investment projects raises doubts about the quality and reliability of environmental footprint analyses, if any, undertaken in these sites.[34]

5.7 South–South Integration and Institutional Development

As discussed in the previous four chapters, the debates on the effects of South–South and North–South interactions are largely confined to trade, and to a lesser extent finance. As a result, most of the academic discourse on the whole subject of development has ignored the indirect effects, such as those on institutions, democracy and capacity building. There is, however, a growing concern, mostly in Northern policy circles, regarding the political and institutional effects of growing South–South trade and finance on host countries. In this section we will be discussing this issue and trying to provide answers to questions about the impacts of increasing South–South

---

34. For further a discussion, see Deininger and Byerlee (2011), Wise (2014a, 2014b, 2014c, 2015). Particularly, see UNCTAD (2009) for an in-depth analysis of the effects of FDI in agricultural sectors in developing countries.

financial flows on various elements of institutional development, including democratization, increased transparency, attacks on corruption, promotion of human rights and rule of law?

While there is a growing consensus in economics that institutions matter for long-run development and growth, this discussion has a Eurocentric bias towards European–North American institutions. While the direction of causality is open to debate, it is generally accepted that development and growth go hand in hand with the parallel development of social, legal and political institutions. A corollary to this theory is that the Northern countries have better institutions than the Southern ones do, and therefore Southern countries need to harmonize their institutions with those of Northern ones, reducing heterogeneity between the two.[35] Nevertheless, there is no consensus on what causes institutional heterogeneity across countries. Broadly speaking, there are two approaches to understanding the causes of institutional change—"top-down" and "bottom-up" (Easterly, 2008). While the top-down approach sees institutions as creations of political actors, the bottom-up sees them as a product of historical, cultural and environmental factors with a high level of path-dependency. Not surprisingly, these two views have quite different implications regarding the speed at which institutions change. According to the top-down view, change can be fast and furious, done at any time once there is the will. The bottom-up view, however, sees transition as evolutionary rather than revolutionary (Easterly, 2006).

Academic work on the bottom-up view of institutions focuses on the effects of a natural resource base (Leite and Weidmann, 1999; Ades and Di Tella, 1999); economic openness (Laffont and N'Guessan, 1999; Ades and Di Tella, 1999, Rigobon and Rodrik, 2005); colonial institutions (Acemoglu et al., 2001, 2005) and slave trade (Nunn and Wanchekon, 2011); initial wealth (Engerman and Sokoloff, 2002); ethnic structures (Michalopoulos and Papaioannou, 2013) and ethnic fragmentation (Easterly and Levine, 1997); pre-colonial governance structures (Gennaioli and Rainer, 2007, Hariri, 2012); and past rulers and governments (Caselli and Morelli, 2004).

In contrast, the top-down view explores the effects of domestic as well as international actors on institutions. Among the international actors, the World Bank and the IMF have long advocated and pushed for top-down changes through structural adjustment programs (based on the first and second Washington Consensus) in member-country institutions through their conditionality requirements. A related example of the top-down approach is shock therapy, as applied in former Soviet Union countries. As discussed in chapters 2 and 3, international investment treaties (BITs) and preferential trade agreements (PTAs) have also been instrumental in initiating top-down institutional change (Dahi and Demir, 2013; Thrasher and Gallagher, 2008; UNCTAD, 2011, 2012, 2015c; Neumayer and Spess, 2005; Busse et al., 2010; Yackee, 2009). Regional

---

35. For a review of this long (and obviously Eurocentric) literature, see, for example, Shleifer and Vishny (1993); Knack and Keefer (1995), Wei (1997) La Porta et al. (1998), Kaufmann et al. (1999b); Rodrik (1999), Hall and Jones (1999), Acemoglu et al. (2001, 2002), Levchenko (2007), Alfaro et al. (2008).

unions, such as the European Union, have also been in for reducing institutional heterogeneity through a centralized decision making mechanism.

The implication of the top-down approach is that a universal set of "correct" institutions produces the best outcomes for long-run development and growth. Moreover, in this view it is also commonly agreed that the frontier for these correct institutions is established by Western European and North American countries—so much so that theirs are taken as the international gold standard.[36] The original Washington Consensus, as well as the revised version, is a byproduct of this belief. In contrast, bottom-up economists are more prepared to accept that there may be myriad correct institutions, and that different societies may flourish using diverse sets of institutions without ever converging upon a single standard (Rodrik, 1996, 2006, 2008). They argue further that we may not even know what it is that we do not know about the best path to development in all cases and that the only way to find it is through experimentation (Rodrik, 2001, 2004, 2005).[37] The mainstream research on this topic used to assume that good institutions would appear effortlessly from the magical hat of growth. Both the top-down and bottom-up view, however, see institutional development as a necessary precondition of growth; they just disagree how to achieve that precondition. There is also substantial confusion over whether or not to give different priority to different institutions, and whether or not all institutions are equally significant for long-run growth. Furthermore, since most of the key institutional reforms that are advocated today for the South were absent in Western Europe and North America until those regions were already developed, the debate about which institutions precede development, and therefore which is cause and which is effect becomes even more complex (Chang, 2000, 2008).

In global economic relations, developed countries as well as bilateral and multilateral institutions controlled by those countries[38] are known to adopt the top-down approach with strong conditionality requirements in their economic exchanges with foreign governments. In developed countries, legal barriers also put pressure on foreign governments to synchronize their regulatory and institutional environment with those of the home economies. For example, the US Foreign Corrupt Practices Act of 1977 bans US firms from bribing foreign governments or businesses. Meanwhile, no such law exists in China or India. Likewise, 34 of the 40 countries that have signed the

---

36. For example, legal code, based on British, French, German or Scandinavian code has long been pointed out as a major source of institutional and economic development and comparative advantage. The same is true for the effects of other Western style institutions.

37. We take the liberty of quoting the following prophetic words from Rodrik (2001, p. 11): "One needs to guard against the common journalistic error of supposing that one set of institutional arrangements must dominate the others in terms of overall performance. Hence the fads of the decade: with its low unemployment, high growth and thriving culture, Europe was the continent to emulate throughout much of the 1970s; during the trade-conscious 1980s, Japan became the exemplar of choice; and the 1990s have been the decade of US-style freewheeling capitalism. It is anybody's guess which set of countries will capture the imagination *once the effects of the correction of the US stock market play themselves out*" (italics added).

38. IMF and WB are usually considered Northern country institutions, as developed countries control the majority of votes.

OECD Anti-Bribery Convention of 1997 are OECD members.[39] In addition to their direct effects, such legal conditions may have indirect effects, encouraging developing countries to adopt similar standards if they want to expand their economic relations with developed countries.

In contrast, developing countries reportedly attach fewer, if any, conditionality requirements to their economic exchanges with other developing countries. As shown in chapter 2, they are also much less aggressive bringing charges against each other in international courts on trade and investment disputes. One cause for this difference may be increasing rivalry between key emerging markets, such as those of China and Brazil, and the West in gaining access to Southern countries, either for natural resources or for market access. Another may be the reported comparative advantage of developing country investors, in their ability to operate in poor institutional environments.[40] Like supporters of the bottom-up view, China has often justified its lack of conditionality requirements as respecting national sovereignty—a hint at the Bandung Conference principles—by not imposing its institutions on their partner governments. Furthermore, Chinese officials have been quite vocal in calling on Southern countries to explore freely their "diversified paths of development," reflecting their "unique characteristics" (Ministry of Foreign Affairs of China, 2015). Southern countries may also be understood to operate on the implicit understanding that South–South interactions do not carry imperialistic overtones, as is assumed to be the case in North–South interactions.[41] Some critics also argue that the faster disbursement of funds from Emerging South investors and donors makes these sources of funding more efficient than the slow Northern governments, which take significantly longer to move through the long channel of bureaucracy.

The Emerging South countries, which have become a major source of investment, development finance and aid for the South also appear to bypass existing reporting systems for transparency, such as the OECD's Creditor Reporting System or the International Aid Transparency Initiative. For example, at the 2011 High Level Forum on Aid Effectiveness in Busan, South Korea, the Northern and the Southern governments were clearly divided, the former arguing that the new Southern actors, such as

---

39. Six non-member countries are Argentina, Brazil, Bulgaria, Colombia, Russia and South Africa.

40. Cuervo-Cazurra and Genc (2008), Darby et al. (2010); Aleksynska and Havrylchyk (2013) and Demir and Hu (2015) explore the idea that investors in developing countries have a comparative advantage in dealing with challenging institutional and political environments because of their own similar experiences at home. This advantage may help them overcome their disadvantaged position in other areas, including technology, operational and management capabilities, experience, internal and external financing sources (including international debt and equity markets), marketing and advertisement and size.

41. In a recent high-level roundtable on South–South Cooperation, co-hosted by China and the United Nations at the UN headquarters in New York, Chinese president Xi said that "South–South cooperation, as a great pioneering measure uniting the developing nations together for self-improvement, is featured by equality, mutual trust, mutual benefit, win-win result, solidarity and mutual assistance" (Ministry of Foreign Affairs of China, 2015).

China and Brazil, need to increase transparency regarding their aid activities, while the Southern governments argued that South–South cooperation engagements are structurally different from Northern aid flows and therefore not subject to the traditional aid principles (Fraeters, 2011; Tran, 2012; Strange et al., 2013). China even went so far as to argue explicitly that the "principle of transparency should apply to North–South cooperation, but [...] it should not be seen as a standard for South–South cooperation" (Tran, 2011).[42]

As a result of this lack of conditionality, South–South economic exchanges, particularly those involving financial flows, are singled out by the conventional wisdom of Western politicians, neoclassical economists, Eurocentric political pundits and others as undermining Western efforts to improve the institutional settings of developing countries. China, for example, has frequently been accused by the West of "neglecting human rights offences in recipient nations, supporting corrupt authoritarian regimes," undermining environmental and labor standards, and thereby damaging Northern countries' efforts to improve the institutional quality and economic and political infrastructure of developing countries (Strange et al., 2013; *Economist*, 2006; Warmerdam, 2012; Mbaye, 2011; Dreher et al., 2015a, 2015c).[43] According to this narrative, China's quest for energy resources has propelled it to extend lifelines to rogue states and dictatorial regimes such as that of Sudan and the Central African Republic.[44] For example, although a military coup in the Central African Republic was condemned in the West, China's government offered the new government an interest-free loan and a state visit.[45] Similarly, China

---

42. Strange et al. (2013) from *AidData* provides the most comprehensive account of Chinese official investment activities in Africa, including a discussion of pros and cons of these activities.
43. For further discussion, see Mbaye (2011), Graham-Harrison (2009), Strange et al. (2013). Moreover, the 2013 Human Development Report of UNDP (titled *The Rise of the South*) includes an entire chapter on the issue of re-aligning the institutional structures of the South with the North, including those involving trade policy, business environment, transparency and rule of law.
44. In a recent executive briefing from the US International Trade Commission, Butcher and Yuan (2015) argued that Chinese official development assistance to Africa is "driven mainly by China's desire to secure natural resources in Africa."
45. There is a growing criticism that China is trying to expand its influence and export its cultural values to other Southern countries through cultural and educational initiatives. For example, the Confucius Institutes, founded in 2004 and funded and supervised by the government of China, have recently been a center of attention. There are currently 438 Confucius Institutes in 115 countries, and a fifth of them, numbering 95, are in the United States. Among the Southern countries, South Korea (with 20) and Russia (with 18) are at the top of the list (as of June 2015). The main criticism of the Confucius Institutes centers on the suppression of freedom of speech, as these ostensibly educational institutions are under the direct control of the Chinese government. Having statements by Politburo members such as those by Li Changchun, who famously announced that Confucius institutes are "an important part of China's overseas propaganda setup" do not help much to reduce their image as being Trojan Horses. As Sahlins (2013) put it, the close control of these institutes "effectively stipulates that students will acquire their knowledge of China only in ways acceptable to the Chinese state." Suppression of free speech on issues of human-rights violations in China, environmental issues, democracy movements, or criticisms of the Communist Party, and so

and Russia have supplied arms to the Sudanese government, even while it was being condemned for atrocities in Darfur and elsewhere. Likewise, Turkey invited the president of Sudan, Omar al-Bashir, to Ankara when the International Criminal Court was prosecuting him for war crimes and genocide in Darfur.

Another reason why Northern and Southern investors may have different effects on Southern institutions is the demonstration and professionalization effect. Through their demonstration of ethical business conduct and raising the bar for professionalism and managerial skills demanded of their employees, the MNCs can introduce new business practices that "challenge the legitimacy of existing patterns and stimulate debates on better business practice in the host country" (Kwok and Tadesse, 2006). There may also be structural reasons why the effects of FDI flows may differ depending on the direction of those flows. For example, for better or worse, greater institutional and cultural similarity, not to mention technological and preference structures, among Southern countries (as discussed in chapter 3) may increase the potential for institutional and governance spillovers from foreign firms.

However, it is also possible that increasing financial flows, independent of where they come from, may worsen the institutional quality in host countries. Robertson and Watson (2004) and Kwok and Tadesse (2006), for example, argue that FDI may result in more corruption in recipient countries by increasing the total supply of money (i.e., bribery potential) and increasing the cutthroat competition by foreign investors for host country natural resources and market access.

Despite the widespread criticism of Southern governments by various observers in the North, however, very little empirical evidence supports the view that, whether through trade or through financial flows, including aid, developed countries have had any positive effect on host country institutions. Likewise, there is no evidence showing that Southern governments act any differently from their Northern counterparts when it comes to their motivations for humanitarian aid disbursements (Dreher et al., 2011, 2015a, 2015b, 2015c). On the contrary, some evidence shows that developed countries have often rewarded bad behavior in developing countries. Easterly and Pfutze (2013), for example, convincingly show that the percentage of aid from the North going to corrupt countries actually increased during the 1990s as those countries became more corrupt. Furthermore, multilateral institutions that are controlled by developing countries, such as the African Development Bank, are found be favoring corrupt countries less, in their financial aid programs, than do many developed countries, including the United States, the United Kingdom and Japan (Easterly and Pfutze, 2008). Regarding the example set by aid agencies themselves on issues such as transparency, many Western multilateral agencies reportedly perform worse than their developing-country counterparts. These authors have found that the African Development Bank and the Asian Development Bank have a higher level of transparency in their operations than the

---

forth, is reported to be the way of life in these institutes. Similar objections have arisen to similar institutes funded by other Southern governments with the goal of advancing their own interests. For example, the Yunus Emre institute of Turkey serves a similar purpose.

Nordic Development Fund, the European Bank for Reconstruction and Development, HellenicAid, IrishAid, Japan's Ministry of Foreign Affairs, New Zealand Aid, the Spanish Agency for International Cooperation, the German Development Bank, or the IMF.

Furthermore, even the economics orthodoxy acknowledges that Western countries often intervene in developing countries for their own economic benefits. Berger et al. (2013), for example, provide strong evidence that the United States used its political influence through CIA interventions in developing countries during the Cold War years to increase US export penetration in these countries. The same finding applies to developed countries' motivations for development aid disbursements (Dreher et al., 2011, 2015a, 2015b, 2015c). Like the pot calling the kettle black, the situation represents hypocrisy in terms of both the historical legacy of Europe and current US and European policy, which has created alliances with human rights abusers and international law violators around the world. Still, it is important to keep in mind that the demand for accountable, democratic and effective governance is first and foremost a demand by social movements and civil society in the developing countries themselves.

Regarding Chinese official flows to Africa, based on a media-based data gathering exercise, Strange et al. (2013) found that the top three sectors are government and civil society, health and education. In other words, China appears to be doing what the Northern governments have claimed to be doing themselves.[46] Meanwhile, contrary to what is usually suggested by the Northern politicians and media pundits, "industry, mining and construction" ranks only 14th on China's list. Also, in a comparison of official flows to Africa, for the United States the number one recipient is Egypt; for the rest of the OECD development assistance committee (DAC) countries combined it is Nigeria. This pattern most likely reflects these respective governments' foreign policy goals, geopolitics in the case of Egypt and oil in the case of Nigeria and in both cases has clearly not resulted in market improvement in institutions, governance, human rights, or democracy.[47] In contrast, the top recipient from China is Ghana, a major cocoa producer that has no military or security connections with China. Even for China, Nigeria ranks second, followed by Sudan, but Chinese official finance flows appear to be scattered all over Africa with no clear concentration in any particular region, except that they are lower for those countries that have recognized Taiwan. Sectoral distribution of these flows from China follows no clear pattern either, with the exception of "general environmental protection" (Strange et al., 2013, p. 35).[48]

---

46. These three items rank much lower in aid priorities for many DAC countries and the World Bank. For example, in the case of the United States, health and education, respectively, received only 5.4 percent and 3.3 percent of the total US aid budget in 2013 (OECD, 2015b).

47. It is no surprise that the choice of top recipients of aid from the United States is based on its strategic interests. During the 1990s, 2000s and 2010s, the countries that were frequently at the top of the list were Israel, Egypt, Iraq and Afghanistan.

48. Also see Geda and Meskel (2010) for a case study of China in Ethiopia.

In a similar study focusing on the impact of Chinese financial flows to Latin America, Gallagher et al. (2012) find that the sets of recipient countries and sectors differ between those receiving funds from China and those depending on more traditional lenders such as international financial institutions and Western banks. For example, for China, the top three borrowers are Venezuela, Brazil and Argentina, while for the World Bank they are Brazil, Mexico and Argentina. Likewise, housing and infrastructure sectors receive the lion's share from Chinese lending, while the public administration sector receives the most from World Bank. The sectoral distribution of concessional loans from China to the rest of the world shows a similar pattern with "economic infrastructure" receiving 61 percent and "energy and natural resource development" receiving only 8.9 percent of the total at the end of 2009. In contrast, during the same period, economic infrastructure received less than 1percent of aid commitments from the traditional DAC countries (Warmerdam, 2015, pp. 112–13). Gallagher et al. (2012) also find that Chinese lenders attach no conditions to borrowing governments, but they require repurchase agreements. However, these agreements show that China Development Bank loans may be more relaxed regarding environmental standards. Independent monitoring and review, as well as public consultation with communities affected by development projects, are not included in the guidelines of the China Development Bank. Moreover, Chinese investment and development assistance activities in the South are decidedly less than transparent. Therefore, we believe, the concerns regarding the impact of Chinese investment activities in the South will only increase in the coming years, and rightly so.

With regard to the effects of financial flows on institutional development, however, Kwok and Tadesse (2006) and Demir (2016) are the only studies we are aware of that have explored the topic empirically. Kwok and Tadesse (2006) report that aggregate FDI flows have a significantly negative effect on host-country corruption levels. Demir (2016) empirically tests the validity of Northern criticism regarding the institutional effects of South–South FDI flows, by exploring the following two questions: Do bilateral FDI flows narrow the institutional development gaps between home and host countries? And is there any difference between the effects of Northern and of Southern investors on institutional change in host countries? The empirical results suggest that the institutional development effects of bilateral FDI flows from developed to developing countries, as well as those from developing to developing countries, are not significant and are not different from each other. In either case, no significant convergence or divergence effect of FDI flows on the institutional development gap between host and home countries is apparent, and neither is any significant effect of aggregated North–South FDI flows on host country institutions. However, some evidence suggests that aggregate South–South flows have a significantly negative effect on host country institutions. Also South–South FDI flows may be harmful to institutional development in host countries that are rich in natural resources. A similar exercise on the trade side is lacking.[49] While ample evidence suggests that institutions matter for trade and even for trade structure

---

49. International trade not only can diffuse cultural and institutional patterns globally, but also may be more effective in harmonizing institutional structures between two countries.

(Levchenko, 2013), the research has so far tested only whether trade openness is a significant determinant of institutional change.

Measuring of institutional development is not an easy task. Acemoglu et al. (2002, 2005), among others, argue that institutional development encompasses overlapping economic and political institutions, and that it includes various degrees of development of government bureaucracy, law and order, civil institutions, democracy, level of corruption, and so forth. To proxy all these different aspects of institutional development, we use the International Country Risk Guide (ICRG), a political risk rating constructed by the for-profit organization, Political Risk Services. The ICRG rating has several advantages over other institutional quality measures. First, it exhibits ample variation within and between countries (i.e., it is time- and cross-section variant). Second, it has been reported for most countries since 1984.[50] The ICRG is determined by a composite index that includes political, legal and bureaucratic institutions and that takes account of government stability, socioeconomic conditions, the country's investment profile, internal conflict, external conflict, corruption, involvement of the military in politics, the role of religion in politics, law and order, ethnic tensions, democratic accountability and bureaucracy quality. It ranges from 0 to 100, with 100 reflecting the best institutional environment.

We can use the ICRG index to compare the level of institutional development between countries in the North and the South. To this end, we use the following method from Kogut and Singh (1988), which measures weighted institutional distance between two countries, i and j, along 12 dimensions:

$$Institutional\ Development\ Gap\left(Inst\right) = \frac{1}{12}\sum_{d=1}^{12}\left(Inst_{dit} - Inst_{djt}\right)^2 / V_d$$

where d indicates the dimensions of the index; V_d indicates the variance of the dth dimension; $Inst_{dit}$ and $Inst_{djt}$ refer to the institutional quality index of order d for country i and j at time t.

Figure 5.5 displays the evolution of average institutional development (based on a simple average of all 12 components) in the Rest of South, the Emerging South and the North. As evident from this figure, the North averages a higher institutional development score and greater homogeneity, followed by the Emerging South, while the Rest of South has the lowest level of institutional development. Figure 5.6 shows the average institutional distance, based on the Kogut and Singh (1988) method above, in five directions. The institutional distance is the lowest between developed country pairs and the highest between the Rest of South and the North. The institutional distance is significantly lower between Emerging South pairs than between those in the Rest of South. Interestingly, the distance within the Rest of South, and between the Rest of South and the Emerging South, appear almost identical, suggesting that the

---

50. There is a high level of correlation between the ICRG and various other ratings such as Polity IV, Transparency International and so forth.

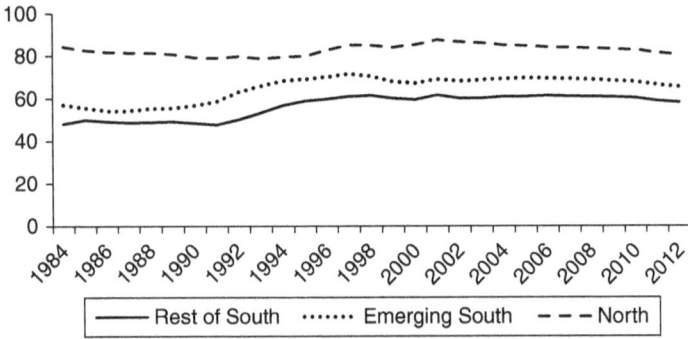

Figure 5.5 Average institutional development in the South vs. the North, 1984–2012
Note: The values refer to the average institutional development for 67 Rest of South, 50 Emerging
South and 23 North countries.
Source: For Figures 5.5–5.6, PRS and authors' calculations.

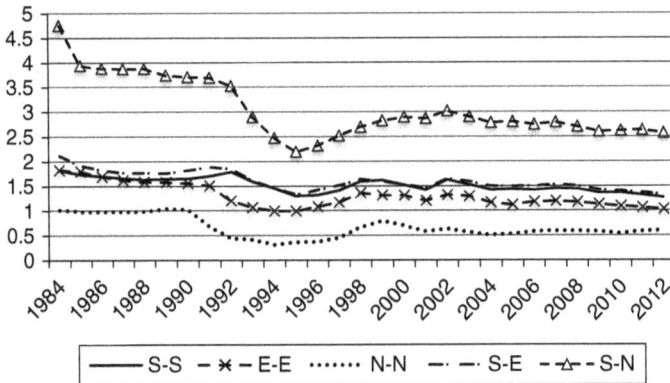

Figure 5.6 Institutional distance across countries, South vs. North, 1984–2012
Note: The values refer to bilateral institutional distance (measured by Kogut and Singh's (1988) method)
between countries that had a trading relationship (as reported by the IMF DOTS) in a given year. S,
E and N refer to the Rest of South, the Emerging South and the North.

institutional heterogeneity within the Rest of South is similar to the one found between
the Emerging South and the Rest of South. The heterogeneity within the Emerging
South, however, appears to be lower, as shown by the lower institutional distance in
that direction. We also see this heterogeneity in the simple variation level (measured by
the standard deviation), which is significantly higher among Southern countries (13.95),
than within the Emerging South (10.86) or the North (8.35).

As discussed in this and previous chapters, the higher level of institutional similarity
among South countries, compared to the lower level between countries of the South and
of the North, together with the closer proximity of technological and preference structures within the South may promote positive spillovers through economic exchanges in
trade and finance. This similarity in institutions may also facilitate capabilities-sharing
and know-how transfer, and it may enhance policy coordination among Southern

countries. Furthermore, there is no denying that increasing donor competition and the availability of a larger pool of financial flows, including both debt and equity, allows developing countries to shop around for the best deal regarding their own interests and their development programs (Warmerdam, 2015). Furthermore, the new multipolar investment and aid landscape may facilitate the acceptance of a more pluralistic attitude by Northern policy makers towards institutions within the South, and it may allow for experimentation as to what works best.

5.8 South–South Exchanges and New Developmentalism: A Policy Framework

In this section we present a general policy framework to analyze the rise in South–South relations and to consider how these relations may promote greater economic development. This framework builds on our own work along with the work of other authors, particularly Kaplinsky (2008) in analyzing China–Africa relations.

Table 5.17 shows eight transmission channels of South–South relations that have a direct impact on development.[51] As discussed earlier in the chapter, countries hoping to forge a new-developmentalist path will focus on industrial policy, experimentation, knowledge spillovers, human capital and technological acquisition, governance and institutions building. The rise of the Emerging South presents all South countries with opportunities for new partnerships in all those domains. However, taking advantage of those opportunities must be purposeful, and it should not be left to the whims of the market to decide. South–South partnerships and investment and trade agreements, not unfettered free trade, are the answer. The conceptual framework developed below provides a road map for key issues that both the Emerging South and the Rest of South should consider when contemplating expanding South–South relations.

5.8.1 Trade

As discussed in chapters 3 and 4, South–South trade in merchandise goods has increased steadily since the early 1990s, reaching 31 percent of world trade and 58 percent of total Southern trade in 2013. This trade comes with the potential to help Southern countries climb the development ladder, as it is increasingly skill-intensive. An increasing share of Southern manufactures exports is targeted to other Southern countries: from 42 percent in 1995 to 53 percent in 2009. Additionally, South–South trade involves increasing concentration of manufactured goods, reaching 23 percent of world manufactures trade in 2009, up from its 1995 level of 13 percent, and the skill intensity of those manufactures is increasing as well. Theoretically speaking, South–South trade in manufactures, particularly skill-intensive ones, holds the promise of industrial upgrading. Both as intermediate products and as final consumer goods, Southern manufactures are also

---

51. Kaplinsky (2008) includes aid and migrants. We included aid under financial flows (investment/capital) and leave out the issue of migrants, focusing instead on domestic labor standards as a more generalizable issue.

Table 5.17 Framework for assessing South–South relations

	Complementary	Competitive
1. Trade		
2. Technology transfer		
3. Investment/Capital flows		
4. Institutional development		
5. Trade and Investment Agreements & Policy Space		
6. Labor		
7. Environment		
8. Global governance		

Table 5.18 Share of Southern exports by product groups in world trade in 2012

	Emerging South	Rest of South	China
Number of countries	53	154	
% Share in world exports in			
Primary goods	43.1%	22.7%	2.0%
Res-Intense-Man	41.1%	3.3%	6.6%
Low	56.8%	2.8%	30.1%
Medium	35.8%	1.4%	10.3%
High	55.5%	0.4%	24.8%
Total manufactures	45.5%	7.9%	16.8%

Source: Authors' calculations based on COMTRADE data from MIT Media Lab (2015).

likely to be more appropriate for other Southern consumers and producers, particularly those at similar income levels. Furthermore, growing South–South trade can reduce Southern growth dependence on the North.

Nevertheless, as shown earlier in this and previous chapters, there are great imbalances in South–South trade. We believe the term "South–South" itself is no longer meaningful as an analytical category to describe Southern trade relations, given the great divergence between Emerging South and the Rest of South countries. As Table 5.18 shows, in 2012, 53 Emerging South countries controlled 45 percent of world manufactures trade and 55.5 percent of high-skill manufactures trade. In contrast, the share of 154 Rest of South countries in world manufactured goods trade was less than 8 percent, and their share in high-skill manufactures was even smaller, a bare 0.4 percent. In fact, China alone produced 65 times more high-skill manufactures than all those 154 countries combined. Furthermore, most of South–South trade—75 percent—in manufactures is between Emerging South countries. The Rest of South also has a very high concentration of its exports in a few commodities and in a few markets. In addition to the highly skewed nature of South trade, the continuing process of primarization of exports in the South, driven by trade with Emerging South, chiefly China, has been leading to the de-industrialization in the Rest of South.

Export quality also appears to be higher in South–North trade than in South–South trade, as reflected by higher export unit values across all product groups. Given that export unit prices increase with skill-intensity of goods, this finding suggests a higher export earnings potential and skills-upgrading from North–South rather than South–South trade. The level of intra-industry trade, which signals convergence in trade structures of trading country pairs, remains particularly low in South–South trade. The level of intra-industry trade is the highest in North–North trade, three times of its level in intra-Emerging South and nine times the level of trade within the Rest of South. We also observe an increasing level of intra-industry trade within the Emerging South and between the Emerging South and the North. The Rest of South, however, shows no convergence trend in intra-industry trade in any direction. In fact, in the 1990s and 2000s we even see a decrease in the level of intra-industry trade between the Rest of South and both Emerging South and the North.

Therefore, any discussion on how to use South–South trade for development needs to address the growing disparities between the Rest of South and Emerging South, as described above.

5.8.2 Technology Transfer

According to mainstream economic theory, the greater the gap in development the greater the potential for technology transfers between the pioneer and the laggard. As in the case of trade however, similar technological sophistication presents opportunities for transfer of knowledge and know-how within the South, and in fact South–South technology transfer has grown significantly in the last two decades. Traditionally throughout the postwar period, there has been significant South–South technology transfer and cooperation in agriculture. For example, the four-country cotton project brings Brazilian expertise in producing cotton varieties to the Cotton-4 (C-4) countries: Burkina Faso, Benin, Chad and Mali. This collaboration was part of a larger Brazilian–African initiative of the Agricultural Innovation Marketplace, dedicated to sharing expertise in natural resource management, land reclamation, food security and conservation, among other initiatives.[52]

However, the UNCTAD 2012 Technology and Innovation Report, *Innovation, Technology and South–South Collaboration*, recognized the potential for across-the-board cooperation, particularly in industrial development (UNCTAD 2012). The similarity of development experiences of South countries makes them ideal partners and makes South–South technology transfer an ideal complement to North–South technology transfer. However, as shown by the downward changes in the trade structures of the Rest of South and of many Emerging South countries, we doubt that this sort of transfer

---

52. http://www.mktplace.org/site/

can be solely left to the free market, as South–based firms with advanced technological capacity may not find it profitable to engage with other South firms, or as these firms export products of lower quality and inferior technology products to their smaller and poorer Southern partners. The low levels of R&D spending in Southern host countries by Southern MNCs support this view. Therefore states need to initiate purposeful joint ventures and collaborations initiated by states with the support of the international community at three levels: exchange of experiences in policy making and in devising policy frameworks for technology transfer; technology exchange and flows aimed at increasing technology-absorptive capacity of the private and public sectors; and transfer of technologies in key sectors of importance to public well-being, such as agriculture, health, climate change and renewable energy (UNCTAD 2012: xix).

5.8.3 *Investment/Capital Flows*

As discussed in chapters 4 and 5, the Emerging South has now become a major source of foreign capital for the South. The significant increase and availability of South–South debt and equity as well as international aid flows are welcome news for the Rest of South, as they open up new possibilities and increase the bargaining power of the borrowing nations. Previously the North had a monopoly in global capital markets, and its power was only worsened by the conditionality requirements attached to capital flows, including aid disbursements. In fact, approval by the IMF with sealing off by one of its country programs has long been an implicit requirement by foreign lenders. Lower conditionality requirements and greater funding for development projects, either directly or through South–South cooperation agencies, are expected to change the playing field in global capital markets, making them more level. The South–South direct investment flows also differ from North–South flows, with a larger share of greenfield investments than M&A, the primary form of FDI from the North. The sectoral distribution of these flows, including aid flows, is also different from that of the North–South flows. The net effects of South–South investment (both debt and equity) and aid flows on investment, productivity, technology transfer, human capital and production structure, however, remain to be tested empirically (Lall, 2002).

5.8.4 *Institutions*

In Section 5.7 we discussed in detail the interaction between institutional change and South–South integration. While we agree that the institutional footprint of Northern countries in the South is highly problematic and that the institutional effects of existing North–South economic and political exchanges leave much to be desired, we do not think that South–South exchanges are immune to the same type of critiques. The beauty, we are afraid, might again be found in the eye of the beholder here. Whether the South–South exchanges, particularly those between the Emerging South and the Rest of South, will have a positive impact on Southern institutional development, including rule of law, democracy, human rights and environment, depends on the structure of these exchanges as well as on public awareness at home and abroad in these countries.

However, one welcome effect of the rise of the Emerging South with highly heterogeneous institutional backgrounds has been the discussion of institutional diversity and its role in economic development, helping diminish the influence of one-size-fits-all dogma.

5.8.5 Trade and Investment Agreements and Policy Space

Policy space, which refers to a country's own ability to set its economic development policies and priorities, is needed for the new-developmentalism to work, yet this policy space has been limited by the IMF, the World Bank, the WTO and various trade and investment treaties. Thrasher and Gallagher show that South–South trade agreements contain the greatest policy space, opening up opportunities that can be expanded. The growing importance of China both as a source of financial flows to the South and as a market for Southern exports has allowed the South to have a choice regarding development policy.[53] The previous one-party system of international financial institutions (IFI) under Washington Consensus has been slowly replaced by a more pluralistic policy space. We can expect this change to have an effect on the conditions of PTAs and BITs, as well as on the conditionality requirements of international lending and aid flows between the North and the South. We should, however, note that the success of the Chinese model, at least for the foreseeable future, relies on its export growth, which necessitates access to other markets, including those in the South. Furthermore, as discussed in chapter 2, despite the growing number of PTAs and BITs with each other, and unlike their experiences with the North, the countries of the South have not confronted each other in international trade or investment related disputes, allowing them more policy space. This may change as the Emerging South countries are becoming more combative against each other at the WTO dispute settlements and bilateral investor-state disputes. As discussed in chapter 2, UNCTAD and other critics of trade and investment treaties have been advocating for a new generation of those treaties with clearly defined proposals to make them development-enhancing and in particular including government "right to regulate" clauses in various aspects of development objectives such as sustainable development, environmental protection, public health or other social objectives.

5.8.6 Labor Standards

We have not discussed the case of labor rights and environmental policy implications of South–South exchanges in detail in this book—not because they are unimportant but, on the contrary, because they deserve an entire book of their own, which we hope, future work will pick up. Nevertheless, we should note that labor standards in many leading South countries, including China, leave much to be desired by way of improvement. In China, for example, still an authoritarian country, labor rights are yet to be

---

53. Warmerdam (2015) shows that the sectoral distribution of Chinese aid flows to the South is highly influenced by its own development experience and priorities, which are different than those of the Northern countries.

recognized. Labor unions, while they exist, are under government control, and freedom to assembly and speech is greatly restricted. Furthermore, many policy makers and elites in the South perceive labor rights as a Northern country luxury, or they accuse any attempts to improve labor conditions in their own countries as a Northern "Trojan Horse" to undermine the competitiveness of Southern workers. Occupational injuries are high, child labor is still common, informal markets cover half or more of labor markets, and social security is nonexistent in most countries of the South.[54]

As recently noted by the ILO, serious data reporting problems on labor market indicators, including labor safety, limit the possibility of any corrective action. Data from the ILO are unfortunately either unavailable for most developing countries or are significantly underreported. On this issue, however, the ratification information on critical ILO conventions may be suggestive of considerable room for improvement. The "Freedom of Association and Protection of the Right to Organise Convention, 1948 (No. 87)," for example, is not ratified by 33 countries, 32 of which are from the South, including heavyweights Brazil, China, India, South Korea and Malaysia. Likewise, the "Right to Organise and Collective Bargaining Convention, 1949 (No. 98)" is not ratified by 22 countries, 20 of which are from the South, including China, India, Mexico and Thailand. The "Forced Labour Convention, 1930 (No. 29)" is still not ratified by China or South Korea, which makes them among eight countries worldwide that have not yet ratified the agreement. (One is from the North, the United States, as in almost all other ILO conventions.) Even the "Abolition of Forced Labour Convention, 1957 (No. 105)" is not signed by China and South Korea.[55] We believe that if South–South exchanges are to differ from the dark side of North–South exchanges of the last few centuries, they need to follow the better examples from the North *today* rather than following their examples from last century.[56]

5.8.7 Environment

The North–South exchanges, including those by the multilateral institutions such as the IMF, have been criticized for either ignoring or directly undermining environmental protection initiatives in the South. Under the theoretical cover-up of Ricardian models, increasing specialization has pushed most countries in the South to a very lopsided and concentrated production and export pattern, turning them into pollution havens. We should also emphasize that the lack of environmental protection by today's developed countries during their industrialization is the main culprit for today's climate change crisis. The Southern leaders frequently exploit this issue in their opposition to assuming any responsibility or to curbing their own carbon

---

54. For a discussion, see the collection of articles in Mosoetsa and Williams (2012).
55. Accessed from http://www.ilo.org/dyn/normlex/en/f?p=1000:11001:0::NO on 11/23/2015.
56. For example, in the aftermath of a deadly mine accident in Turkey in 2014 that left over 300 people dead, the Turkish president, R. T. Erdogan, defended his government against criticism on worker safety laws by using the example of a mine accident in Britain in 1862, adding that "these types of accidents are in the nature of this kind of work".

emissions. Many in the South also perceive Northern attempts to impose environmental standards on their North–South economic exchanges as an implicit protectionism against Southern exports.

However, South–South exchanges appear to suffer from similar type of problems. China has become the top polluter in the world, its release of CO_2 emissions surpassing that of the United States and likely to continue increasing before leveling off. Even though the Chinese authorities acknowledge this problem, particularly its sustainability, we should not expect any rapid correction of this trend.[57] Plenty of evidence also suggests that a lack of strict environmental standards at home causes Chinese investors, including official sources, to place lower conditionality requirements on host countries of the South. The growing demand for carbon as well as for bio-fuels has also increased pressure on the Rest of South to tolerate deforestation, biodiversity loss and the worsening of monocropping practices in agriculture. China has become the world's largest importer of environmentally problematic crops such as soya and oil palm, which are also two of the most planted crops in overseas land deals. We find similar trends in the case of other emerging South economies.

On the positive side, we see an increasing awareness among Emerging South countries on climate change. For example, China announced that it will introduce a cap-and-trade system in 2017 and will increase fuel standards in its auto market. China has also pledged new funding to help developing countries tackle climate change.[58] In 2015, the US–China Joint Presidential Statement on Climate Change included this announcement:

> China will lower carbon dioxide emissions per unit of GDP by 60 percent to 65 percent from the 2005 level by 2030 and increase the forest stock volume by around 4.5 billion cubic meters on the 2005 level by 2030. China will promote green power dispatch, giving priority, in distribution and dispatching, to renewable power generation and fossil fuel power generation of higher efficiency and lower emission levels. China also plans to start in 2017 its national emission trading system, covering key industry sectors. [...] China commits to promote low-carbon buildings and transportation, with the share of green buildings reaching 50% in newly built buildings in cities and towns by 2020 and the share of public transport in motorized travel reaching 30 percent in big- and medium-sized cities by 2020. It will finalize next-stage fuel efficiency standards for heavy-duty vehicles in 2016 and implement them in 2019. (White House, 2015)

In this summit China also announced that it will set up the China South–South Climate Cooperation Fund, with an initial endowment of $3.1 billion, to support Southern countries in fighting climate change and to help build capacity for their access to this fund (White House, 2015). This has been a part of an ongoing Chinese attempt to help South–South cooperation for climate change. Already at the UN meeting on

---

57. China has also become the number one producer of some renewable energy sources such as solar panels. However, even if China went through a complete transformation using all its renewable energy potential, it would be far short of meeting its energy demand.

58. http://www.ccchina.gov.cn/WebSite/CCChina/UpFile/File300.pdf

sustainable development in June 2012 in Rio de Janeiro, China promised to contribute USD6 million to a United Nations Environment Programme (UNEP) trust fund to help Southern countries raise environmental protection capacity, and it pledged a further $31.7 million to help small and least-developed countries tackle climate change.[59] This is a significant change in Chinese attitudes since 1990s, marking a long evolution from the Kyoto climate talks in the 1990s, when, China and most other countries of the South were exempted from the carbon-emission reductions required by the Kyoto protocol. The increasing political will and power of the Emerging South may also allow the Rest of South countries to broker a deal on an international subsidy mechanism to tackle the impacts of climate change.

5.8.8   *Global Governance*

In terms of global governance, South–South exchanges have opened new possibilities for countries of the South, including the formation of coalitions within the WTO, such as the Like Minded Group, the G-90, which blocked the Quad in Cancun and Hong Kong, as discussed in detail in chapter 2. South–South cooperation has also helped block the push for further liberalization in the WTO. However, the rise of China and the rest of the BRICS has posed another challenge for the South, namely the issue of representation. Who is speaking on behalf of the South? To take an illustrative example, when World Bank voting rights were redistributed in 2010, China and other dynamic emerging economies gained, while Africa's voting rights were reduced (Wade 2011). Likewise, after the IMF's reallocation of voting and quota shares in 2008 and 2010, heralded as significant reforms, the voting share of developed economies fell from 60.6 percent to 55.2 percent, with the share of the United States dropping from 17 percent to 16.5 percent. As a result, the share of developing Asia increased from 10.4 percent to 16.1 percent while that of Africa fell from 6 percent to 5.7 percent and that of the Middle East fell from 7.6 percent to 6.8 percent. The biggest increase was enjoyed by China, whose share jumped from 2.9 percent to 6 percent.

Table 5.19 shows by region and income group the numbers of countries that experienced changes in their voting shares. Voting shares were reduced in 63 countries, of which 26 were high-income while 37 were low- and middle-income. In contrast, of the 123 countries that enjoyed an increase in their voting shares, 97 were low- and middle-income. In terms of the regional representation of developing countries that enjoyed an increase in their voting rights, the highest number were from sub-Saharan Africa followed by East Asia and Pacific.

However, these numbers mask the significantly uneven nature of the reallocation of voting shares. For further illumination, Table 5.20 shows the total percentage point change in voting shares across regions and income groups. Despite the large number of countries in sub-Saharan Africa enjoying an increase in their voting shares, the total voting share of developing countries in this region fell. In contrast, the share of developing Asia, including both East Asia and Pacific and South Asia, increased by more

---

59. https://sustainabledevelopment.un.org/partnership/?p=1053

Table 5.19 Changes in IMF voting shares by region and income group in 2008 and 2010 (number of countries)

Region/Income level	Decrease			Increase		
	High	Middle	Low	High	Middle	Low
East Asia & Pacific	3	1	0	2	19	3
Europe & Central Asia	14	9	0	16	10	1
Latin America & Caribbean	4	7	0	3	17	1
Middle East & North Africa	3	6	0	4	6	0
North America	2	0	0	0	0	0
South Asia	0	2	1	0	3	2
Sub-Saharan Africa	0	10	1	1	10	25
Totals	26	35	2	26	65	32

Note: High-income includes both OECD and non-OECD.
Source: For Tables 5.18–5.19, IMF, 2011b. https://www.imf.org/external/np/sec/pr/2011/pdfs/quota_tbl.pdf, and authors' calculations.

than five percentage points. Even though the increase in the share of Asia came at the expense of high-income European and Middle Eastern countries, the changes are not sufficient to bring about any major transformation in IMF politics. The total increase in the voting share of Latin America and the Caribbean, for example, was only 0.82 percentage points.

Furthermore, as discussed in chapter 2, the countries of the Rest of South are left out of international dispute mechanisms. For example, between 1995–2015, low-income South countries accounted for only 6.8 percent of complainants at the WTO as opposed to 44.6 percent for lower- and upper middle-income countries. Overall, while it is true that the rise of the emerging South led to a more multipolar world, as a recent World Bank report called it (World Bank, 2011a), this is not an all-inclusive club and the Rest of South is not a member, at least not yet.

5.9 Conclusion

In their development perspectives, visions, motivations and approaches to the Rest of South, the economies of the Emerging South are ominously heterogeneous. The evidence since 1990s suggests that South–South cooperation is as complicated as North–South cooperation, and that the encounters between the economies of the leading countries in the South and those of the Rest of South will inevitably create diverse outcomes, some negative and some positive. Cultural and social dynamics in home and host countries, as well as power politics, have a significant impact on the structure and future development trajectories of South–South cooperation (Scoones et al., 2013).[60]

---

60. Scoones et al., 2013 also shows that the drive for capital accumulation and new market access, both for inputs and outputs, appears to be a key engine of South–South encounters from Emerging South.

Table 5.20 Percentage point change in IMF voting shares by region and income group in 2008 and 2010

Region/Income level	High	Middle	Low	Totals
East Asia & Pacific	0.09	3.68	0.98	4.75
Europe & Central Asia	–3.46	0.12	0.01	–3.33
Latin America & Caribbean	–0.08	0.81	0.01	0.75
Middle East & North Africa	–1.15	–0.42		–1.57
North America	–1.27			–1.27
South Asia		0.64	0.01	0.65
Sub-Saharan Africa	0.03	–0.41	0.32	–0.06
Totals	–5.83	4.41	1.34	

We should also note that the growing South–South economic exchanges have been made possible only by earlier interventions from dominant Northern countries, and they must be judged in this historical background (Amanor, 2013, pp. 9–10). In other words, the current South–South integration, at least in its current form, would not be possible without the neoliberal push by the Bretton Woods institutions and Western lenders and donors, who have required conditions in their exchanges with the South. The liberalization policies in trade and finance during the 1980s and 1990s as well as the accompanying changes in institutional and legal structures have facilitated the significant growth of South–South economic exchanges—and this, we believe, is also the Achilles' heel of this whole process. Overall, despite the rhetoric of a new paradigm, there is little evidence yet to suggest that the new rising powers in the South are behaving any differently from the old powers of the North.

The promise of an economic utopia in which economic integration would lead to peace and prosperity for both sides has been a key element in legitimizing both the earlier neoliberal expansion and the current South–South discussions. Notwithstanding their significant differences, these two worldviews converge as they regard the South–South integration process and its expected outcomes. Many Emerging South countries share the neoliberal economic view that domestic economic (but not necessarily political) liberalization, and a free hand to do business under the auspices of unfettered economic integration into the global economy in trade and finance as a harbinger for prosperity and power consolidation. In many respects, therefore, the new South–South integration debates are far from the original South–South integration efforts of the Cold War years.

On the scoreboard of South–South exchanges, increasing primarization and deindustrialization appears as the most noticeable negative development. With it come the environmental costs of natural resource and monoculture based economic development. As dissenting development economists have long warned, export growth does not necessarily mean export-led growth, a point completely ignored by neoclassical economists. The human cost behind the success stories of late developers should not be ignored either. In many cases, the recent successes of Emerging South came at significant human expense, including the suppression and violation of human and workers' rights. The environmental and social sustainability of the growth modes followed by the Emerging South is also questionable. Renewed attention to the binding constraints of Southern development and South–South integration needs to be brought back to policy debates on the issue. Particular care should be given to the conditions under which industrial and technology transfer and capacity building can be materialized. The Emerging South also needs to resist the temptation to repeat the mistakes of the North in global governance, and it needs to adopt a more inclusive policy stance towards the Rest of South. After all, what is good for China may not be good for the Rest of South. Ultimately, all efforts to promote greater economic development worldwide must emphasize experimentation in development policy, without any reversal to the one-size-fits-all orthodoxy.

Chapter Six

CONCLUDING THOUGHTS

6.1 A Brief Recap

From the early 1950s into the 1980s, South–South trade was a black box into which many development economists and Third World intellectuals projected their hopes and upon which mainstream economists poured their scorn. For the sympathetic economists, two appealing possibilities stood out for South–South trade. One was that, because the countries of the South were on more equal footing vis-à-vis one another than they were against the North, their more equal bargaining power meant they could enter into more equitable relationships and could ally themselves against the North, progressively changing the rules of the global economic game. The second was that, since South–South trade was more focused on manufactures, it offered possibilities for greater industrial development than South–North trade, which caught the South in the colonial pattern of exporting raw materials for industrial goods.

For mainstream economists, Southern efforts to change this second pattern represented all that was wrong with development policy during those decades. From their perspective, developing countries were pursuing a wrong-headed economic model when they focused on import substitution industrialization (ISI). Instead of focusing on their comparative advantage in raw materials, they were turning out low-quality industrial products, whether intermediate capital goods or final consumer products: machines and machine parts, refrigerators, televisions and so on. Or so went the argument. As these economists saw it, South–South trade was more likely than not an attempt to offload such products on nearby developing countries, because their low quality and high price meant no chance of their being exported to Northern markets. Even so, this trade did not amount to much and, thus, any argument over its worth remained muted, a sideshow to more pressing debates over ISI, foreign debt, trade policy, multinational corporations, foreign aid and other issues. In fact, it was a contrived or proxy debate over deeper ideologies; being pro- or anti-South–South trade was code for being a partisan of a larger intellectual debate about the superior merits of developmentalist or neoclassical thinking, of being a statist or a free marketeer.

In the last four decades the picture has changed and the debate itself has shifted dramatically, with support for South–South trade coming both from within and from outside respectable economic-policy opinion. Meanwhile, South–South trade (and increasingly finance) has risen from a nearly negligible amount of global trade to something significant, and it seems likely to continue to grow. Throughout this book we have tried to document this shift in detail and to discuss its implications. In so doing, we have found that we can no longer map economic relations between various developing countries by trying to make them all fit into larger developmental positions, whether traditional or radical, in any sort of one-to-one correspondence.

There are valid theoretical and empirical reasons both to support and to criticize South–South economic relations. On the positive side, since the start of the 2000s the growing power and assertiveness of leading Southern countries has produced a South–South renaissance in economics. The World Bank and the IMF have begun to reconsider their own evaluations of the costs and benefits of South–South integration. The calls for restructuring the Fund and the Bank to make them more representative of the economic facts of twenty-first century than of 1945 have also intensified, accompanied by renewed efforts to change the quotas and accompanying voting powers of member states. The rise of the Emerging South has also opened up new possibilities for development financing, know-how and technology transfer and capacity building, creating a more level playing field with the North in trade, finance and global governance. The Emerging South, particularly China, has become a major investor in the South, and it now rivals the North in its international aid programs.

As many observers have pointed out, the lack of a colonial history between countries of the South has also allowed cooperation based on their mutual benefit. In fact, China often uses the rhetoric of the nonaligned movement and Third World era in its efforts to promote its South–South initiatives as win-win attempts to initiate the "collective rise of developing countries" for "development and prosperity" (Jinping, 2015). South–South exchanges also make possible greater technology transfer, both through trade and through FDI, because of their higher technology and skill content and their similarity in endowments, consumer preferences and institutional infrastructure, not to mention the political will of the countries involved. The burgeoning number of bilateral and multilateral trade and investment agreements also creates new possibilities for collaboration and offers a breathing space for countries in the Rest of South that are hard pressed by the North to enter similar, but more one-sided, agreements with it.

The Asian Infrastructure Investment Bank and the New Development Bank BRICS, are generally positive developments. As its president, K. V. Kamath, has put it, the BRICS Bank offers "an alternative to the existing US-dominated World Bank and International Monetary Fund." Being based on the principle of one-country, one-vote, rather than on the one-dollar, one-vote governing system of the World Bank, the BRICS Bank allows members, particularly smaller Southern ones, an equal voice. Similarly, none of its members has veto power, unlike the situation in the IMF and WB, where the United States holds unilateral veto power, thanks to its large voting share. South–South cooperation is at the forefront of the goals of the BRICS Bank, and addressing "sustainable development" goals of "emerging market economies and developing countries" is its stated primary purpose. We also find it promising that the BRICS Bank has underlined the common development goals of the Emerging South and the Rest of South without merging them together into one homogeneous group.

We also witness an increasing assertiveness of the Emerging South in multilateral institutions such as the WTO, the World Bank and the IMF. Leading countries in the South are increasingly resorting to the same dispute settlement mechanisms that had long been employed by the North quite monopolistically. This practice applies both to trade disputes and to disputes about international investment, and the fact that China has become the second-largest foreign investor in the world suggests the continuation of this trend. For the moment, however, the Rest of South is being left out of this process. Furthermore, the slow reform of the IMF and World Bank leaves the North largely in control of those institutions, and so the rise of new South-based multilateral institutions may make them less vital for the South or may encourage further reform.

Reflecting these developments, the economics field is going through a significant shift in its approach to South–South exchanges. Even the paragons of economic orthodoxy such as the World Bank and the IMF, or top mainstream economics journals such as the *Quarterly Journal of Economics* or the *American Economic Review* are opening themselves, for the first time since the 1970s, to different theoretical possibilities in their analysis of such exchanges. It is no longer blasphemy to suggest that South–South exchanges may offer something that is missing in North–South exchanges. From this perspective, South–South is better seen as a complement to, rather than as a substitute for, North–South cooperation. Another significant change in economics orthodoxy has been the recognition that real world economics is not characterized by perfect markets or static comparative advantage, and that what you export matters for economic development.

At the same time, unless there is a serious effort to address the sharp imbalances, we may be witnessing a second great divergence in the global economy. The first divergence, essentially starting in the nineteenth century, created the large gap between Western Europe and North America on one hand and the rest of the world on the other; this time such a divergence may be arising within the global South itself. Yes, South–South trade has grown significantly, accounting for more than half (52 percent) of all Southern manufactures trade in 2012. Furthermore, 58 percent of all high-skill manufactures exports of the South that year went to other Southern countries. However, the distribution of this trade is lopsided, and a there is now a sharp split, a bifurcation, that we have tried to capture by recognizing the global South as two distinct groups: Emerging South and Rest of South.

The 55 Emerging South countries, which claim 75 percent of the global South population, accounted for more than 96 percent of total Southern manufactures exports and 99 percent of high-skill manufactures exports in 2012, from among 212 countries in all of the global South. In fact, these 55 countries also account for more than 88 percent of all South–South trade in manufactured goods. The same lopsidedness is found in South–North trade, where the Emerging South accounted for 97 percent of all South–North manufactured goods exports and 99.5 percent of all high-skill manufactures trade. Meanwhile, in 2012, 74 percent of all Rest of South exports were of primary commodities, and one single product, petroleum oils, accounted for 57.5 percent of all their exports in that year. These stylized facts remain unchanged even if we drop many countries from our current list of Emerging South, including low performers such as Syria, Paraguay or Algeria. Such a divide between the two categories, even while including a relatively liberal definition of "Emerging," is indicative of the great width of the divergence.

Given the positive correlation between the structure of a country's exports and its income levels, with a bias towards high-skill manufactured goods, the future for the Rest of South, even for many Emerging South countries, is not bright. After all, the higher the percentage share of high- and medium-skill manufactured goods exports in a country's export bundle, the higher is its income. Furthermore, higher-skill manufactures account for a majority of export earnings for most countries. For example, in East Asia and the Pacific, high-skill manufactures account for 25 percent of export revenues yet only 1 percent of export volume. In contrast, primary goods and resource-intensive manufactures each account for more than 40 percent of this region's export volume but bring in less than 20 percent of its export earnings.

These circumstances do not mean that all is well within the Emerging South. UNCTAD, in its various publications, and Dani Rodrik have warned of "premature deindustrialization" in many countries in the global South—that is, of the process in many advanced countries of a decline in the manufacturing sector accompanied by a rise of output in the low-productivity and low-value added services sectors. As Rodrik further argues, however, manufacturing today is not what it used to be. It has become much more capital- and skill-intensive, with greatly diminished potential to absorb large amounts of labor. Moreover, while global supply chains have facilitated entry into manufacturing, they have also reduced the gains in terms of value added that accrue at home. Many traditional industries, such as textiles and steel, are likely to face shrinking global markets and overcapacity, driven by demand shifts and environmental concerns.

Rodrik (2013) points to Brazil and India, two countries that have done well recently. In Brazil, manufacturing's share of employment barely budged from 1950 to 1980, rising from 12 percent to 15 percent. Since the late 1980s, Brazil has begun to deindustrialize, a process which recent growth has done little to stop or reverse. India presents an even more striking case: Manufacturing employment there peaked at a meager 13 percent in 2002 and has since trended downward. On the economic front, it is clear that early deindustrialization impedes growth and delays convergence with the advanced economies. Nevertheless, we view growth in industrial development as a necessary, but not sufficient, condition. It may not deliver on high human development, but its lack implies that any growth-increases—due to commodity booms or otherwise—will be short-lived and unsustainable.

Other fault lines in South–South exchanges need to be emphasized again. First, whether the Emerging South can replace the North as the engine of growth for the global South is yet to be seen. As discussed in detail in chapters 4 and 5, countries in the Rest of South are going through a structural change in their economies, and this change is in the direction of primarization of their productive capabilities—that is, greater emphasis, as in colonial and early postcolonial times, on their production of raw materials. The export-led growth model of the leading South countries, China particularly, also leaves little room for replicability in the already-saturated world markets.

Deep concerns continue on several sides. For example, the environmental sustainability of the Chinese growth model is questionable at best, as are institutional reforms in

South–South exchanges. Labor rights as well as environmental protections are by no means embraced uniformly across Southern countries, and they remain the Achilles' heel of South–South relations. The often-heralded goal of equal treatment of each member in South–South relations is also inaccurately stated, imprecise and misleading. For example, despite the claim by its president, each member of the BRICS Bank is actually not equal to every other, and its president is elected only from one of its five founding members, who together retain 55 percent of the total votes. In the Asian Infrastructure Investment Bank we find a similar story, with China controlling just below 30 percent of the shares.

Another pressing challenge is climate change, the effects of which will be felt more severely in the South, both for geographic reasons and also for its limited capacity to mitigate the negative effects. On this front, China has stepped up as the flag bearer for the Southern countries, pledging more than the sum committed by developed countries, over $5 billion as of 2015. Equally important, through initiatives such as the China South–South Climate Cooperation Fund or China–UN and China–UNDP initiatives, China has intensified its efforts to help Southern countries share technology, know-how and experience to help address climate change, and it is helping build global momentum to take climate change seriously. This change in position, from being a major cause of the problem—as revealed during the debates surrounding Chinese exemption form the Kyoto protocol –to being a flag bearer, is significant and stands in stark contrast to the US attitudes to climate change. And again, as by now even casual observers have noticed, China has become a game-changer in development aid flows, allowing more choice to the least-developed countries of the South.

6.2   The Road Ahead

We believe that our book provides a framework through which to evaluate the trajectory of South–South relations, to describe those relations and to consider how they may continue to develop in ways most healthy and most equitable for all the countries involved. Moving forward, scholars interested in this subject can pursue a variety of paths. One fruitful path is to pursue more case studies of South–South networks driven by Southern corporations. For example, the shift of the Mumbai-based Indian Sun Pharmaceutical Industries (Sun Pharma) from focusing on home and US markets to focusing on other emerging markets conforms both to the theoretical frameworks (such as Linder) discussed in chapter 2 as well as to the empirical patterns shown in chapter 4. As stated by Uday Baldota, Sun Pharma's CFO:

> The demographics, per capita income and other factors are similar in [other developing] countries, so your ability to promote your products has an advantage. You have a natural starting advantage there, as you understand the dynamics at that level of income. You can carry the practices from your home market to other markets. (Quoted in *Economist* Intelligence Unit 2015, p. 16)[1]

---

1. *Economist* Intelligence Unit (2015) Available at: http://growthcrossings.economist.com/south-south-trade

These words tend to confirm Linder's hypothesis and our general approach in showing how South–South exchange can be uniquely beneficial. More broadly the case studies will enable researchers to better understand where and how value is added from regional supply chains and to determine whether the main drivers behind these value additions are lowering costs, operational efficiency, or influencing other factors.

Another fruitful path is to examine the economic impact of the infrastructural projects sponsored by China and the newly founded Asian Infrastructure Investment Bank. Undoubtedly the infrastructural upgrading needs of the global South are significant. The IMF and World Bank estimate a 2-percent loss in GDP each year for all of Africa because of its inadequate infrastructure, most significantly in roads and transportation, telephone mainlines and ICT technology and power-generating capacity. A 2010 study found that 30 African countries face regular power shortages. In 1970, sub-Saharan Africa had three times the power generation capacity per million population as South Asia, whereas in 2000, the latter had twice as much per million population as sub-Saharan Africa (Foster and Briceno-Garmendia, 2010). Though not to the same extent, infrastructural needs are also urgent in Latin America, MENA and even within East Asia itself. At the same time, the economic payoff of large infrastructural adjustments can vary dramatically from one country to another, especially if poor governance results in misplaced priorities of what projects are launched and inefficient implementation of the projects themselves. Such inconsistencies, multiplied by so many variables, underscore the complexity of the challenges in global economic development. They can be frustrating; they need not be discouraging.

South–South relations after World War II started out as a battle for global equality waged by countries that were economically poor and militarily weak. That same battle persists today, even if the cast of characters has changed.

APPENDIX

A1. Country Classification: North, Emerging South and Rest of South

The CEPII BACI dataset is available for 1995–2009 and includes bilateral trade data (both values and quantities) for 231 countries consisting of 23 in the North, 55 in the Emerging South, 154 in the Rest of South. The IMF Direction of Trade Statistics for 1948–2013, on the other hand, includes bilateral merchandise trade data (only trade values) for 223 countries. The data from the IMF are adjusted for mirror data. Depending on data availability and length-of-time series data, we corrected the export data using the import data of trading partners after adjusting for an average 5 percent cif/fob correction. For consistency, when using the mirror data from importing trade partners, we replaced the data for all years for country i rather than simply filling in missing years.

The North refers to the following countries: Austria, Australia, Belgium, Canada, Denmark, Germany, Finland, France, Greece, Iceland, Israel, Italy, Japan, Luxembourg, Netherlands, New Zealand, Norway, Portugal, Spain, Sweden, Switzerland, United Kingdom and United States. The Emerging South includes: Algeria, Angola, Argentina, Armenia, Azerbaijan, Bosnia and Herzegovina, Bolivia, Brazil, Bulgaria, Chile, China, Colombia, Costa Rica, Croatia, Cyprus, Czech Republic, Dominican Republic, Ecuador, Egypt, Estonia, Guatemala, Hong Kong, Hungary, India, Indonesia, Ireland, Jordan, Kazakhstan, Korea, Latvia, Lithuania, Malaysia, Mexico, Morocco, Oman, Pakistan, Paraguay, Peru, Philippines, Poland, Romania, Russian Federation, Singapore, Slovakia, Slovenia, South Africa, Syria, Taiwan, Thailand, Tunisia, Turkey, Ukraine, Uruguay, Venezuela and Vietnam. All other countries are classified as the Rest of South.

A2. Product Classification

The product classifications are based on the following three-digit product codes using SITC Rev2.

High-skill manufactures: 716, 718, 751, 752, 759, 761, 764, 771, 774, 776, 778, 524, 541, 712, 792, 871, 874, 881.

Medium-skill manufactures: 781, 782, 783, 784, 785, 266, 267, 512, 513, 533, 553, 554, 562, 572, 582, 583, 584, 585, 591, 598, 653, 671, 672, 678, 786, 791, 882, 711, 713, 714, 721, 722, 723, 724, 725, 726, 727, 728, 736, 737, 741, 742, 743, 744, 745, 749, 762, 763, 772, 773, 775, 793, 812, 872, 873, 884, 885, 951.

Low-skill manufactures: 611, 612, 613, 651, 652, 654, 655, 656, 657, 658, 659, 831, 842, 843, 844, 845, 846, 847, 848, 851, 642, 665, 666, 673, 674, 675, 676, 677, 679, 691, 692, 693, 694, 695, 696, 697, 699, 821, 893, 894, 895, 897, 898, 899.

Resource-intensive manufactures: 012, 014, 023, 024, 035, 037, 046, 047, 048, 056, 058, 061, 062, 073, 098, 111, 112, 122, 233, 247, 248, 251, 264, 265, 269, 423, 424, 431, 621, 625, 628, 633, 634, 635, 641, 281, 282, 286, 287, 288, 289, 323, 334, 335, 411, 511, 514, 515, 516, 522, 523, 531, 532, 551, 592, 661, 662, 663, 664, 667, 688, 689.

Primary products: 001, 011, 022, 025, 034, 036, 041, 042, 043, 044, 045, 054, 057, 071, 072, 074, 075, 081, 091, 121, 211, 212, 222, 223, 232, 244, 245, 246, 261, 263, 268, 271, 273, 274, 277, 278, 291, 292, 322, 333, 341, 681, 682, 683, 684, 685, 686, 687.

Unclassified goods: All remaining products not included in any of above groups

A3. List of PTAs

The list below includes the bilateral and multilateral free-trade agreements with the corresponding countries, country groups and starting dates specified in parentheses (the number of countries for the European Community refer to the number of members as the Community enlarged).

Afghanistan (India, 2003); Albania (Turkey, 2008); Andean Community (1988); Armenia (Georgia, 1999; Kazakhstan, 2002; Kyrgyz Republic, 1996; Moldova, 1996; Russia, 1993; Turkmenistan, 1997; Ukraine, 1997); ASEAN (Australia and New Zealand, 2010; China, 2005; India, 2010; AFTA, 1993; Japan, 2009); Australia (Papua New Guinea, 1977; Chile, 2009; New Zealand, 1983; Thailand, 2005); Azerbaijan (Georgia, 1997; Russia, 1993; Ukraine, 1997); Bangkok Agreement (now Asian Pacific Trade Agreement, APTA) (Accession of China, 2002); Bangkok Agreement (now Asian Pacific Trade Agreement, APTA, 1976, Kazakhstan–Russian Federation, 1998; Russian Federation, 1993; Ukraine, 2007); Bhutan (India, 2007); Brunei Darussalam (Japan, 2009); Canada (Chile, 1998; Colombia, 2012; Costa Rica, 2003; Israel, 1997; Peru, 2010); CARICOM (1974); CEFTA (2006); CEMAC (1999); Central American Common Market (1962); Chile (China, 1998; Colombia, 2009; Costa Rica, 2002; El Salvador, 2002; Guatemala, 2010; Honduras, 2009; India, 2008; Japan, 2008; Korea, 2004; Malaysia, 2012; Mexico, 2000; Panama, 2008; Peru, 2009; Turkey, 2011); China (Costa Rica, 2012; Hong Kong, 2004; Macao, 2004; New Zealand, 2009; Pakistan, 2008; Peru, 2010; Singapore, 2009); Colombia (Mexico, 1995; Northern Triangle (El Salvador, Guatemala, Honduras), 2010; United States, 2012); Common Economic Zone (2004); Common Market for Eastern and Southern Africa (1995); Community of Independent States Free Trade Agreement (2005); Costa Rica (Mexico, 1995; Panama, 1973); Croatia (Turkey, 2004); Dominican Republic,(El Salvador, 2001; Guatemala, 2001; Honduras, 2001; Costa Rica, 2002; Nicaragua, 2002; United States, 2006); East African Community (2001; Accession of Burundi and Rwanda, 2008); EC (Treaty of Rome, 1958); EC (9 countries, 1973; 10 countries, 1981; 12 countries, 1981; 15 countries, 1995; 25 countries, 2004; 27 countries, 2007); European Community (Albania,

2007; Algeria,1977; Andorra, 1992; Bosnia–Herzegovina, 2009; Cameroon, 2010; CARIFORUM States EPA, 2009; Chile, 2003; Cote d'Ivoire, 2009; Eastern and Southern Africa States Interim EPA, 2012; Egypt, 1977; Faroe Islands, 1997; FYROM, 2001; Iceland, 1973; Jordan, 2002; Republic of Korea, 2012; Lebanon, 2003; Mexico, 2001; Montenegro, 2008; Morocco, 2000; Norway, 1974; OCT, 1971; Palestine, 1998; Papua New Guinea/Fiji, 2010; San Marino, 2002; Serbia, 2010; South Africa, 2000; Switzerland and Liechtenstein, 1973; Syria, 1978; Tunisia, 1998; Turkey, 1996); Economic Cooperation Organization (1992); ECOWAS (1994); EFTA (Albania, 2011; Canada, 2010; Chile, 2004; Colombia, 2012; Croatia, 2002; Egypt, 2008; Hong Kong, 2013; Israel, 1993; Jordan, 2002; Korea, 2007; Lebanon, 2007; Mexico, 2002; Montenegro, 2013; Morocco, 2000; Palestine, 2000; Peru, 2012; Serbia, 2011; Singapore, 2003; Macedonia, 2001; Tunisia, 2005; Turkey, 1992; Ukraine, 2012); EFTA (Stockholm Convention, 1960; Accession of Iceland, 1970; SACU, 2007); Egypt (Turkey, 2007); El Salvador (Honduras, Taiwan, 2008; Panama, 2003); Eurasian Economic Community (1998); Faroe Islands (Iceland, 1994; Norway, 1994; Switzerland, 1995); Macedonia (Turkey, 2001; Ukraine, 2002); Georgia (Kazakhstan, 2000; Russia, 1994; Turkey, 1994; Turkmenistan, 2000; Ukraine, 1996); GSTP (1989); Guatemala (Taiwan, 2007); Honduras (Panama, 1974); Hong Kong (New Zealand, 2011); India (Japan, 2012); India (Malaysia, 2012; Nepal, 1992; Singapore, 2006; Sri Lanka, 2002); Israel (Mexico, 2001); Japan (Indonesia, 2009; Mexico, 2005; Peru, 2012; Singapore, 2003; Switzerland, 2010; Thailand, 2008; Vietnam, 2010; Malaysia, 2007; Philippines, 2009); Jordan (Singapore, 2006; Turkey, 2011); Kazakhstan (Kyrgyzstan, 1996; Russia, 1993; Ukraine, 1999); Korea (Rep) (Peru, 2012; United States, 2012); Kyrgyzstan (Moldova, 1997; Russia, 1993; Ukraine, 1998; Uzbekistan, 1998); Laos (Thailand, 1991); Latin American Integration Association (1981); Malaysia (New Zealand, 2011); Malaysia (Pakistan, 2008); Melanesian Spearhead Group (1994); MERCOSUR (1992); MERCOSUR (India, 2009); Mexico (Nicaragua, 1999; Peru, 2012); Moldova (Russia, 1993; Ukraine, 2005); Montenegro (Turkey, 2010); New Zealand (Thailand, 2006); Nicaragua (Panama, 2010; Taiwan, 2008); North American Free Trade Agreement (NAFTA) (1994); Pacific Island Countries Trade Agreement (PICTA) (2003); PAFTA (1998); Pakistan (Sri Lanka, 2005); Palestine (Turkey, 2005); Panama (Peru, 2012; Taiwan, 2004; United States, 2013); Peru (Singapore, 2010); Protocol on Trade Negotiations (PTN) (1973); Russia (Serbia, 2006; Tajikistan, 1993; Turkmenistan, 1993; Uzbekistan, 1993; Ukraine, 1994); SADC (2002); SAFTA (2006); Serbia (Turkey, 2011); Singapore (Australia, 2004, New Zealand, 2001; Panama, 2007); South Asian Preferential Trade Arrangement (1996); South Pacific Regional Trade and Economic Cooperation Agreement (1981); Southern African Customs Union (2005); Syria (Turkey, 2007); Tajikistan (Ukraine, 2003); Trans-Pacific Strategic Economic Partnership (2006); Tunisia (Turkey, 2006); Turkey (Bosnia and Herzegovina, 2004); Turkmenistan (Ukraine, 1996); United States (Australia, 2005; Bahrain, 2007; Chile, 2004; Israel, 1986; Jordan, 2002; Morocco, 2006; Oman, 2009; Peru, 2009; Singapore, 2004); WAEMU (2000).

REFERENCES

Aarts, P. 1999. The Middle East: A region without regionalism or the end of exceptionalism? *Third World Quarterly* 20(5): 911–25.

Acemoglu, D., Johnson, S. and Robinson, J. A. 2001. The colonial origins of comparative development: An empirical investigation. *American Economic Review* 91(5): 1369–1401.

Acemoglu, D., Johnson, S. and Robinson, J. A. 2002. Reversal of fortune: Geography and institutions in the making of the modern world income distribution. *The Quarterly Journal of Economics* 117(4): 1231–94

Acemoglu, D., Johnson, S. and Robinson, J. 2005. The rise of Europe: Atlantic trade, institutional change, and economic growth. *American Economic Review* 95(3): 546–79.

Adejumobi, S. and A. Olukoshi. 2008. *The African Union and New Strategies for Development in Africa.* New York: Cambria Press.

Ades, A. and Di Tella, R. 1999. Rents, competition, and corruption. *American Economic Review* 89(4): 982–93.

Ahmad, E. 1981. The NeoFascist State: Notes on the Pathology of Power in the Third World. *Arab Studies Quarterly* April 1: 170–80.

Ahmad, E. 2006. The neofascist state: Notes on the pathology of power in the Third World. In C. Bengelsdorf, M. Cerullo and Y. Chandrani (eds.) *The Selected Writings of Eqbal Ahmad*, 142–45. New York: Columbia University Press.

Aitken, B. and Harrison, A. 1999. Do domestic firms benefit from direct foreign investment? Evidence from Venezuela. *American Economic Review* 89(3): 605–18.

Akamatsu, K. 1962. A historical pattern of economic growth in developing countries. *Journal of Developing Economies* 1(1): 3–25.

Akbulut, B., Adaman, F. and Madra, Y. M. 2015. The Decimation and Displacement of Development Economics. *Development and Change* 46(4): 733–61.

Akin, C. and Kose, M. A. 2007. Changing Nature of North-South Linkages: Stylized Facts and Explanations. IMF Working paper. WP/07/280

Aleksynska, M. and Havrylchyk, O. 2013. FDI from the South: The role of institutional distance and natural resources. *European Journal of Political Economy* 29: 38–53.

Amanor, K. 2013. South–South Cooperation in Africa: Historical, Geopolitical and Political Economy Dimensions of International Development. *IDS Bulletin*, 44.4. Institute of Development Studies.

Amar, P. 2013. The Security Archipelago: Human-Security States, Sexuality Politics, and the End of Neoliberalism. Durham, NC: Duke University Press.

Amighini, A. and Sanfilippo, M. 2014. Impact of South–South FDI and trade on the export upgrading of African economies. *World Development* 64: 1–17.

Amin, S. 1976. *Unequal Development: An Essay on the Social Formations of Peripheral Capitalism.* New York: Monthly Review Press.

Amin, S. 1990. *Delinking: Towards a Polycentric World.* London: Zed Books.

Amsden, A. 1980. The industry characteristics of intra-Third World trade in manufactures. *Economic Development and Cultural Change* 29(1): 1–19.

Amsden, A. 1983. De-skilling, skilled commodities, and the NIC's emerging competitive advantage. *American Economic Review*; Papers and Proceedings 73(2): 333–37.

Amsden, A. 1984. The division of labor is limited by the rate of growth of the market: The Taiwanese machine tool industry revisited. Harvard Business School, mimeo.

Amsden, A. 1987. The directionality of trade: Historical perspective and overview. In O. Havrylyshin (ed.), *World Bank Symposium: Exports of Developing Countries: How Direction Affects Performance*, 123–38. Washington, DC: World Bank.

Amsden, A. 1989. *Asia's Next Giant: South Korea and Late Industrialization*. New York: Oxford University Press.

Amsden, A. 2001. *The Rise of the "Rest."* New York: Oxford University Press.

Amsden, A. 2007. *Escape from Empire: The Developing World's Journey through Heaven and Hell*. Cambridge, MA: MIT Press.

An, G. and Iyigun, M. F. 2004. The export skill content, learning by exporting and economic growth. *Economics Letters* 84: 29–34.

Andrew, H. and David, S. 2015. European powers say they will join China-led bank. *The New York Times*, March 17, 2015. http://www.nytimes.com/2015/03/18/business/france-germany-and-italy-join-asian-infrastructure-investment-bank.html?_r=0

Angeles, L. 2007. Income inequality and colonialism. *European Economic Review* 51(5): 1155–76.

Antweiler, W. and Trefler, D. 2002. Increasing returns and all that: A view from trade. *American Economic Review* 92(1): 93–119.

Asian Development Bank and Asian Development Bank Institute. 2009. *Infrastructure for a Seamless Asia*, Tokyo: Asian Development Bank and Asian Development Bank Institute.

Asian Infrastructure and Investment Bank (AIIB). 2015. "About Us." http://www.aiibank.org/ Accessed on July 14, 2015.

Bacha, E. L. 1978. An interpretation of unequal exchange from Prebisch-Singer to Emmanuel. *Journal of Development Economics* 5(4): 319–330.

Bacha, O. I. 2008. A common currency area for ASEAN? Issues and feasibility. *Applied Economics* 40(4): 515–529.

BACI: International Trade Database at the Product-Level. The 1994–2007 Version CEPII Working Paper, No. 2010–23, Octobre 2010 Guillaume Gaulier, Soledad Zignago.

Bagchi, A. K. 2008. Historical perspectives on development. In A. K. Dutt and J. Ros (eds.) *International Handbook of Development Economics*, vol. 1. 16–31. Northampton, MA: Edward Elgar.

Bagley, B. M. and Defort, M. (eds.) 2015. *Decline of U.S. Hegemony? A Challenge of ALBA and a New Latin American Integration of the Twenty-First Century*. Lanham, MD: Lexington Books.

Bagwell, K. and Staiger, R. W. 1997a. Strategic export subsidies and reciprocal trade agreements: The natural monopoly case. *Japan and the World Economy* 9(4): 491–510.

Bagwell, K. and Staiger, R. W. 1997b. Multilateral tariff cooperation during the formation of customs unions. *Journal of International Economics* 42(1–2): 91–123.

Bahar, D., Hausmann, R. and Hidalgo, C. A. 2014. Neighbors and the evolution of the comparative advantage of nations: Evidence of international knowledge diffusion? *Journal of International Economics* 92(1): 111–23.

Baird, S., Chirwa, E., McIntosh, C. and Ozler, B. 2010. The short-term impacts of a schooling conditional cash transfer program on the sexual behavior of young women. *Health Economics*, September Supplement: 55–68.

Balakrishnan, R. 2003. *International Law from Below: Development, Social Movements, and Third World Resistance*. Cambridge: Cambridge University Press.

Baldwin, R. and Robert-Nicoud, F. 2014. Trade-in-goods and trade-in-tasks: An integrating framework. *Journal of International Economics* 92(1): 51–62.

Baldwin, R. E. 1979. Determinants of trade and foreign investment: Further evidence. *Review of Economics and Statistics* 61(1): 40–48.

Bandung Conference. 1955. Final Communiqué of the Asian-African Conference of Bandung. available at http://franke.uchicago.edu/Final_Communique_Bandung_1955.pdf (last accessed July 21, 2016).

Baran, B. 1957. *The Political Economy of Growth*. New York: Monthly Review Press.

Baran, P. 1976. *The Political Economy of Growth*. New York: Monthly Review Press.

Bastos, P. and Silva, J. 2010. The quality of a firm's exports: Where you export to matters. *Journal of International Economics* 82(2): 99–111.

Beck, T. 2002. Financial development and international trade: Is there a link? *Journal of International Economics* 57: 107–31.

Beck, T. 2003. Financial dependence and international trade. *Review of International Economics* 11(2): 107–31.

Becker, G. S., Murphy, K. M. and Tamura, R. F. 1990. Human capital fertility and economic development. *Journal of Political Economy* 98: 12–37.

Behar, A. and Cirera-i-Criville, L. 2013. Does it matter who you sign with? Comparing the impacts of North-South and South-South trade agreements on bilateral trade. *Review of International Economics* 21(4): 765–82.

Berger, D., Easterly, W., Nunn, N. and Satyanath, S. 2013. Commercial imperialism? Political influence and trade during the Cold War. *American Economic Review* 103(2): 863–96.

Bergsten, F. C. 1998. Reviving the Asian Monetary Fund. *Peterson Institute for International Economics*, Policy Brief 98-8.

Bergstrand, J. H. and Egger, P. 2013. What determines BITs? *Journal of International Economics* 90(1): 107–22.

Bhagwati, J. 1993. Regionalism and multilateralism: An overview. In J. de Melo and A. Panagriya (eds.), *New Dimensions in Regional Integration*, 22–51. Cambridge: Cambridge University Press.

Bhagwati, J. 1995. U.S. trade policy: The infatuation with free trade areas. In J. Bhagwati and A. O. Krueger, *The Dangerous Drift to Preferential Trade Agreements*, 1–18. Washington, DC: AEI Press.

Bhagwati, J. and Panagariya, A. 1996. Preferential trading areas and multilateralism: Strangers, friends or foes? In J. Bhagwati and A. Panagariya (eds.), *The Economics of Preferential Trading Agreements*, 1–78. Washington, DC: AEI Press.

Bhagwati, J. N., Panagariya, A. and Srinivasan, T. N. 1998. *Lectures on International Trade*. Cambridge, MA: MIT Press.

Bhagwati, J. N. 1994. Free trade: Old and new challenges. *Economic Journal* 104: 231–46.

Bond, P. and A. Garcia, eds. 2015. *BRICS: An Anti-capitalist Critique* London, UK: Pluto Press.

Botto, M. and A. Bianculli. 2006. *The Impact of Research in Trade Policy in the Southern Cone: The Construction of the Capital Goods Protocol and the Common External Tariff within MERCOSUR. FLACSO*, Argentina.

BP. 2015. *BP Statistical Review of World Energy*. 64th Edition, British Petroleum.

Brewer, A. 1990. *Marxist Theories of Imperialism. A Critical Survey*. London: Routledge and Kegan Paul, 2nd edition.

Bureau of Inter-American Affairs. 1974. LAFTA Reorganization. US Department of State. December 1974. Declassified on June 30, 2005. https://www.wikileaks.org/plusd/cables/1974MONTEV03635_b.html Accessed on March 5, 2016.

Busse, M., Königer, J. and Nunnenkamp, P. 2010. FDI Promotion through Bilateral Investment Treaties: More Than a Bit? *Review of World Economics* 146(1): 147–77.

Butcher, A. and Yuan, W. J. 2015. China's official assistance and corresponding trade flows to Africa; Executive Briefings on Trade, US International Trade Commission, March.

Caglayan, M., Dahi, O. S. and Demir, F. 2013. Trade flows, exchange rate uncertainty, and financial depth: Evidence from 28 emerging countries. *Southern Economic Journal* 79(4): 905–27.

Campbell, J. and Pedersen, O. (eds.) 2001. *The Rise of Neoliberalism and Institutional Analysis*. Princeton: Princeton University Press.

Carkoglu, A., Eder, M. and Kirisci, K. 1998. *The Political Economy of Regional Cooperation in the Middle East*. New York: Routledge.

Carmody, P. 2013. *The Rise of the BRICS in Africa: The geopolitics of South-South Relations*. London, UK: Zed Books.

Caselli, F. and Morelli, M. 2004. Bad politicians. *Journal of Public Economics* 88(3): 759–82.

Cassiolato, J. E. and Vitorino, V. (eds.) 2009. *BRICs and Development Alternatives*. Anthem Press: New York.

Cernat, L. 2001. *Assessing Regional Trade Arrangements: Are South-South RTAs More Trade Diverting?* UNCTAD Policy Issues in International Trade and Commodities Study Series, No. 16. New York: UNCTAD.

Chan, S. 2013. *The Morality of China in Africa: The Middle Kingdom and the Dark Continent*. London: Zed Books.

Chang, H.-J. 2002. *Kicking Away the Ladder: Development Strategy in Historical Perspective*. London: Anthem Press.

Chang, H.-J. 2006. *The East Asian Development Experience: The Miracle, the Crisis and the Future*. London: Zed Books.

Chang, H.-J. 2008. *Bad Samaritans*. London: Random House.

Chang, H-J. and Grabel, I. 2004. *Reclaiming Development: An Alternative Economic Policy Manual*. London: Zed Books.

Chase-Dunn, C. 1990. Resistance to imperialism: Semiperipheral actors. *Review* (Fernand Braudel Center): 1–31.

Chattopadhyay, R. and Duflo, E. 2004. Women as policy makers: Evidence from a randomized policy experiment in India. *Econometrica* 72(5): 1409–43.

Cheong, J., Kwak, D. W. and Tang, K. K. 2015. Heterogeneous effects of preferential trade agreements: How does partner similarity matter? *World Development* 66: 222–36.

Chichilnisky, G. 1994. North-South trade and the global environment, *American Economic Review* 84(4): 851–74.

China Statistical Yearbook, 2014. National Bureau of Statistics of China. http://www.stats.gov.cn/tjsj/ndsj/2014/indexeh.htm

Chudnovsky, D. 1983. The entry into the design and production of complex capital goods: The experiences of Brazil, India, and South Korea. In M. Fransman (ed.), *Machinery and Economic Development*, 54–92. New York: St. Martin's Press.

CIA, 1963. *Special Report: Latin American Free Trade Association*. Fairfax, VA: CIA.

Cline, W. ed. 1979. *Policy Alternatives for a New International Economic Order: An Economic Analysis*. New York: Praeger.

Copeland, B. and Kotwal, A. 1996. Product quality and the theory of comparative advantage. *European Economic Review*: 40: 1747–60.

Copeland, B. R. and Taylor, M. S. 2005. *Trade and the Environment: Theory and Evidence*. Princeton: Princeton University Press.

Cuervo-Cazurra, A. and Genc, M. 2008. Transforming disadvantages into advantages: Developing-country MNEs in the least developed countries. *Journal of International Business Studies* 39(6): 957–79.

Dahi, O. S. and Demir, F. 2013. Preferential trade agreements and manufactured goods exports: does it matter whom you PTA with? *Applied Economics* 45(34): 4754–72.

Darby, J., Desbordes, R. and Wooton, I. 2010. Does public governance always matter? How experience of poor institutional quality influences FDI to the South. *CESifo Working Paper No. 3290*. Munich.

Darity, W. Jr. 1990. The fundamental determinants of terms of trade reconsidered: Long run and long-period equilibrium. *American Economic Review* 80(4): 816–27.

Darity, W. Jr. 1992. A model of "Original Sin": Rise of the West and lag of the rest. *American Economic Review Papers and Proceedings* 82(2): 162–67.

Darity, W. Jr., and Davis, L. S. 2005. Growth, trade and uneven development. *Cambridge Journal of Economics* 29: 141–70.

Davis, M. 2002. *Late Victorian Holocausts: El Niño Famines and the Making of the Third World*. London: Verso.

de la Torre, A., Didier, T., Ize, A., Lederman, D. and Schmukler, S. L. 2015. *Latin America and the Rising South: Changing World, Changing Priorities*. Washington, DC: World Bank.

Deardorff, A. V. 1987. The directions of developing country trade: Examples of pure theory. World Bank symposium: Exports of developing countries: How direction affects performance: 9–22. Washington, DC: World Bank.

Deaton, A. 2009. Instruments of development: Randomization in the tropics, and the search for the elusive keys to economic development. NBER Working Paper. 14690.

Deininger, K. and Byerleee, D. 2011. The rise of large farms in land abundant countries: Do they have a future? Working Paper, World Bank.

Demir, F. 2016. Effects of FDI flows on institutional development in the South: Does it matter where the investors are from? *World Development* 78, 341–59.

Demir, F. and Dahi, O. S. 2011. Asymmetric effects of financial development on South–South and South–North trade: Panel data evidence from emerging markets. *Journal of Development Economics* 94, 139–49.

Demir, F. and Hu, C. 2015. Institutional differences and the direction of bilateral foreign direct investment flows: Are South–South flows any different than the rest? *The World Economy*. Advance online publication doi: 10.1111/twec.12356

Demirguc-Kunt, A. and Maksimovic, V. 1998. Law, finance and firm growth. *Journal of Finance* 53: 2107–37.

Devlin, R. and Ffrench-Davis, R. 1995. The great Latin America debt crisis: A decade of asymmetric adjustment. *Revista de Economia Politica* 15(3) (July–September): 117–42.

Diamond, L. 2010. Why are there no Arab democracies? *Journal of Democracy* 21(1): 93–112.

Diaz-Alejandro, C. F. 1973. Some characteristics of recent export expansion in Latin America. Economic Growth Center Discussion Paper no. 183. Yale University.

Diaz-Alejandro, C. F. 1984. Latin American Debt: I don't think we are in Kansas anymore. *Brookings Papers on Economic Activity* 2: 335–403.

DiCaprio, A. and K. Gallagher. 2006. The WTO and the shrinking of development space: How big is the bite? *Journal of World Investment and Trade* 7(5): 781–803.

Djankov, S. and Hoekman, B. 2000. Foreign investment and productivity growth in Czech enterprises. *The World Bank Economic Review* 14(1): 49–64.

Doctor, M. 2007. Why bother with inter-regionalism? Negotiations for a European Union-Mercosur agreement. *Journal of Common Market Studies* 45(2): 281–314.

Dorraj, M. and English, J. 2013. The dragon nests: China's energy engagement of the Middle East. *China Report* 47.

Draper, P. and Sally, R. 2005. *Developing country coalitions in multilateral trade negotiations: Aligning the majors?* South African Institute of International Affairs.

Dreher, A. and Fuchs, A. 2015. Rogue aid? An empirical analysis of China's aid allocation. *Canadian Journal of Economics* 48(3): 988–1023.

Dreher, A., Fuchs, A., Parks, B., Strange, A. M. and Tierney, M. J. 2015a. Apples and dragon fruits: The determinants of aid and other forms of state financing from China to Africa. Working paper 15. Aid Data.

Dreher, A., Fuchs, A., Hodler, R., Parks, B. C., Raschky, P. and. Tierney, M. J. 2015b. Aid on demand: African leaders and the geography of China's foreign assistance. CEPR Discussion Paper #10704. London: Centre for Economic Policy Research.

Dreher, A., Nunnenkamp, P. and Thiele, R. 2011. Are 'new' donors different? Comparing the allocation of bilateral aid between non-DAC and DAC donor countries. *World Development* 39(11): 1950–68.

Dumenil, D. and Levy, D. 2004. *Capital Resurgent: Roots of the Neoliberal Revolution*. Cambridge, MA: Harvard University Press.

Dumenil, D. and Levy, D. 2011. *The Crisis of Neoliberalism*. Cambridge, MA: Harvard University Press.

Dutt, A. K. 1986. Vertical trading and uneven development. *Journal of Development Economics* 20(2): 339–59.

Dutt, A. K. 1987. Keynes with a perfectly competitive goods market. *Australian Economic Papers* 26(49): 275–93.

Dutt, A. K. 1989. Uneven development in alternative models of North–South trade. *Eastern Economic Journal* 15(2): 91–106.

Dutt, A. K. 1990. *Growth, Distribution, and Uneven Development*. Cambridge, UK: Cambridge University Press.

Dutt, A. K. 1992. The NICs, global accumulation and uneven development: Implications of a simple three-region model. *World Development* 20(8): 1159–71.

Dutt, A. K. 1996. Southern primary exports, technological change and uneven development. *Cambridge Journal of Economics* 20(1): 73–89.

Dutt, A. K. 2012. Distributional dynamics in Post Keynesian growth models. *Journal of Post Keynesian Economics* 34(3): 431–52.

Eagleton-Pierce, M. D. 2012. The competing kings of cotton: (Re)framing the WTO African cotton initiative. *New Political Economy* 17(3): 313–37.

Easterly, W. and Levine, R. 1997. Africa's growth tragedy: Policies and ethnic divisions. *The Quarterly Journal of Economics* 1203–50.

Easterly, W. and Pfutze, T. 2008. Where does the money go? Best and worst practices in foreign aid. *Journal of Economic Perspectives* 22(2).

Easterly, W. 2006. *The White Man's Burden: Why the West's Efforts to Aid the Rest Have Done So Much Ill and So Little Good*. London: Penguin.

ECLAC, 2015. Integrated Database of Trade Disputes for Latin America and the Caribbean. http://idatd.cepal.org/omc.htm?perform=estadisticasandnumero=1

Economic and Social Commission for Asia and Pacific (ESCAP). 2009. *Asia-Pacific Trade and Investment Report: Trade Led Recovery and Beyond*. New York: United Nations.

Economist. 2006. Africa and China: African heads of state gather for a summit in China. November 3. http://www.economist.com/node/8126261/print?story_id=8126261

Economist. 2011. The Chinese in Africa: Trying to pull together, Africans are asking whether China is making their lunch or eating it. April 20. http://www.economist.com/node/18586448?story_id=18586448

Economist, 2015. Japan and the AIIB: To join or not to join. May 30. http://www.economist.com/news/asia/21652351-will-japan-lend-its-muscle-chinas-new-asian-infrastructure-bank-join-or-not-join

Economist Intelligence Unit. 2015. Theme: South-South trade, chain reactions. http://growth-crossings.economist.com/chain-reactions

Eichengreen, B. 1998. Does Mercosur need a single currency? (NBER Working Papers 6821). National Bureau of Economic Research, Inc.

Eichengreen, B. and Bayoumi, T. 1996. Is Asia an optimum currency area? Can it become one? Regional, global and historical perspectives on Asian monetary relations. Center for International and Development Economics Research (CIDER) (Working Papers C96-081). Berkeley: University of California at Berkeley.

Emmanuel, A., Bettelheim, C. and Pearce, B. 1972. *Unequal Exchange: A Study of the Imperialism of Trade*. New York: Monthly Review Press.

Engerman, S. L. and Sokoloff, K. L. 2002. Factor endowments, inequality, and paths of development among new world economics (No. w9259). National Bureau of Economic Research.

Escobar, A. 1992. Imagining a post-development Era? Critical thought, development and social movement. In *Social Text*, No. 31/32. Third World and Post-Colonial Issues, 20–56. Duke University Press.

Escobar, A. 1995. *Encountering Development: The Making and Unmaking of the Third World.* Princeton: Princeton University Press.

Escobar, A. 2000. Beyond the search for a paradigm? Post-development and beyond. *Development* 43(4): 11–14.

Ethier, W. 1998. The new regionalism. *The Economic Journal* 108, 1149–61.

European Commission. 2015. http://ec.europa.eu/budget/explained/myths/myths_en.cfm Accessed on October 12, 2015.

Evans, P. 1995. *Embedded Autonomy: States and Industrial Transformation.* Princeton: Princeton University Press.

External Direct Investment Statistics of Hong Kong. 2014. Hong Kong. http://www.censtatd.gov.hk/hkstat/sub/sp260.jsp?productCode=B1040003

Fawzy, S. 2003. Assessing corporate governance in Egypt. Egyptian Center for Economic Studies Working Paper (82) 1–45.

Feenstra, R. C. *et al.* 2005. World trade flows, 1962–2000. NBER working paper 11040.

Feenstra, R. C. 1996. Trade and uneven growth. *Journal of Development Economics* (49): 229–56.

Final Communique of the Asian-African Conference. 1955. Available at: http://franke.uchicago.edu/Final_Communique_Bandung_1955.pdf

Finlday, R. 1978. Relative backwardness, direct foreign investment, and the transfer of technology: a simple dynamic model. *The Quarterly Journal of Economics* 92(1): 1–16.

Findlay, R. 1980. The terms of trade and equilibrium growth in the world economy. *American Economic Review* 70(3): 291–99.

Findlay, R. 1984. Growth and development in trade models. In R. Jones and P. Kenen (eds.), *Handbook of International Economics*, vol. 1. Amsterdam: Elsevier Science.

Findlay, R. 1992. The roots of divergence: Western economic history in comparative perspective. *American Economic Review Papers and Proceedings* 82(2): 158–61.

Forum on China-Africa Cooperation. 2000. Beijing Declaration of the Forum on China-Africa Cooperation http://www.fmprc.gov.cn/zflt/eng/zyzl/hywj/t157833.htm Accessed May 1, 2015.

Foster, V. and Briceño-Garmendia, C., 2010. Africa's infrastructure. *A Time for Transformation. A co-publication of the Agence Française de Développement and the World Bank.* Washington DC: The World Bank.

Fraeters, Han. 2011. Three-way-learning. The South–South agenda in Busan. http://blogs.worldbank.org/voices/three-way-learning-the-south- south-agenda-in-busan Accessed December 1, 2011.

Frank, A. G. 1966. *The Development of Underdevelopment.* Boston: New England Free Press.

Frank, A. G. 1998. *ReOrient: Global Economy in the Asian Age.* Berkeley: University of California Press.

Frankel, J. A., Stein, E., and Wei, S. 1995. Trading blocs and the Americas: The natural, the unnatural and the supernatural. *Journal of Development Economics* 47(1): 61–96.

Fugazza, M. and Nicita, A. 2011. On the importance of market access for trade. UNCTAD Blue Series Papers, No. 50.

Fugazza, M. and Robert-Nicoud, F. 2006. Can South-South trade liberalization stimulate North-South trade? *Journal of Economic Integration* 21: 234–53.

Fujita, M., Kuroiwa, I. and Kumagai, S. (eds.) 2011. *The Economics of East Asian Integration: A Comprehensive Introduction to Regional Issues.* Northampton, MA: Edward Elgar.

Furtado, C. 1964. *Development and Underdevelopment.* Berkeley: University of California Press.

Furtado, C. 1976. *Economic Development in Latin America: Historical Background and Contemporary Problems.* Cambridge: Cambridge University Press.

Galal, A. and Hoekman, B. (eds.) 2003. *Arab Economic Integration: Between Hope and Reality.* Washington, DC: Brookings Institution Press.

Gallagher, K. P., Irwin, A. and Koleski, K. 2012. *The New Banks in Town: Chinese Finance in Latin America.* Inter-American Development Bank Report.

Gallagher, K. P. and Porzecanski, R. 2010. *The Dragon in the Room: China and the Future of Latin American Industrialization*. Palo Alto: Stanford University Press.

Gardini, G. L. 2006. Government-business relations in the construction of MERCOSUR. *Business and Politics* (8) 1:1–26.

Geda, A. and Meskel, A. G. 2010. *Impact of China–Africa investment relations: Case study of Ethiopia.* Final Draft Prepared for AERC Collaborative Research on the Impact of China on Africa. Mombasa, Kenya

Gennaioli, N. and Rainer, I. 2007. The modern impact of precolonial centralization in Africa. *Journal of Economic Growth* 12(3): 185–234.

Gilbert, J. 2013. What kind of thing is "neoliberalism?" *New Formations: A Journal of Culture/Theory/Politics* (80)1: 7–22.

Gordon, D. M., Edwards, R. and Reich, M. 1982. *Segmented Work, Divided Workers: The Historical Transformation of Labor in the United States*. Cambridge: Cambridge University Press.

Graham-Harrison, E. 2009. China Trade Outweighs Corruption Fears for Africa. Reuters. http://www.reuters.com/article/2009/11/05/businesspro-us-china-africa-corruption-a-idUSTRE5A44I220091105

Grosmann, G. M. and Helpman, E. 1991. *Innovation and Growth in the Global Economy*. Cambridge, MA: MIT Press.

Hakimian, H. and Nugent, J. B. 2003. *Trade Policy and Economic Integration in the Middle East and Africa*. New York: Routledge.

Hanieh, A. 2011. *Capitalism and Class in the Gulf Arab States*. New York: Palgrave Macmillan.

Hanieh, A. 2013. *Lineages of Revolt: Issues of Contemporary Capitalism in the Middle East*. Chicago: Haymarket Press.

Hardt, M. 2002. Today's Bandung? *New Left Review*, March–April (14): 112–18.

Hariri, J.G. 2012. The autocratic legacy of early statehood. *American Political Science Review* 106(03): 471–94.

Harris, R. and Robinson, C. 2002. The effect of foreign acquisitions on total factor productivity: Plant-level evidence from UK manufacturing, 1987–1992. *Review of Economics and Statistics*, 84(3): 562–68.

Harrison, A. and Rodriguez-Claire, A. 2010. Trade, foreign investment, and industrial policy for developing countries. In D. Rodrik and M. Rosenzweig (eds.), *Handbook of Development Economics*, vol. 5. 4039–4214. Amsterdam: Elsevier.

Harvey, D. 2005. *A Brief History of Neoliberalism*. Oxford: Oxford University Press.

Hausman, R., Hwang, J. and Rodrik, D. 2007. What you export matters. *Journal of Economic Growth* 12: 1–25.

Havrylyshyn, O (ed.) 1987. *Exports of Developing Countries: How Direction Affects Performance*. Washington, DC: The World Bank.

Havrylyshyn, O. and Wolf, M. 1983. *Recent Trends Among Developing Countries*. Washington, DC: World Bank.

Hettne, B. 2005. Beyond the "new regionalism." *New Political Economy* 10(4): 543–71.

Hettne, B., Inotai, A. and Sunkei, O. (eds.) 1999. *Globalism and the New Regionalism*. New York: Palgrave Macmillan.

Hochschild, A. 1998. *King Leopold's Ghost: A Story of Greed, Terror, and Heroism in Colonial Africa*. Boston: Mariner.

Hoekman, B., Mattoo, A. and English, P. 2002. *Development, Trade, and the WTO: A Handbook*. Washington, DC: The World Bank.

Hojman, D. E. 1981. The Andean Pact: Failure of a model of economic integration? *JCMS: Journal of Common Market Studies* 20(2): 139–60.

Hook, G. D., Gilson, J., Hughes, C. W. and Dobson, H. 2011. *Japan's International Relations: Politics, Economics, and Security*. London: Routledge.

Hughes, C. W. 2000. Japanese policy and the East Asian currency crisis: Abject defeat or quiet victory? *Review of International Political Economy* 7(2): 219–53.

Hur, J., Raj, M. and Riyanto, Y. E. 2006. Finance and trade: A cross-country empirical analysis on the impact of financial development and asset tangibility on international trade. *World Development* 34(10): 1728–41.

Hveem, H. 1999. Political regionalism: Master or servant of economic internationalization? In B. Hettne, A. Inotai, and O. Sunkei (eds.), *Globalism and the New Regionalism*. New York: Palgrave Macmillan.

Iida, K. 1988. Third World Solidarity: The Group of 77 in the UN General Assembly. *International Organization* 42(2): 375–95.

Imbs, J. and Wacziarg, R. 2003. Stages of diversification. *American Economic Review* 93(1): 63–86.

IMF. 2011a. *Emerging Markets Tackle Risks, Cement Global Power*, IMF Survey http://www.imf.org/external/pubs/ft/survey/so/2011/NEW041811A.htm. Accessed on September 10, 2015.

IMF, 2011b. Quota and Voting Shares Before and After Implementation of Reforms Agreed in 2008 and 2010. https://www.imf.org/external/np/sec/pr/2011/pdfs/quota_tbl.pdf

IMF. 2013. *World Economic Outlook*. April. IMF IMF_Apr2013 WEO

IMF. Direction of Trade Statistics. 2014. Direction of Trade Statistics Online Database. Accessed on December 1, 2014.

IMF. 2015. International Financial Statistics. Accessed on December 10, 2015.

Irwin, D. A., Mavroidis, P. C. and Sykes, A. O. 2008. *The Genesis of the GATT.* Cambridge: Cambridge University Press.

Iyer, L. 2010. Direct versus indirect colonial rule in India: Long-term consequences. *Review of Economics and Statistics* 92(4): 693–713.

Jenkins, R. 2009. The Latin American case. In R. Jenkins, and E. D. Peters (eds.), *China and Latin America: Economic Relations in the Twenty-First Century*, 21–64. Bonn and Mexico City: German Development Institute.

Jenkins, R. and Peters, E.D. (eds.) 2009. *China and Latin America: Economic Relations in the Twenty-First Century.* Bonn and Mexico City: German Development Institute.

Kadri, A. 2014. *Arab Development Denied: Dynamics of Accumulation by Wars of Encroachment.* Anthem Press: London.

Kaldor, N. 1967. *Strategic Factors in Economic Development.* Ithaca, NY: Cornell University Press.

Kaltenthaler, K. and Mora, F. O. 2002. Explaining Latin American economic integration: The case of Mercosur. *Review of International Political Economy* 9(1): 72–97.

Kanbur, S.R. and D. Vines. 1986. North-South interaction and commodity control. *Journal of Development Economics* 23(2): 371–87.

Kaplinsky, R. 2013. *Globalization, Poverty and Inequality: Between a Rock and a Hard Place.* New York: John Wiley and Sons.

Kaplinsky, R. and Morris, M. 2008. Do the Asian drivers undermine export-oriented industrialization in SSA? *World Development* 36(2): 254–73.

Karacaovali, B. 2011. Productivity matters for trade policy: Theory and evidence. *International Economic Review* 52: 33–62.

Kee, H. L. Nicita, A. and Olarreaga, M. 2009. Estimating trade restrictiveness indices. *The Economic Journal* 119: 172–99.

Kennan, George. 1948. Review of Current Trends, U.S. Foreign Policy, Policy Planning Staff, PPS No. 23. Top Secret. Included in the U.S. Department of State, Foreign Relations of the United States, 1948, vol. 1, part 2 (Washington DC Government Printing Office, 1976): 509–29 (Memo by George Kennan, Head of the US State Department Policy Planning Staff. Written February 28, 1948, Declassified June 17, 1974.) https://en.wikisource.org/wiki/Memo_PPS23_by_George_Kennan Accessed on November 10, 2015.

Khan, S. R. 2011. Towards new developmentalism: Context, program, and constraints. In S.R. Khan and J. Christiansen (eds.) *Towards New Developmentalism: Market as Means Rather than Master*, 252–79. New York: Routledge.

Khan, S. R. and J. Christiansen, eds. 2011. *Towards New Developmentalism: Market as Means Rather than Master*, New York: Routledge.

Khanna, A. 1987. Market distortions, export performances, and export direction: India's exports of manufactures in the 1970s. World Bank Symposium: Exports of developing countries: How direction affects performance (47–56. Washington, DC: World Bank.

Kletzer, K. and Bardhan, P. 1987. Credit markets and patterns of international trade. *Journal of Development Economics* 27(1–2): 57–70.

Kobayashi-Hillary, Mark (ed.) 2007. *Building a Future with BRICs*. New York: Springer.

Kowalski, P. and Shepherd, B. 2006. South–South trade in goods. OECD Trade Policy (Working Paper No. 40).

Kripa, S. 1998. G-15 and South-South cooperation: Promise and performance. *Third World Quarterly* 19(3): 357–73.

Krishna, P. 1998. Regionalism and multilateralism: A political economy approach. *Quarterly Journal of Economics* 108(1): 227–51.

Krueger, A. 1977. *Growth, Distortions, and Patterns of Trade among Many Countries*. Princeton Studies in International Finance, no. 40. Princeton: Princeton University Press.

Krugman, P. R. 1979. Increasing returns, monopolistic competition, and international trade. *Journal of International Economics* 9(4): 469–79.

Krugman, P. 1981. Trade, accumulation and uneven development. *Journal of Development Economics* 8(2): 149–61.

Krugman, P. 1987. The narrow moving band, the Dutch disease and the consequences of Mrs. Thatcher. *Journal of Development Economics* 27, 41–55.

Krugman, P. 1991a. History versus expectations. *Quarterly Journal of Economics* 196(2): 651–67.

Krugman, P. 1991b. The move to free trade zones. In Policy Implications of Trade and Currency Zones. Symposium sponsored by Federal Reserve Bank, Kansas City.

Krugman, P. 1995a. What do we need to know about the international monetary system? In P. Kenen (ed.), *Understanding Interdependence: The Macroeconomics of the Open Economy*, 509–29. Princeton University Press.

Krugman, P. 1995b. Growing world trade: Causes and consequences. Brookings Papers on Economic Activity 1, 327–77.Kumar, N. 2008. South-South and triangular cooperation in Asia-Pacific: Towards a new paradigm in development cooperation. Research and Information System for Developing Countries RIS Discussion Paper RIS-DP #145.

Kwok, C. C. and Tadesse, S. 2006. The MNC as an agent of change for host-country institutions: FDI and corruption. *Journal of International Business Studies* 37(6): 767–85.

Laffont, J. J. and N'Guessan, T. 1999. Competition and corruption in an agency relationship. *Journal of Development Economics* 60(2): 271–95.

Lall, S. 1975. Is "dependence" a useful concept in analyzing underdevelopment? *World Development* 3(11–12): 799–810.

Lall, S. 2000. The technological structure and performance of developing country manufactured exports, 1985–1998. *Oxford Development Studies* 28(3): 337–70.

Lall, S. 2001. *Competiveness, Technology and Skills*. Cheltenham: Edward Elgar.

Lall, S. 2002. Linking FDI and technology development for capacity building and strategic competitiveness. *Transnational Corporations* 11(3): 39–88.

Lall, S., Ray, A. and Ghosh, S. 1989. The determinants and promotion of south-south trade in manufactured products. In V. Ventura-Dias (ed.), *South-South Trade: Trends, Issues, and Obstacles to its Growth*. New York: Praeger Publishers.

Lancaster, K. 1971. *Consumer Demand: A New Approach*. New York: Columbia University Press.

Lau, C., Schropp, S. and Sumner, D. A. 2015. The 2014 US Farm Bill and its Effects on the World Market for Cotton. *ICTSD Issue Paper No. 58* Geneva, Switzerland.

Lawson, F. 2012. Transformations of Regional Economic Governance in the Gulf Cooperation Council. *Center for International and Regional Studies Georgetown University School of Foreign Service in Qatar* Occasional Paper no. 10: 1–26.

Leite, C.A. and Weidmann, J. 1999. Does mother nature corrupt? Natural resources, corruption, and economic growth (June). IMF Working Paper (99/85).

Lenin, Vladimir I. 1917. Imperialism, the Highest Stage of Capitalism. In *Selected Works*, vol. 1. Moscow: Foreign Languages Publishing House.

Levchenko, A. 2013. International trade and institutional change, *Journal of Law, Economics and Organization* 29(5): 1145–81.

Levy, P. 1997. A political-economic analysis of free-trade agreements. *American Economic Review* 87(4): 58–84.

Lewis, W. A. 1969. *Some Aspects of Economic Development*. Accra: The Ghana Publishing Corporation.

Lewis, W. A. 1980. The slowing down of the engine of growth. *American Economic Review* 70(3): 555–64.

Linder, S. B. 1961. *An Essay on Trade and Transformation*. New York: John Wiley and Sons.

Linder, S. B. 1967. *Trade and Trade Policy for Development*. New York: Praeger Publishers.

Lipscy, P. 2003. Japan's Asian Monetary Fund proposal. *Stanford Journal of East Asian Affairs* 3(1): 93–104.

Liu, Z. 2008. Foreign Direct Investment and technology spillovers: Theory and evidence. *Journal of Development Economics* 85(1–2): 176–93.

Lucas, R. E. 1988. On The Mechanics Of Economic Development. *Journal of Monetary Economics* 22(1), 3-42.

Luciani, G. and Salamé, G. (eds.) 2015. *The Politics of Arab Integration*. London: Routledge.

Luxemburg, R. 1913. *The Accumulation of Capital* (transl. from German, 1951). London: Routledge and Kegan Paul.

Maddison, A. 2003. *The World Economy: Historical Statistics*. Paris: OECD.

Maddison, A. 2005. *Growth and Interaction in the World Economy: The Roots of Modernity*. Washington, DC: The AEI Press.

Manova, K. B. and Zhang, Z. 2012. Export prices across firms and destinations. *The Quarterly Journal of Economics* 127: 379–436.

Marx, K. 1853. The future of British rule in India. *New-York Daily Tribune*, June 25. https://www.marxists.org/archive/marx/works/1853/06/25.htm. Accessed on September 20, 2015.

Marx, K. 1867. *Capital 1*. Preface to the German Edition. https://www.marxists.org/archive/marx/works/1867-c1/p1.htm. Accessed on July 1, 2015.

Marx, K. 1879. Letter to Nikolai Danielson in St. Petersburg. https://www.marxists.org/archive/marx/works/1879/letters/79_04_10.htm. Accessed on July 1, 2015.

Marx, K. and Engels, F. 1848[1969] *Manifesto of the Communist Party*. In Marx/Engels Selected Works, vol. 1. 98–137. Moscow: Progress Publishers. https://www.marxists.org/archive/marx/works/download/pdf/Manifesto.pdf. Accessed on July 1, 2015.

Marx-Engels Correspondence. 1929 [1853]. *Engels to Marx in London*. Source: *MECW* vol. 39, 335. First published in full in *MEGA*, Berlin.

Masset, E. 2015. *Northern Ghana Millennium Villages Impact Evaluation:* Preliminary Report on the Second Round of Data. Itad, Hove (edited by Chris Barnett). http://opendocs.ids.ac.uk/opendocs/bitstream/handle/123456789/5902/2014_MV%20Eval_Year%202%20 Report 24Feb15 submitted.pdf;jsessionid=0D86932FEEEEA2D3496A13C1DE4589C0?s equence=1. Accessed on September 1, 2015.

Matsushita, M., Schoenbaum, T. J. and Mavroidis, P. C. 2003. The World Trade Organization. *Law, Practice, and Policy* 2: 141.

Matsuyama, K. 1991. Increasing returns, industrialization and indeterminacy of equilibrium. *Quarterly Journal of Economics* 106(2): 617–50.

Mbaye, H.A. 2011. Political Decisions and Management Dilemmas Facing National and Local Officials in Complying with European Union Policies. *Midsouth Political Science Review* 11(1): 59–82.

McMillan, M. and Rodrik, D. 2011. Globalization, Structural Change, and Productivity Growth. NBER Working Paper 17143. Cambridge, MA: NBER.

Medvedev, D. 2010. Preferential trade agreements and their role in world trade. *Review of World Economies* 146: 199–222.

Michalopoulos, S. and Papaioannou, E. 2013. Pre-colonial ethnic institutions and contemporary African development. *Econometrica* 81(1): 113–52.

Ministry of Foreign Affairs of China. 2015. Xi Jinping delivers speech at high-level roundtable on South-South cooperation, expounding on cooperation Initiatives on South-South cooperation in the new era and stressing to uplift South-South Cooperation cause to a new high. 2015/09/27. http://www.fmprc.gov.cn/mfa_eng/zxxx_662805/t1302399.shtml Accessed on November 24, 2015.

Mirowski, P. 2013. *Never Let a Serious Crisis Go to Waste: How Neoliberalism Survived the Financial Meltdown*. London: Verso.

Mirowski, P. and Plehwe, D. (eds.) 2009. *The Road from Mont Pelerin: The Making of the Neoliberal Thought Collective*. Cambridge, MA: Harvard University Press.

MIT Media Lab. 2015. *The Atlas of Economic Complexity*. Center for International Development at Harvard University. http://atlas.media.mit.edu/en/resources/data/ Accessed on March 1, 2015.

Mkandawire, T. 2005. *African Intellectuals: Rethinking Politics, Language, Gender and Development*. London: Zed Books.

Mosoetsa, S. and Williams, M. (eds.) 2012. *Labour in the Global South: Challenges and Alternatives for Workers*. Geneva: International Labour Office (ILO).

Mukand, S. W. and Rodrik, D. 2005. In search of the Holy Grail: Policy convergence, experimentation, and economic performance. *American Economic Review* 95(1): 374–83.

Mundell, R. A. 1968. *International Economics*. New York: Macmillan.

Mundell, R. A. 2002. National economic policies, currency areas and Arab monetary integration. Discussion Papers 0102-31, Columbia University, Department of Economics.

Murphy, K. M. and Shleifer, A. 1997. Quality and trade. *Journal of Development Economics* 53(1): 1–15.

Myrdal, G. 1956. *An International Economy*. London: Routledge and Kegan Paul.

Najam, A. and Thrasher, R (eds.) 2012. *The Future of South-South Economic Relations*. London: Zed Books.

Narlikar, A. and Odell, J. 2003. The strict distributive strategy for a bargaining coalition: The Like Minded Group in the World Trade Organization. *Negotiating Trade: Developing Countries in the WTO and NAFTA*, 115–44.

Narlikar, A. 2003. *International Trade and Developing Countries: Bargaining Coalitions in the GATT and WTO*, vol. 13. London: Taylor and Francis.

National Science Foundation (NSF). 2014. Science and Engineering Indicators 2014, NSF. http://www.nsf.gov/statistics/seind14/index.cfm/appendix/tables.htm#c4. Accessed on December 8, 2015.

Nehru, J. 1955. Reference on Bandung Conference. In Ravinder Kumar and H. Y. Sharada Prasad (eds.) *Selected Works of Jawaharlal Nehru*, vol. 28. New Delhi: Jawaharlal Nehru Memorial Fund; Oxford University Press, 2001.

Nelson, R. and Pack, H. 1999. The Asian miracle and modern growth theory. *Economic Journal*, 109(457): 416–36.

Neumayer, E. and Spess, L. 2005. Do bilateral investment treaties increase foreign direct investment to developing countries? *World Development* 33(10): 1567–85.

New York Times. 1955. Editorial. Issues at Bandung, April 18.

Nunn, N. and Wantchekon, L. 2011. The slave trade and the origins of mistrust in Africa; forthcoming in *American Economic Review*.

Nurkse, R. 1952. Some international aspects of the problem of economic development. *American Economic Review* May: 571–83.

Nurkse, R. 1953. *Problems of Capital Formation in Underdeveloped Countries*. New York: Oxford University Press.

Nyqvist, M. B., Corno, L., Walque, D. and Svensson, J. 2015. Using lotteries to incentivize safer sexual behavior evidence from a randomized controlled trial on HIV prevention. Policy Research Working Paper 7215. World Bank.

Ocampo, J. A. 2013. The Latin America Debt Crisis in Historical Perspective. Paper prepared for International Economic Association project. http://policydialogue.org/publications/network_papers/the_latin_american_debt_crisis_in_historical_perspective/. Accessed on September 5, 2015.

OECD. 2015. Development Finance Statistics. www.oecd.org/dac/stats. Accessed on December 15, 2015. http://www.oecd.org/dac/stats/

OECD. 2015b. Statistics on resource flows to developing countries. http://www.oecd.org/dac/stats/statisticsonresourceflowstodevelopingcountries.htm. Accessed on January 10, 2016.

Otsubo, S. 1998. New regionalism and South-South trade: Could it be an entry point for the South toward global integration? APEC Discussion Paper, No. 18.

Owen, R. 1993. *The Middle East in the World Economy, 1800–1914*. London: IB Tauris.

Pack, H. and Saggi, K. 1997. Inflows of foreign technology and indigenous technological development. *Review of Development Economics* 1(1): 81–98.

Palma, G. 2008. Structuralism. In A.K. Dutt and J. Ros (eds.) *International Handbook of Development Economics* vol. 1: 136–43. Northhampton, MA: Edward Elgar.

Panagariya, A. 2000. Preferential trade liberalization: The traditional theory and new developments. *Journal of Economic Literature* 287–331.

Panitch, L. and Gindin, S. 2012. *The Making of Global Capitalism*. London: Verso Books.

Paz, L. S. 2014. Intermediate inputs and premature deindustrialization: An analysis of the Brazilian case. Working Paper. Syracuse University.

Peters, E. D. 2005. Economic opportunities and challenges posed by China for Mexico and Central America. Bonn: Dt. Inst. Fur Entwicklungspolitik.

Pfeifer, K. 2010. Social structure of Accumulation Theory for the Arab World: The economies of Egypt, Jordan, and Kuwait in the regional system. In McDonough, T., Reich, M. and Kotz, D. (eds.), *Contemporary Capitalism and its Crises: Social Structure of Accumulation Theory in the 21st Century*. Cambridge: Cambridge University Press.

Phillips, N. 2001. Regionalist governance in the new political economy of development: "Relaunching" the Mercosur. *Third World Quarterly* 22(4): 565–83.

Phillips, N. 2003. The rise and fall of open regionalism? Comparative perspectives on regional governance in the Southern Cone of Latin America. *Third World Quarterly* 24(2): 217–34.

Phillips, N. 2004. *The Southern Cone Model: The Political Economy of Regional Capitalist Development in Latin America*. RIPE Series in Global Political Economy. New York: Routledge.

Phillips, N. 2009. Regionalist governance in the new political economy of development: "Relaunching" the Mercosur. In F. Lawson (ed.) *Comparative Regionalism*. London: Ashgate.

Porrata-Doria, R. A. 2005. *MERCOSUR: The Common Market of the Southern Cone*. Durham, NC: Carolina Academic Press.

Prashad, V. 2007. *The Darker Nations: A People's History of the Third World*. New York: The New Press.

Prashad, V. 2012. *The Poorer Nations: A Possible History of the Global South*. London: Verso Books.

Prebisch, P. 1950. *The Economic Development of Latin America and Its Principal Problems*. New York: United Nations Department of Economic Affairs.

Prebisch, R. 1976. A critique of peripheral capitalism. *Cepal Review* 1.

Pritchett, L. 1997. Divergence, big time. *Journal of Economic Perspectives*, 11(3): 3–17.

Proctor, R. N. 2012. *Golden Holocaust: Origins of the Cigarette Catastrophe and the Case for Abolition*. Berkeley: University of California Press.

Puga, D. and Venables, A. J. 1997. Preferential trading arrangements and industrial location. *Journal of International Economics* 43: 347–68.

Radice, H. 2009. Halfway to paradise? Making sense of the semiperiphery. In O. Worth and P. Moore (eds.) *Globalization and the "New" Semi-Peripheries.* 25–39. Basingstoke: Palgrave.

Rajagopal, B. 2003. *International Law from Below: Development, Social Movements and Third World Resistance.* Cambridge: Cambridge University Press.

Rajan, R. G. and Zingales, L. 1998. Financial dependence and growth. *American Economic Review* 88: 559–86.

Regolo, J. 2013. Export diversification: How much does the choice of the trading partner matter? *Journal of International Economics* 91: 329–42.

Reuters, 2012. China Ex-Minister Says Foreign Auto JV Policy "like opium," http://www. reuters.com/article/2012/09/03/china-autos-foreign-idUSL4E8K314620120903 Accessed September 5, 2012.

Rigobon, R. and Rodrik, D. 2005. Rule of law, democracy, openness, and income. *Economics of Transition* 13(3): 533–64.

Rodney, W. 1982. *How Europe Underdeveloped Africa.* Washington, DC: Howard University Press.

Rodriguez, F. and Rodrik, D. 2001. Trade policy and economic growth: A skeptic's guide to the cross-national evidence. In *NBER Macroeconomics Annual 2000*, vol. 15: 261–338. Cambridge, MA: MIT Press.

Rodrik, D. 1994. Getting interventions right: How South Korea and Taiwan grew rich (No. w4964). National Bureau of Economic Research.

Rodrik, D. 2001. Development Strategies for the Next Century. Seminar "Development Theory at the Threshold of the Twenty-First Century." Commemorative event to mark the centenary of the birth of Ratil Prebisch. Santiago, Chile, 28–29 August 2001.

Rodrik, D. 2004. Industrial policy for the twenty-first century. C.E.P.R. Discussion Papers, No. 4767. London, Centre for Economic Policy Research.

Rodrik, D. 2006. Goodbye Financial Consensus, Hello Washington Confusion? A review of the World Bank's economic growth in the 1990s: Learning from a decade of reform. *Journal of Economic Literature* (44): 973–87.

Rodrik, D. 2008. Second-Best Institutions. *American Economic Review* 98(2): 100–104.

Rodrik, D. 2008a. The New Development economics: We shall experiment but how shall we learn? In J. Cohen and W. Easterly (eds.) *What Works in Development? Thinking Big vs. Thinking Small.* Washington, DC: Brookings Institution Press.

Rodrik, D. 2013. Unconditional convergence in manufacturing. *The Quarterly Journal of Economics* 128(1): 165–204.

Rogoff, K. 2015. Will China's infrastructure bank work? *The Guardian*, April 7. http://www. theguardian.com/business/2015/apr/07/will-chinas-infrastructure-bank-work. Accessed on July 1, 2015.

Rolland, S. 2007. Developing country coalitions at the WTO: In search of legal support. *Harvard International Law Journal* 48(2): 483–551.

Romer, P. M. 1990. Human capital and growth: theory and evidence. In *Carnegie-Rochester Conference Series on Public Policy* 32, May: 251–86.

Ros, J. 2001. *Development Theory and Economic of Growth.* Ann Arbor: University of Michigan Press.

Ros, J. 2008. Classical development theory. In A. K. Dutt and J. Ros (eds.), *International Handbook of Development Economics* vol. 1. 111–24. Northampton, MA: Edward Elgar.

Ros, J. 2013. Latin America's trade and growth patterns, the China Factor, and Prebisch's Nightmare. *Journal of Globalization and Development* 3(2): 1–16. DOI: 10.1515/jgd-2012-0031

Rosenstein-Rodan, P. 1943. Problems of industrialization of Eastern and Southeastern Europe. *Economic Journal* June-September: 202–11.

Rosenstein-Rodan, P. 1984. Natura Facit Saltum: Analysis of the disequilibrium growth process. In G. Meier and D. Seers (eds.) *Pioneers in Development*. New York: Oxford University Press.

Roubini, N. and Mihm, S. 2010. *Crisis Economics: A Crash Course in the Future of Finance*. London: Penguin.

Saad-Filho, A. and Johnston, D. (eds.) 2005. *Neoliberalism: A Critical Reader*. London: Pluto Press.

SAARC. 2015. http://www.saarc-sec.org/SAARC-Charter/5/. Accessed on July 14, 2015.

Sachs, J. D. 1988. International policy coordination: The case of the developing country debt crisis. In *International Economic Cooperation*, M. Feldstein (ed.) 233–78. Chicago: University of Chicago Press.

Sahlins, M. 2013. China U. *The Nation*, October 30. http://www.thenation.com/article/china-u/. Accessed on May 1, 2014.

Schiff, M. 2003. The Unilateral/Bilateral/Regional/Multilateral approaches to trade liberalization. Background paper for *Trade for Development UN Millennium Project*. New York.

Schiff, M. and Wang, Y. 2006. North-South and South-South trade-related technology diffusion: An industry-level analysis of direct and indirect effects. *Canadian Journal of Economics* 39(3): 831–44.

Schiff, M. and Wang, Y. 2008. North-South and South-South trade-related technology diffusion: How important are they in improving TFP growth? *Journal of Development Studies* 44(1): 49–59.

Schiff, M. and Wang, Y. and Ollareaga, M. 2002. Trade-related technology diffusion and the dynamics of North-South and South-South integration. The World Bank Policy Research Working Paper, No. 2861.

Scoones, I., Cabral, L. and Tugendhat, H. (eds.) 2013. China and Brazil in African agriculture. IDS Bulletin.

Scott, J. C. 2000. *Seeing Like a State: How Certain Schemes to Improve the Human Condition Have Failed*. New Haven: Yale University Press.

Scott, J. W. 2010. The European Union, the Emerging Neighbourhood and Geopolitics of Inclusion and Exclusion. In G. Gorzelak, J. Bachtler and M. Smetkowski (eds) *Regional Development in Central and Eastern Europe*, London and New York: Routledge, 188–212.

Secretary-General of the United Nations. 2004. Address to the 58th session of the General Assembly. State of South-South Cooperation. Background paper.

Seck, D. (ed.) 2013. *Regional Economic Integration in West Africa*. New York: Springer.

Shaw, T. M. and Soderbaum, F. (eds.) 2004. *Theories of New Regionalism: A Palgrave Reader*. Hampshire and New York: Palgrave Macmillan.

Singer, H. W. 1975. *The Strategy of International Development: Essays in the Economics of Backwardness*. A. Cairncross and M. Puri (eds.) London: Macmillan.

Singer, H. W. 1950. The distribution of gains between investing and borrowing countries. *American Economic Review Papers and Proceedings* 40(2): 473–85.

South Asian Association for Regional Cooperation (SAARC). 2015. SAARC Charter. 2015 http://www.saarc-sec.org/SAARC-Charter/5/. Accessed December 10, 2015.

State Council. 2014. Second White Paper on China's foreign aid. Information Office of the State Council, The People's Republic of China, July 2014, Beijing.

Stewart, F. 1992. *North-South and South-South: Essays on International Economics*. Hong Kong: St. Martin's Press.

Stiglitz, J. 2015. In Defence of the Asian Infrastructure Investment Bank. *The Guardian*, April 14. http://www.theguardian.com/business/2015/apr/14/in-defence-of-the-asian-infrastructure-investment-bank. Accessed on July 1, 2015.

Strange, A., Parks, B., Tienney, M. J., Fuchs, A., Dreher, A. and Ramachandran, V. 2013. China's Development Finance to Africa: A Media-Based Approach to Data Collection. Center for Global Development, Working Paper 323.

Strange, G. 2009. Globalization, accumulation by dispossession and the rise of the semi-periphery: Towards global post-Fordism and crisis? In Worth, O. and Phoebe, V. M. (eds.) *Globalization and the 'New' Semi-Peripheries* London: Palgrave Macmillan, 40–57.

Stuenkel, O. 2015. *The BRICS and the Future of Global Order* Lanham, MD: Lexington Books.

Sutcliffe, B. 2008. Marxism and development. In A. K. Dutt and J. Ros (eds.) *International Handbook of Development Economics*, vol. 1: 144–61. Northampton, MA: Edward Elgar.

Svaleryd, H. and Vlachos, J. 2005. Financial markets, the pattern of industrial specialization and comparative advantage: Evidence from OECD countries. *European Economic Review* 49: 113–44.

Taylor, L. 2004. *Reconstructing Macroeconomics*. Cambridge, MA: Harvard University Press.

Taylor, L. 1981. South-North trade and Southern growth: Bleak prospects from a structuralist point of view. *Journal of International Economics* 11(4): 589–602.

Taylor, M. A. 1993. Quality ladders' and Ricardian trade. *Journal of International Economics* 34(3/4): 225–43.

Thrasher, R. D. and Gallagher, K. 2008. 21st century trade agreements: Implications for long-run development policy. The Pardee Papers, no. 2. Boston: Boston University.

Torre, D. L. A., Didier, T., Ize, A., Lederman, D. and Schmukler, S. L. 2015. *Latin America and the Rising South: Changing World, Changing Priorities*. World Bank: Washington, DC.

Tran, M. 2011. Transparency could be the sticking point for China at Busan. The Guardian's Poverty Matters Blog. http://www.theguardian.com/global-development/poverty-matters/2011/nov/14/busan-aid-china-rejects-transparency Accessed on December 14, 2011.

Tran, M. 2012. Nigerian and Indonesian officials join post-Busan Aid Effectiveness Panel. *The Guardian*. August 7, 2012.United Nations Conference on Trade and Development (UNCTAD). 2003. *Trade and Development Report*. Geneva: UNCTAD.

United Nations Conference on Trade and Development (UNCTAD). 2005a. *Trade and Development Report*. Geneva: UNCTAD.

United Nations Conference on Trade and Development (UNCTAD). 2005b. *World Investment Report* Geneva: UNCTAD.

United Nations Conference on Trade and Development (UNCTAD). 2006. *Trade and Development Report*. Geneva: UNCTAD.

United Nations Conference on Trade and Development (UNCTAD). 2007. *Trade and Development Report*. Geneva: UNCTAD.

United Nations Conference on Trade and Development (UNCTAD). 2009. *World Investment Report 2009*. New York and Geneva: United Nations.

United Nations Conference on Trade and Development (UNCTAD). 2011. *World Investment Report 2011*. New York and Geneva: United Nations.

United Nations Conference on Trade and Development (UNCTAD). 2012. *Technology and Innovation Report 2012*. Geneva: UNCTAD.

United Nations Conference on Trade and Development (UNCTAD). 2013. *World Investment Report 2013*. Geneva: UNCTAD.

United Nations Conference on Trade and Development (UNCTAD). 2014. *World Investment Report 2014*. Geneva: UNCTAD.

United Nations Conference on Trade and Development (UNCTAD). 2015a. UNCTAD Online FDI Database. UNCTADSTAT. Accessed on December 1, 2015.

United Nations Conference on Trade and Development (UNCTAD). 2015b. Policy options for IIA reform: Treaty examples and data. Supplementary material to World Investment Report 2015. http://investmentpolicyhub.unctad.org/Upload/Documents/Policy-options-for-IIA-reform-WIR-2015.pdf. Accessed on April 1, 2016.

United Nations Conference on Trade and Development (UNCTAD). 2015c. *World Investment Report 2015*. Geneva: United Nations.

United Nations Conference on Trade and Development (UNCTAD). 2015d. International investment agreements database. http://investmentpolicyhub.unctad.org/IIA> Accessed on December 4, 2015.

United Nations Conference on Trade and Development (UNCTAD). 2015e. Database on Investor-State Dispute Settlements, http://unctad.org/en/pages/DIAE/International%20Investment%20Agreements%20%28IIA%29/IIA-Tools.aspx Accessed on November 18, 2015.

UNDP (United Nations Development Programme). 2013. *Human Development Report 2013. The Rise of the South: Human Progress in a Diverse World.* New York: United Nations.

UNDP. 2015. *United Nations Development Programme in China UNDP–China Partnership on South-South and Global Cooperation 2014 Highlights.* Beijing: UNDP.

UNIDO. 2005. *Industrial Development, Trade and Poverty Alleviation through South-South Cooperation.* New York: United Nations.

UNIDO. 2006. *Industrial Development, Trade and Poverty Reduction through South-South Cooperation.* New York: United Nations. https://www.unido.org/fileadmin/user_media/Publications/Pub_free/Industrial_development_trade_and_poverty_reduction_through_south_south_cooperation.pdf. Accessed on March 5, 2014.

Van Dijk, M. P. (ed.) 2010. *New Presence of China in Africa.* Amsterdam: Amsterdam University Press.

Van Harten, G. 2007. The public–private distinction in the international arbitration of individual claims against the state. *International and Comparative Law Quarterly* 56(02): 371–93.

Venables, A. 1999. Regional integration agreements, a force for divergence or convergence? World Bank Policy Research Working Paper, No. 2260, Washington, DC: World Bank.

Venables, A. 2003. Winners and losers from Regional Integration Agreements. *The Economic Journal* 113: 747–61.

Ventura-Dias, V. 1989. *South-South Trade: Trends, Issues, and Obstacles to its Growth.* Praeger Publishers.

Viner, J. 1950. *The Customs Unions Issue.* New York: The Carnegie Endowment for International Peace.

Wade, R. 1990. *Governing the Market: Economic Theory and the Role of Government in East Asian Industrialization.* Princeton: Princeton University Press.

Wallerstein, I. 1997. Eurocentrism and its avatars: The dilemmas of social science. *New Left Review* 226: 93–108.

Wallerstein, I. 1976. Semi-peripheral countries and the contemporary world crisis. *Theory and Society* 3(4): 461–83.

Wanjala, B. M. and Muradian, R. 2013. Can big push interventions take small-scale farmers out of poverty? Insights from the Sauri Millennium Village in Kenya. *World Development* 45: 147–60.

Warmerdam, W. 2015. Having, Giving, Taking: Understanding China's Development Cooperation in Africa. Unpublished Ph.D. dissertation, Erasmus University Rotterdam.

Wessel, D. 2008. The rise of South-South trade. *Wall Street Journal,* January 3. http://www.wsj.com/articles/SB119931722284263491. Accessed on October 1, 2015.

Wexler, I. 1983. *The Marshall Plan Revisited: The European Recovery Program in Economic Perspective (No. 55).* Westport, CT: Greenwood Press.

White House, 2015. U.S.-China Joint Presidential Statement on Climate Change. September 25. https://www.whitehouse.gov/the-press-office/2015/09/25/us-china-joint-presidential-statement-climate-change Accessed on November 23, 2015.

Wietzke, F-B. 2015. Long-term consequences of colonial institutions and human capital investments: Sub-national evidence from Madagascar. *World Development* 66, 293–307. http://www.iie.com/publications/papers/williamson0904-2.pdf. Accessed July 1, 2015.

Willetts, P. 1978. *The Non-Aligned Movement: The Origins of a Third World Alliance.* London: Pinter.

Williamson, J. 2004. A Short History of the Washington Consensus. Presented in conference "From the Washington Consensus towards a new Global Governance," Barcelona, September 24–25.

Wise, T. A. 2014a. What happened to the biggest land grab in Africa? Searching for ProSavana in Mozambique, Foodtank. December 20. http://foodtank.com/news/2014/12/what-happened-to-the-biggest-land-grab-in-africa-searching-for-prosavana-in. Accessed on September 1, 2015.

Wise, T. A. 2014b. Land grabs and responsible agricultural investment in Africa. *Triple Crisis*. August 4. http://triplecrisis.com/?p=10242. Accessed on September 1, 2015.

Wise, T. A. 2014c. Picking up the pieces from a failed land grab project in Tanzania. June 27. Global Post. http://www.globalpost.com/dispatches/globalpost-blogs/rights/picking-the-pieces-failed-land-grab-project-tanzania. Accessed on September 1, 2015.

Wise, T. A. 2015. The great land giveaway in Mozambique. *DollarsandSense* March/April. Land Matrix (2015) http://www.landmatrix.org Accessed on October 15, 2015.

Wonnacott, R. J. 1996 Trade and Investment in a Hub-and-Spoke System versus a Free Trade Area. *The World Economy* 19: 237–52

Wonnacott, P. and Lutz, M. 1989. Is there a case for free trade areas? In Jeffrey Schott (ed.) *Free Trade Areas and U.S. Trade Policy*: 59–84. Washington, DC: Institute for International Economics.

Wood, R. E. 1986. *From Marshall Plan to Debt Crisis: Foreign Aid and Development Choices in the World Economy*; vol. 15. Berkeley: University of California Press.

World Bank. 2006. *Global Development Finance*. Washington DC: World Bank.

World Bank. 2007. *Agriculture for Development: World Development Report 2008*. Washington, DC: World Bank and Oxford University Press.

World Bank. 2008. *Global Development Finance*. Washington, DC: World Bank.

World Bank. 2010. *Rising Global Interest in Farmland: Can It Yield Sustainable and Equitable Benefits?* Washington DC: The World Bank.

World Bank. 2011. *Global Development Horizons 2011, Multipolarity: The New Global Economy*. Washington, DC: World Bank.

World Bank. 2014. *World Development Indicators*. Washington, DC: World Bank.

World Bank. 2015. World Development Indicators (WDI) Online Database. World Bank. Accessed December 2015.

World Trade Organization (WTO). 2003. *World Trade Report 2003* Geneva: WTO Publications. https://www.wto.org/english/res_e/booksp_e/anrep_e/world_trade_report_2003_e.pdf

World Trade Organization. 2014. WTO Preferential Trade Agreements Database. http://ptadb.wto.org/?lang=1 Accessed on December 11, 2015.

World Trade Organization. 2015. Dispute Settlement Database. https://www.wto.org/english/tratop_e/dispu_e/dispu_status_e.htm. Accessed on December 1, 2015.

Xu, H., Wan, D. and Sun, Y. 2014. Technology spillovers of foreign direct investment in coastal regions of East China: A perspective on technology absorptive capacity. *Emerging Markets Finance and Trade* 50(1S): 96–106.

Yackee, J.. 2009. Do BITs Really Work? Revisiting the Empirical Link between Investment Treaties and Foreign Direct Investment. In K.P. Sauvant and L.E. Sachs (eds.), *The Effect of Treaties on Foreign Direct Investment: Bilateral Investment Treaties, Double Taxation Treaties, and Investment Flows*. Oxford: Oxford University Press, 379–94.

INDEX

9 781785 271847